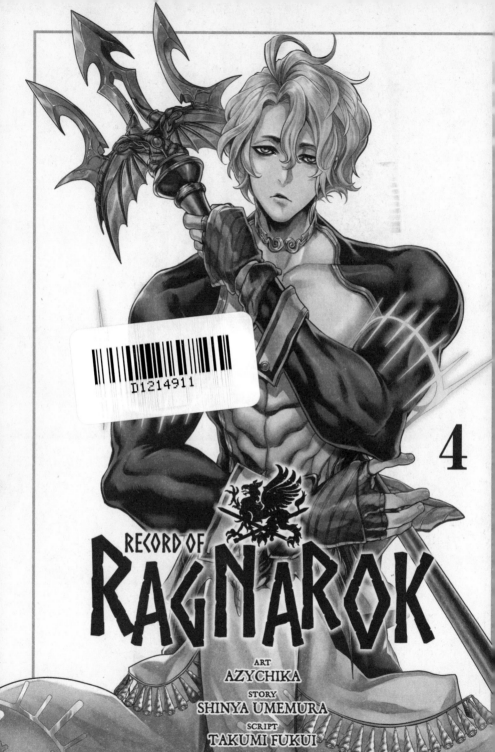

RECORD OF

RAGNAROK

4

ART
AZYCHIKA

STORY
SHINYA UMEMURA

SCRIPT
TAKUMI FUKUI

4

RECORD OF RAGNAROK

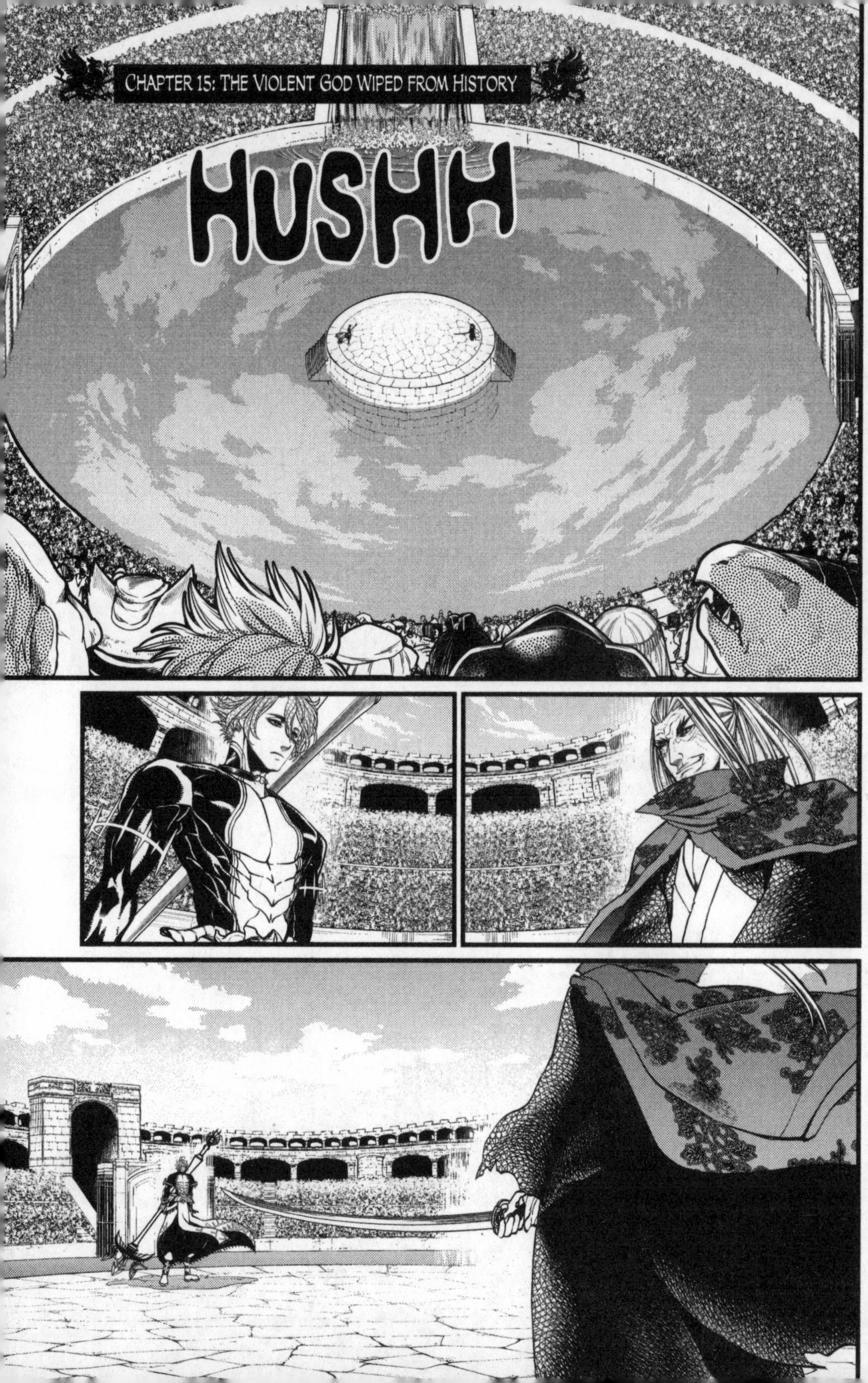
CHAPTER 15: THE VIOLENT GOD WIPED FROM HISTORY
HUSHH

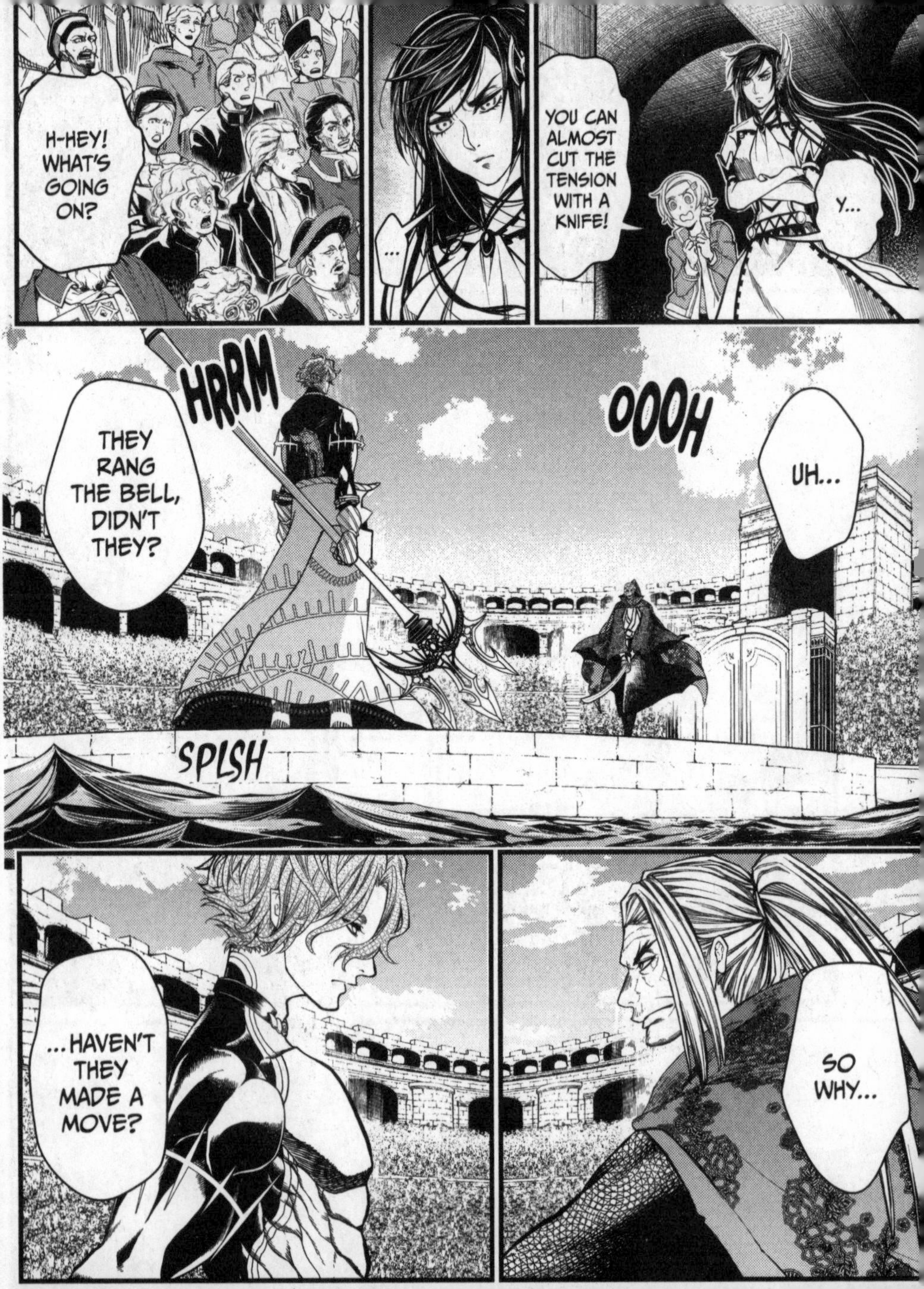
Y...
YOU CAN ALMOST CUT THE TENSION WITH A KNIFE!
...
H-HEY! WHAT'S GOING ON?
UH...
OOOH
HRRM
THEY RANG THE BELL, DIDN'T THEY?
SPLSH
SO WHY...
...HAVEN'T THEY MADE A MOVE?

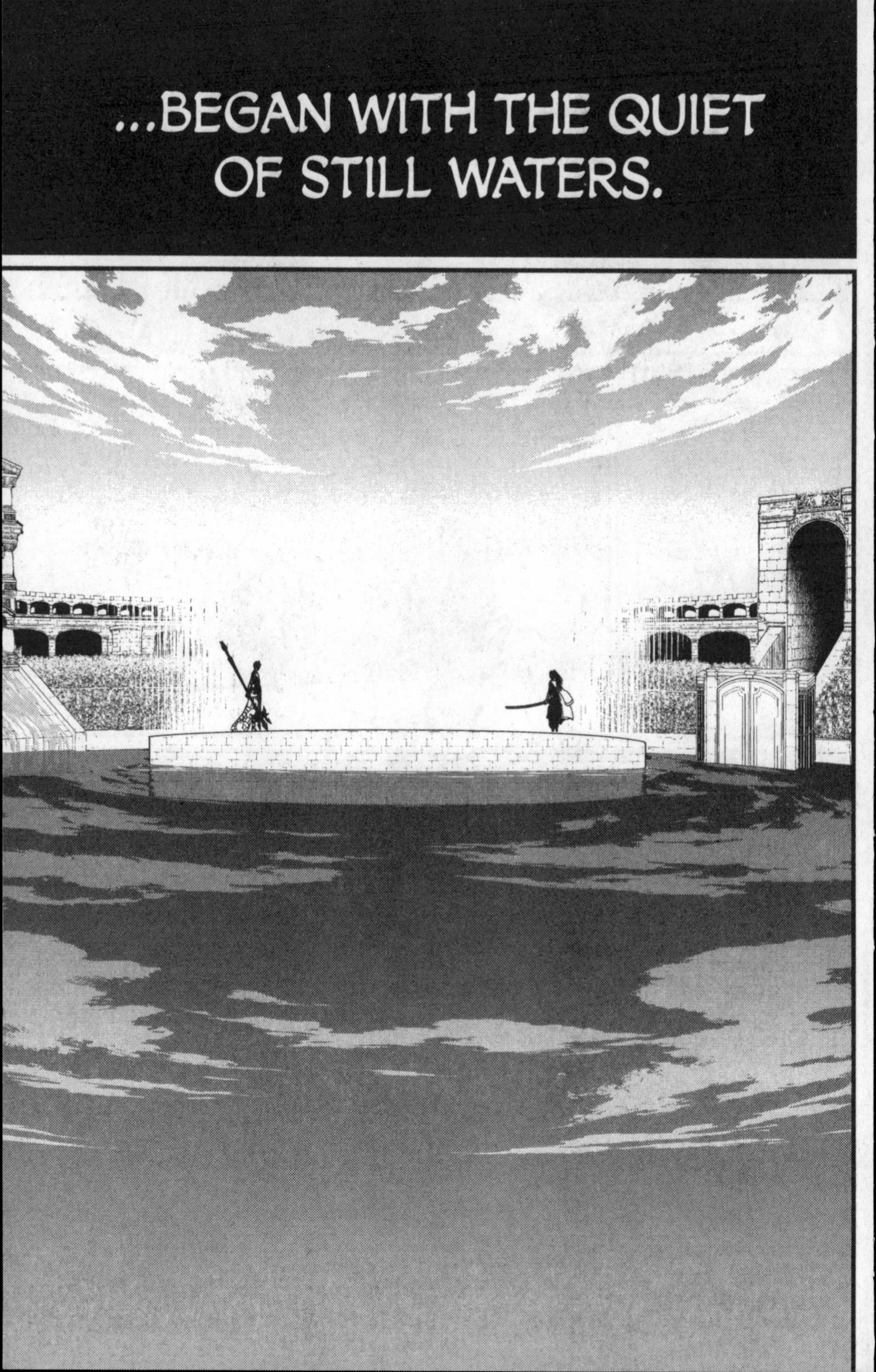
...BEGAN WITH THE QUIET OF STILL WATERS.

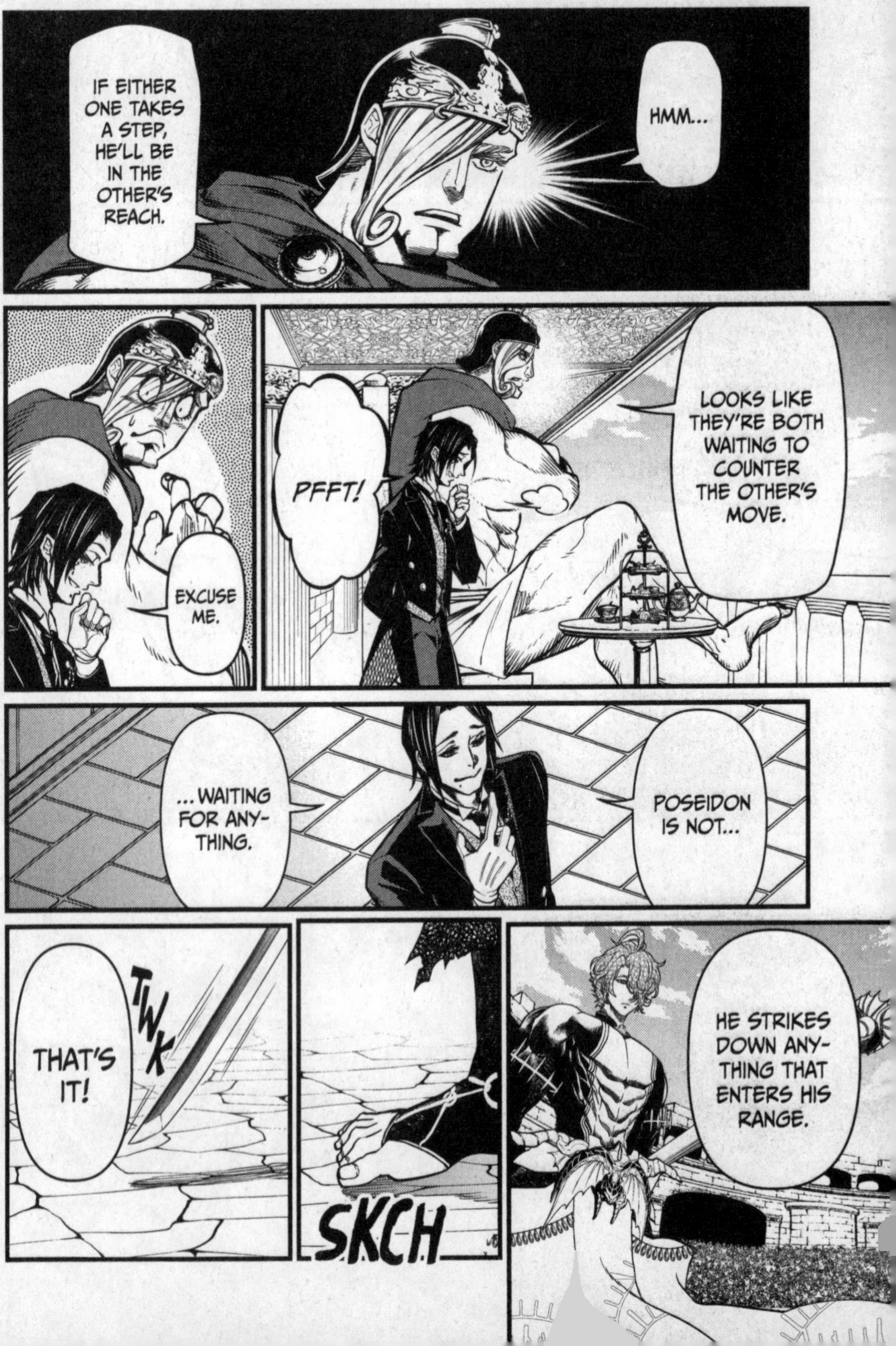
HMM...
IF EITHER ONE TAKES A STEP, HE'LL BE IN THE OTHER'S REACH.
LOOKS LIKE THEY'RE BOTH WAITING TO COUNTER THE OTHER'S MOVE.
PFFT!
EXCUSE ME.
POSEIDON IS NOT...
...WAITING FOR ANY-THING.
HE STRIKES DOWN ANY-THING THAT ENTERS HIS RANGE.
SKCH
TWK
THAT'S IT!

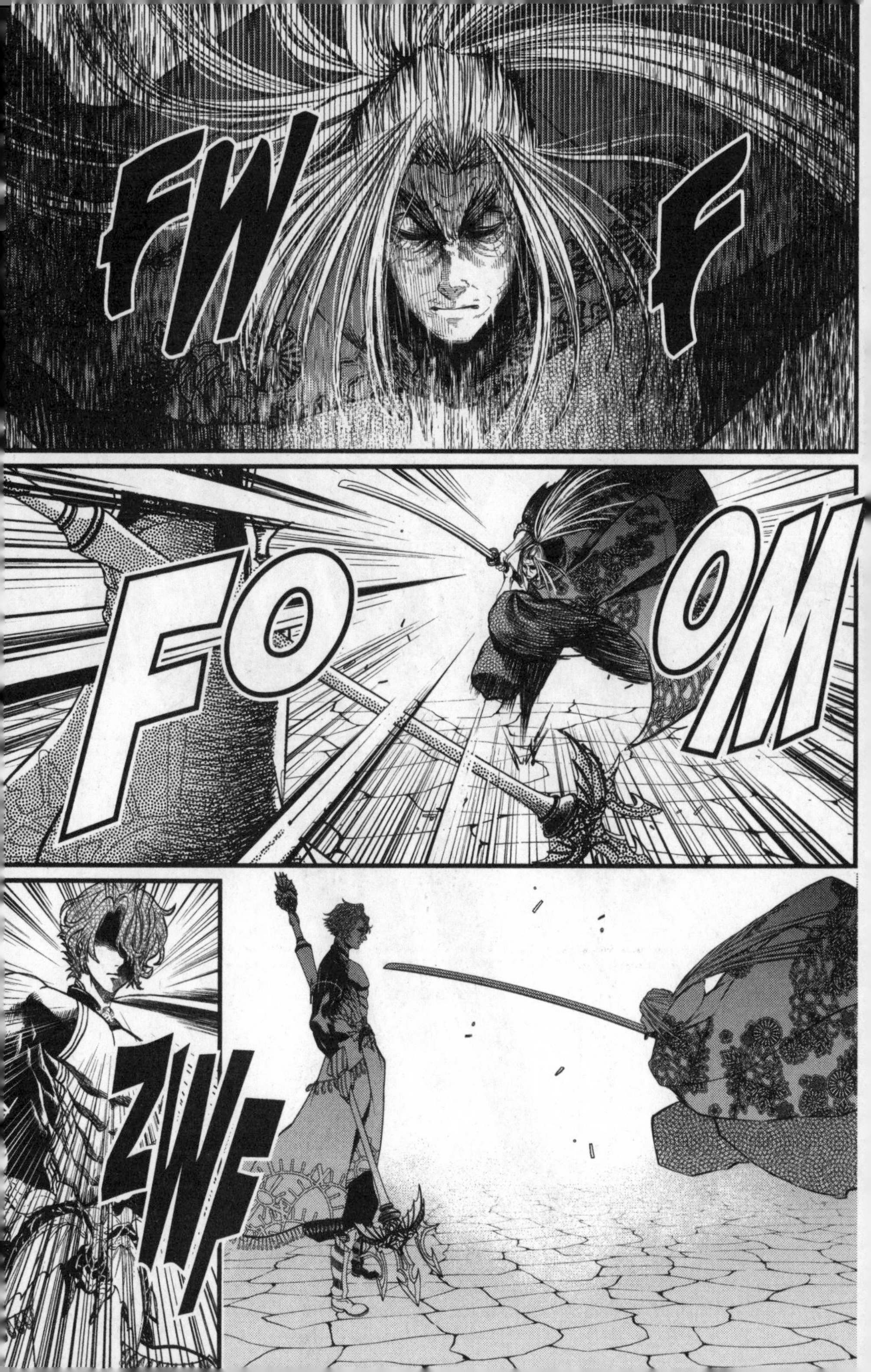
FWF
FOOM
ZWF

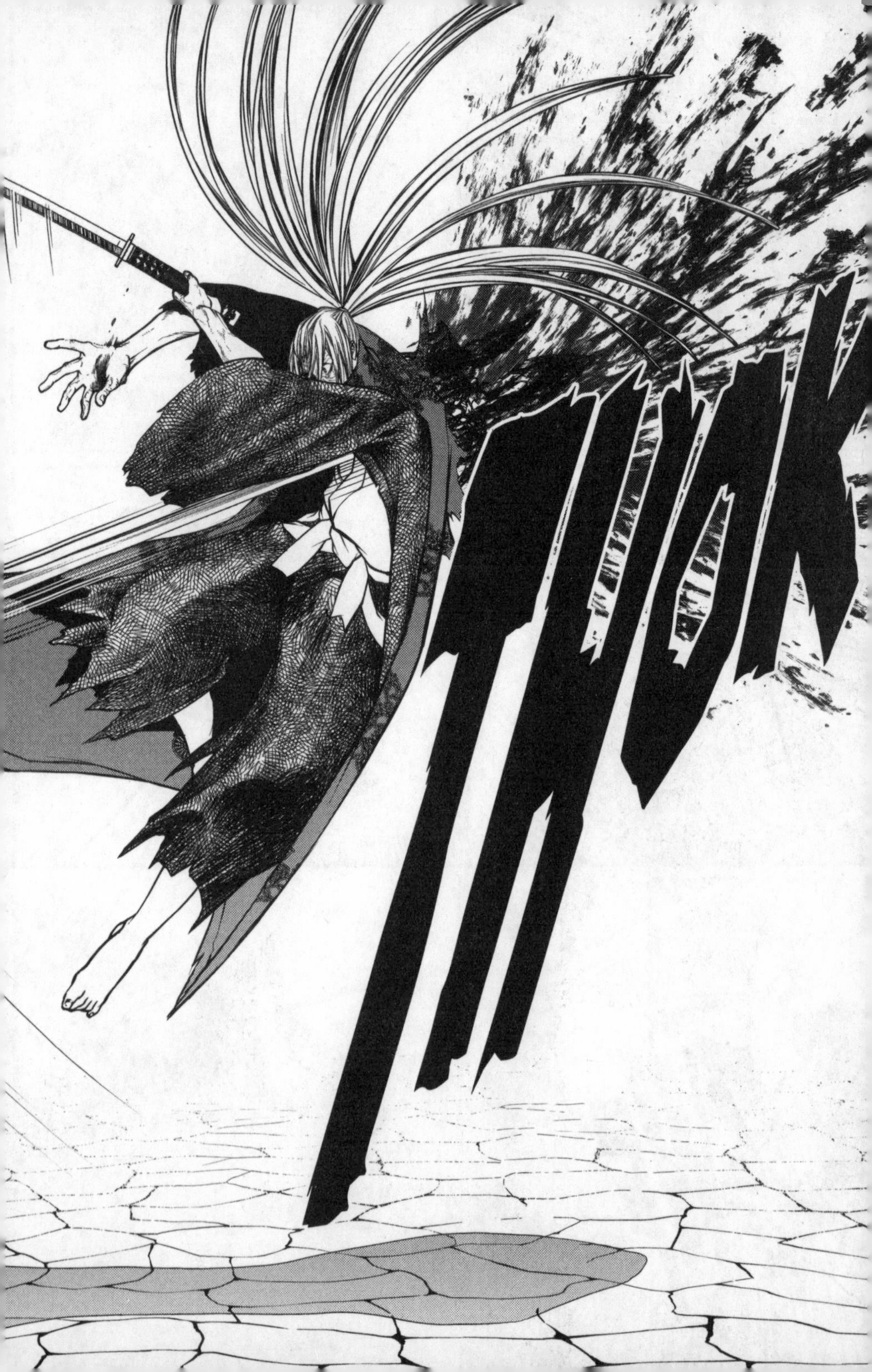
THUNK

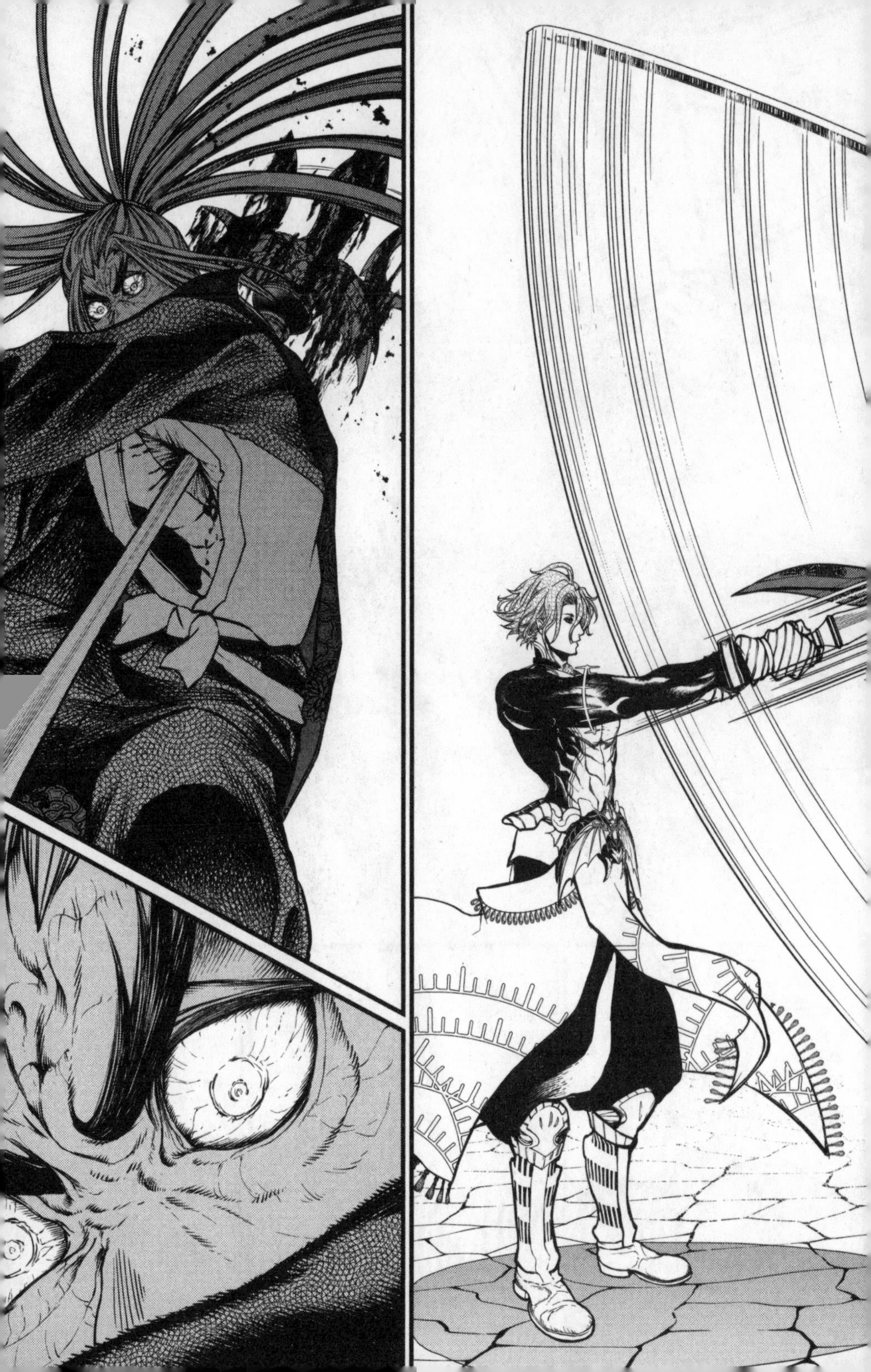

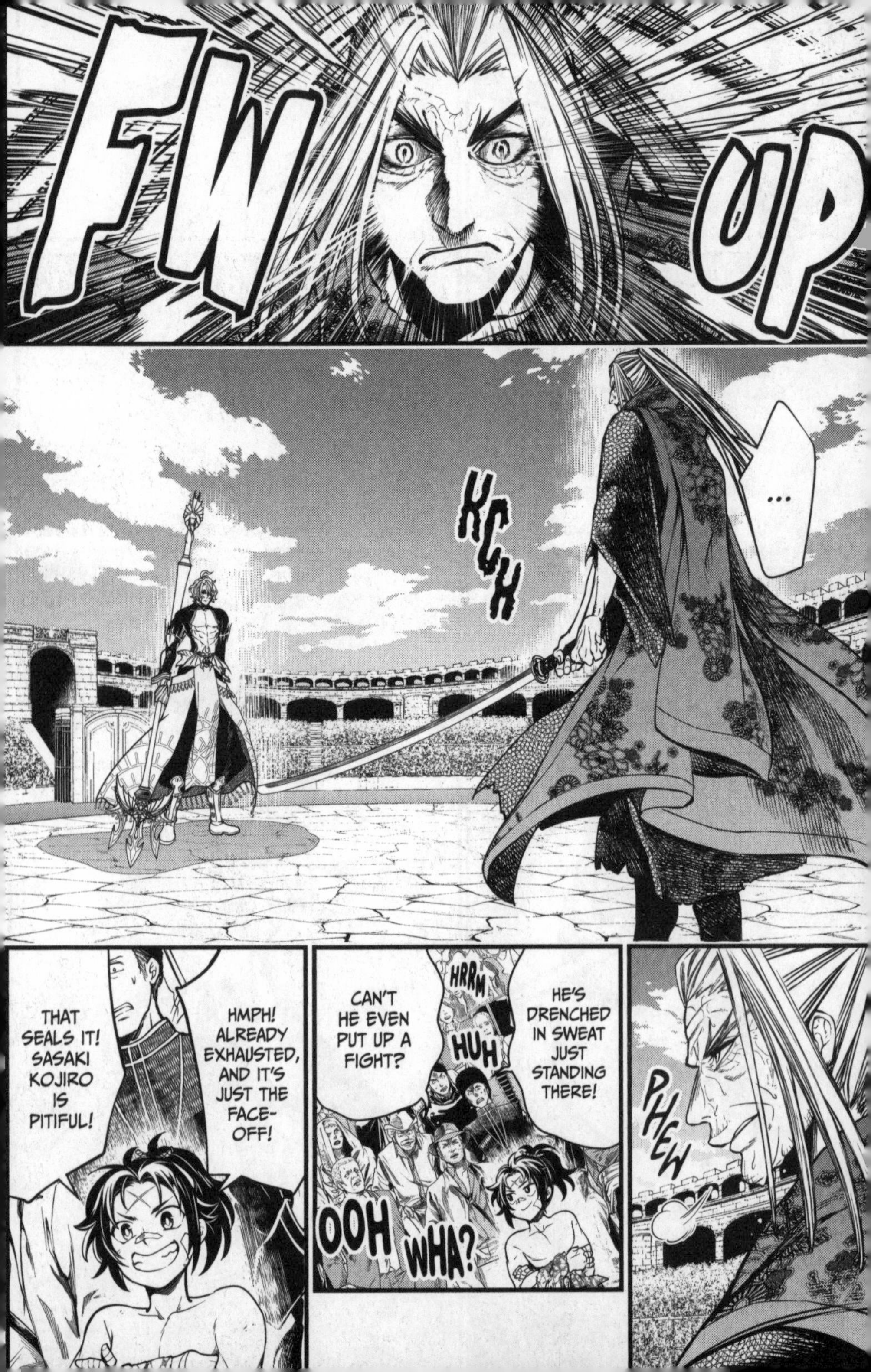
FW UP
...
KCH
PHEW
HE'S DRENCHED IN SWEAT JUST STANDING THERE!
HRRM
CAN'T HE EVEN PUT UP A FIGHT?
HUH
OOH
WHA?
HMPH! ALREADY EXHAUSTED, AND IT'S JUST THE FACE-OFF!
THAT SEALS IT! SASAKI KOJIRO IS PITIFUL!

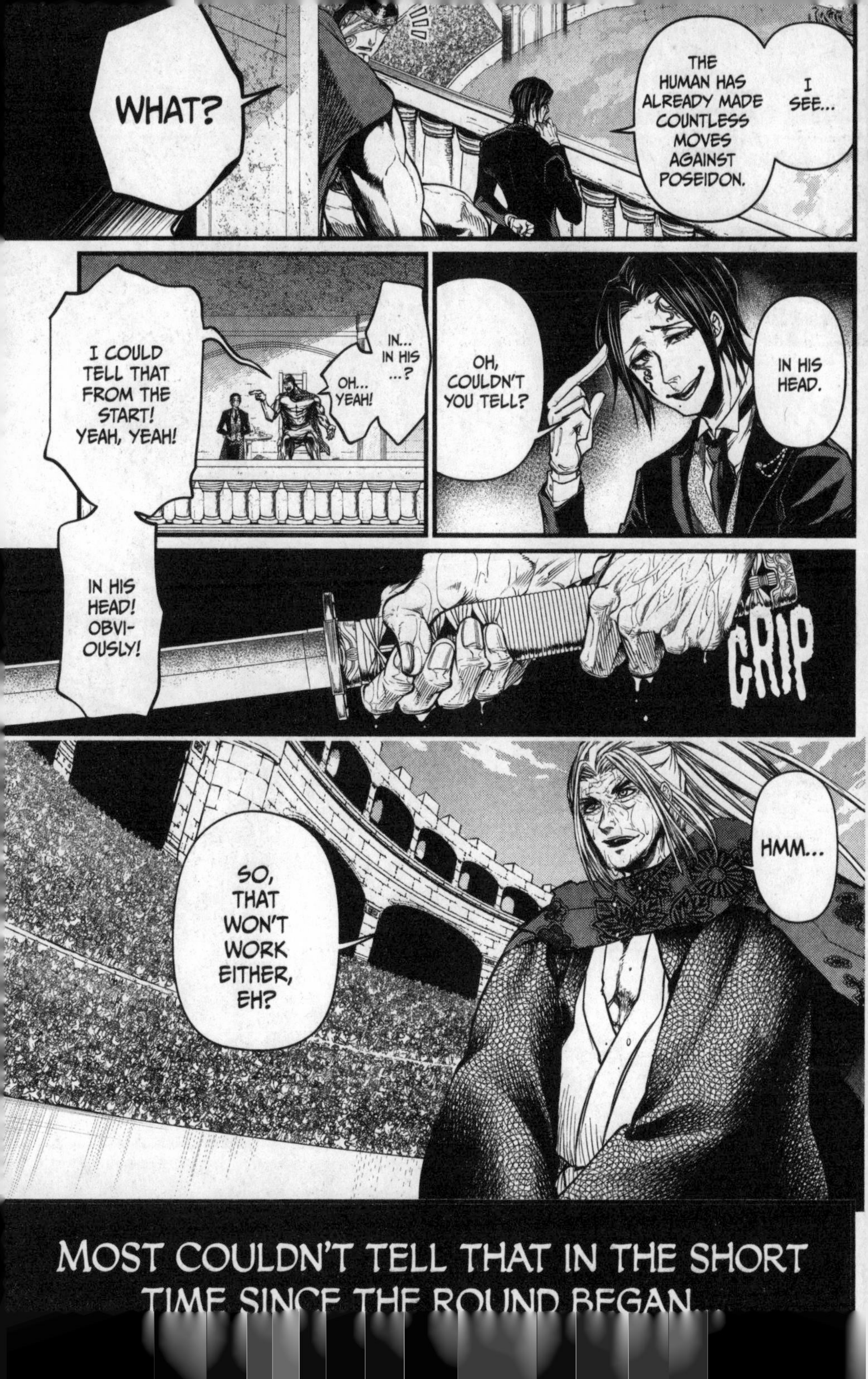
I SEE...
THE HUMAN HAS ALREADY MADE COUNTLESS MOVES AGAINST POSEIDON.
WHAT?
IN HIS HEAD.
OH, COULDN'T YOU TELL?
IN... IN HIS ...?
OH... YEAH!
I COULD TELL THAT FROM THE START! YEAH, YEAH!
IN HIS HEAD! OBVI-OUSLY!
GRIP
HMM...
SO, THAT WON'T WORK EITHER, EH?
MOST COULDN'T TELL THAT IN THE SHORT TIME SINCE THE ROUND BEGAN...

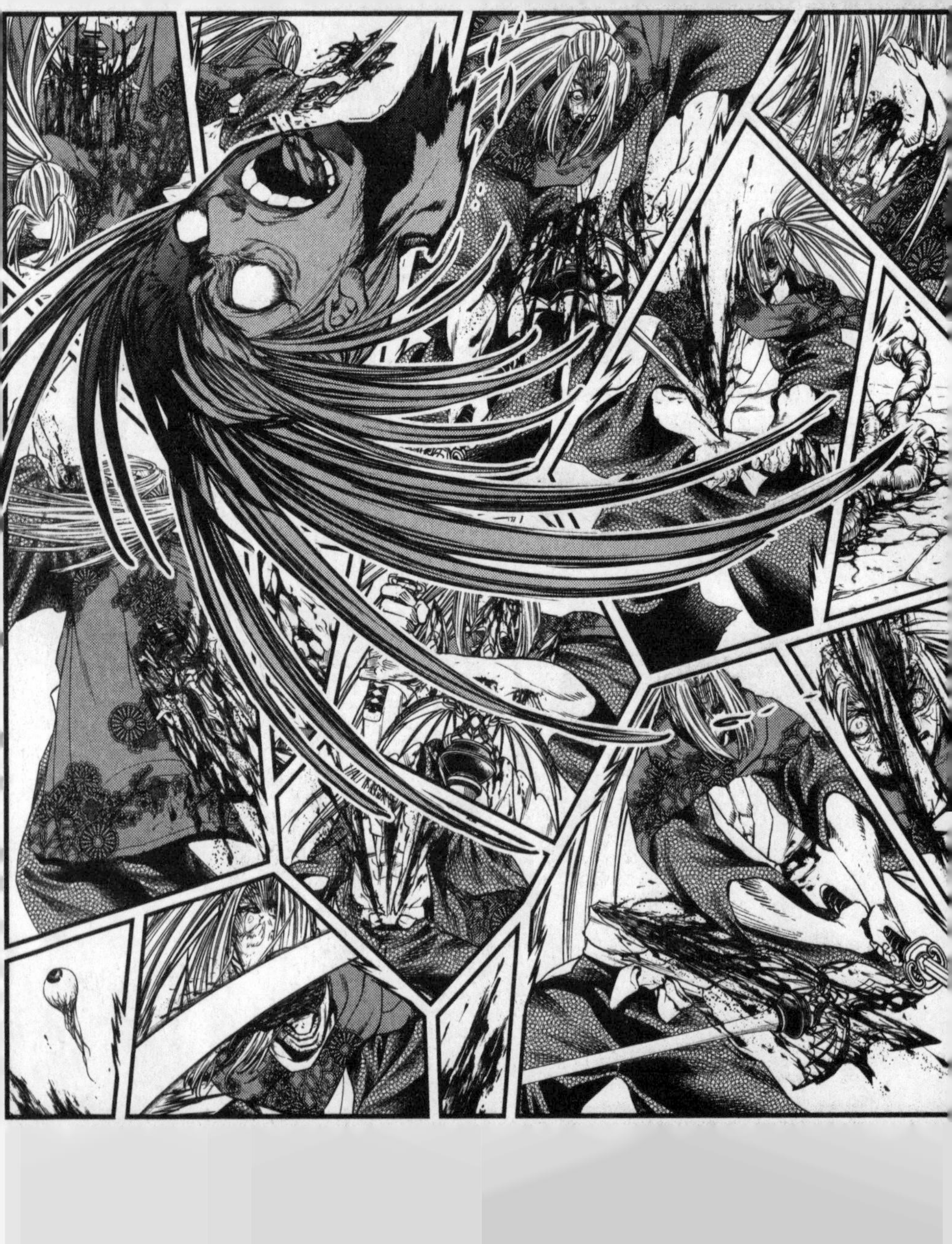

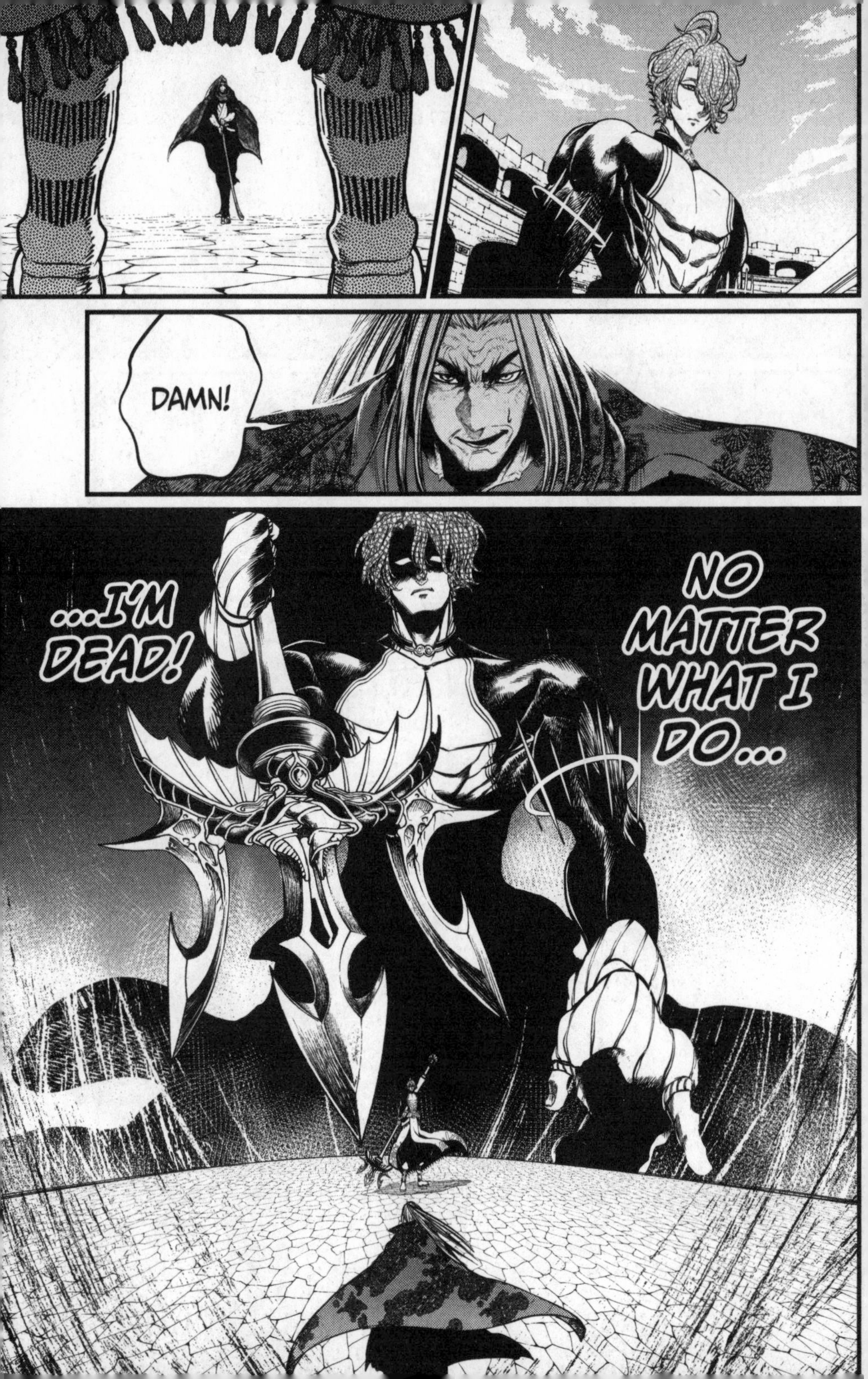
DAMN!
NO MATTER WHAT I DO...
...I'M DEAD!

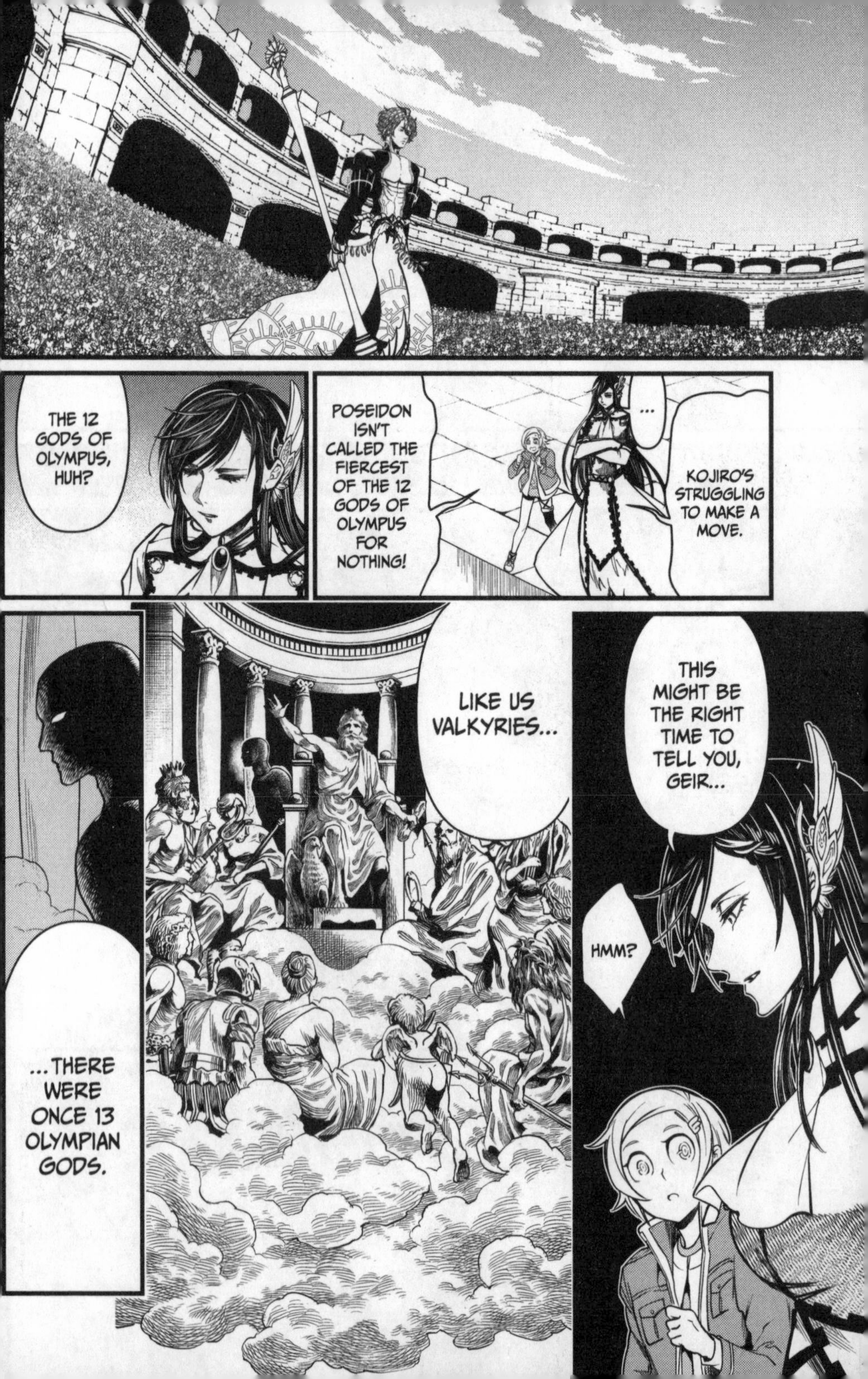
...
KOJIRO'S STRUGGLING TO MAKE A MOVE.
POSEIDON ISN'T CALLED THE FIERCEST OF THE 12 GODS OF OLYMPUS FOR NOTHING!
THE 12 GODS OF OLYMPUS, HUH?
THIS MIGHT BE THE RIGHT TIME TO TELL YOU, GEIR...
HMM?
LIKE US VALKYRIES...
...THERE WERE ONCE 13 OLYMPIAN GODS.

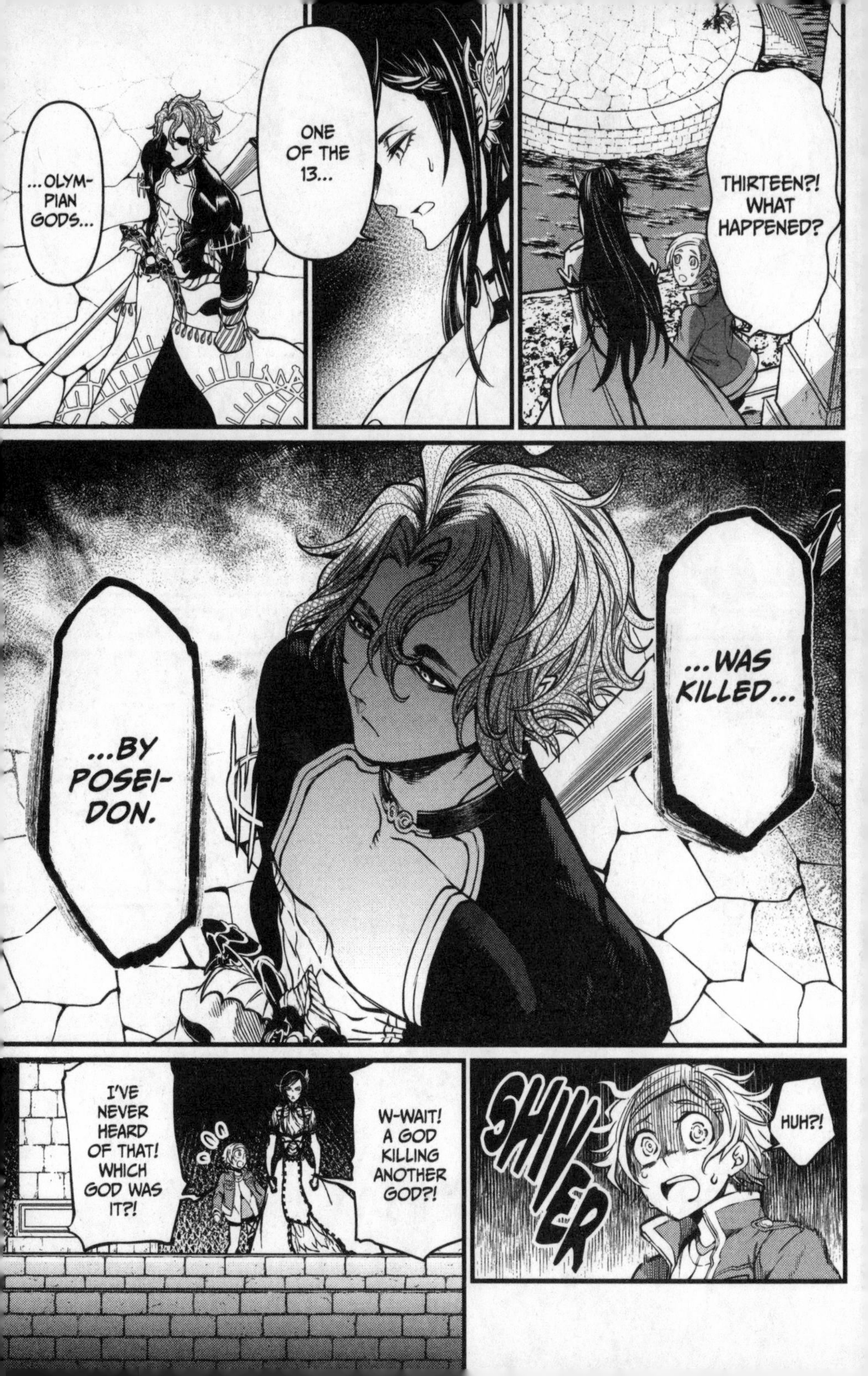
THIRTEEN?! WHAT HAPPENED?
ONE OF THE 13...
...OLYMPIAN GODS...
...WAS KILLED...
...BY POSEIDON.
SHIVER
HUH?!
W-WAIT! A GOD KILLING ANOTHER GOD?!
I'VE NEVER HEARD OF THAT! WHICH GOD WAS IT?!

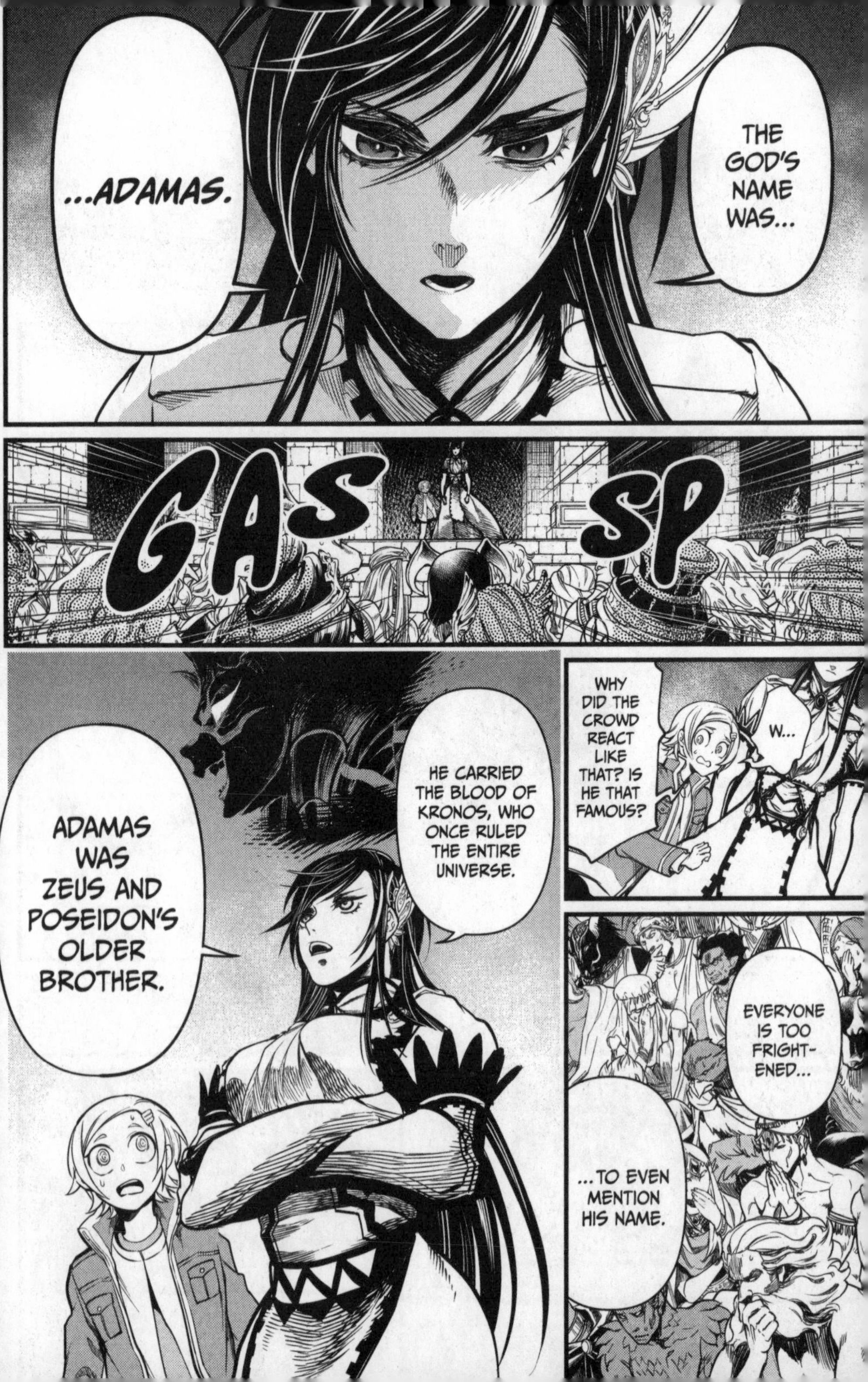
THE GOD'S NAME WAS...
...ADAMAS.
GAS
SP
W...
WHY DID THE CROWD REACT LIKE THAT? IS HE THAT FAMOUS?
EVERYONE IS TOO FRIGHT-ENED...
...TO EVEN MENTION HIS NAME.
HE CARRIED THE BLOOD OF KRONOS, WHO ONCE RULED THE ENTIRE UNIVERSE.
ADAMAS WAS ZEUS AND POSEIDON'S OLDER BROTHER.

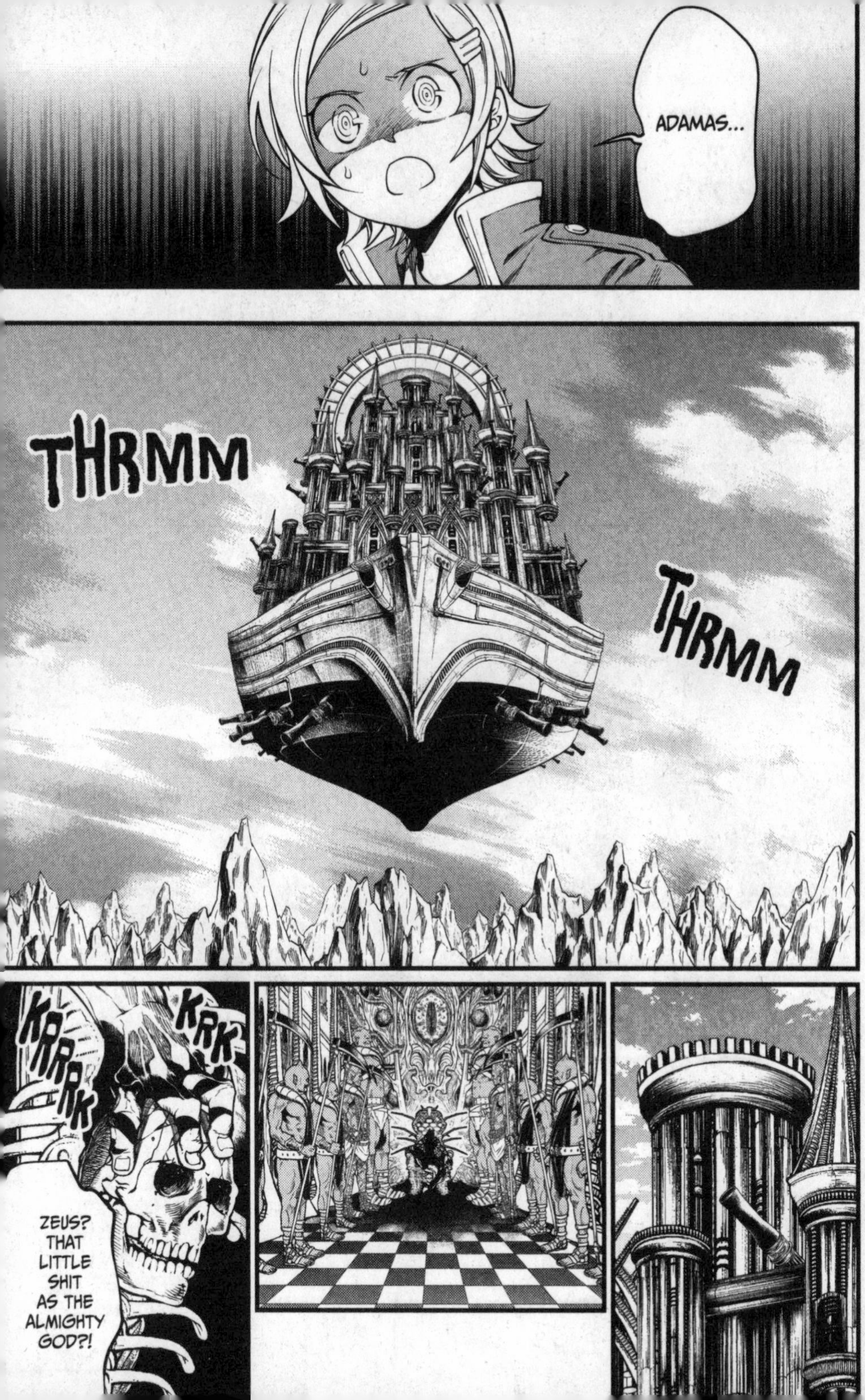
ADAMAS...
THRMM
THRMM
KRK
KRRRK
ZEUS? THAT LITTLE SHIT AS THE ALMIGHTY GOD?!

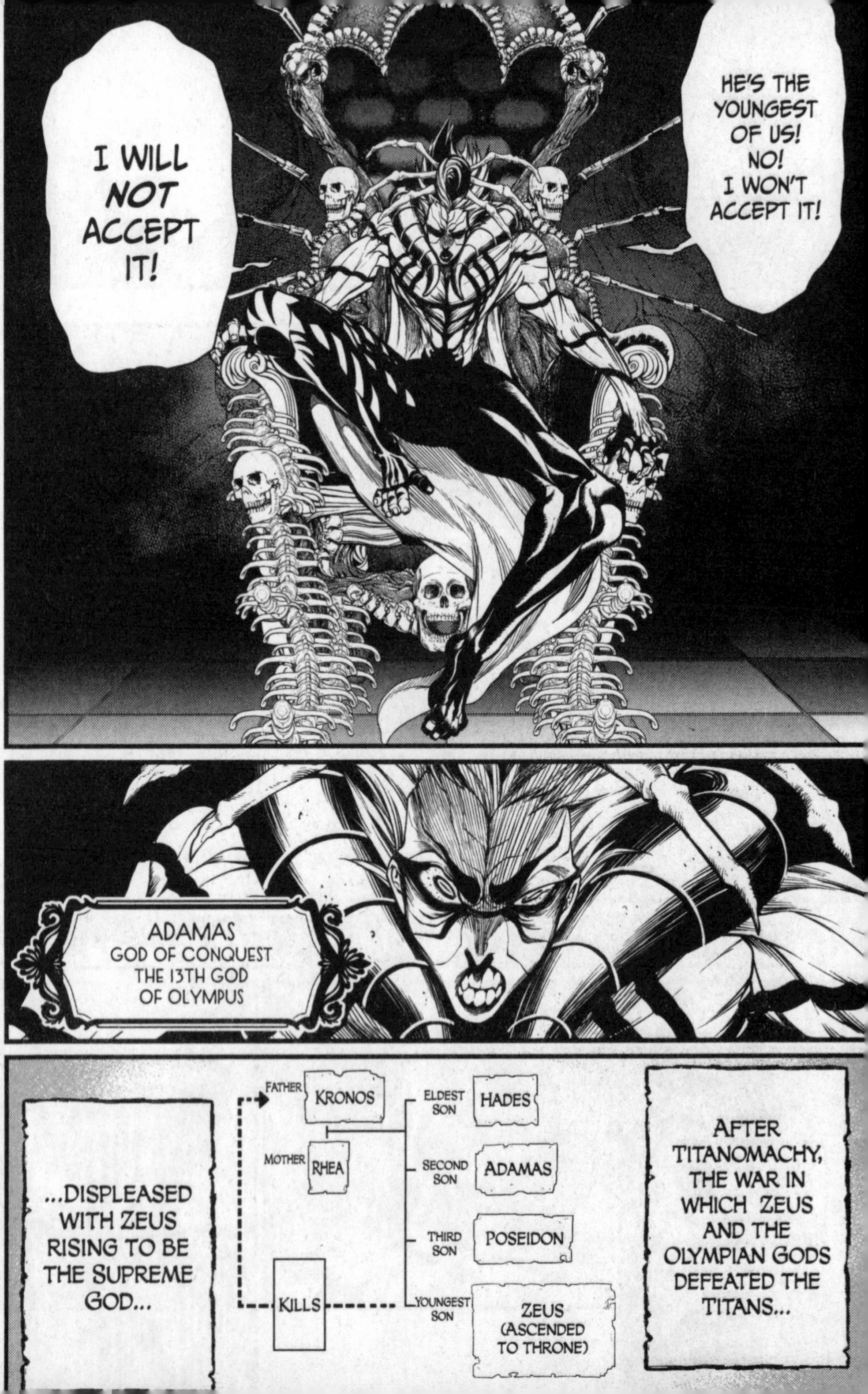
HE'S THE YOUNGEST OF US! NO! I WON'T ACCEPT IT!
I WILL *NOT* ACCEPT IT!
ADAMAS GOD OF CONQUEST THE 13TH GOD OF OLYMPUS
AFTER TITANOMACHY, THE WAR IN WHICH ZEUS AND THE OLYMPIAN GODS DEFEATED THE TITANS...
FATHER KRONOS
MOTHER RHEA
ELDEST SON HADES
SECOND SON ADAMAS
THIRD SON POSEIDON
YOUNGEST SON ZEUS (ASCENDED TO THRONE)
KILLS
...DISPLEASED WITH ZEUS RISING TO BE THE SUPREME GOD...

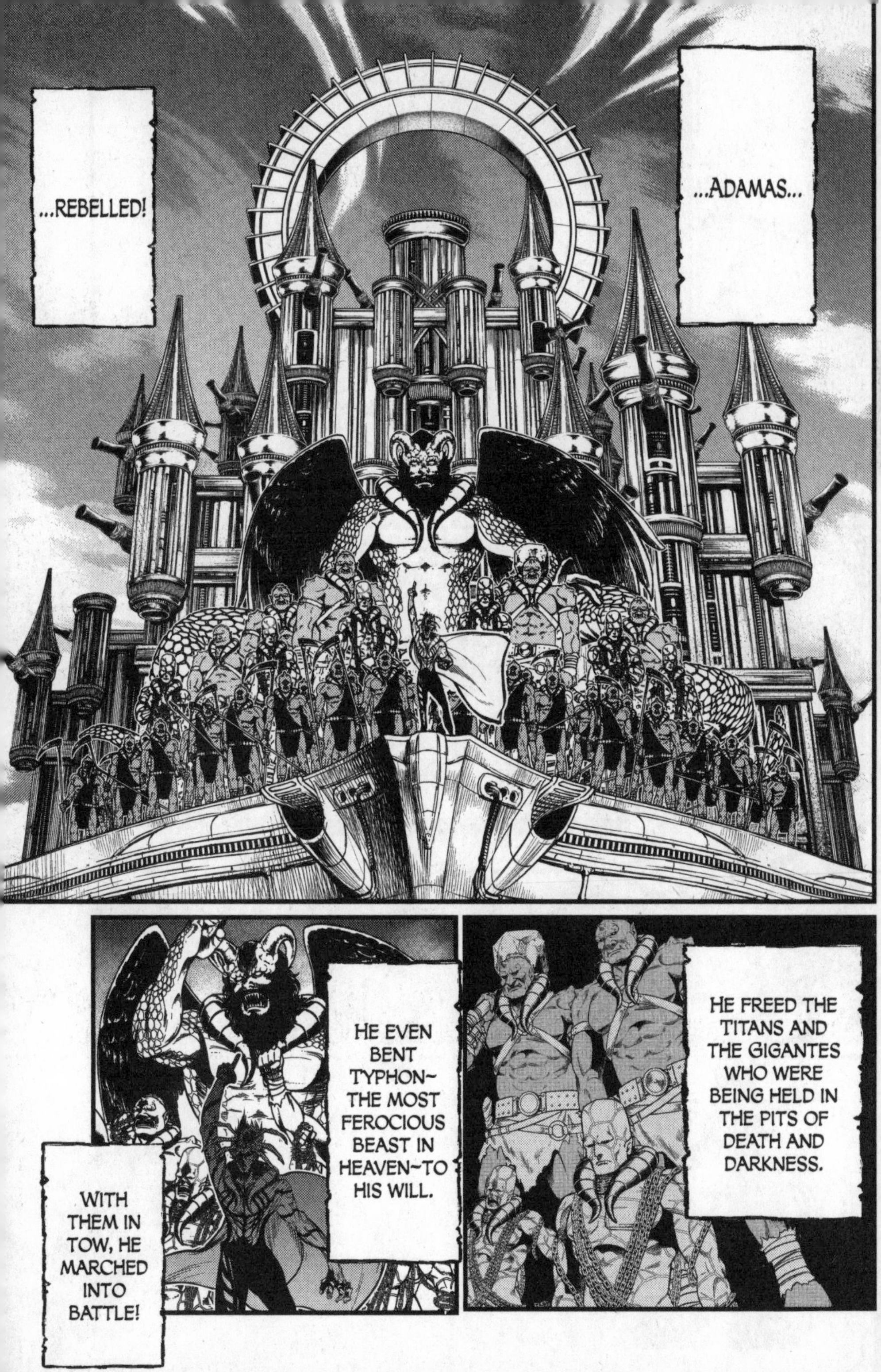
...ADAMAS...
...REBELLED!
HE FREED THE TITANS AND THE GIGANTES WHO WERE BEING HELD IN THE PITS OF DEATH AND DARKNESS.
HE EVEN BENT TYPHON~THE MOST FEROCIOUS BEAST IN HEAVEN~TO HIS WILL.
WITH THEM IN TOW, HE MARCHED INTO BATTLE!

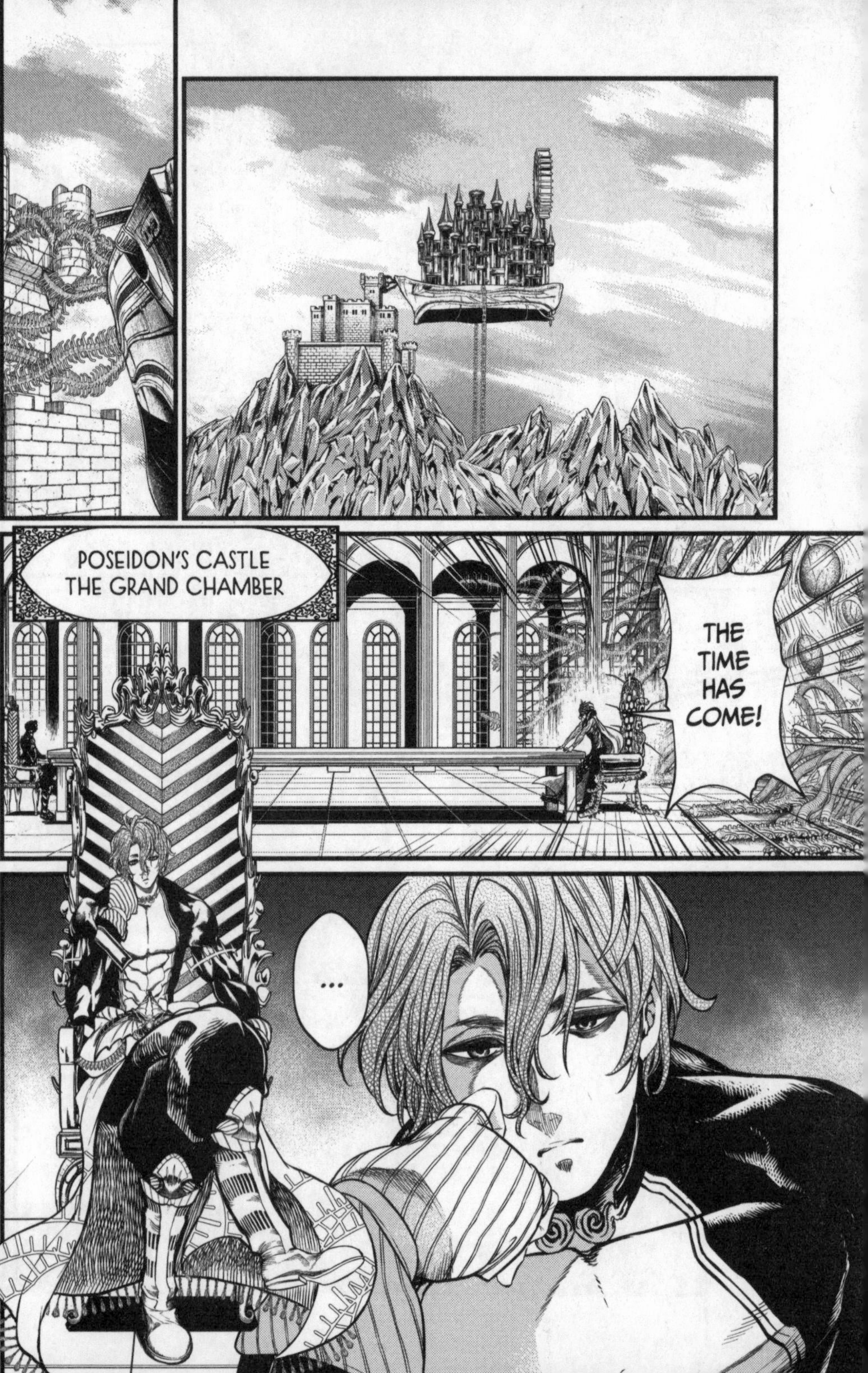
POSEIDON'S CASTLE THE GRAND CHAMBER
THE TIME HAS COME!
...

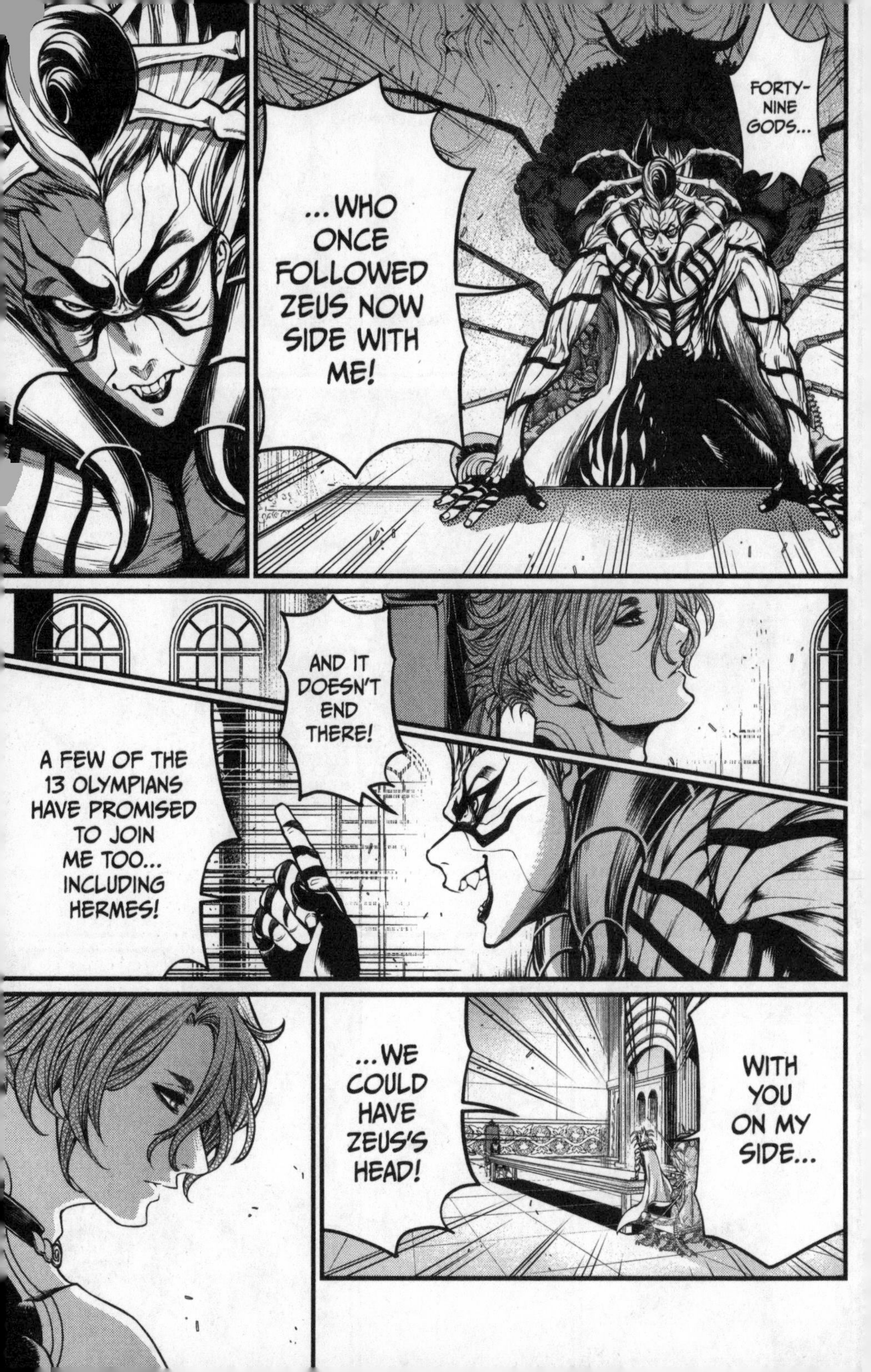
FORTY-NINE GODS...
...WHO ONCE FOLLOWED ZEUS NOW SIDE WITH ME!
AND IT DOESN'T END THERE!
A FEW OF THE 13 OLYMPIANS HAVE PROMISED TO JOIN ME TOO... INCLUDING HERMES!
WITH YOU ON MY SIDE...
...WE COULD HAVE ZEUS'S HEAD!

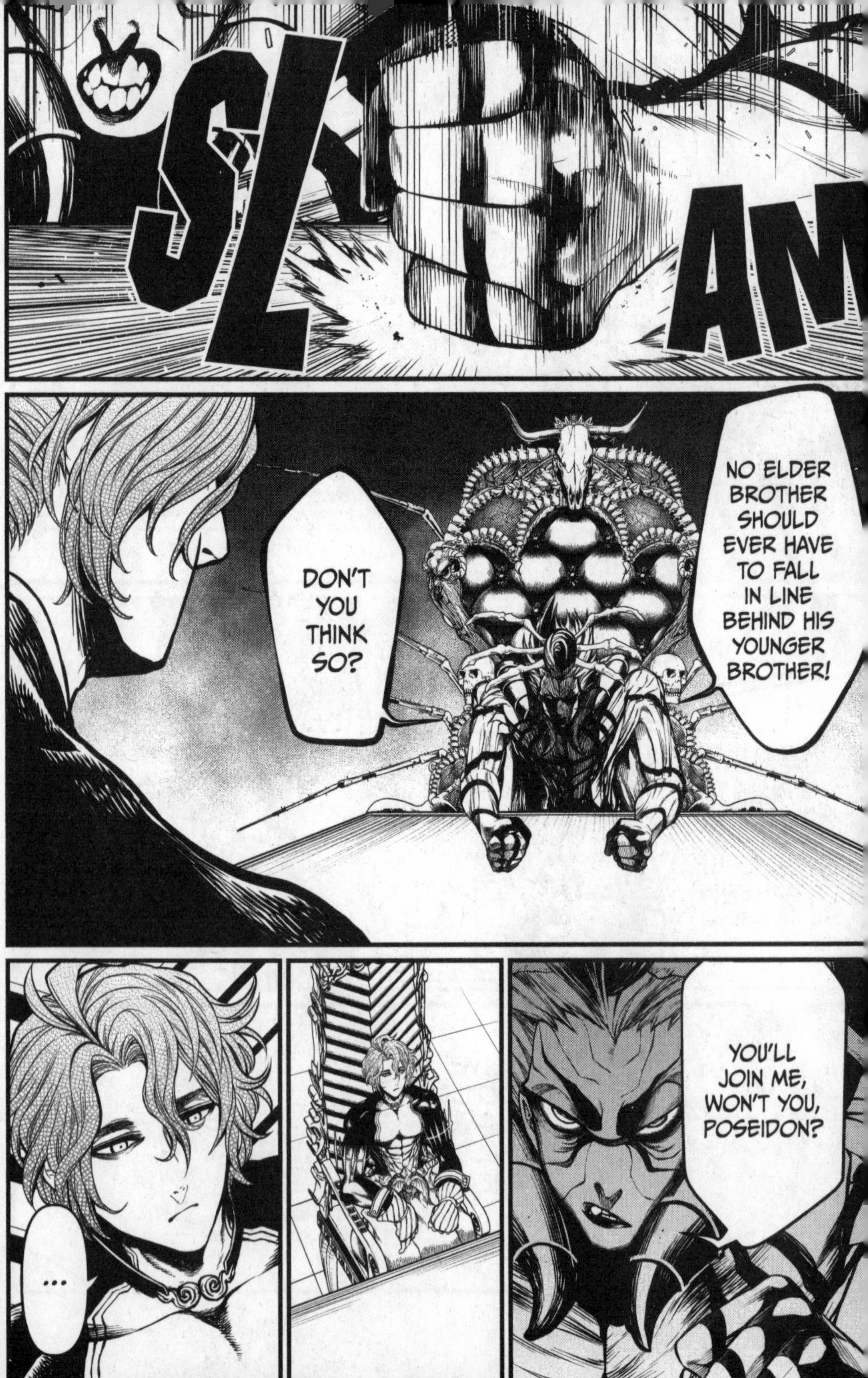
SLAM
NO ELDER BROTHER SHOULD EVER HAVE TO FALL IN LINE BEHIND HIS YOUNGER BROTHER!
DON'T YOU THINK SO?
YOU'LL JOIN ME, WON'T YOU, POSEIDON?
...

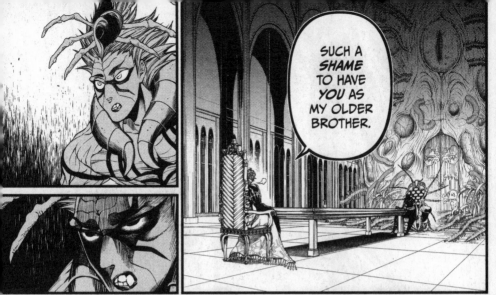

SUCH A *SHAME* TO HAVE *YOU* AS MY OLDER BROTHER.

WHAT WAS THAT?

I'M SORRY...

KR AK

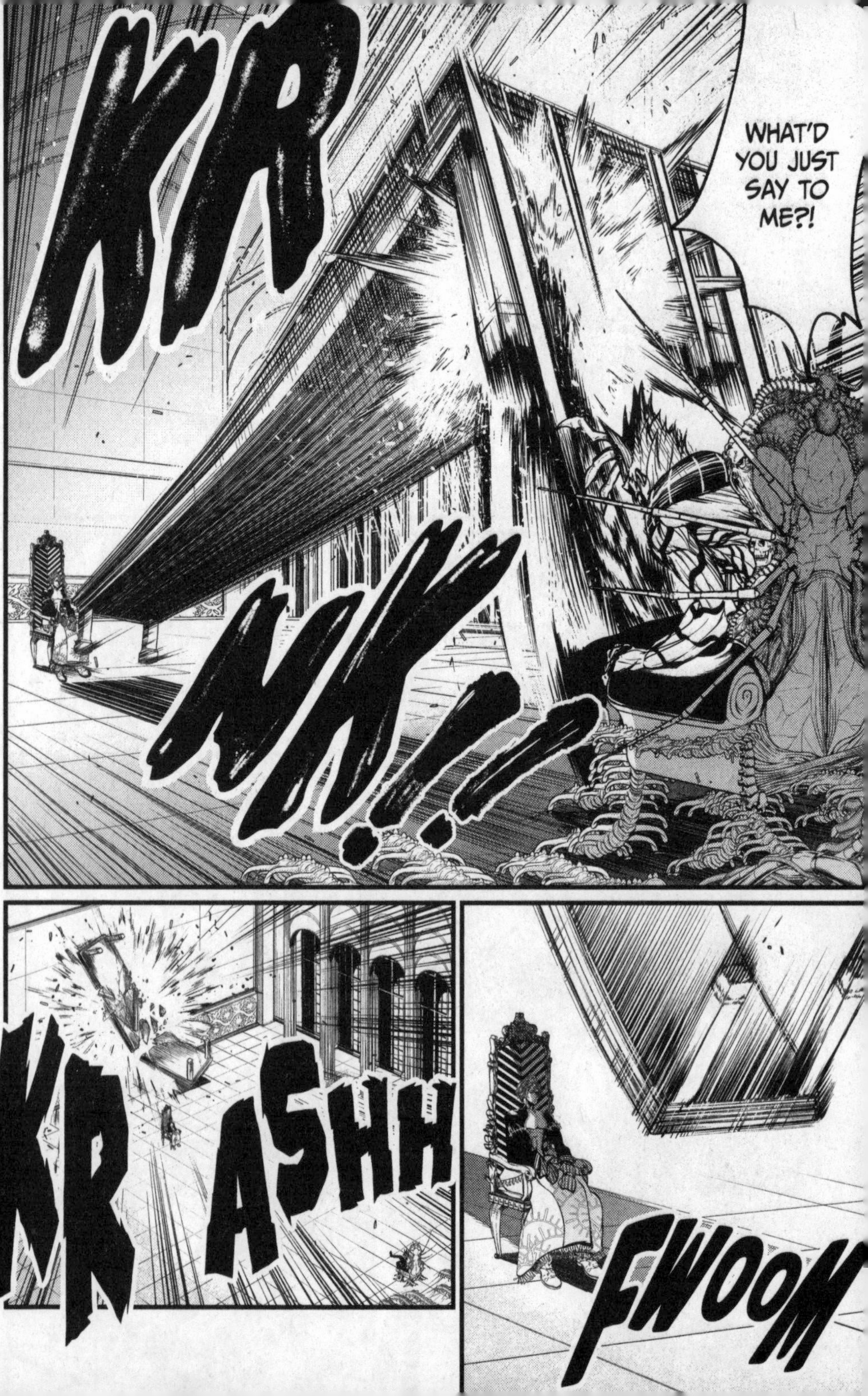
WHAT'D YOU JUST SAY TO ME?!
KRNK!!
FWOOM
KRASHH

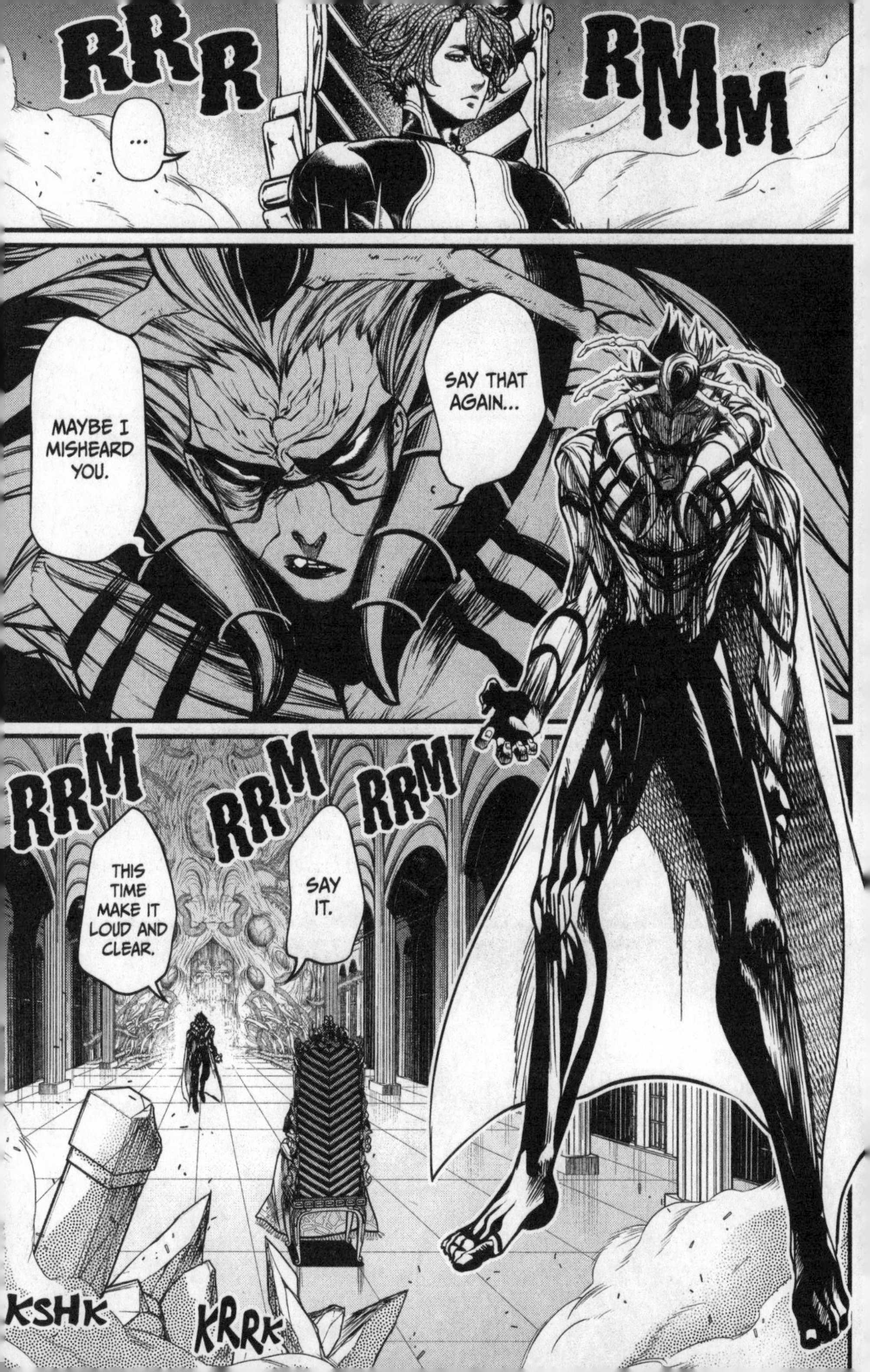
RMM
RRR
...
SAY THAT AGAIN...
MAYBE I MISHEARD YOU.
RRM
RRM
RRM
SAY IT.
THIS TIME MAKE IT LOUD AND CLEAR.
KRRK
KSHK

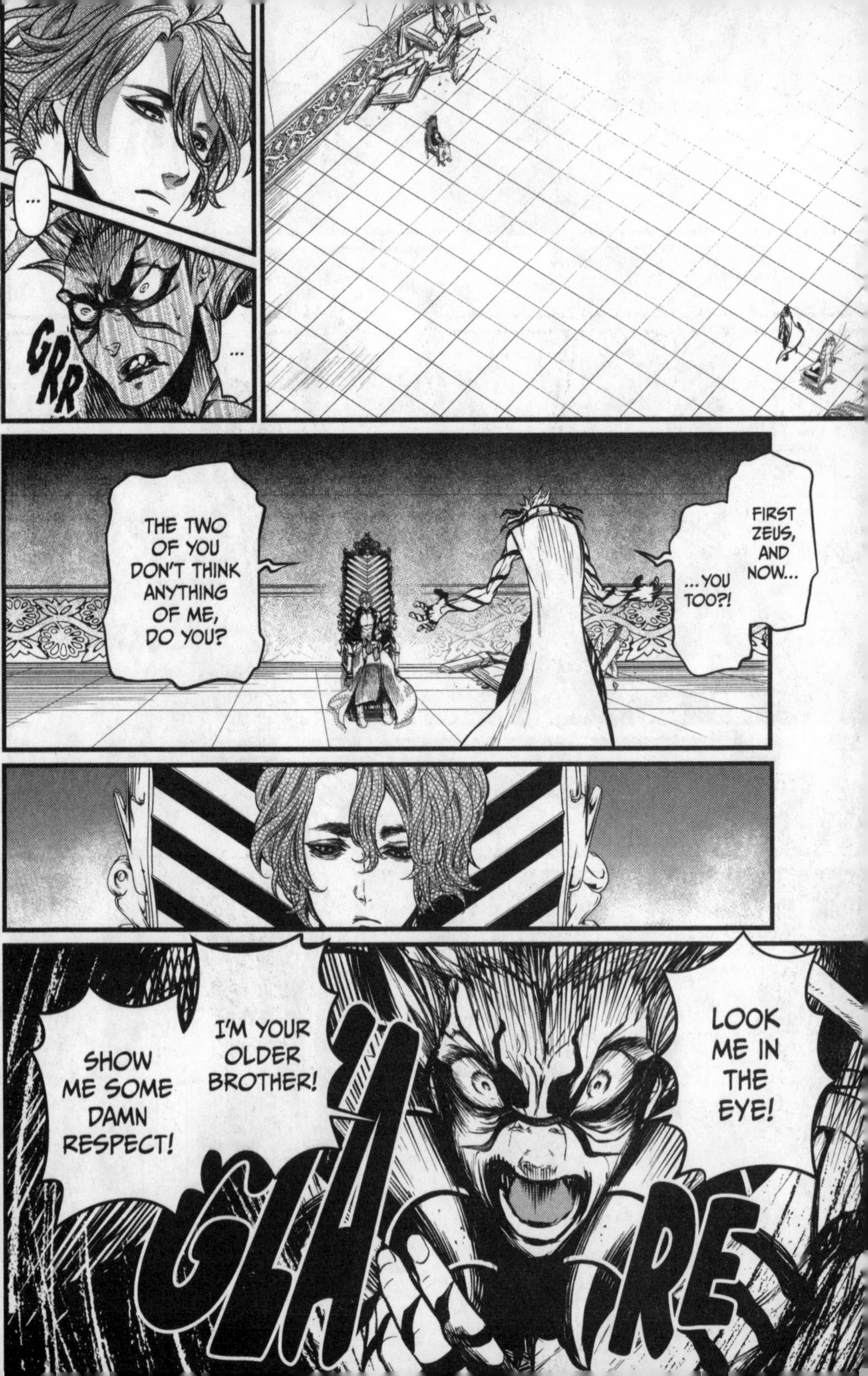
...
GRR
...
FIRST ZEUS, AND NOW...
...YOU TOO?!
THE TWO OF YOU DON'T THINK ANYTHING OF ME, DO YOU?
LOOK ME IN THE EYE!
I'M YOUR OLDER BROTHER!
SHOW ME SOME DAMN RESPECT!

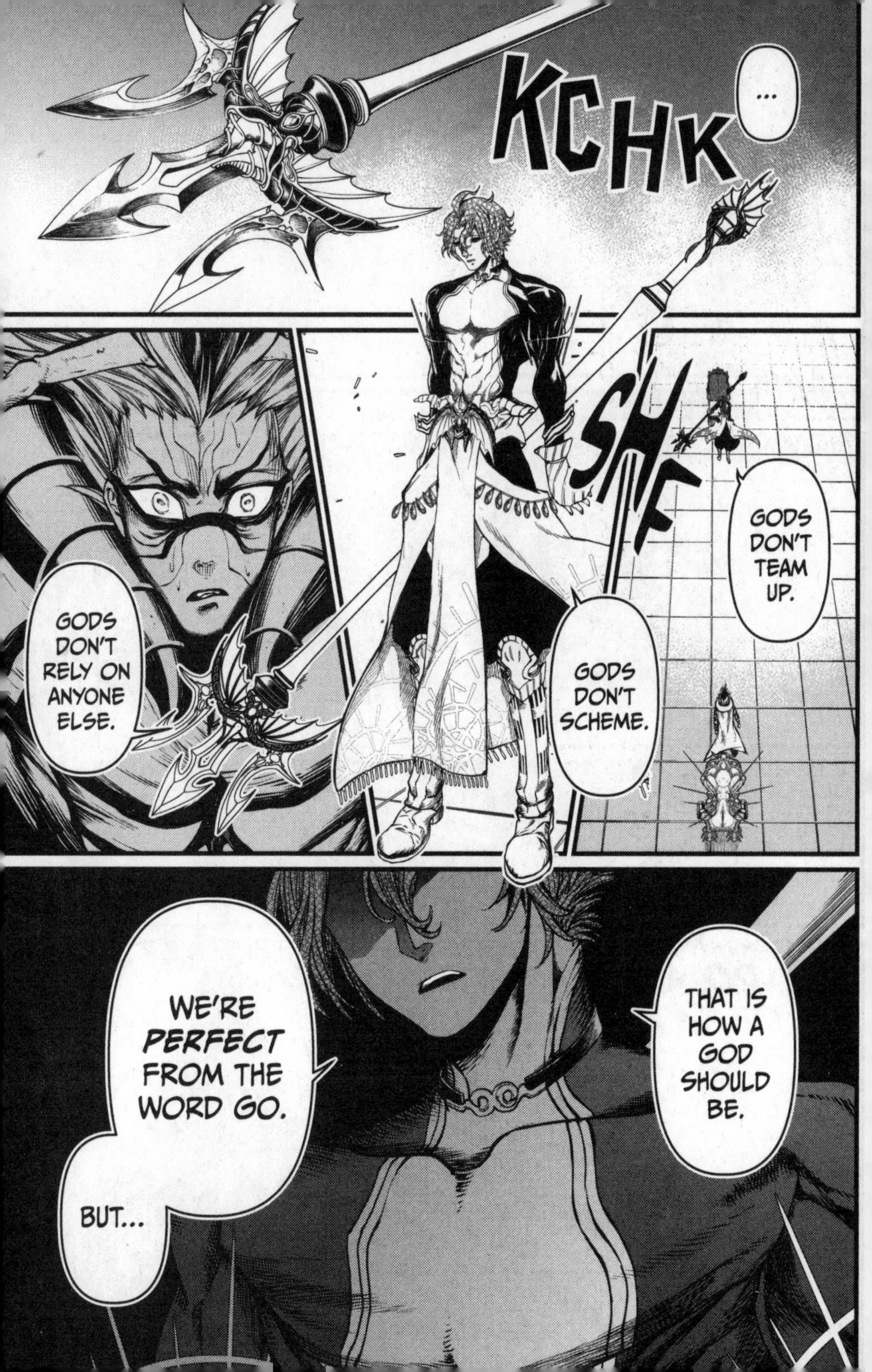

...
KCHK
GODS DON'T TEAM UP.
SHF
GODS DON'T SCHEME.
GODS DON'T RELY ON ANYONE ELSE.
THAT IS HOW A GOD SHOULD BE.
WE'RE *PERFECT* FROM THE WORD GO.
BUT...

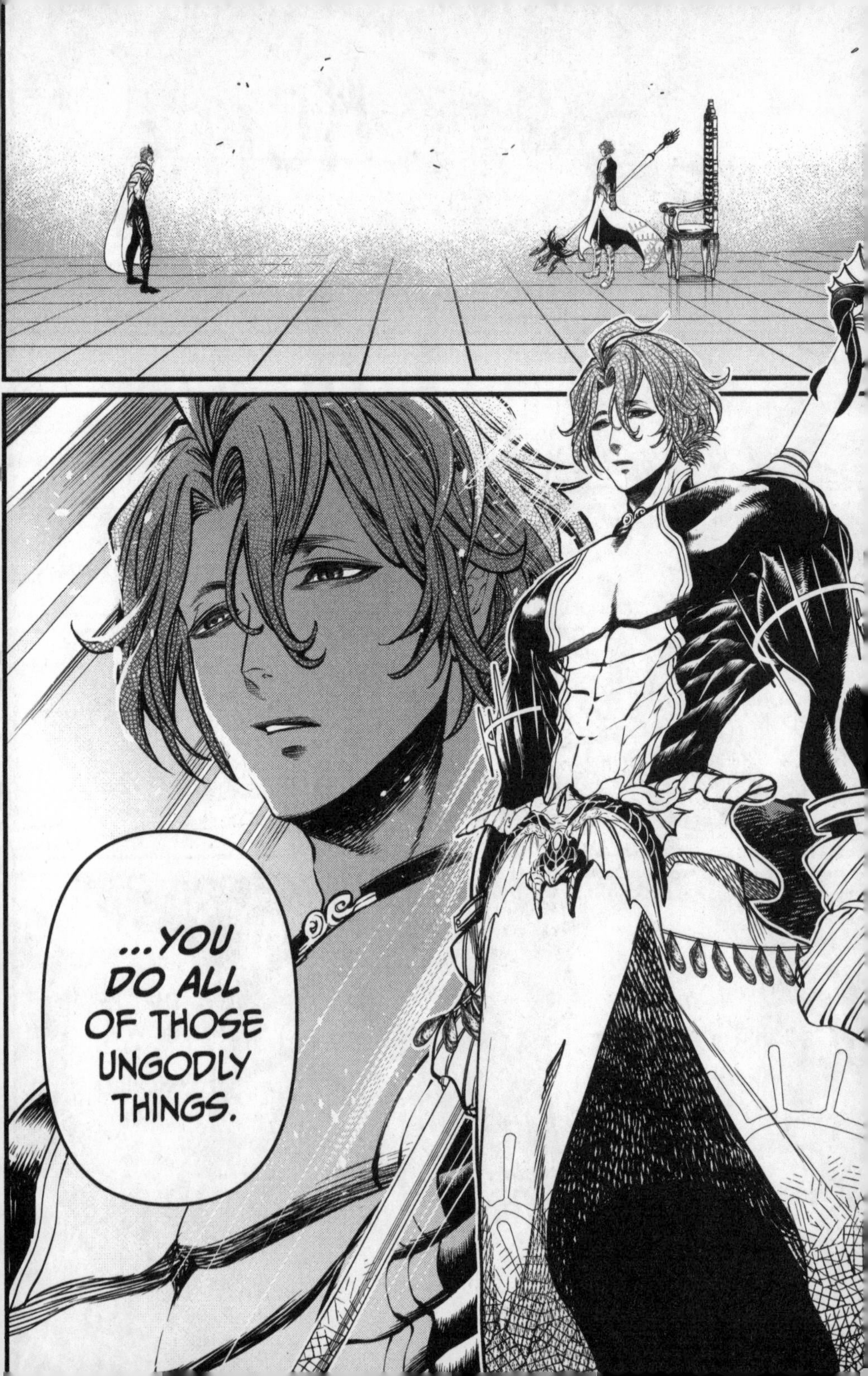
...YOU DO ALL OF THOSE UNGODLY THINGS.

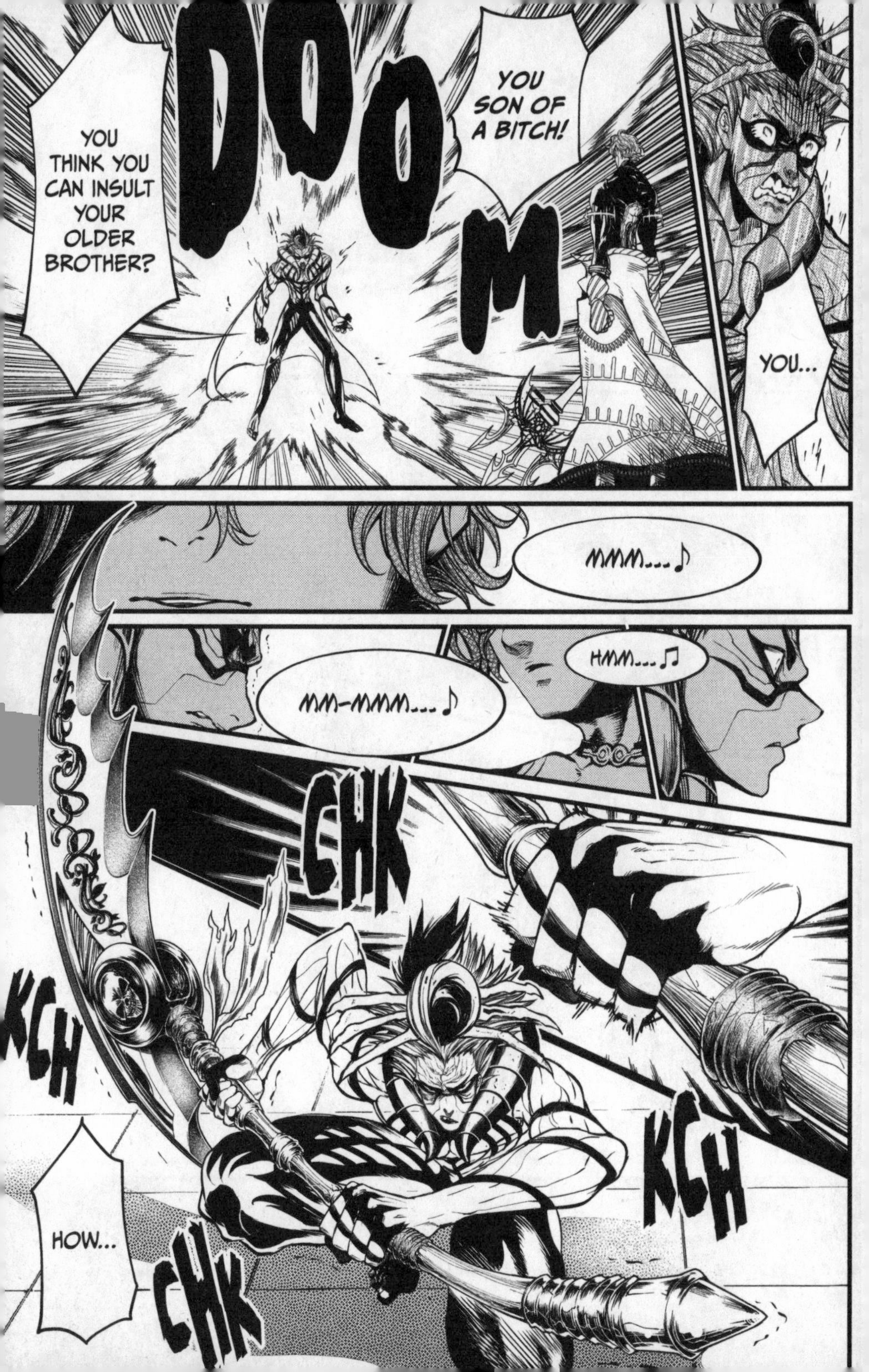
YOU...
YOU SON OF A BITCH!
DOOOM
YOU THINK YOU CAN INSULT YOUR OLDER BROTHER?
MMM...♪
HMM...♫
MM-MMM...♪
CHK
KCH
KCH
HOW...
CHK

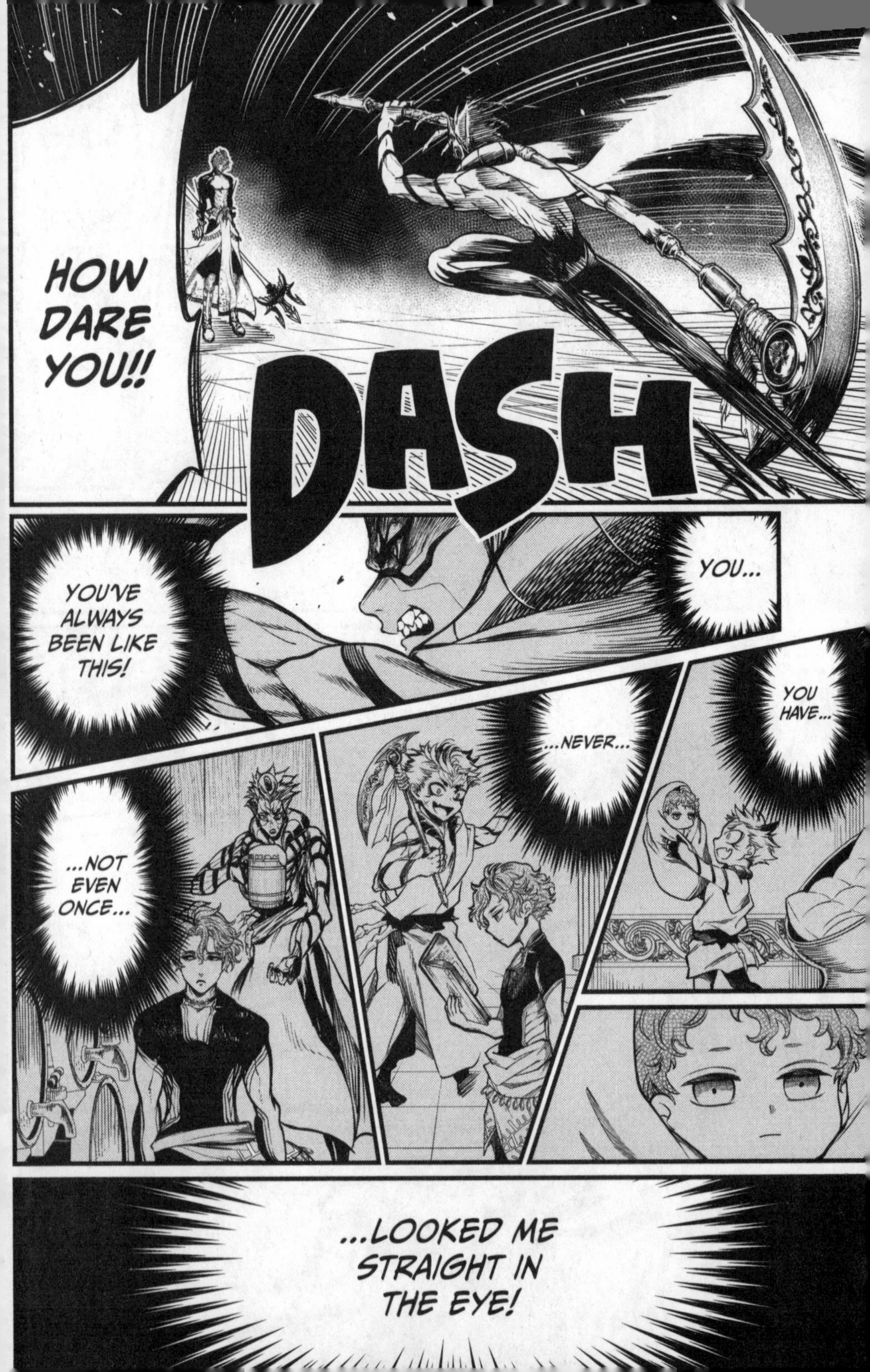
HOW DARE YOU!!
DASH
YOU...
YOU'VE ALWAYS BEEN LIKE THIS!
YOU HAVE...
...NEVER...
...NOT EVEN ONCE...
...LOOKED ME STRAIGHT IN THE EYE!

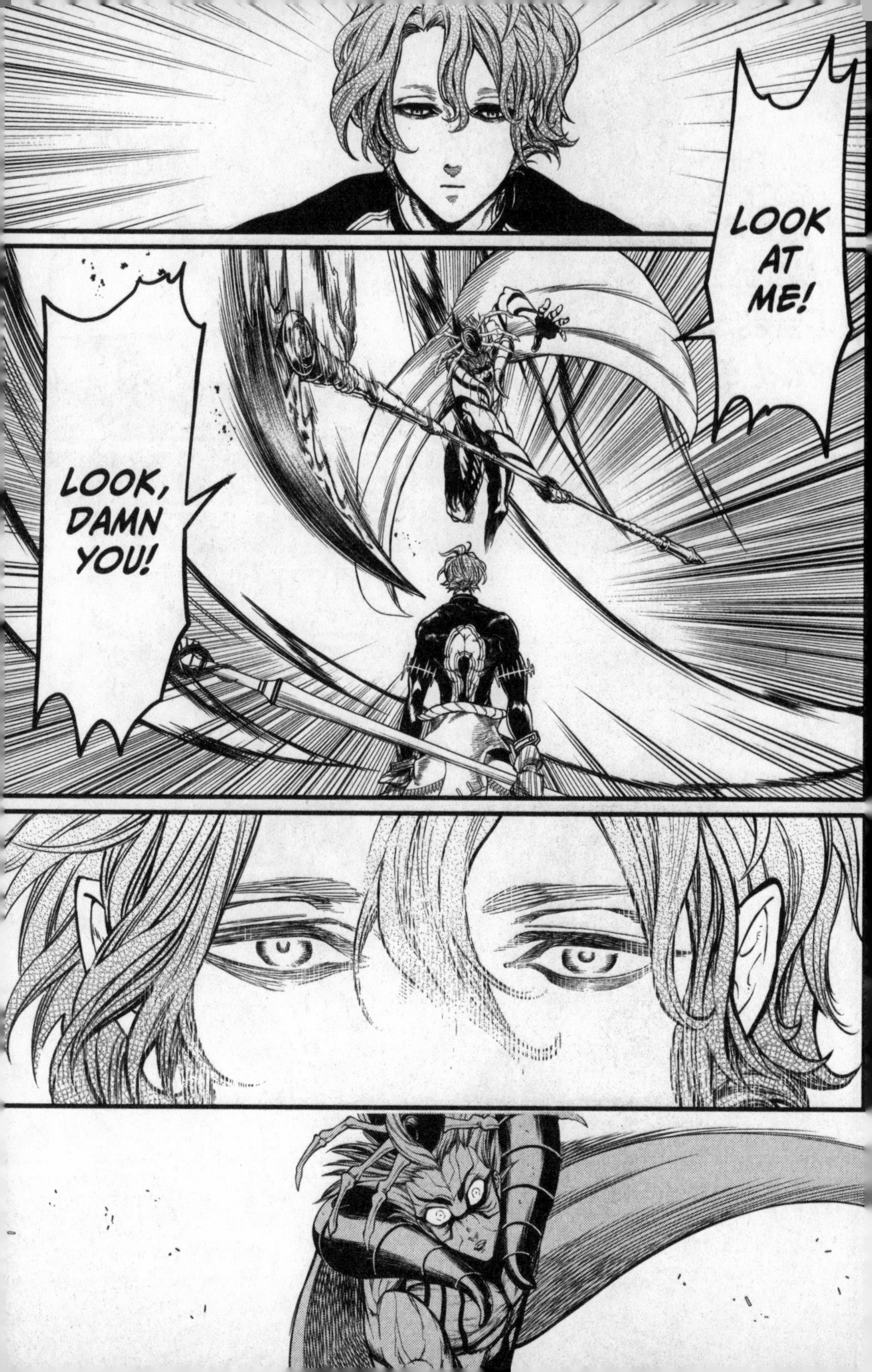
LOOK AT ME!
LOOK, DAMN YOU!

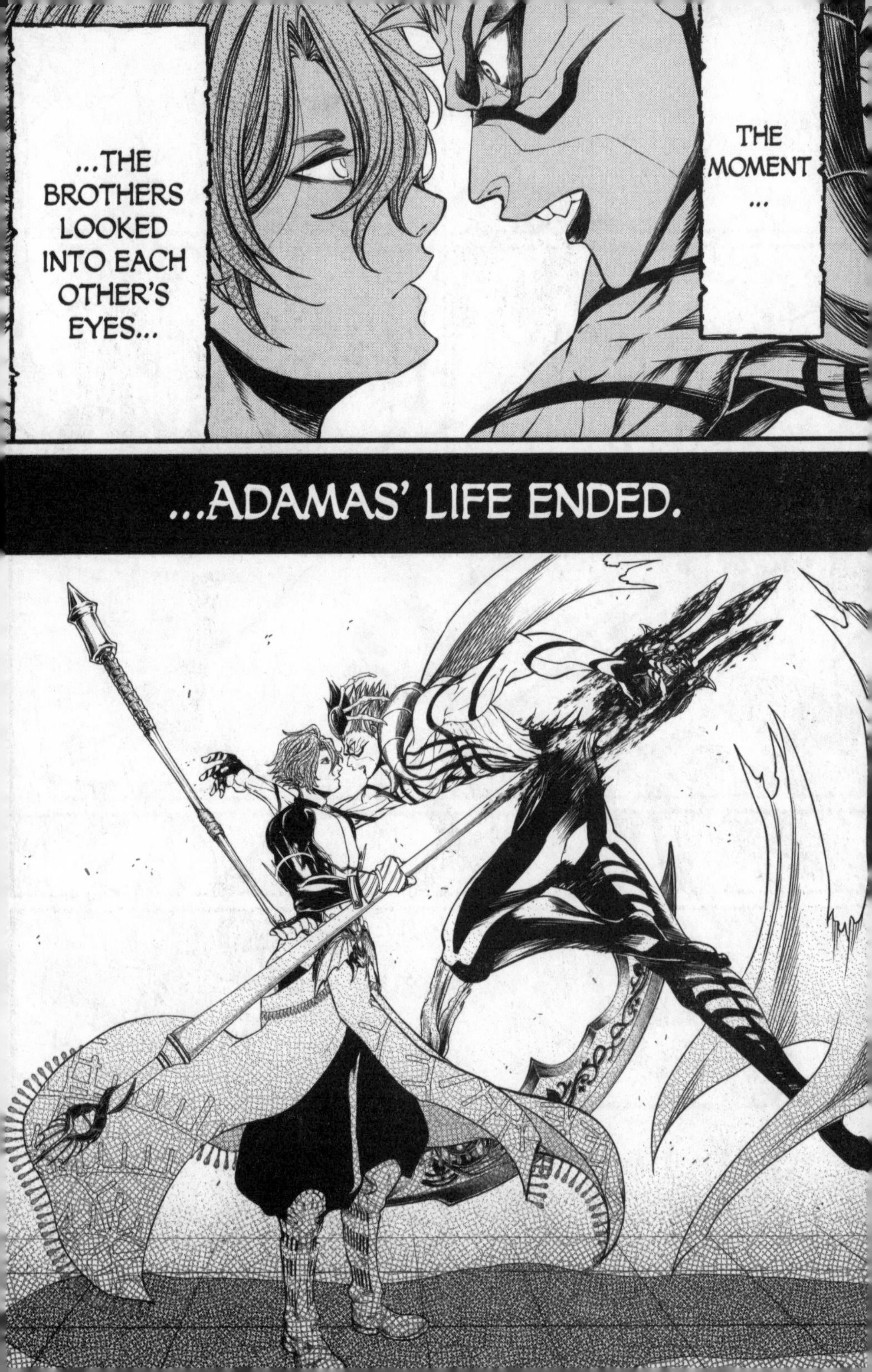
THE MOMENT ...
...THE BROTHERS LOOKED INTO EACH OTHER'S EYES...
...ADAMAS' LIFE ENDED.

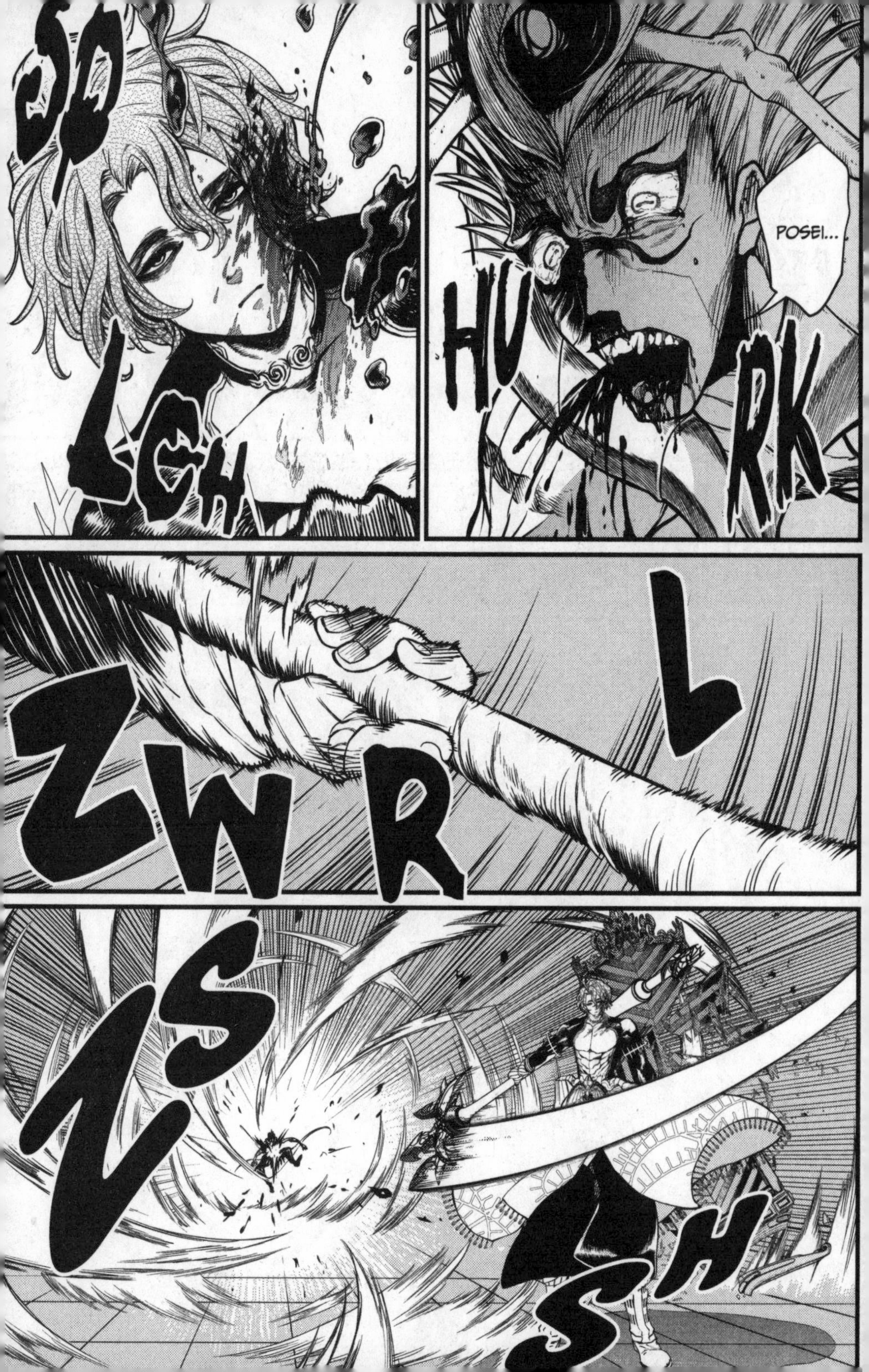
POSEI...
HURK
SPLCH
ZWRL
ZSSH

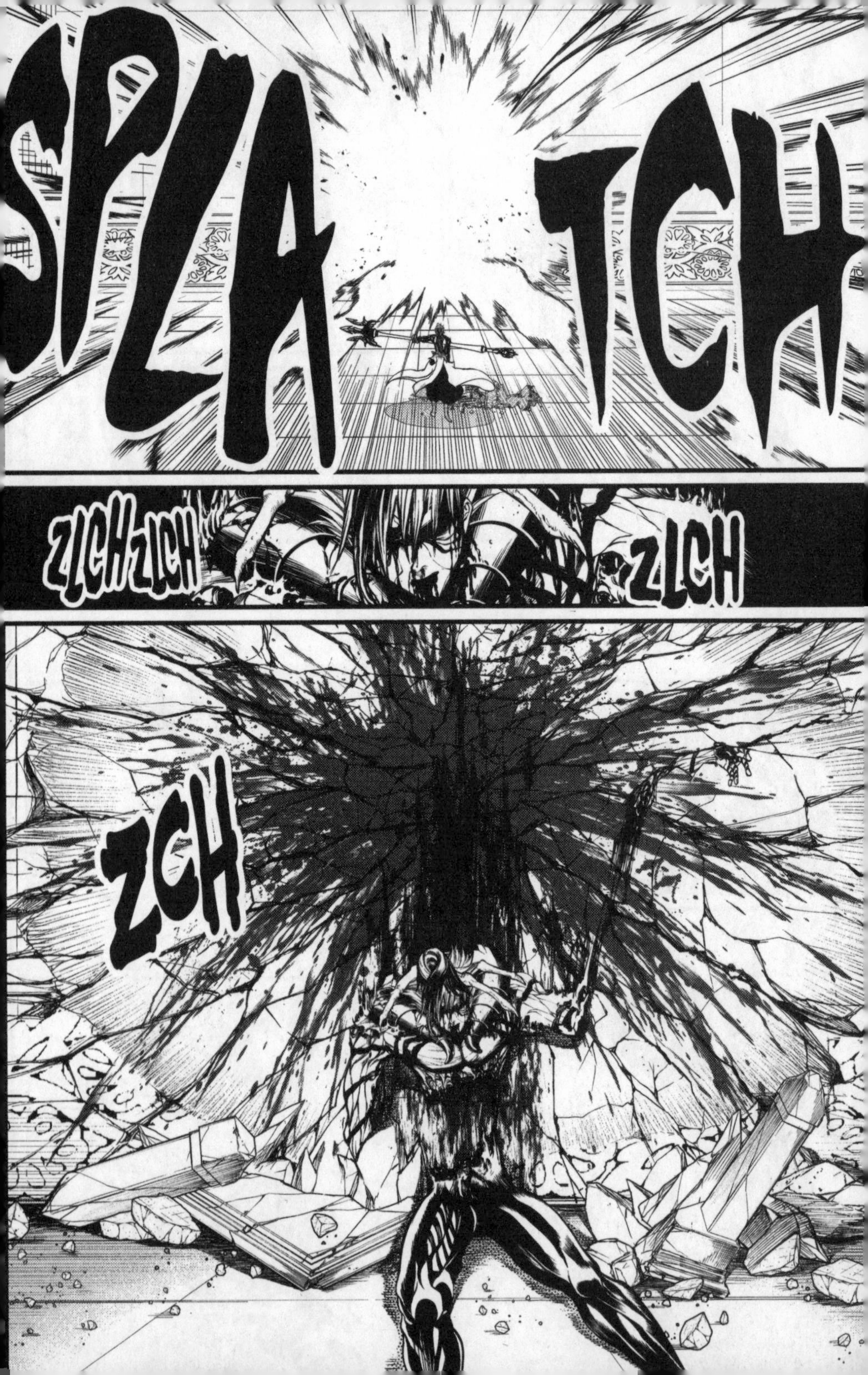
SPLATCH
ZLICH
ZLICH ZLICH
ZCH

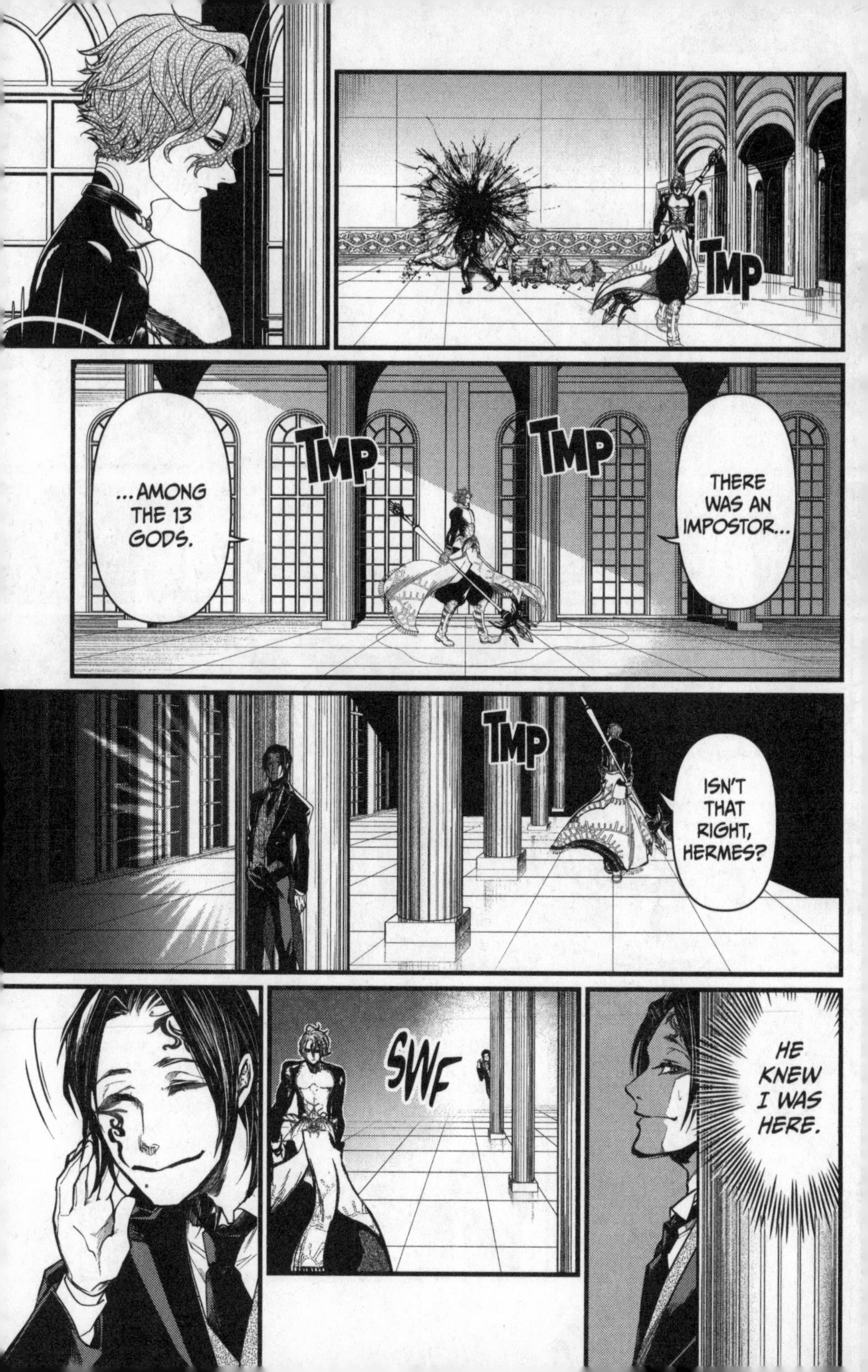
TMP
THERE WAS AN IMPOSTOR...
TMP
TMP
...AMONG THE 13 GODS.
ISN'T THAT RIGHT, HERMES?
TMP
HE KNEW I WAS HERE.
SWF

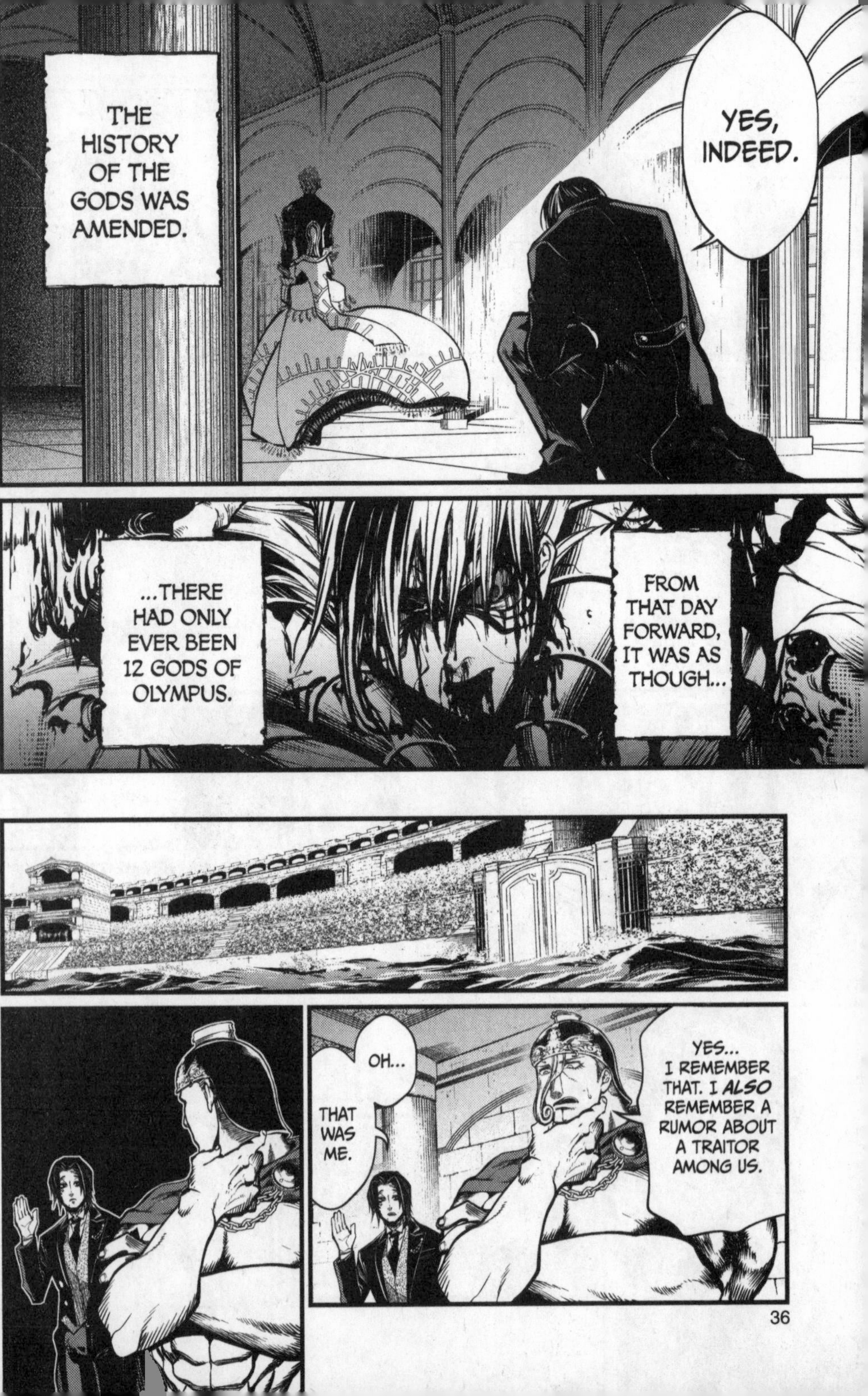
YES, INDEED.
THE HISTORY OF THE GODS WAS AMENDED.
FROM THAT DAY FORWARD, IT WAS AS THOUGH...
...THERE HAD ONLY EVER BEEN 12 GODS OF OLYMPUS.
YES... I REMEMBER THAT. I *ALSO* REMEMBER A RUMOR ABOUT A TRAITOR AMONG US.
OH...
THAT WAS ME.

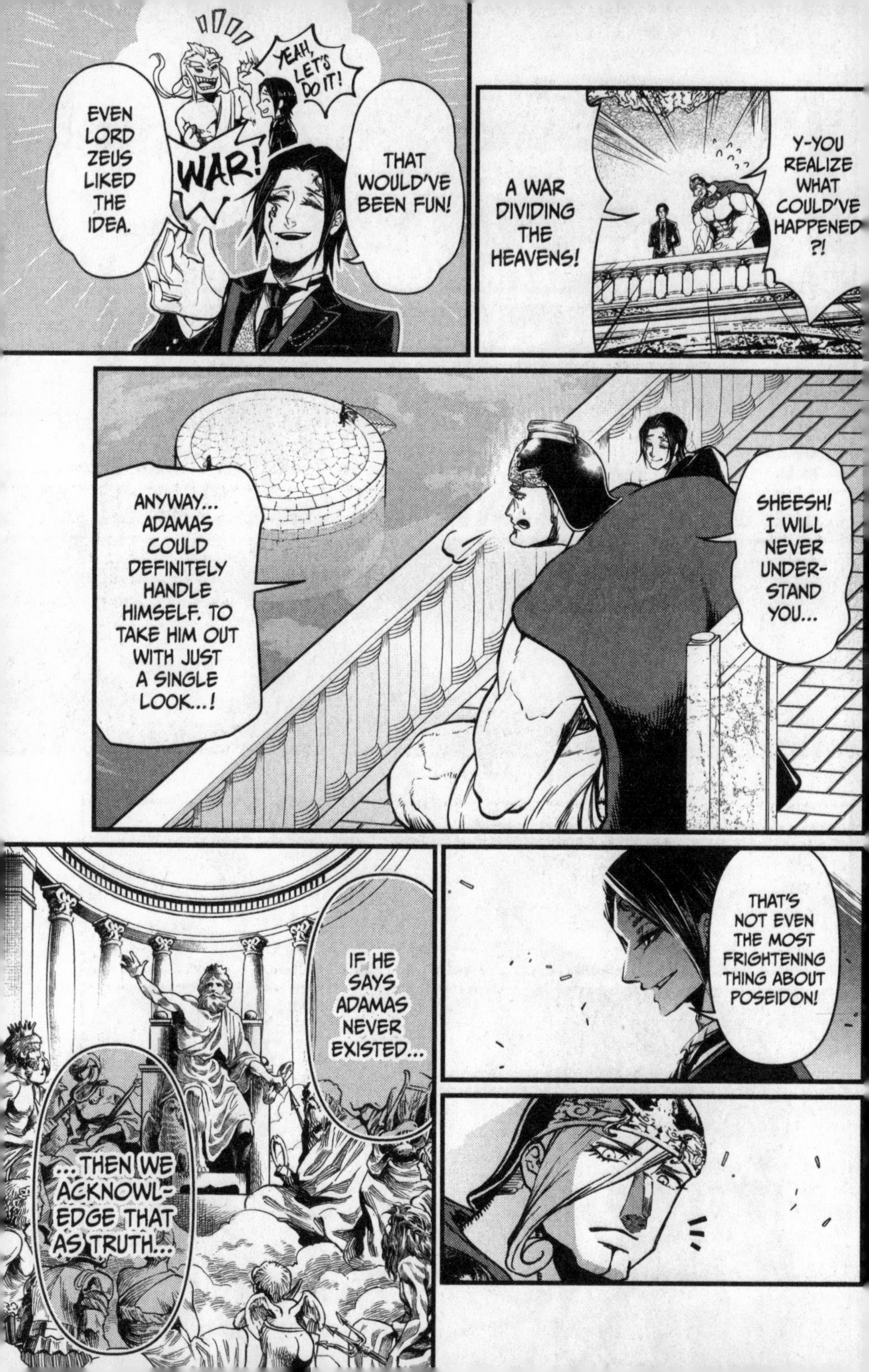
Y-YOU REALIZE WHAT COULD'VE HAPPENED?!
A WAR DIVIDING THE HEAVENS!
YEAH, LET'S DO IT!
THAT WOULD'VE BEEN FUN!
WAR!
EVEN LORD ZEUS LIKED THE IDEA.
SHEESH! I WILL NEVER UNDER-STAND YOU...
ANYWAY... ADAMAS COULD DEFINITELY HANDLE HIMSELF. TO TAKE HIM OUT WITH JUST A SINGLE LOOK...!
THAT'S NOT EVEN THE MOST FRIGHTENING THING ABOUT POSEIDON!
IF HE SAYS ADAMAS NEVER EXISTED...
...THEN WE ACKNOWL-EDGE THAT AS TRUTH...

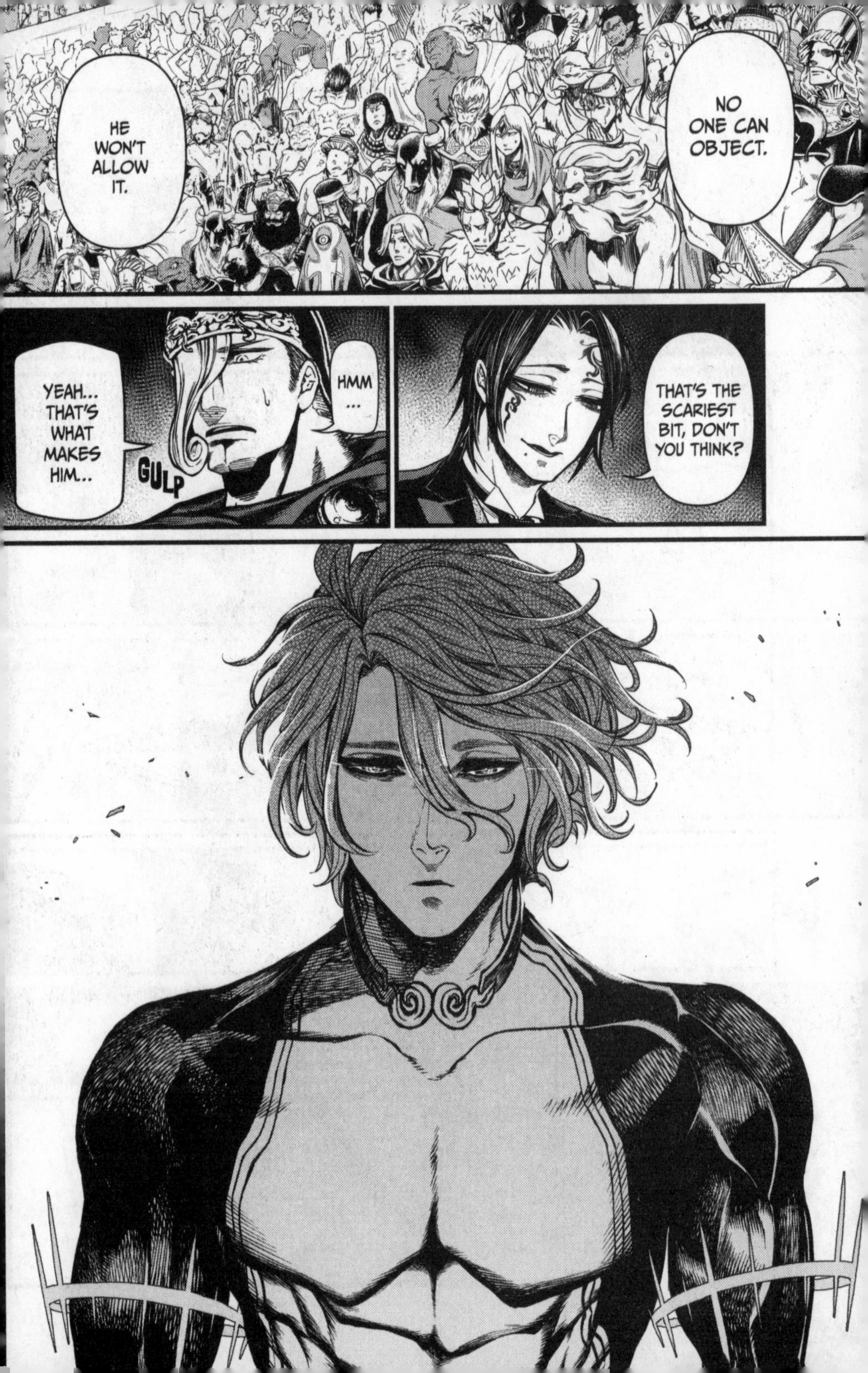
NO ONE CAN OBJECT.
HE WON'T ALLOW IT.
THAT'S THE SCARIEST BIT, DON'T YOU THINK?
HMM ...
YEAH... THAT'S WHAT MAKES HIM...
GULP

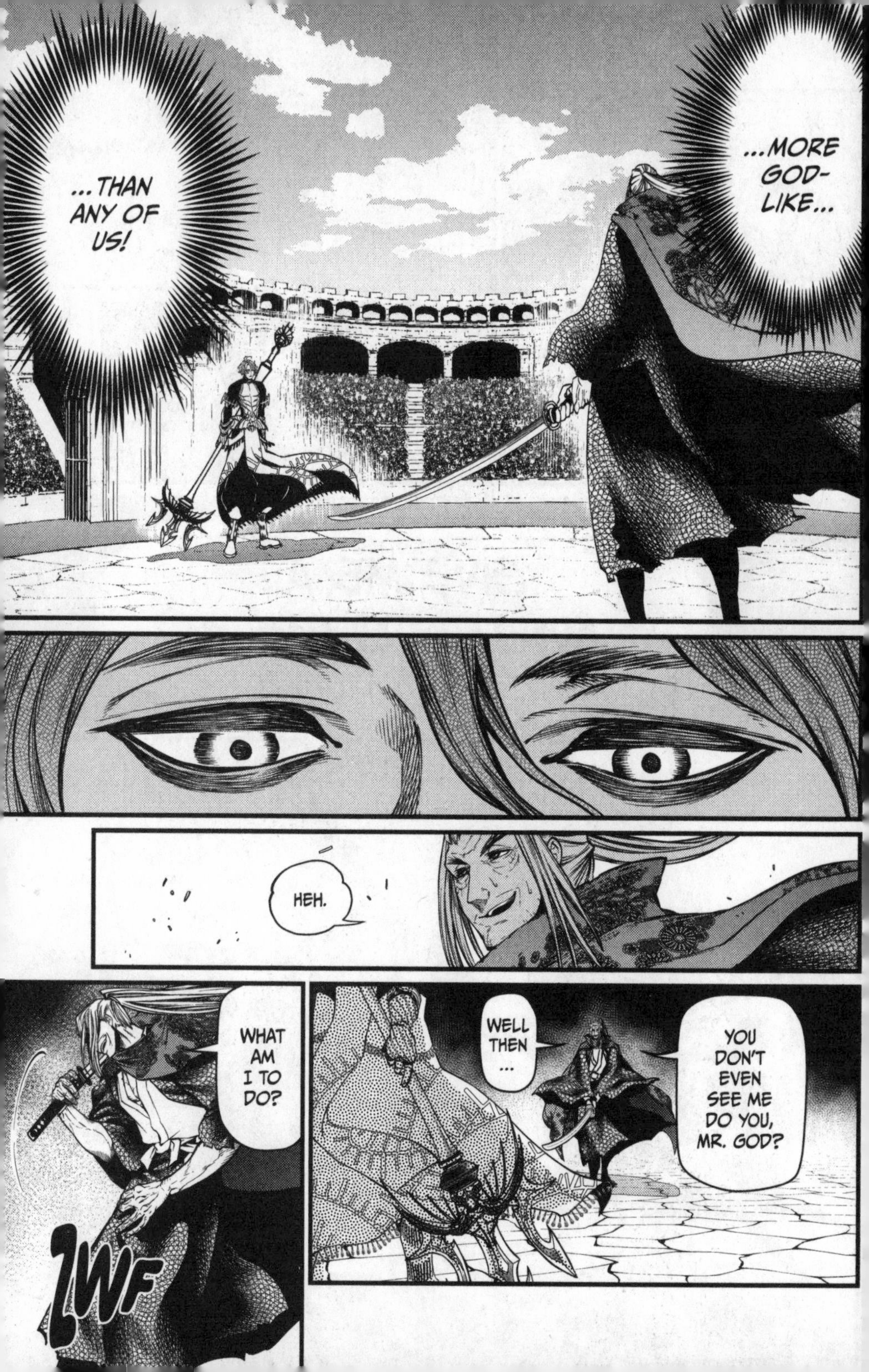
...MORE GOD-LIKE...
...THAN ANY OF US!
HEH.
YOU DON'T EVEN SEE ME DO YOU, MR. GOD?
WELL THEN ...
WHAT AM I TO DO?
ZWF

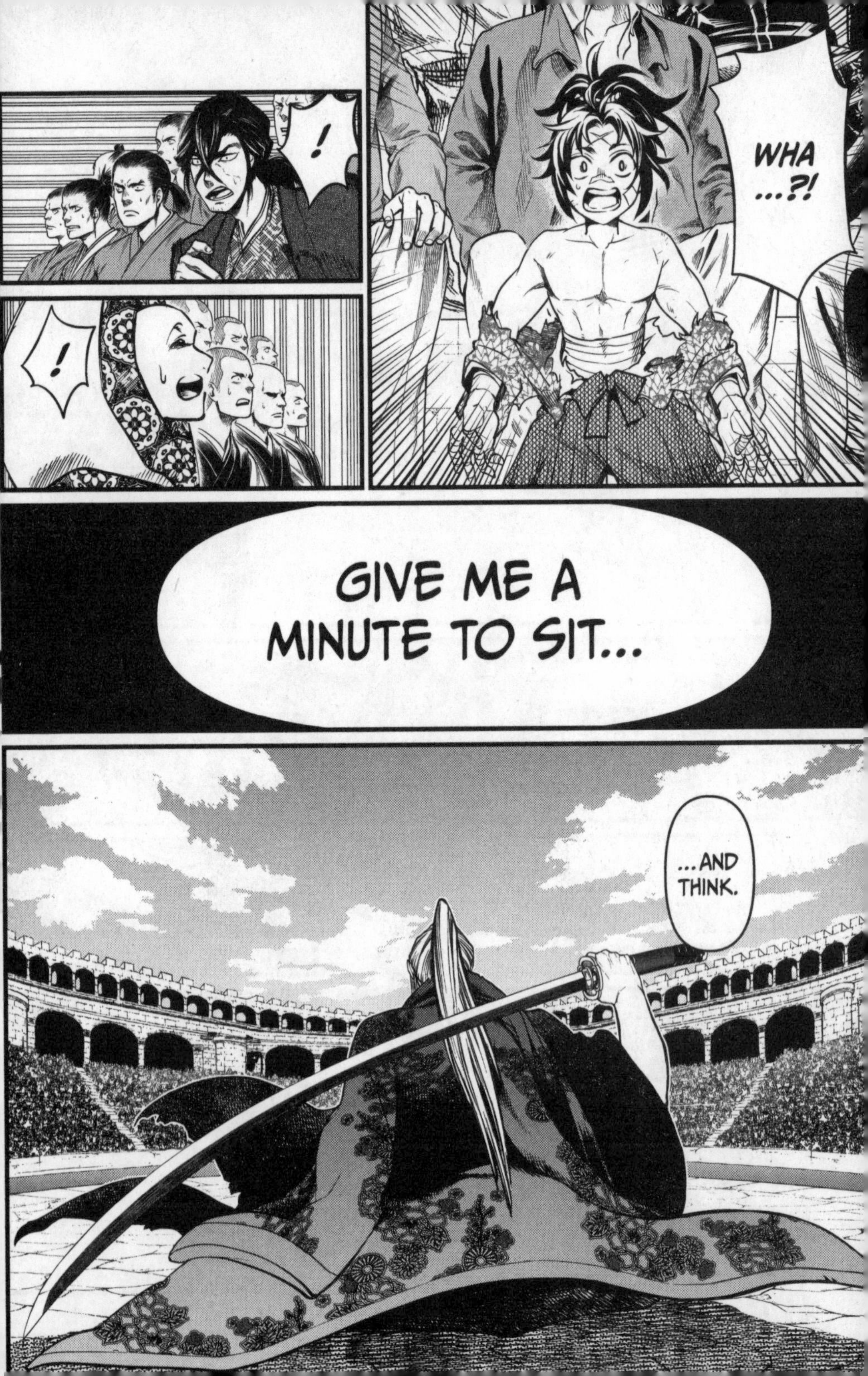
WHA ...?!
!
!
GIVE ME A MINUTE TO SIT...
...AND THINK.

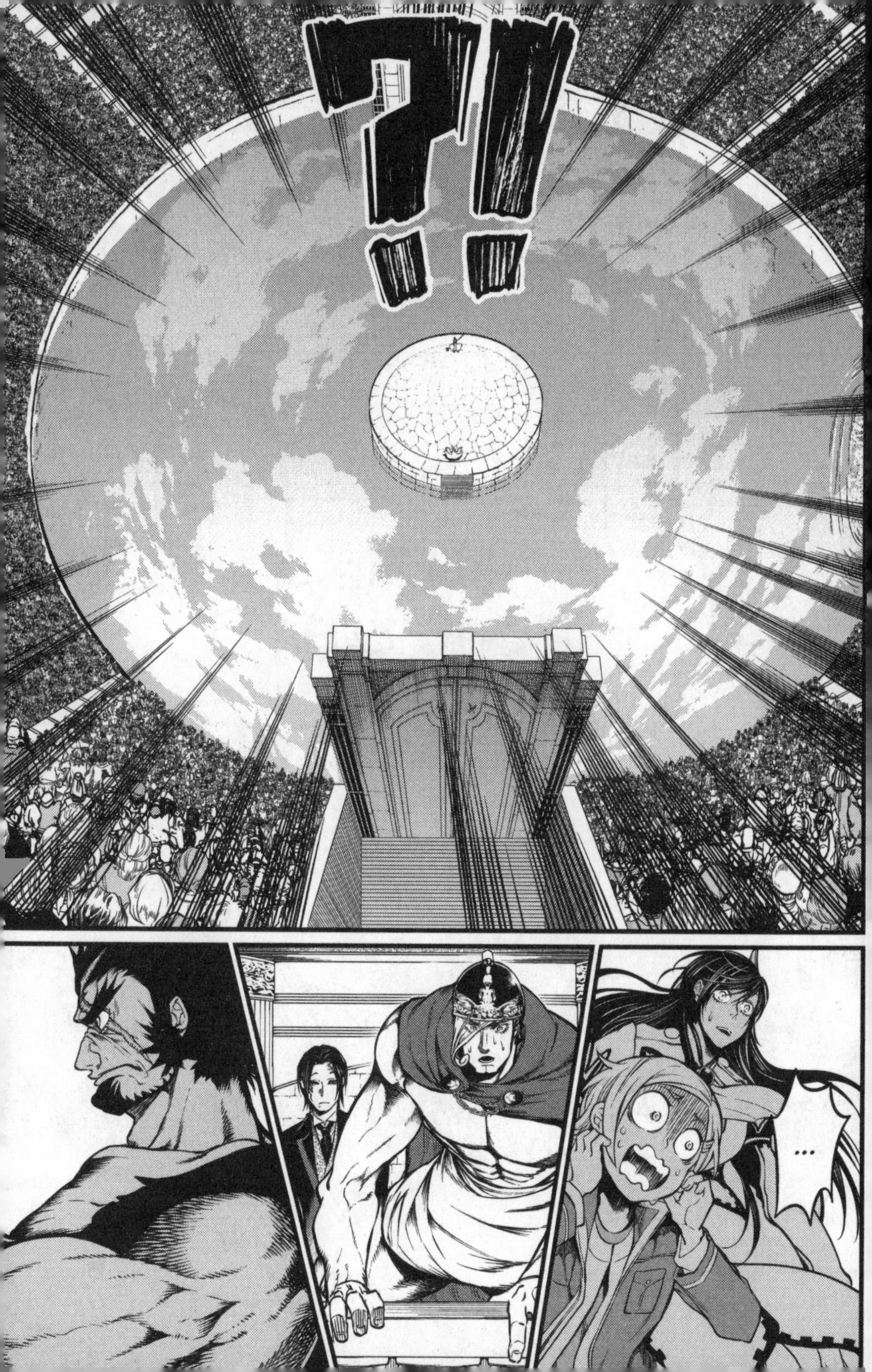
?!
...

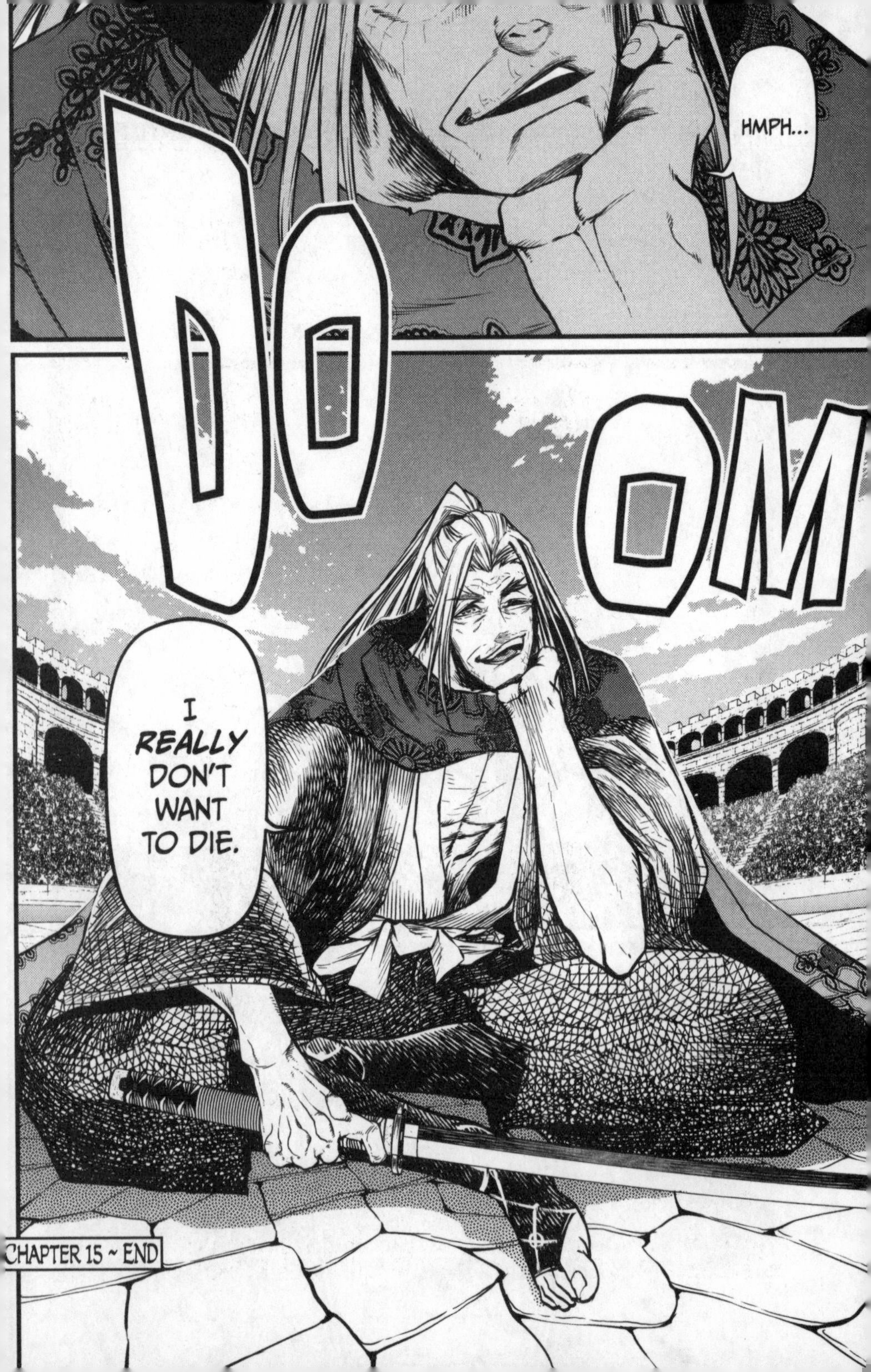
HMPH...
DOOM
I REALLY DON'T WANT TO DIE.
CHAPTER 15 ~ END

A STORY FROM THE PAST

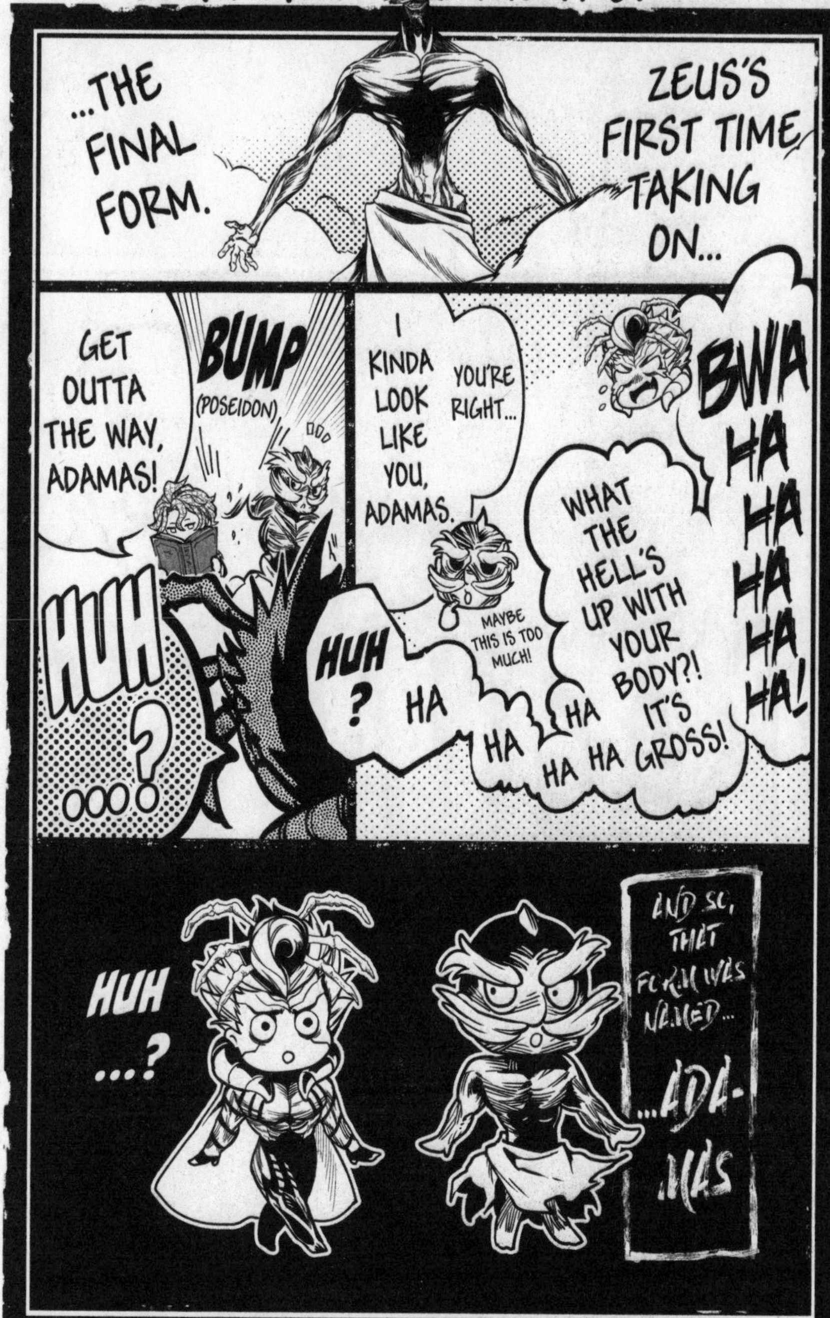
ZEUS'S FIRST TIME TAKING ON...
...THE FINAL FORM.
BWA HA HA HA HA HA!
WHAT THE HELL'S UP WITH YOUR BODY?! IT'S GROSS!
HA HA HA HA HA
YOU'RE RIGHT...
I KINDA LOOK LIKE YOU, ADAMAS.
MAYBE THIS IS TOO MUCH!
HUH?
BUMP
(POSEIDON)
GET OUTTA THE WAY, ADAMAS!
HUH OOO?
AND SO, THAT FORM WAS NAMED...
...ADA-MAS
HUH ...?

RECORD OF

RAGNAROK

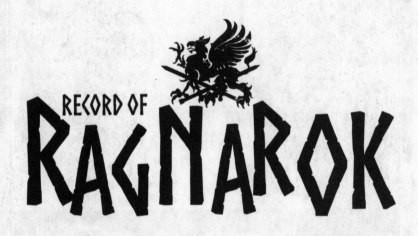

SASAKI KOJIRO NEVER ONCE...

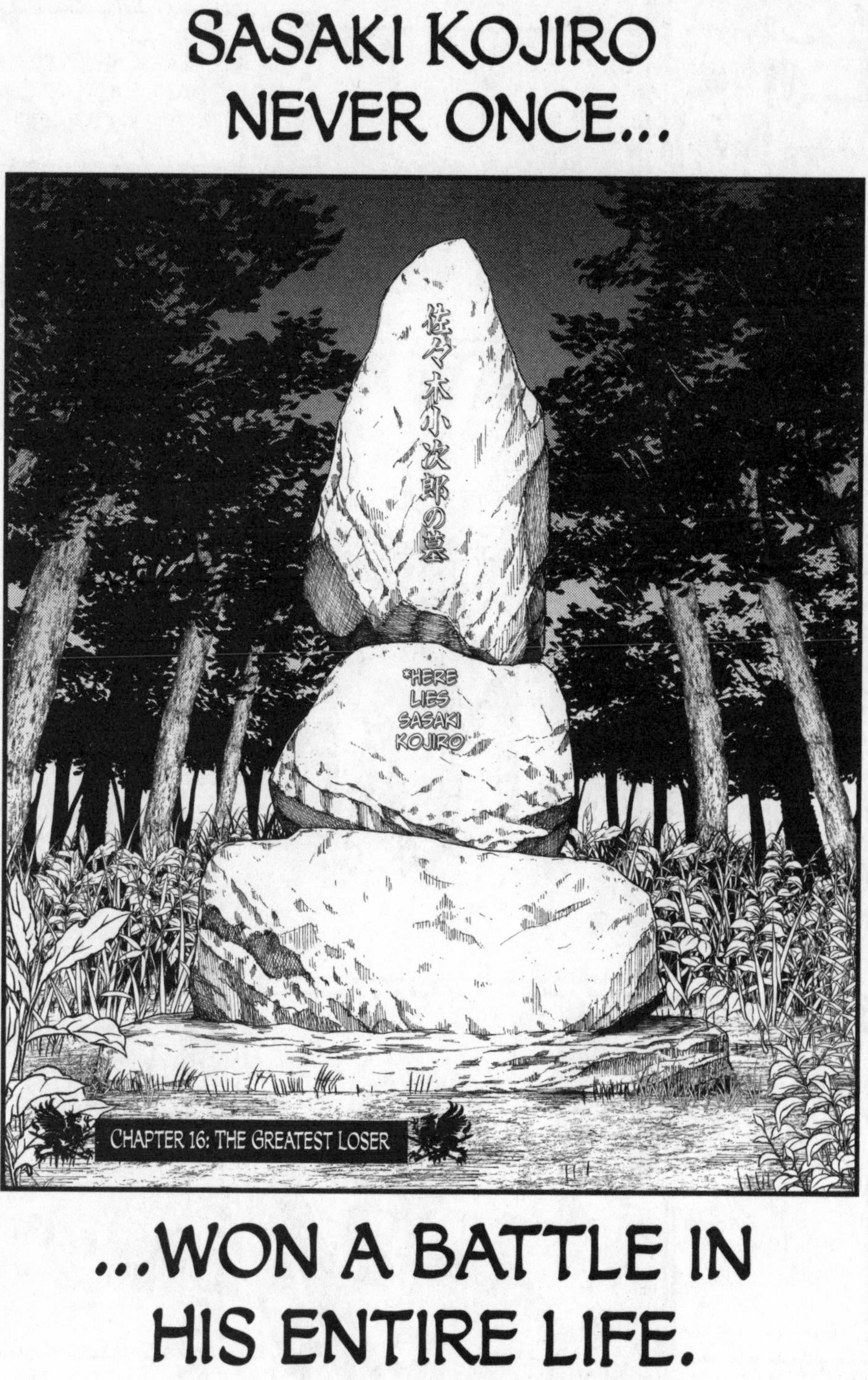
佐々木小次郎の墓
*HERE LIES SASAKI KOJIRO

CHAPTER 16: THE GREATEST LOSER

...WON A BATTLE IN HIS ENTIRE LIFE.

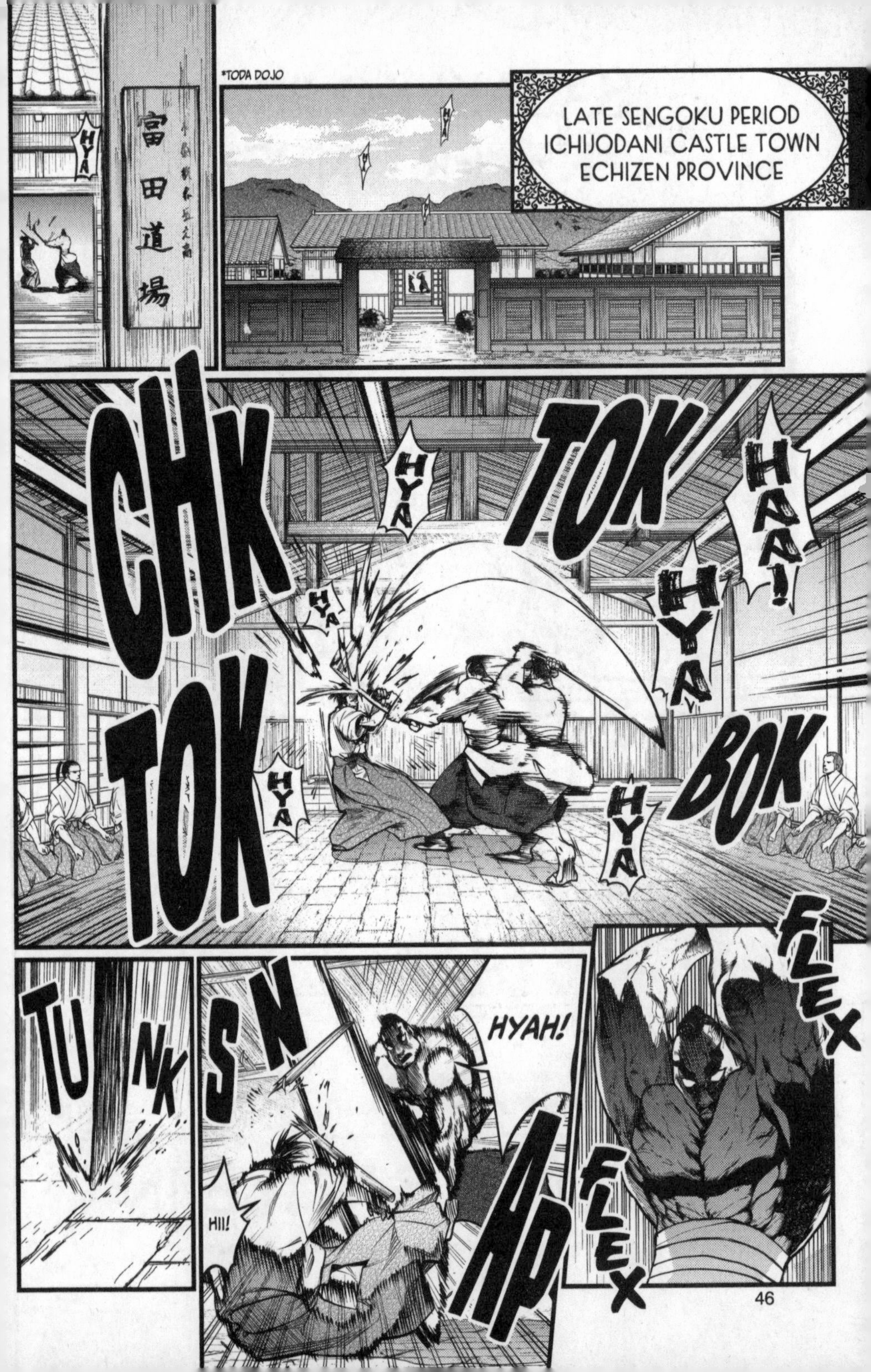
LATE SENGOKU PERIOD
ICHIJODANI CASTLE TOWN
ECHIZEN PROVINCE
HYA
*TODA DOJO
TOK
HAAA!
HYA
BOK
HYA
HYA
HYA
CHK
TOK
HYA
FLEX
FLEX
HYAH!
HII!
TUNK

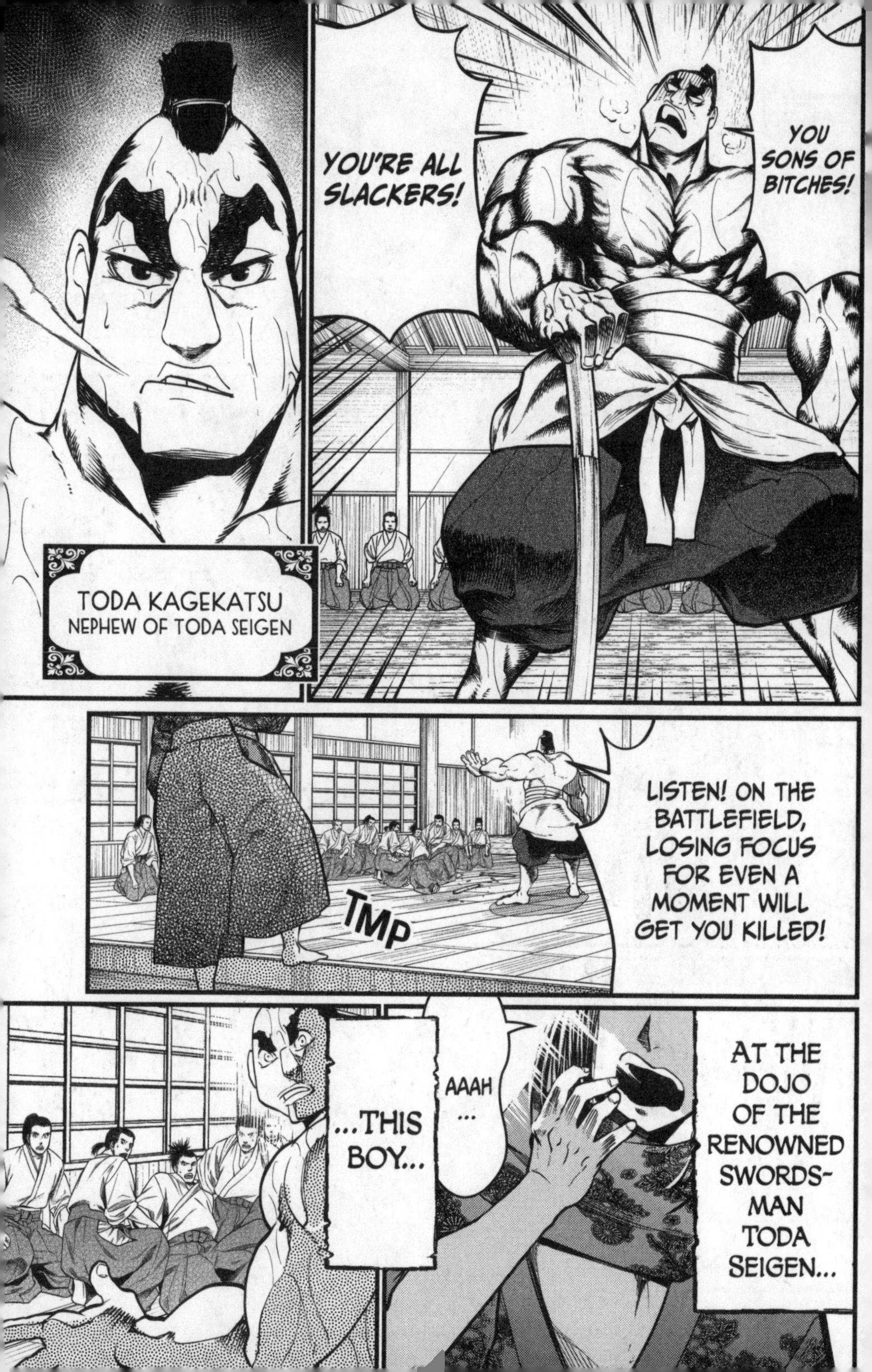
YOU SONS OF BITCHES!
YOU'RE ALL SLACKERS!
TODA KAGEKATSU
NEPHEW OF TODA SEIGEN
LISTEN! ON THE BATTLEFIELD, LOSING FOCUS FOR EVEN A MOMENT WILL GET YOU KILLED!
TMP
AT THE DOJO OF THE RENOWNED SWORDS-MAN TODA SEIGEN...
AAAH ...
...THIS BOY...

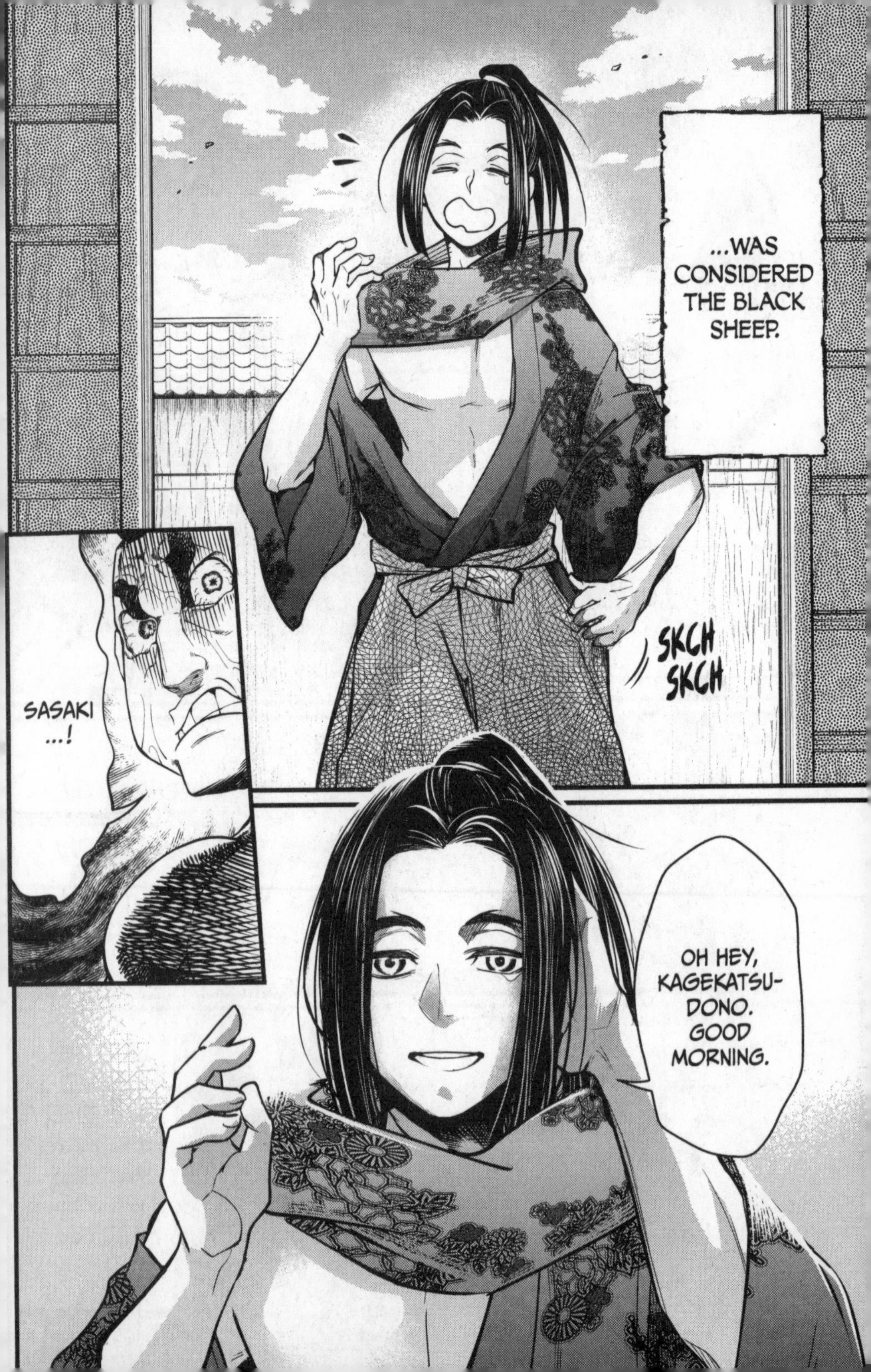
...WAS CONSIDERED THE BLACK SHEEP.
SKCH SKCH
SASAKI ...!
OH HEY, KAGEKATSU-DONO. GOOD MORNING.

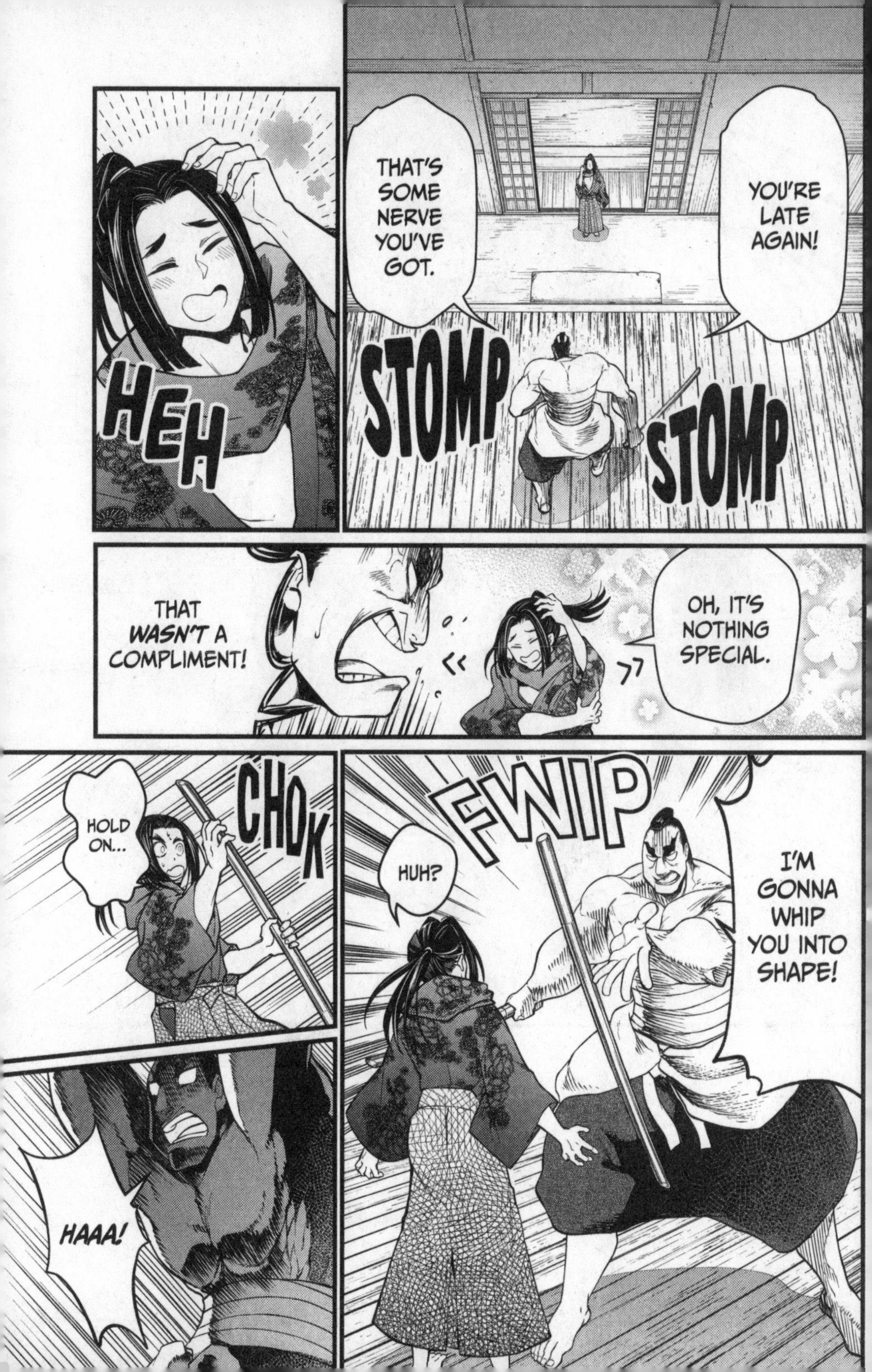

STOMP
YOU'RE LATE AGAIN!
STOMP
THAT'S SOME NERVE YOU'VE GOT.
HEH
OH, IT'S NOTHING SPECIAL.
THAT WASN'T A COMPLIMENT!
I'M GONNA WHIP YOU INTO SHAPE!
FWIP
HUH?
CHOK
HOLD ON...
HAAA!

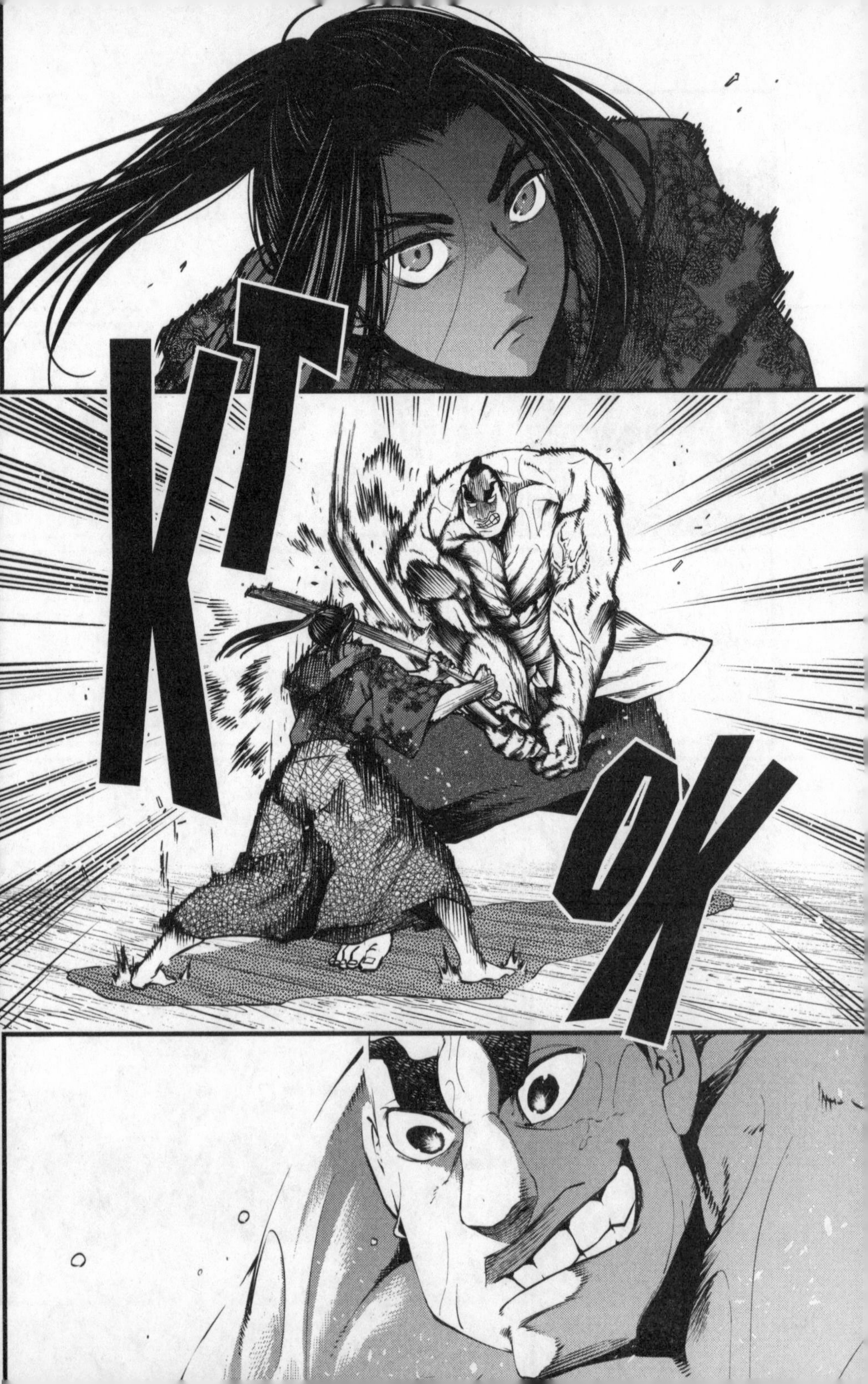
KTOK

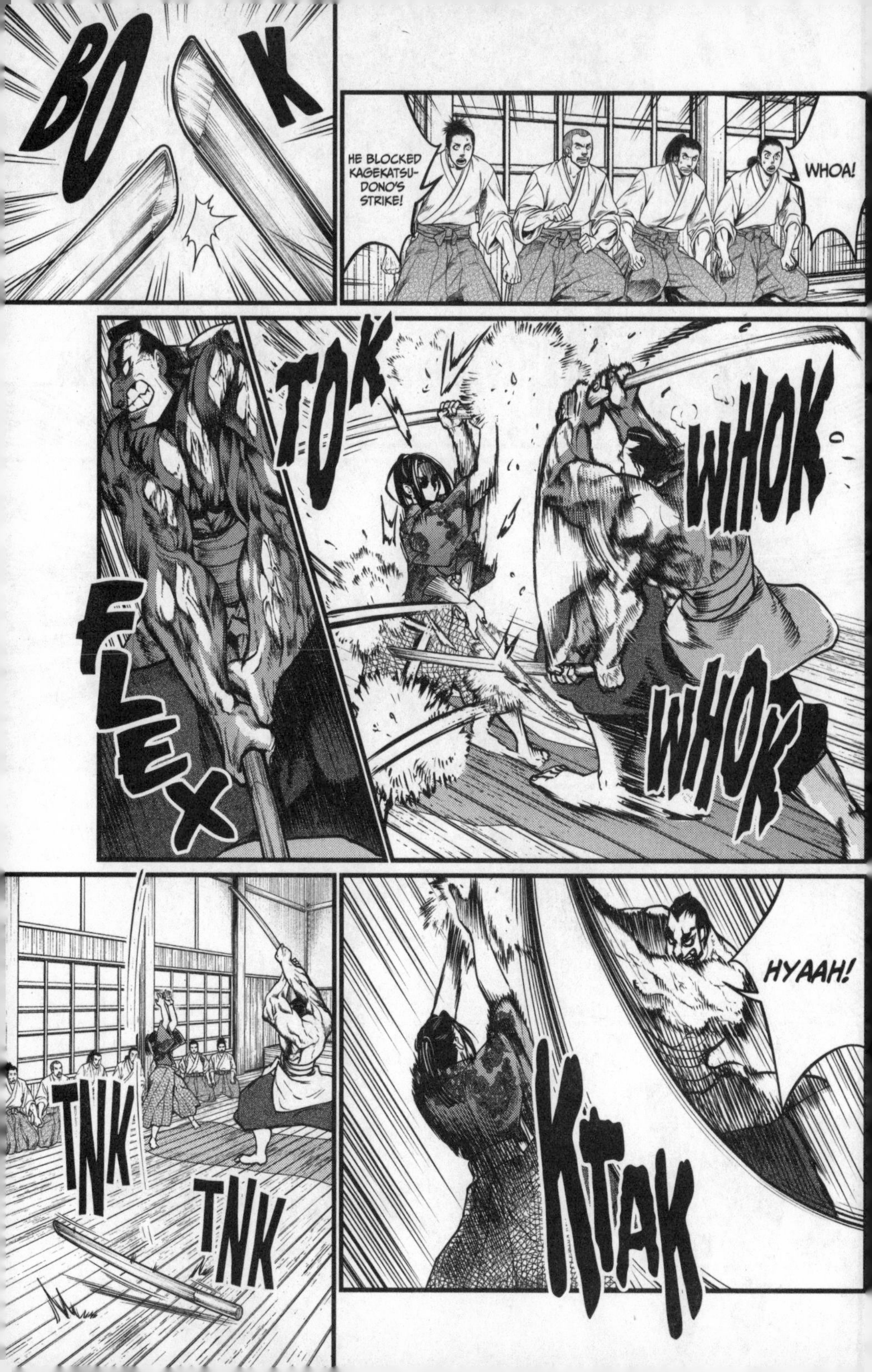
WHOA!
HE BLOCKED KAGEKATSU-DONO'S STRIKE!
BOK
TOK
WHOK
WHOK
FLEX
HYAAH!
KTAK
TNK
TNK

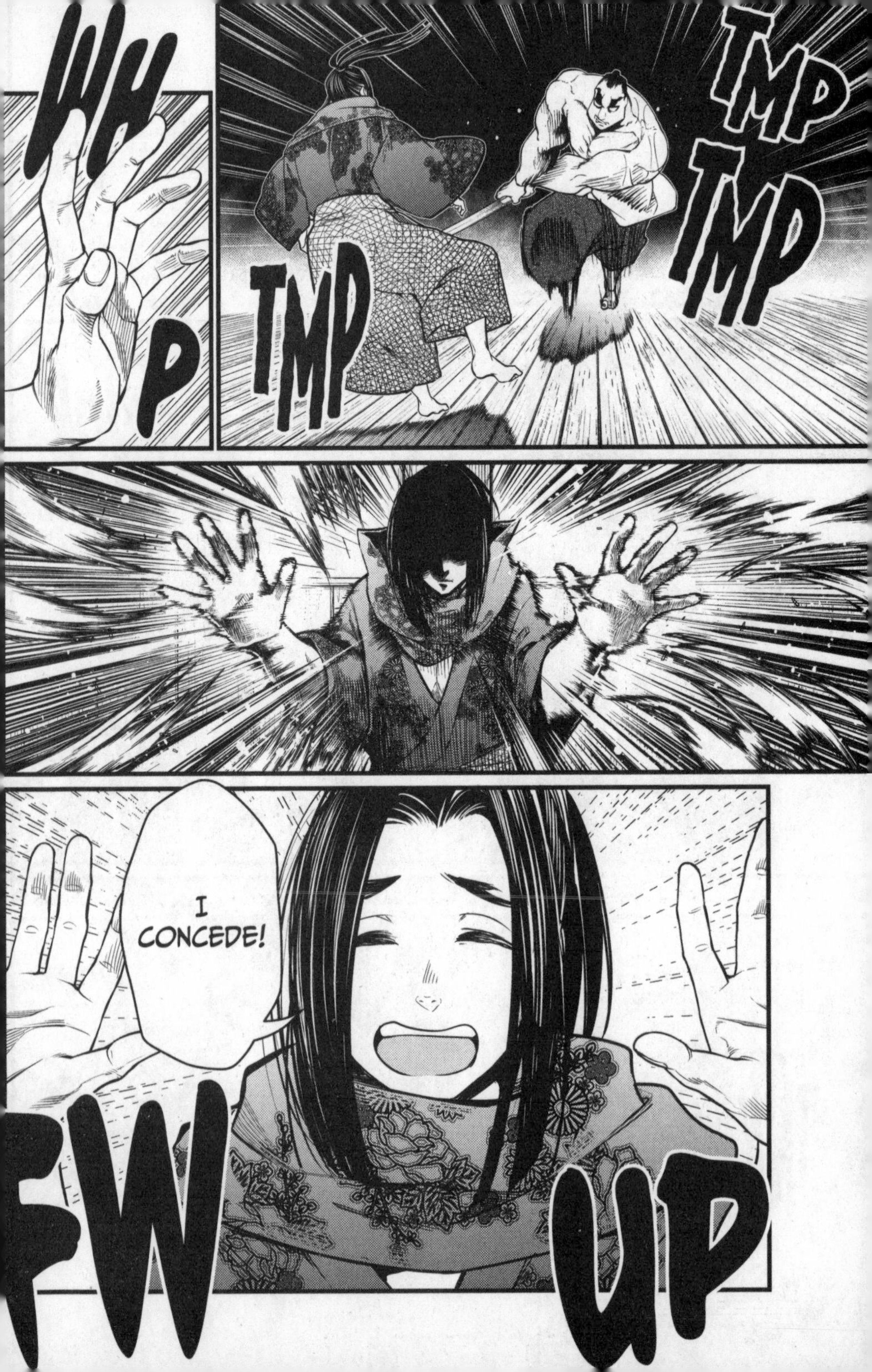

TMP
TMP
TMP
WHP
I CONCEDE!
FWUP

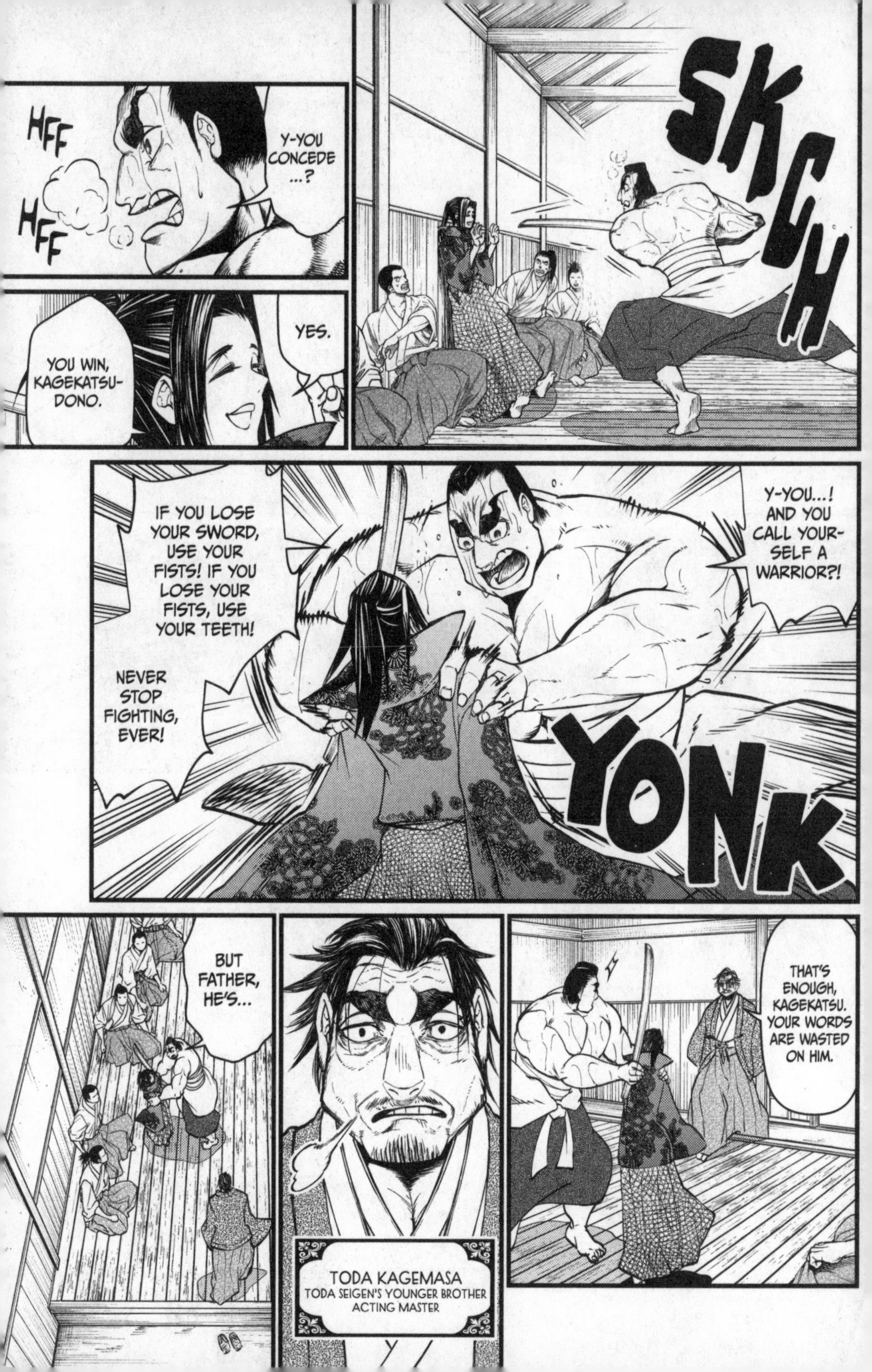
SKCH
HFF HFF
Y-YOU CONCEDE ...?
YES.
YOU WIN, KAGEKATSU-DONO.
Y-YOU...! AND YOU CALL YOUR-SELF A WARRIOR?!
IF YOU LOSE YOUR SWORD, USE YOUR FISTS! IF YOU LOSE YOUR FISTS, USE YOUR TEETH!
YONK
NEVER STOP FIGHTING, EVER!
THAT'S ENOUGH, KAGEKATSU. YOUR WORDS ARE WASTED ON HIM.
TODA KAGEMASA
TODA SEIGEN'S YOUNGER BROTHER
ACTING MASTER
BUT FATHER, HE'S...

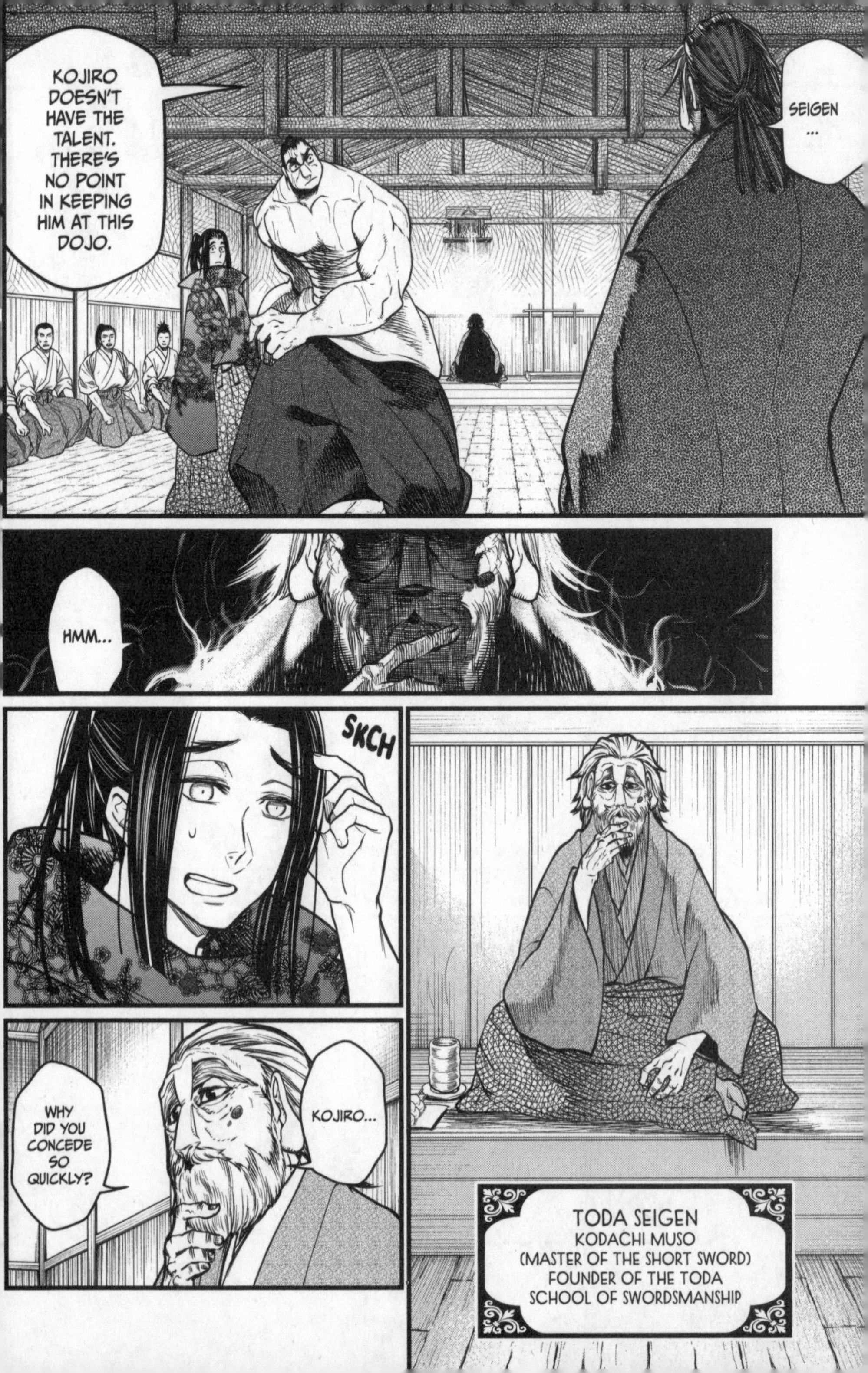
SEIGEN ...
KOJIRO DOESN'T HAVE THE TALENT. THERE'S NO POINT IN KEEPING HIM AT THIS DOJO.
HMM...
TODA SEIGEN
KODACHI MUSO
(MASTER OF THE SHORT SWORD)
FOUNDER OF THE TODA SCHOOL OF SWORDSMANSHIP
SKCH
KOJIRO...
WHY DID YOU CONCEDE SO QUICKLY?

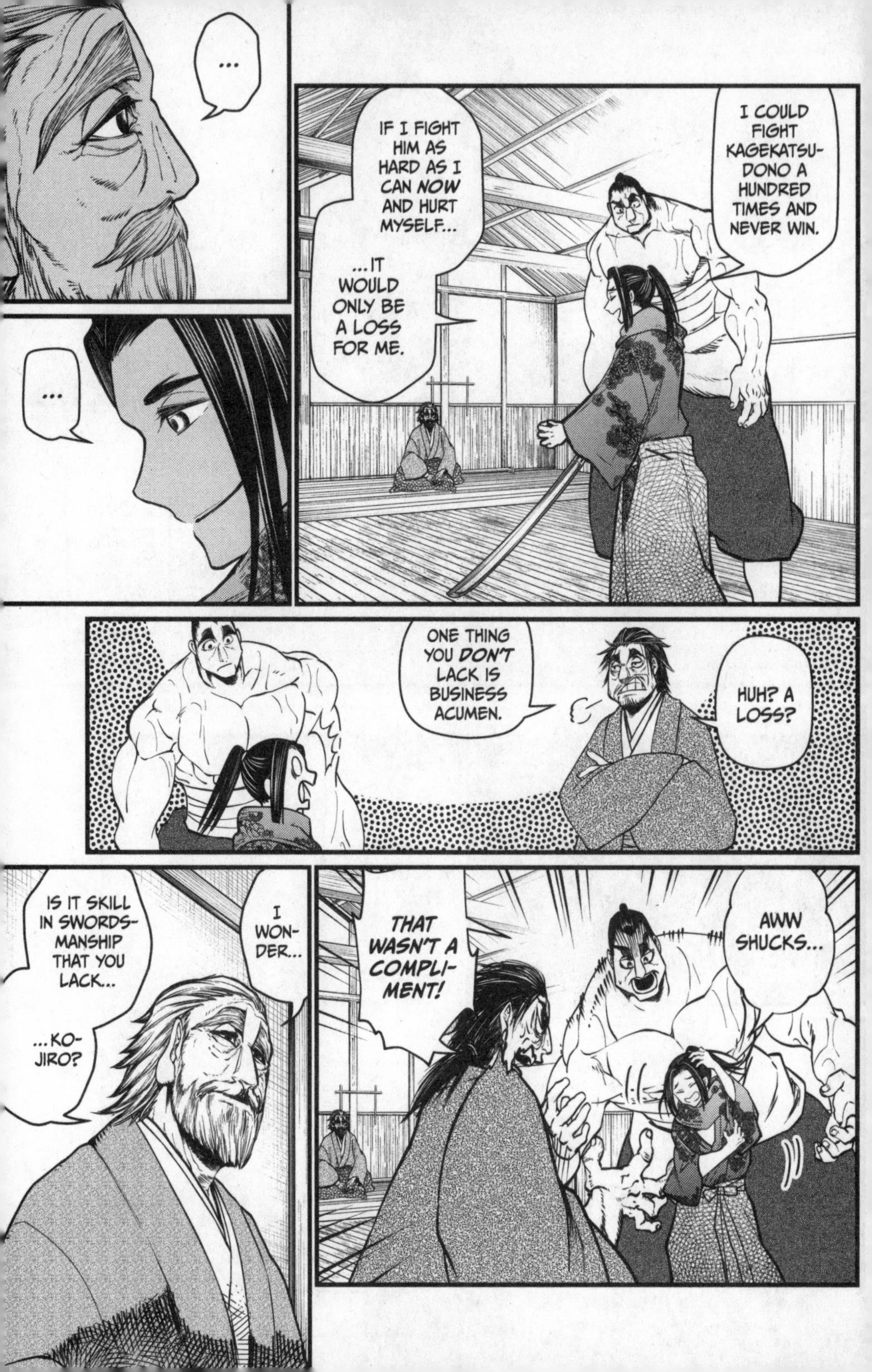
I COULD FIGHT KAGEKATSU-DONO A HUNDRED TIMES AND NEVER WIN.
IF I FIGHT HIM AS HARD AS I CAN *NOW* AND HURT MYSELF...
...IT WOULD ONLY BE A LOSS FOR ME.
...
...
HUH? A LOSS?
ONE THING YOU *DON'T* LACK IS BUSINESS ACUMEN.
AWW SHUCKS...
THAT WASN'T A COMPLIMENT!
I WONDER...
IS IT SKILL IN SWORDSMANSHIP THAT YOU LACK...
...KOJIRO?

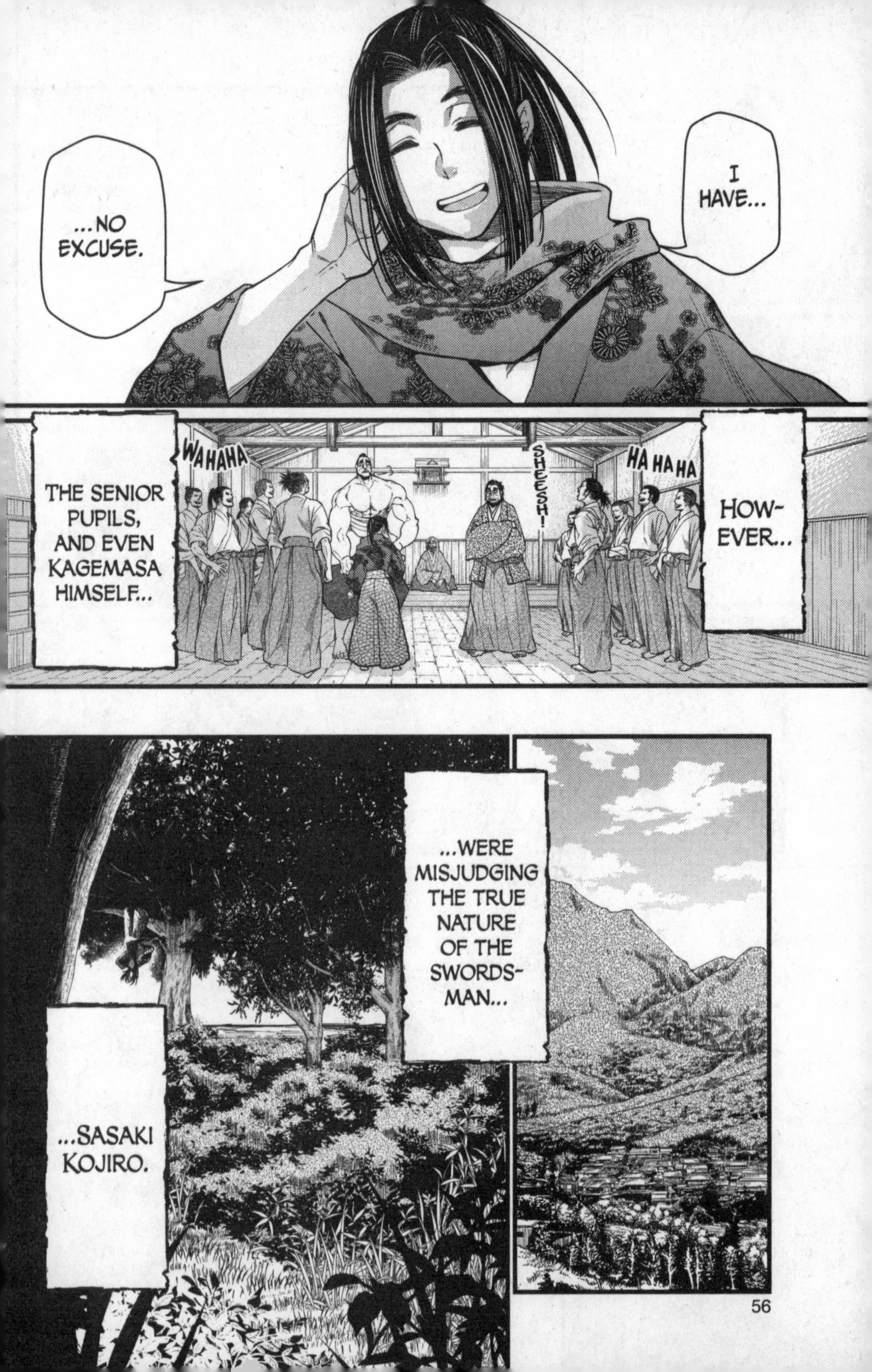
I HAVE...
...NO EXCUSE.
HOW-EVER...
HA HA HA
SHEESH!
WAHAHA
THE SENIOR PUPILS, AND EVEN KAGEMASA HIMSELF...
...WERE MISJUDGING THE TRUE NATURE OF THE SWORDS-MAN...
...SASAKI KOJIRO.

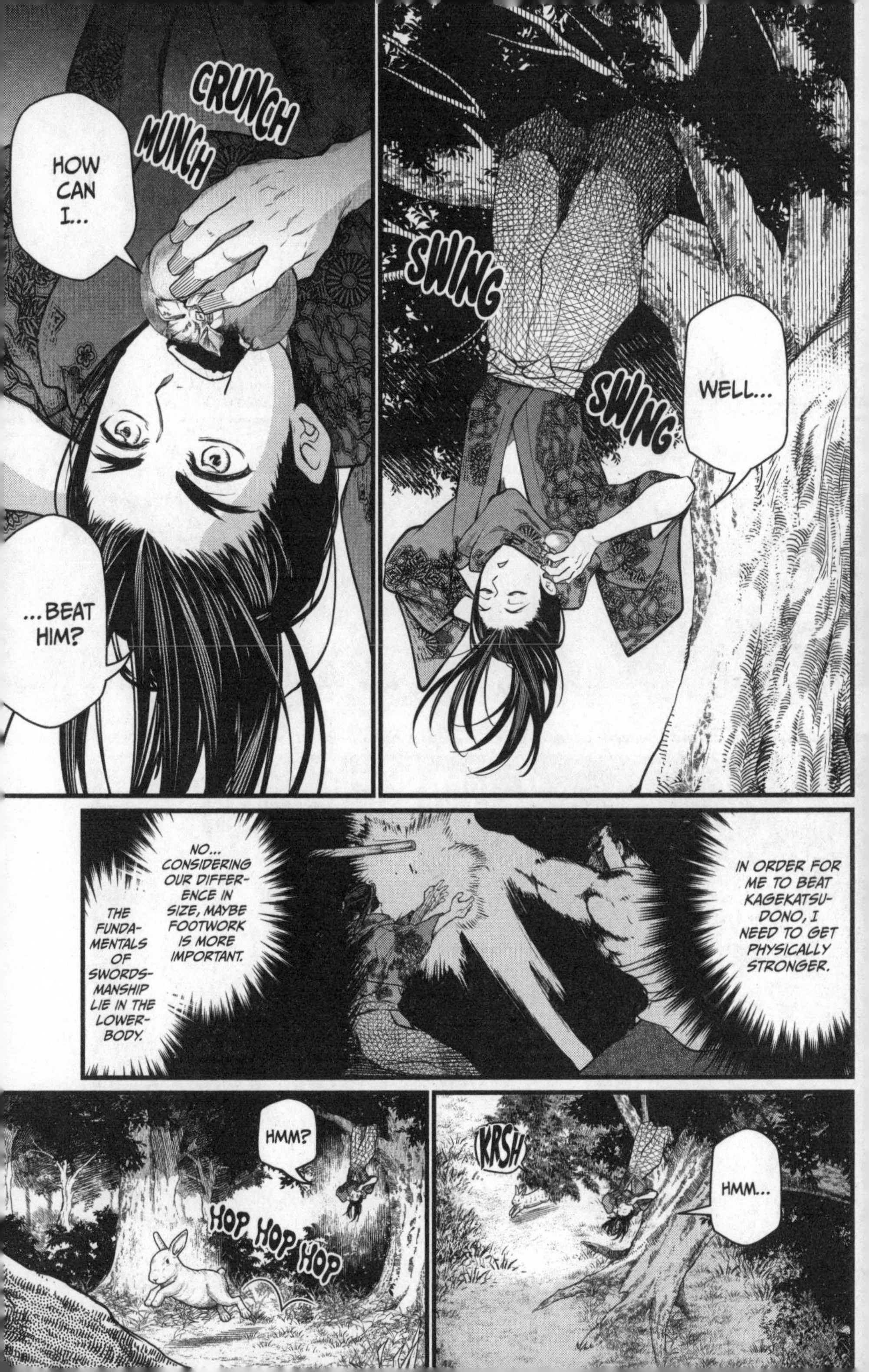
SWING
SWING
WELL...
CRUNCH
MUNCH
HOW CAN I...
...BEAT HIM?
IN ORDER FOR ME TO BEAT KAGEKATSU-DONO, I NEED TO GET PHYSICALLY STRONGER.
NO... CONSIDERING OUR DIFFERENCE IN SIZE, MAYBE FOOTWORK IS MORE IMPORTANT.
THE FUNDAMENTALS OF SWORDSMANSHIP LIE IN THE LOWER-BODY.
KRSH
HMM...
HMM?
HOP HOP HOP

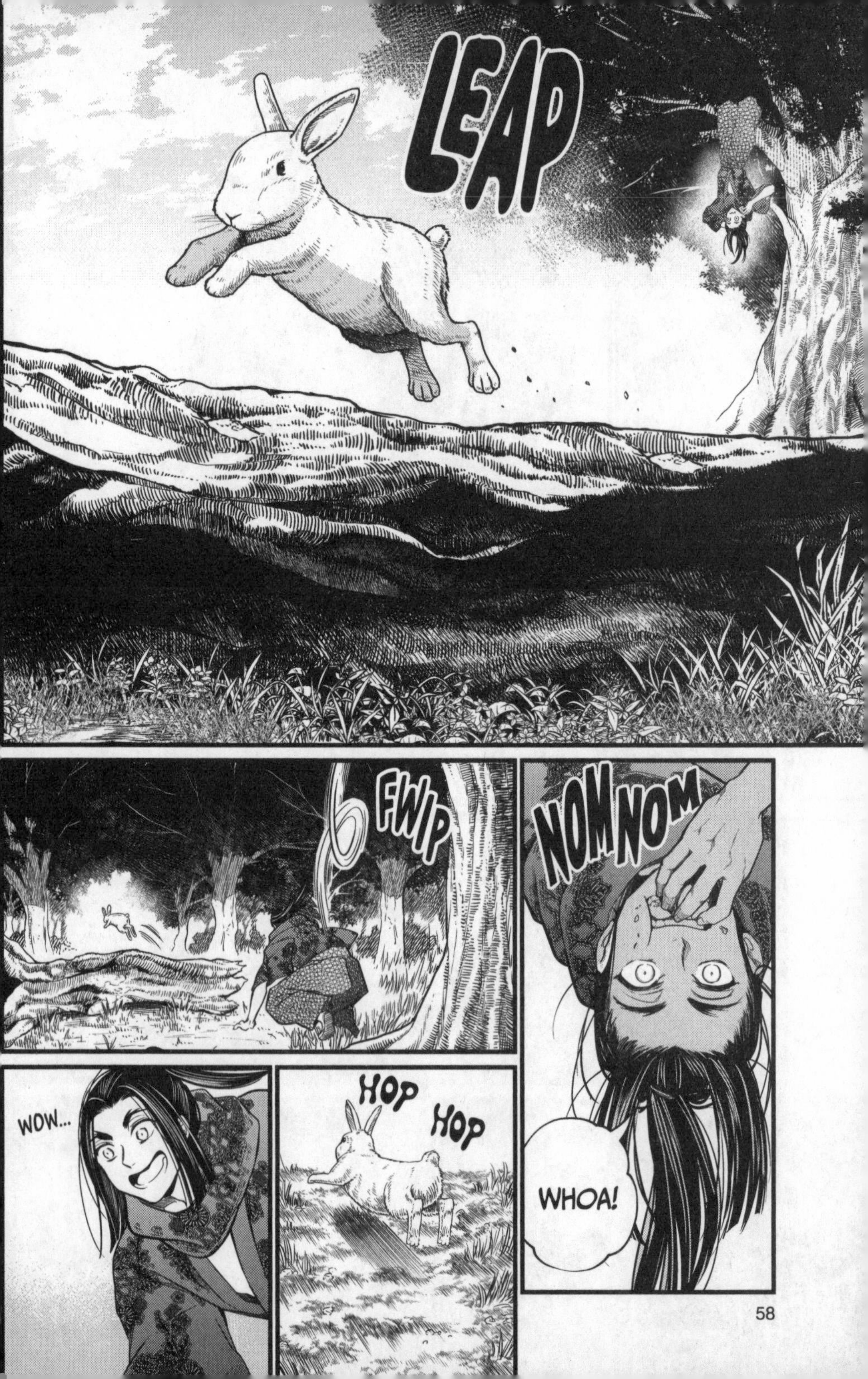
LEAP
NOM NOM
WHOA!
FWIP
HOP HOP
WOW...

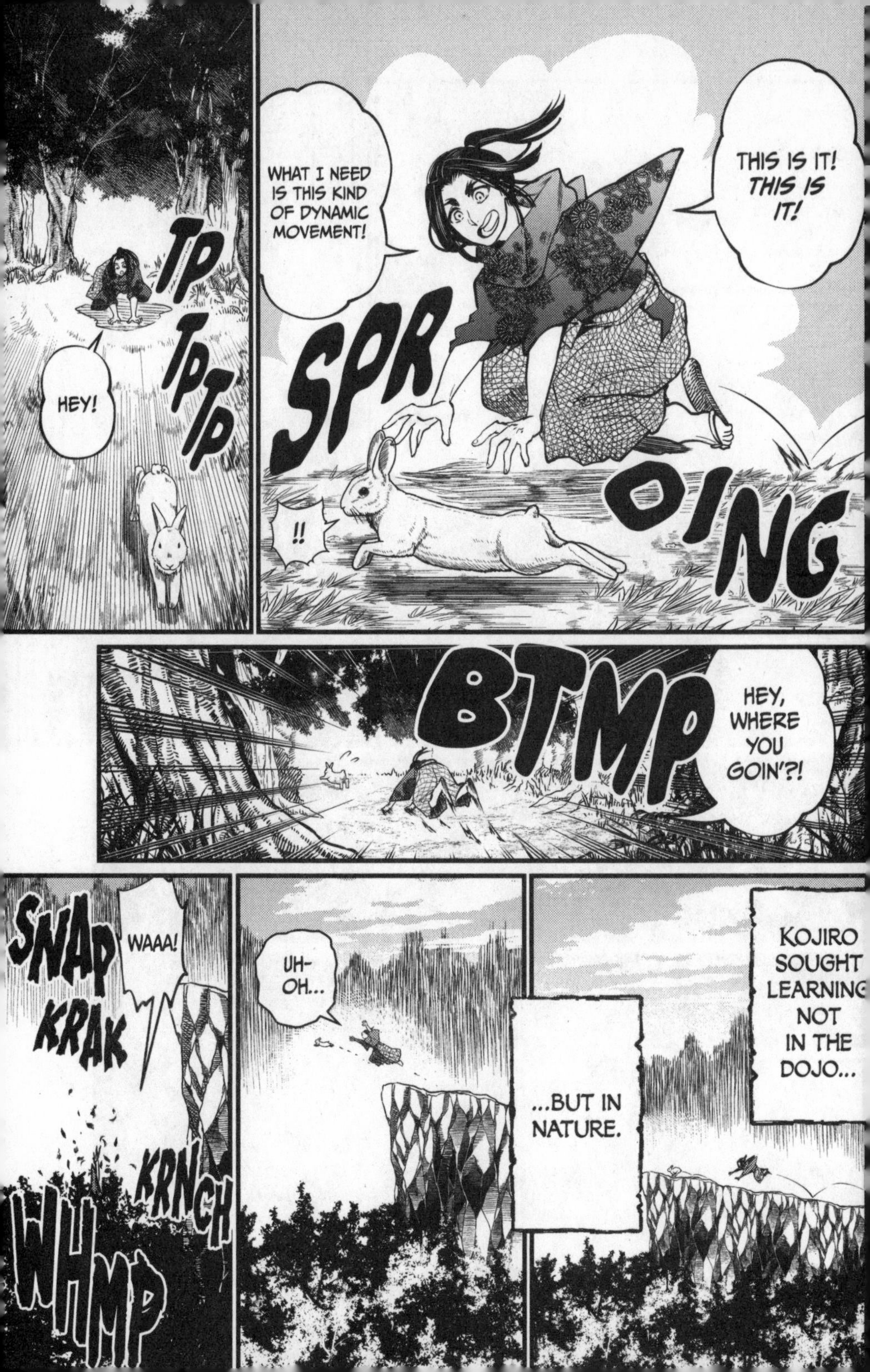
THIS IS IT! THIS IS IT!
WHAT I NEED IS THIS KIND OF DYNAMIC MOVEMENT!
SPR
OING
!!
TP
TPTP
HEY!
HEY, WHERE YOU GOIN'?!
BTMP
KOJIRO SOUGHT LEARNING NOT IN THE DOJO...
...BUT IN NATURE.
UH-OH...
WAAA!
SNAP
KRAK
KRNCH
WHMP

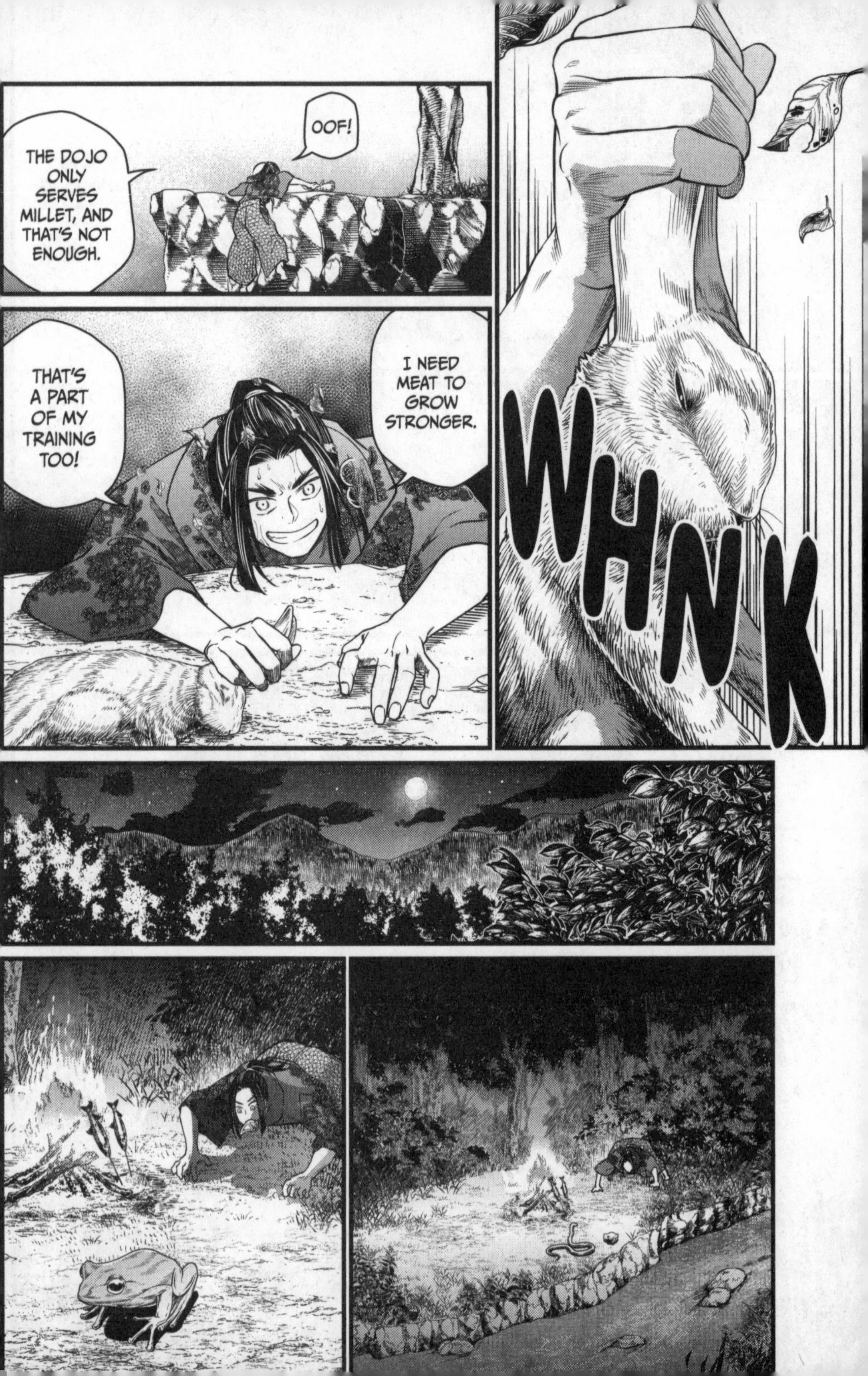

WHNK
OOF!
THE DOJO ONLY SERVES MILLET, AND THAT'S NOT ENOUGH.
I NEED MEAT TO GROW STRONGER.
THAT'S A PART OF MY TRAINING TOO!

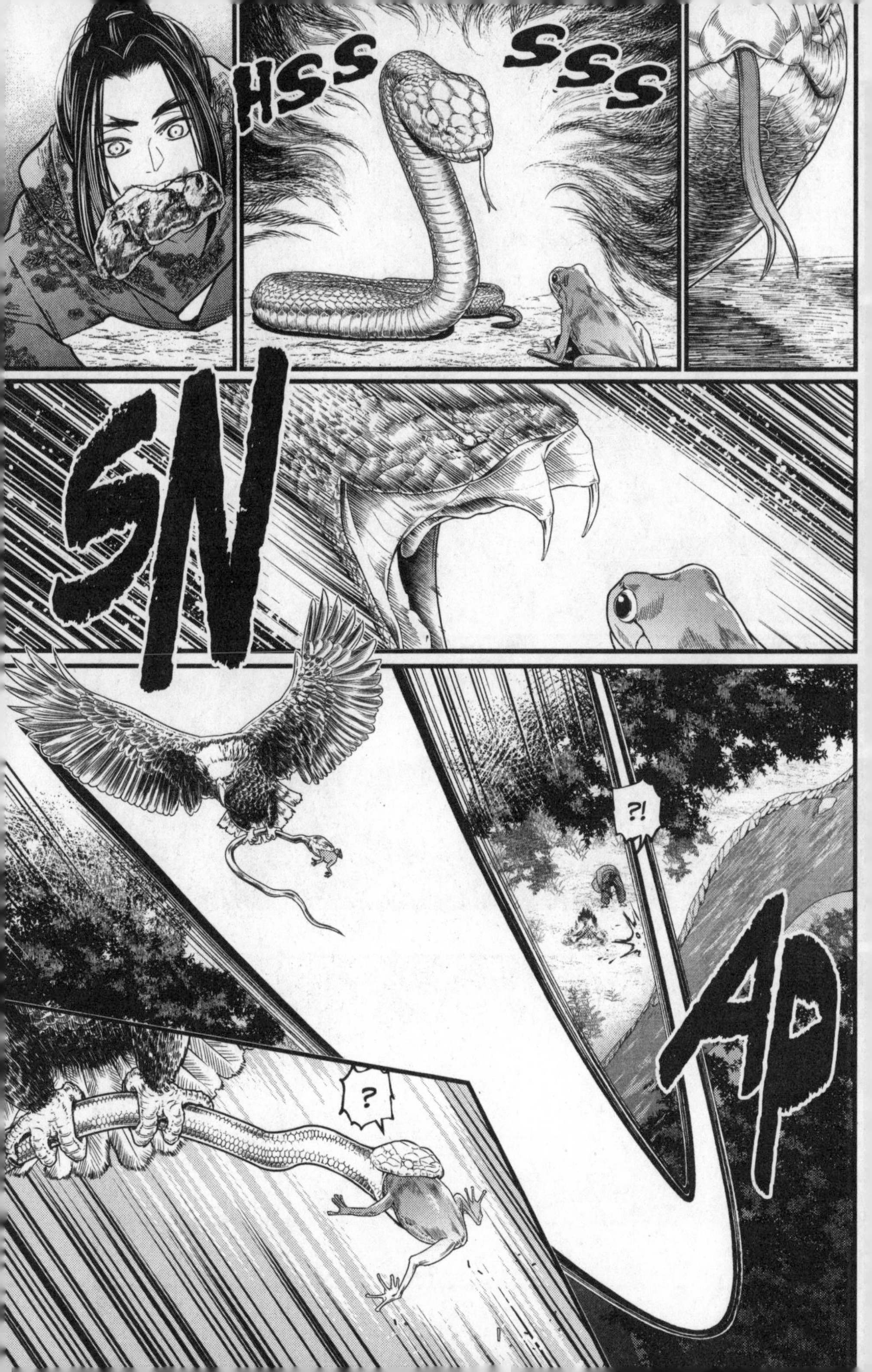
HSS
SSS
SN
?!
AP
?

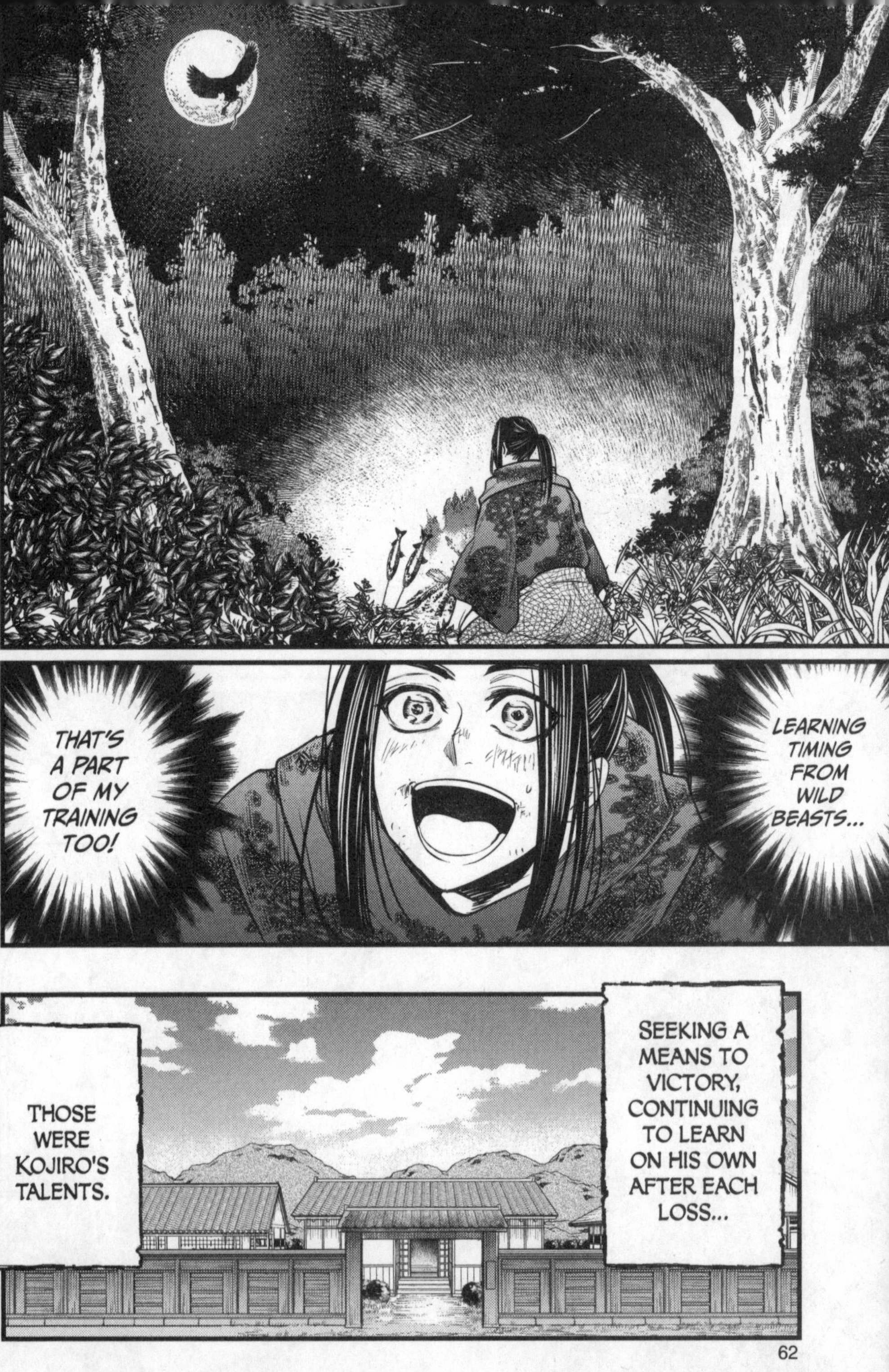
LEARNING TIMING FROM WILD BEASTS...
THAT'S A PART OF MY TRAINING TOO!
SEEKING A MEANS TO VICTORY, CONTINUING TO LEARN ON HIS OWN AFTER EACH LOSS...
THOSE WERE KOJIRO'S TALENTS.

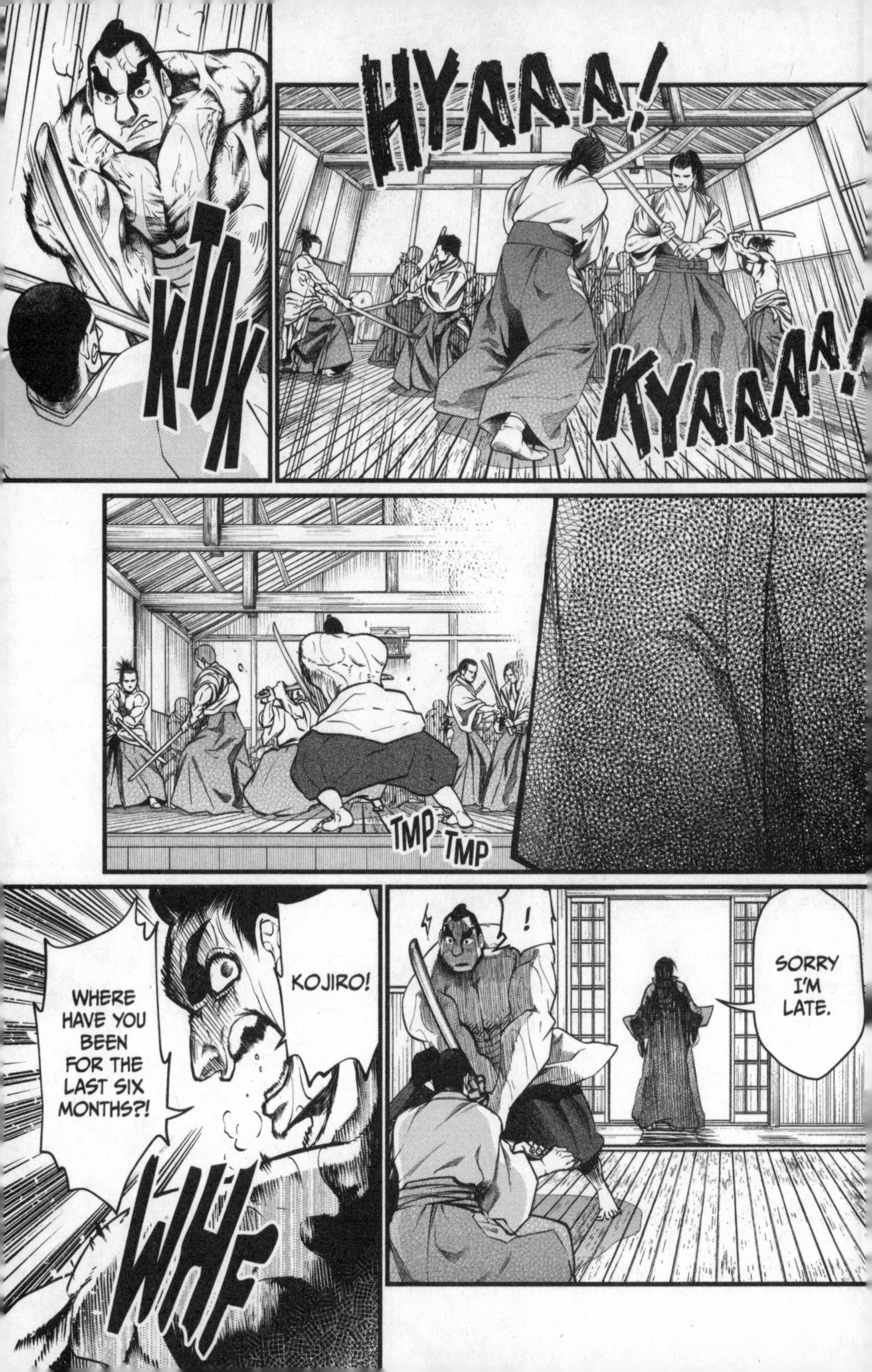
HYAAAA!
KYAAAAA!
KTOK
TMP TMP
!
SORRY I'M LATE.
KOJIRO!
WHERE HAVE YOU BEEN FOR THE LAST SIX MONTHS?!
WHF

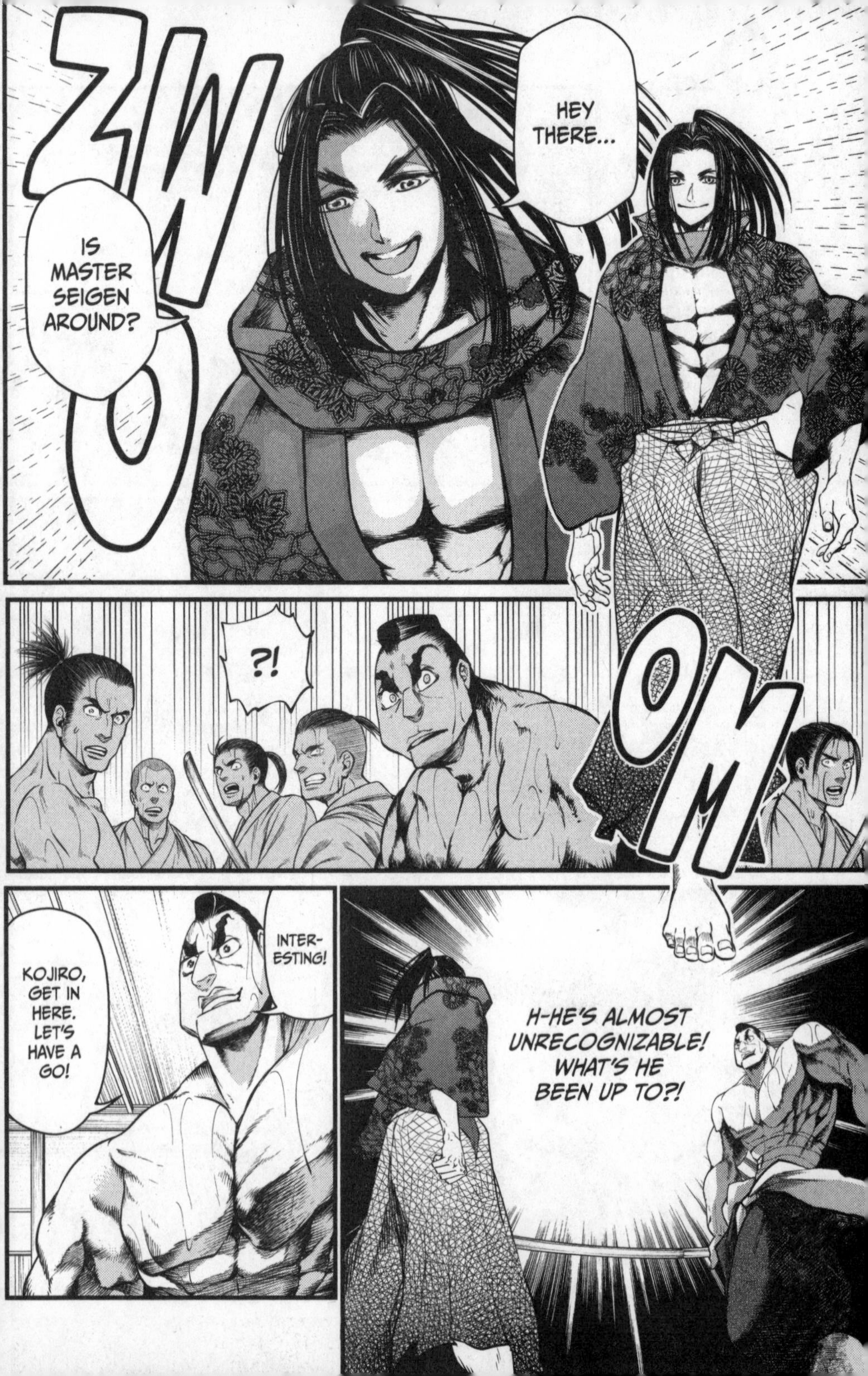
HEY THERE...
ZW
IS MASTER SEIGEN AROUND?
O
OM
?!
H-HE'S ALMOST UNRECOGNIZABLE! WHAT'S HE BEEN UP TO?!
INTER-ESTING!
KOJIRO, GET IN HERE. LET'S HAVE A GO!

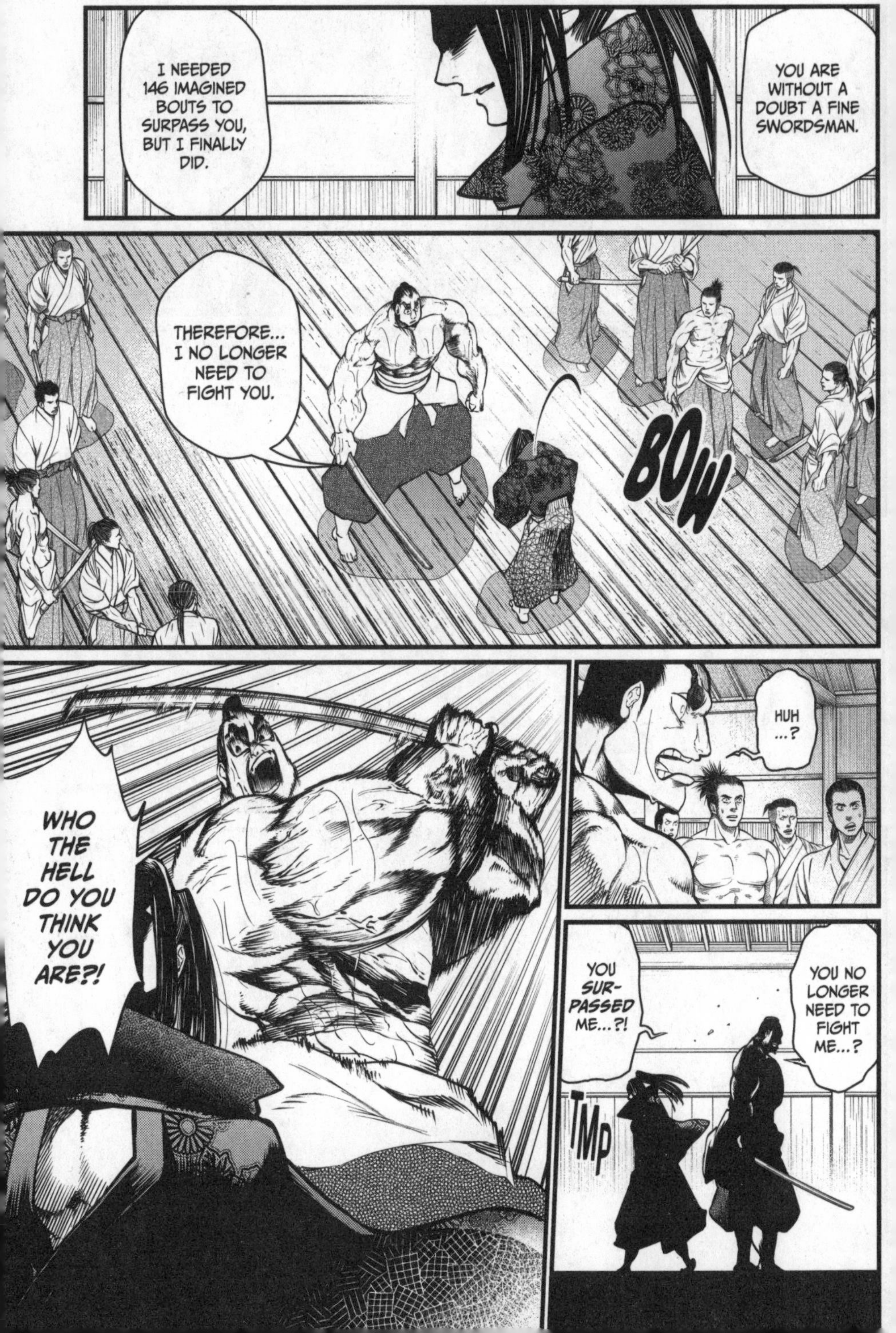
YOU ARE WITHOUT A DOUBT A FINE SWORDSMAN.
I NEEDED 146 IMAGINED BOUTS TO SURPASS YOU, BUT I FINALLY DID.
THEREFORE... I NO LONGER NEED TO FIGHT YOU.
BOW
HUH ...?
YOU NO LONGER NEED TO FIGHT ME...?
YOU SUR-PASSED ME...?!
TMP
WHO THE HELL DO YOU THINK YOU ARE?!

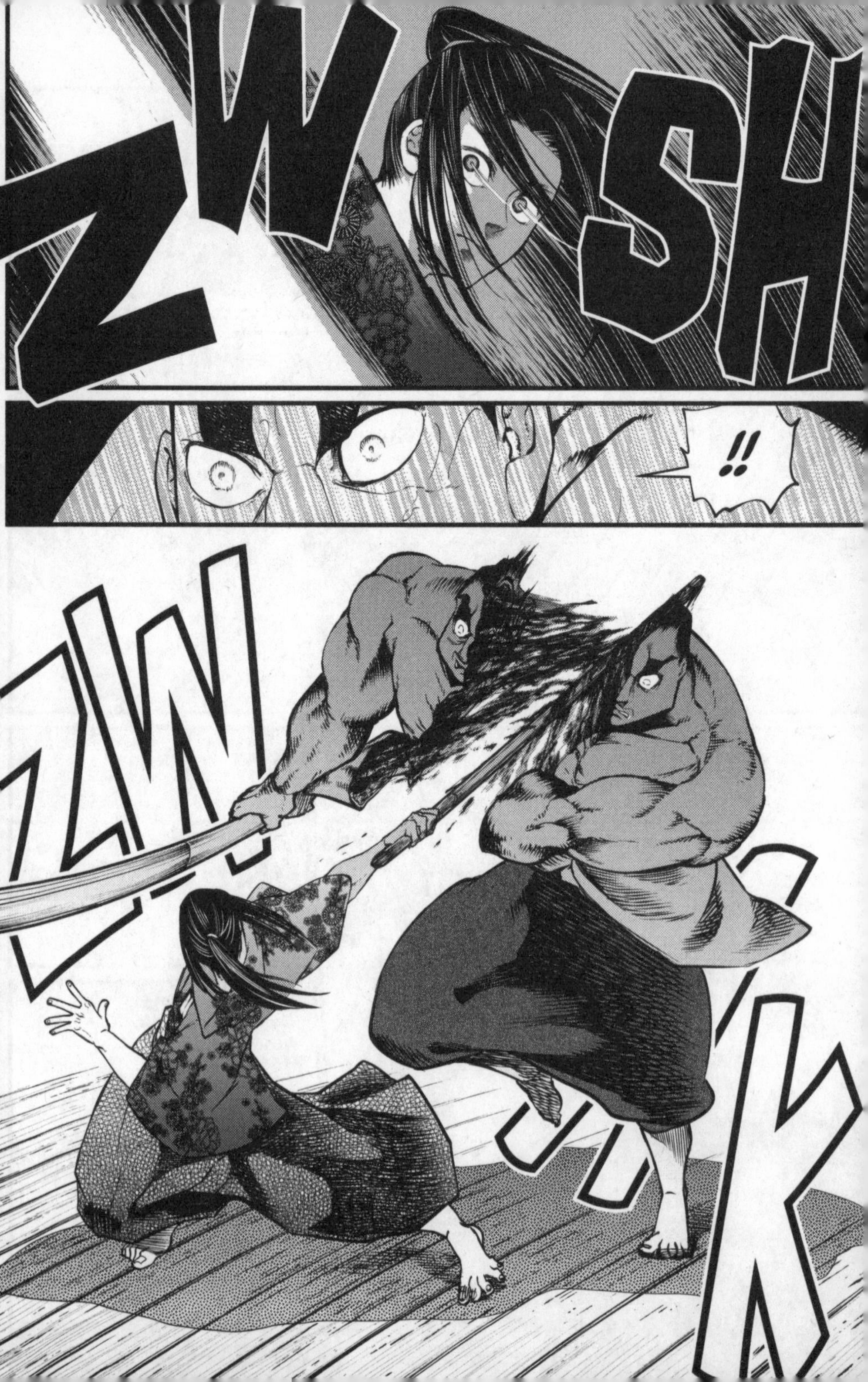
ZWSH
!!
ZW
K

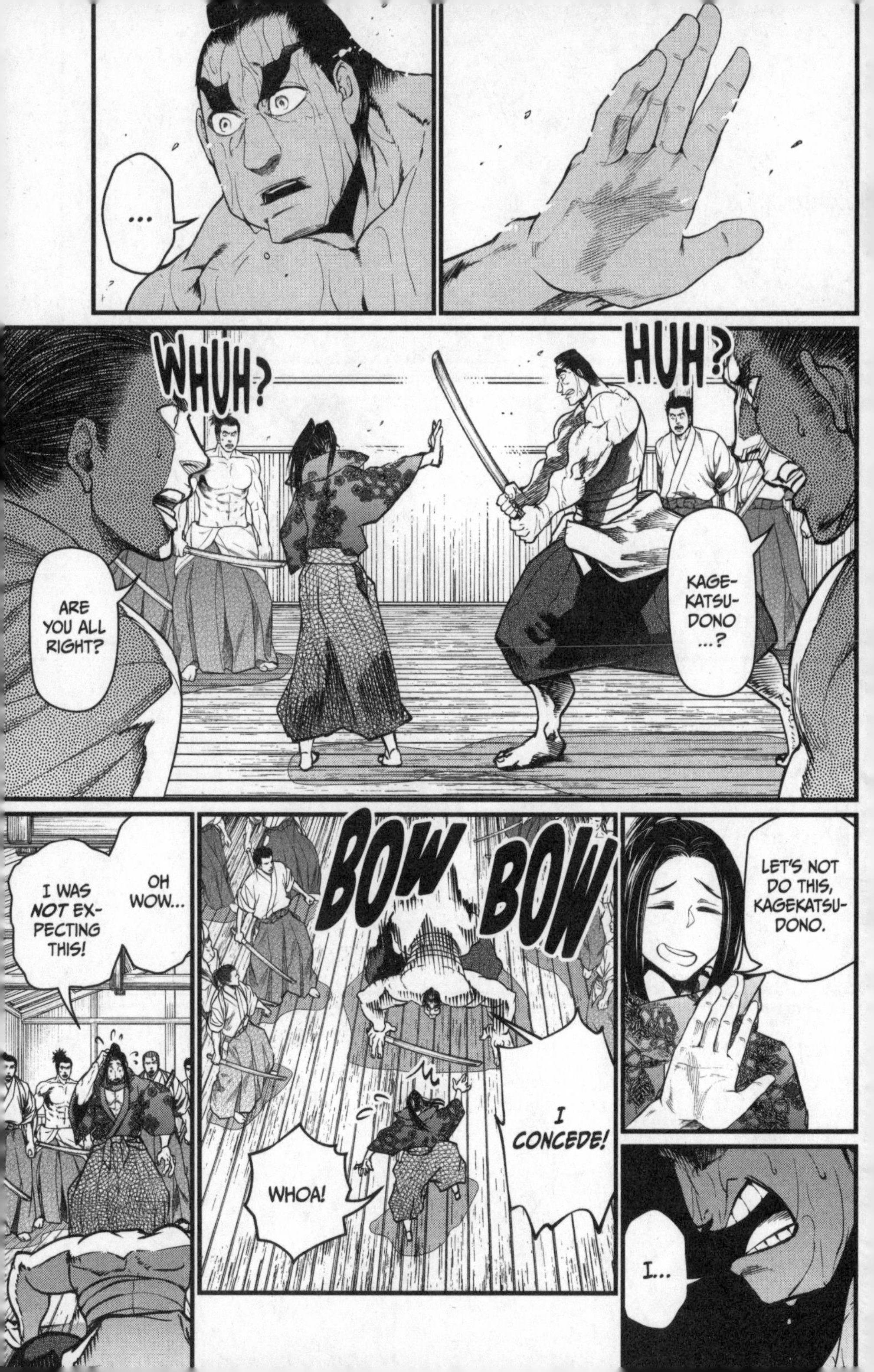
...
HUH?
KAGE-KATSU-DONO ...?
WHUH?
ARE YOU ALL RIGHT?
LET'S NOT DO THIS, KAGEKATSU-DONO.
I...
BOW BOW
I CONCEDE!
WHOA!
OH WOW...
I WAS *NOT* EXPECTING THIS!

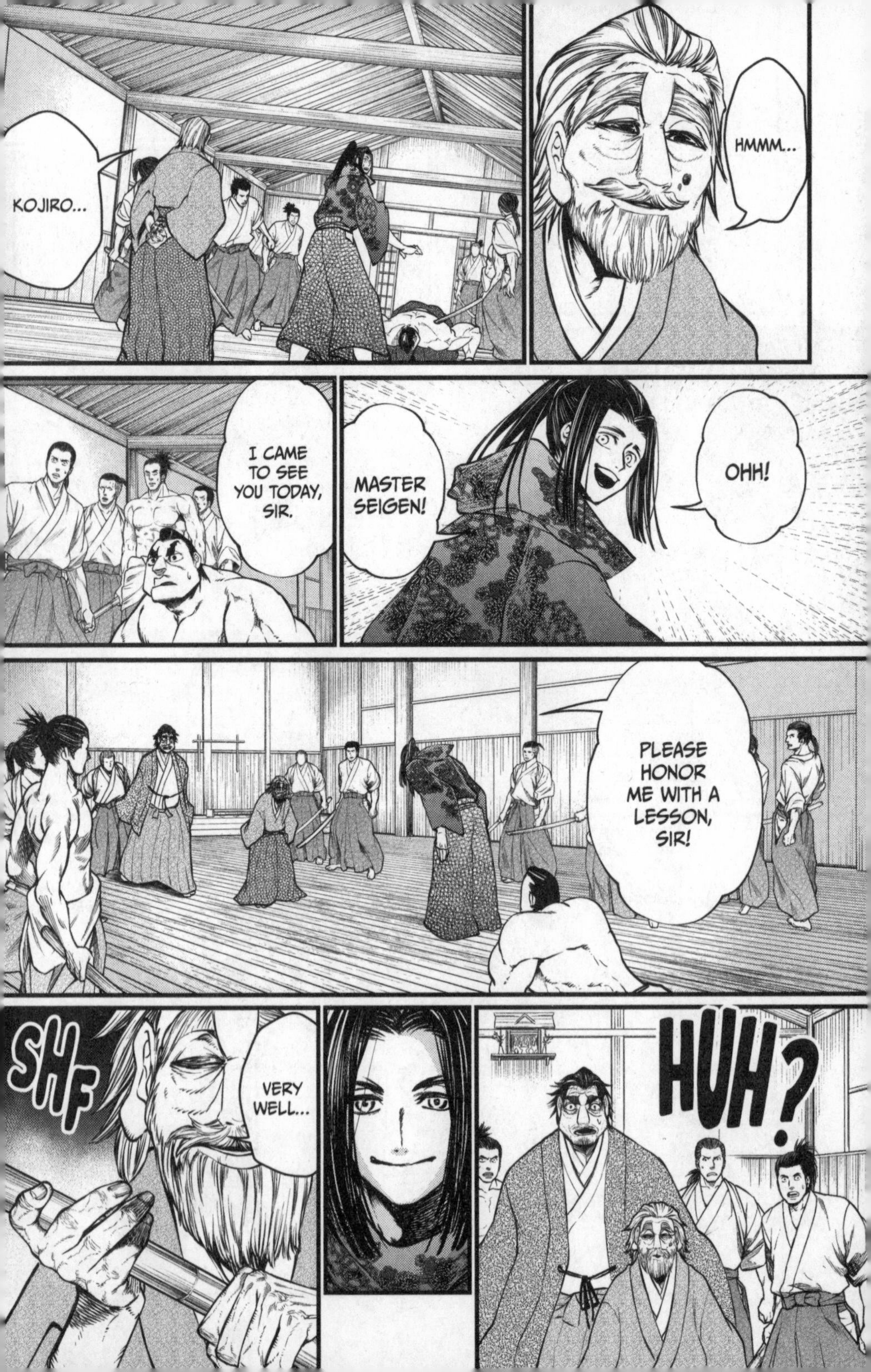
HMMM...
KOJIRO...
OHH!
MASTER SEIGEN!
I CAME TO SEE YOU TODAY, SIR.
PLEASE HONOR ME WITH A LESSON, SIR!
HUH?
VERY WELL...
SHF

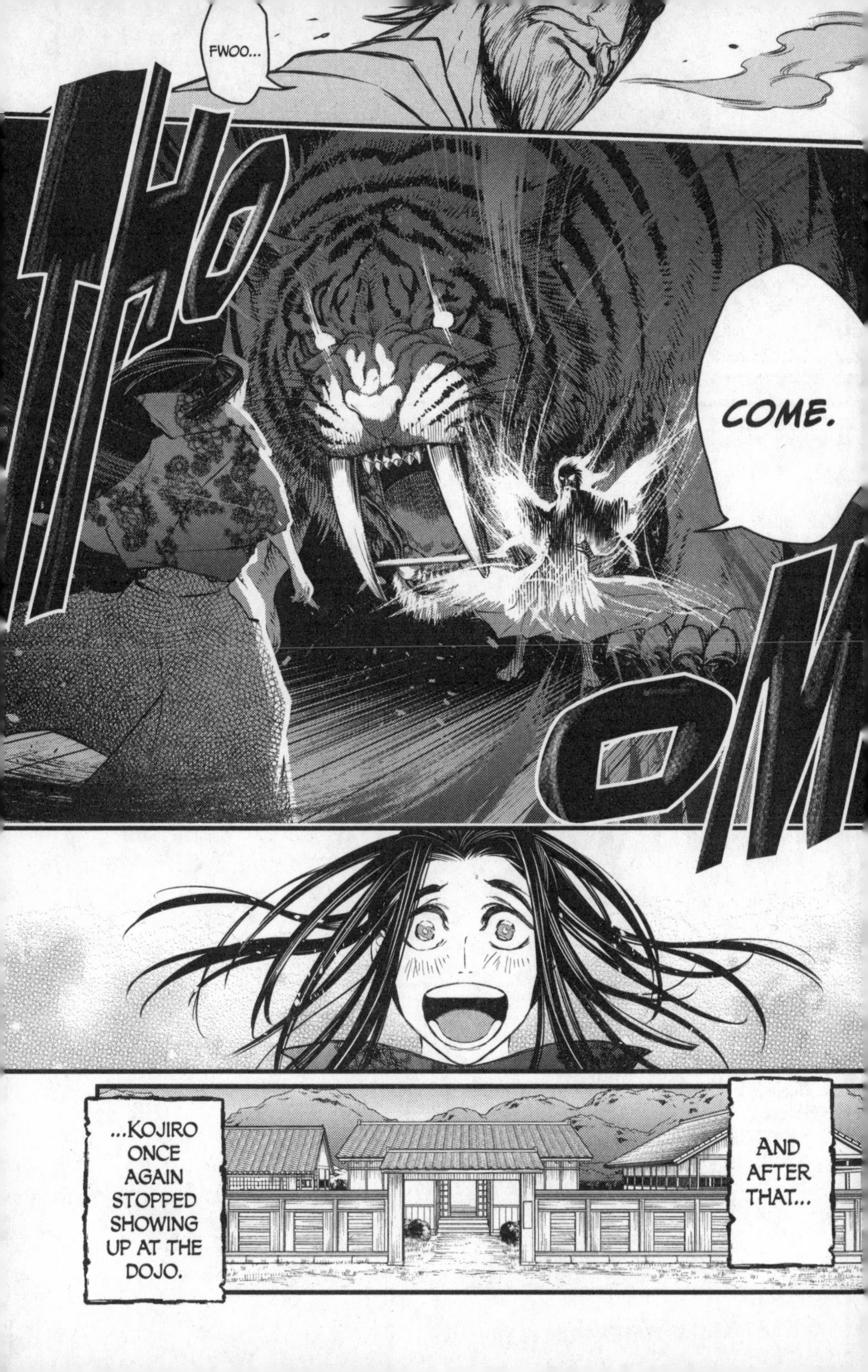
FWOO...
COME.
THOOM
AND AFTER THAT...
...KOJIRO ONCE AGAIN STOPPED SHOWING UP AT THE DOJO.

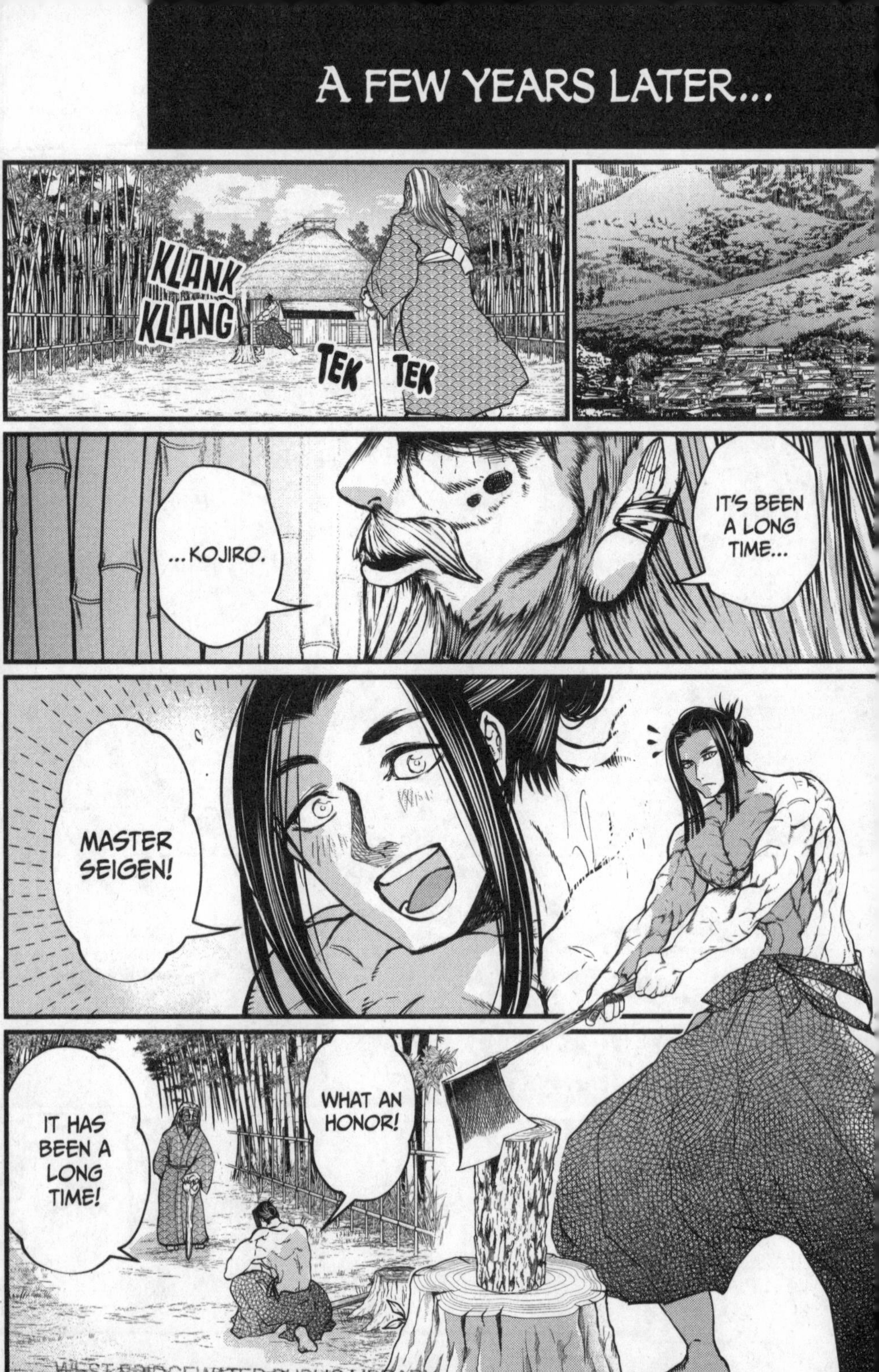
A FEW YEARS LATER...
KLANK KLANG
TEK TEK
IT'S BEEN A LONG TIME...
...KOJIRO.
MASTER SEIGEN!
WHAT AN HONOR!
IT HAS BEEN A LONG TIME!

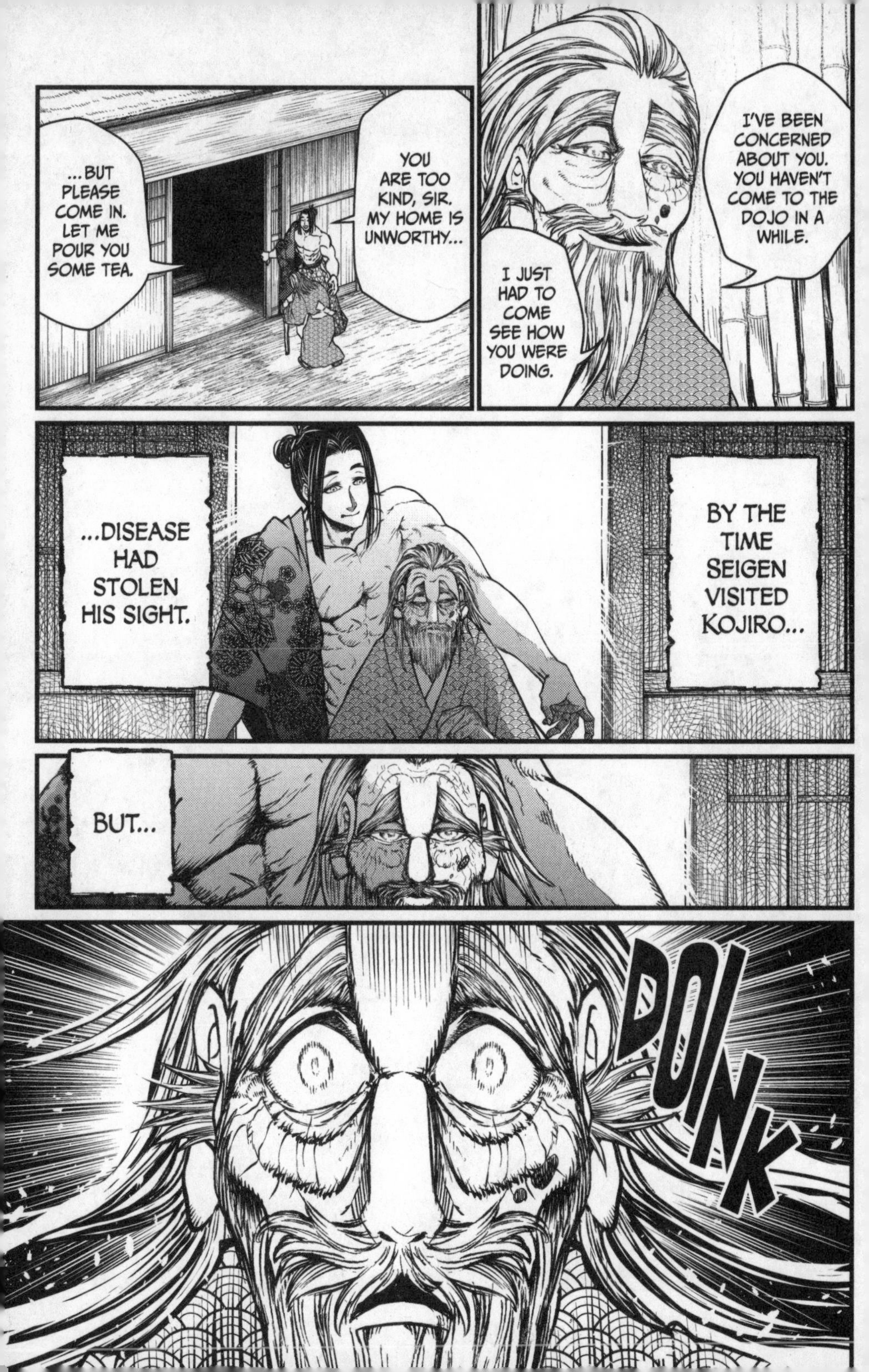
I'VE BEEN CONCERNED ABOUT YOU. YOU HAVEN'T COME TO THE DOJO IN A WHILE.
I JUST HAD TO COME SEE HOW YOU WERE DOING.
YOU ARE TOO KIND, SIR. MY HOME IS UNWORTHY...
...BUT PLEASE COME IN. LET ME POUR YOU SOME TEA.
BY THE TIME SEIGEN VISITED KOJIRO...
...DISEASE HAD STOLEN HIS SIGHT.
BUT...
DOINK

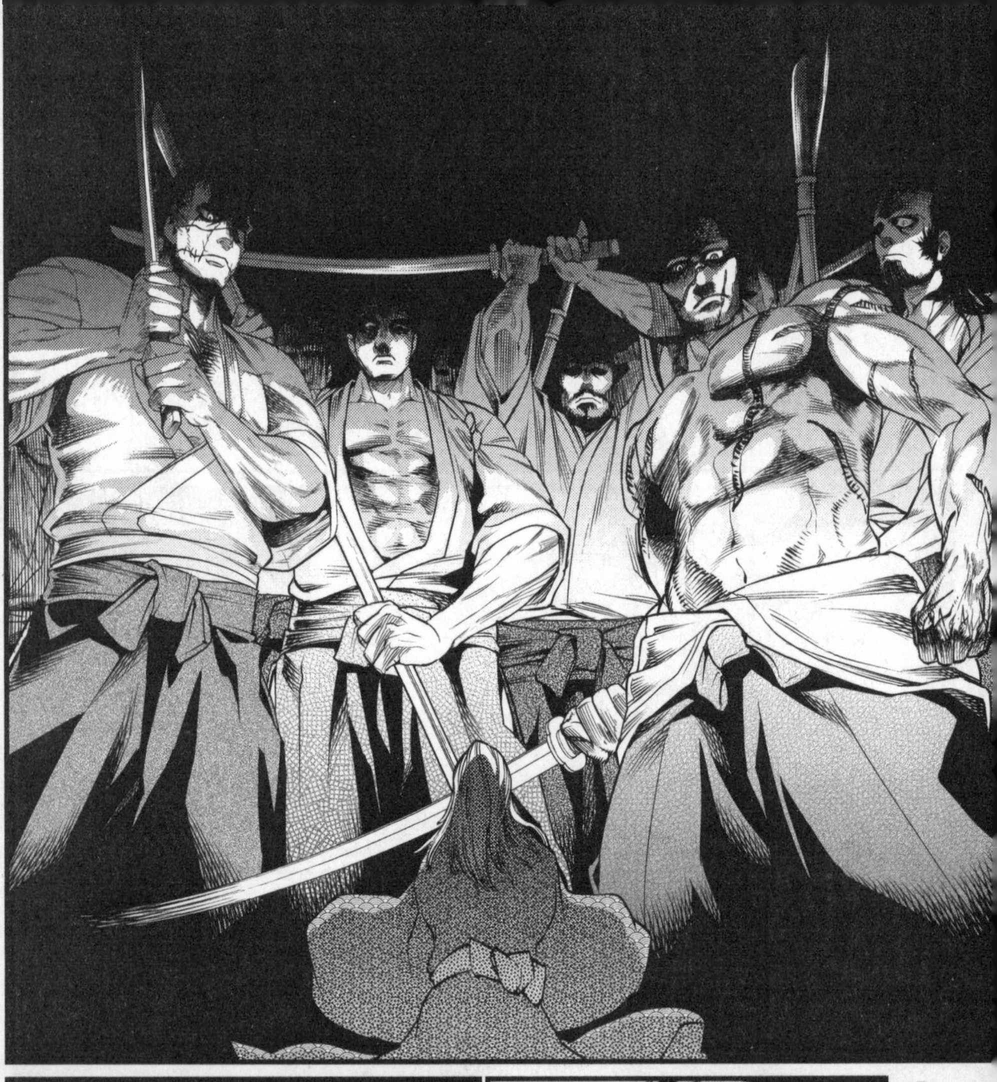
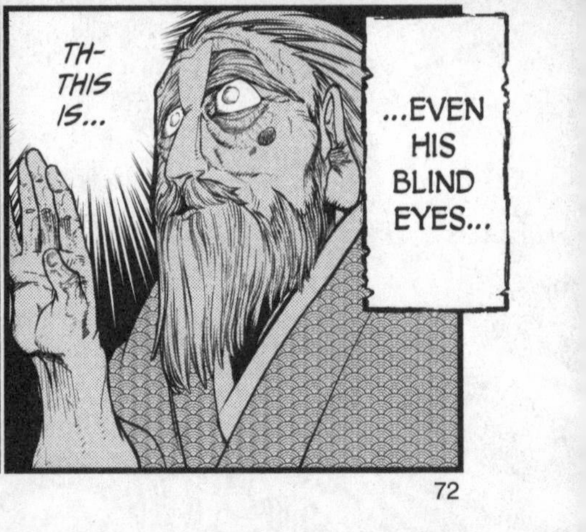
...EVEN HIS BLIND EYES...
TH-THIS IS...
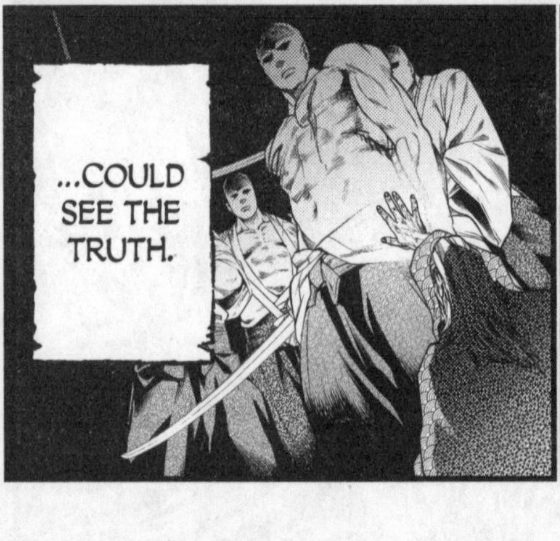
...COULD SEE THE TRUTH.

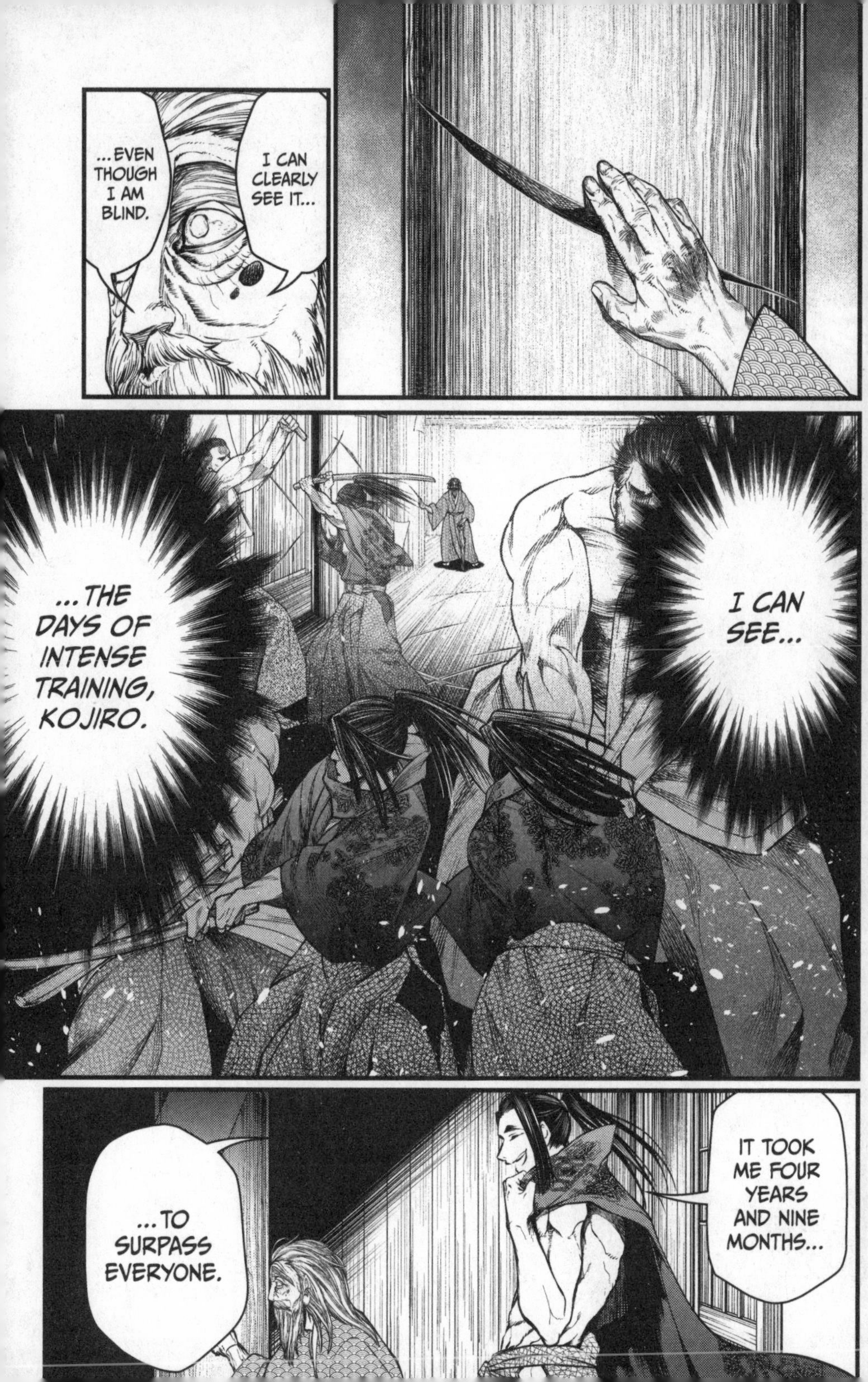
I CAN CLEARLY SEE IT...
...EVEN THOUGH I AM BLIND.
I CAN SEE...
...THE DAYS OF INTENSE TRAINING, KOJIRO.
IT TOOK ME FOUR YEARS AND NINE MONTHS...
...TO SURPASS EVERYONE.

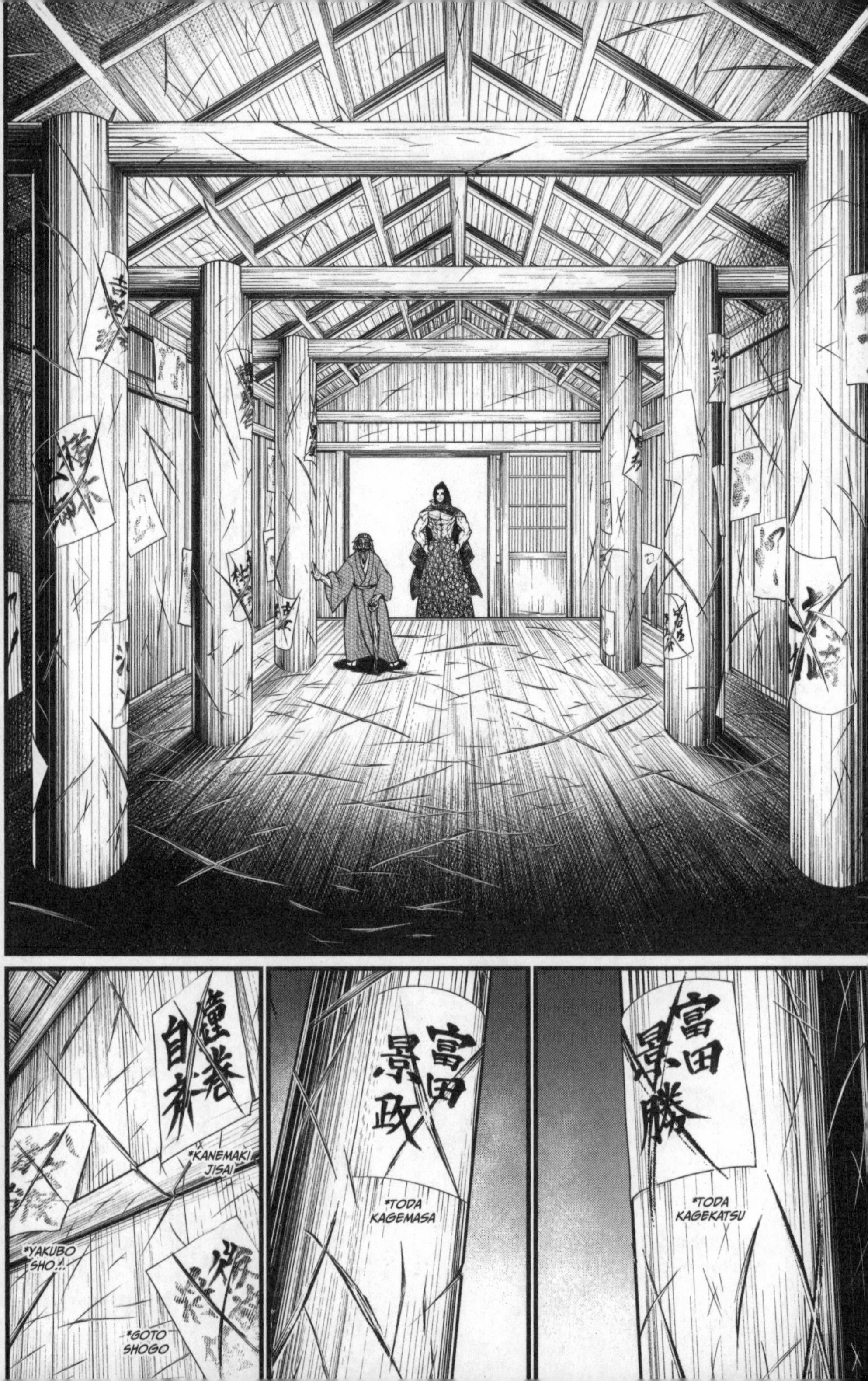
富田景勝
*TODA KAGEKATSU
富田景政
*TODA KAGEMASA
鐘巻自斎
*KANEMAKI JISAI
*YAKUBO SHO...
*GOTO SHOGO

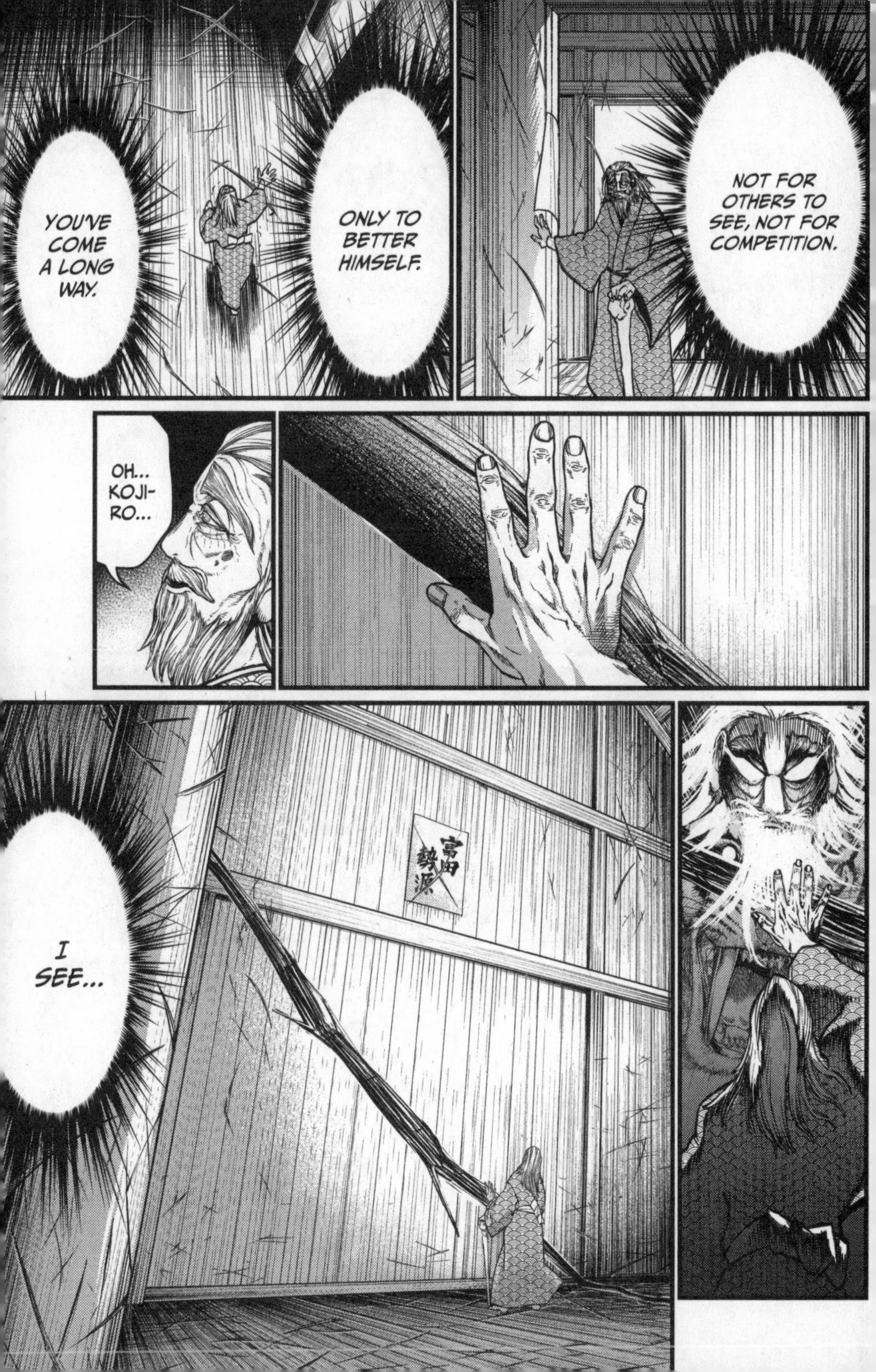
NOT FOR OTHERS TO SEE, NOT FOR COMPETITION.
ONLY TO BETTER HIMSELF.
YOU'VE COME A LONG WAY.
OH... KOJIRO...
富田勢源
I SEE...

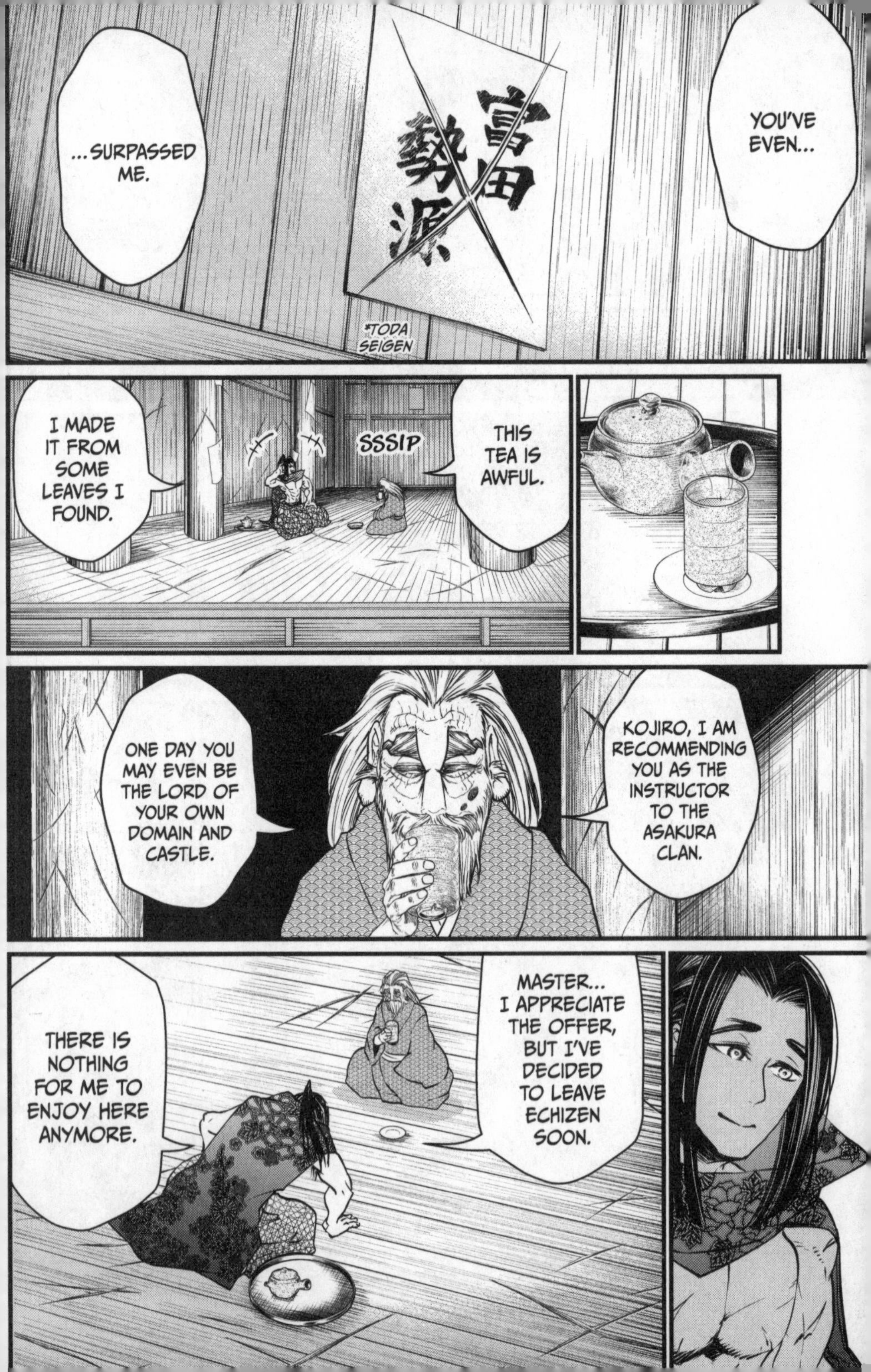
YOU'VE EVEN...
富田勢源
*TODA SEIGEN
...SURPASSED ME.
THIS TEA IS AWFUL.
SSSIP
I MADE IT FROM SOME LEAVES I FOUND.
KOJIRO, I AM RECOMMENDING YOU AS THE INSTRUCTOR TO THE ASAKURA CLAN.
ONE DAY YOU MAY EVEN BE THE LORD OF YOUR OWN DOMAIN AND CASTLE.
MASTER... I APPRECIATE THE OFFER, BUT I'VE DECIDED TO LEAVE ECHIZEN SOON.
THERE IS NOTHING FOR ME TO ENJOY HERE ANYMORE.

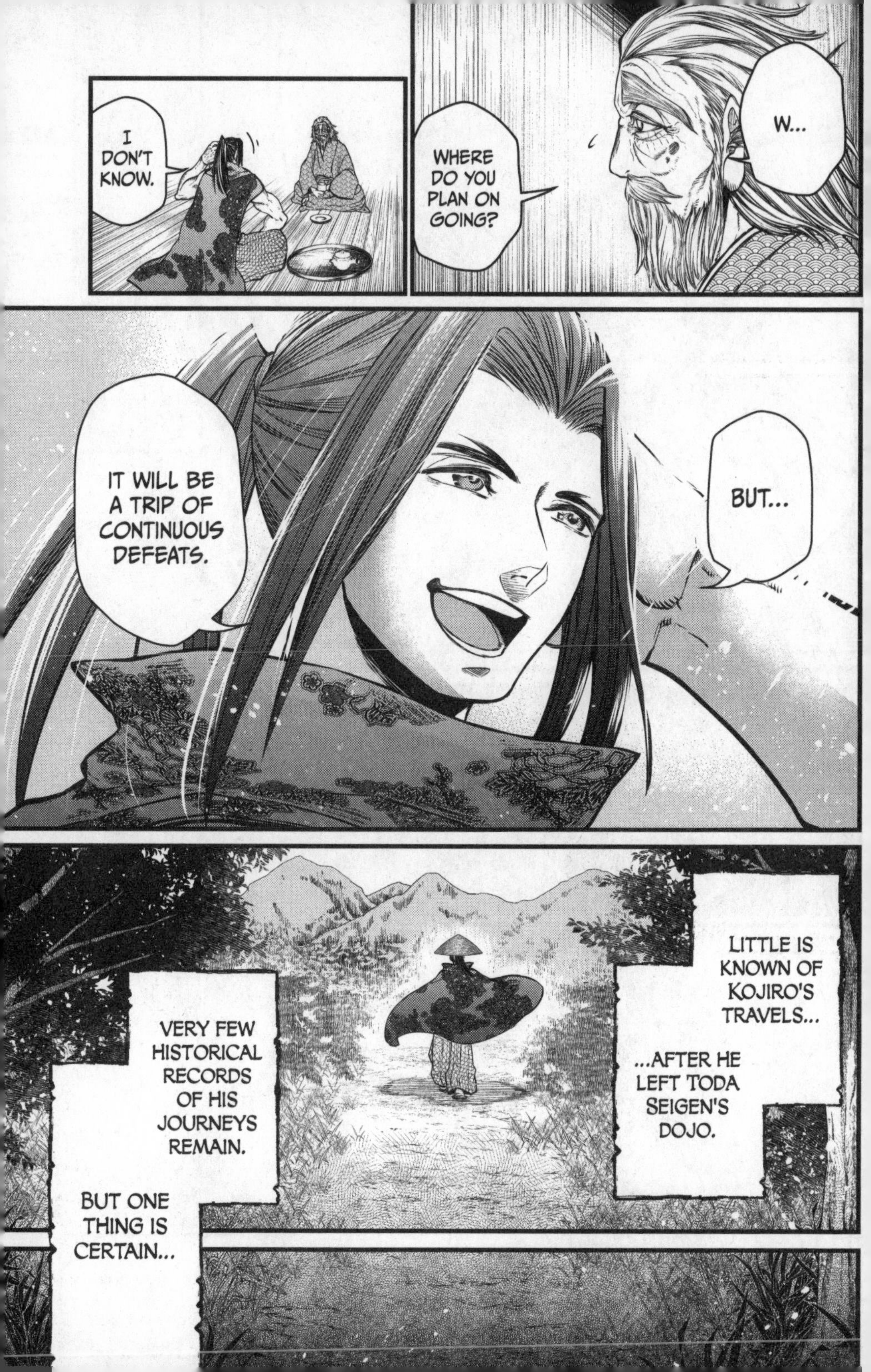
W...
WHERE DO YOU PLAN ON GOING?
I DON'T KNOW.
BUT...
IT WILL BE A TRIP OF CONTINUOUS DEFEATS.
LITTLE IS KNOWN OF KOJIRO'S TRAVELS...
...AFTER HE LEFT TODA SEIGEN'S DOJO.
VERY FEW HISTORICAL RECORDS OF HIS JOURNEYS REMAIN.
BUT ONE THING IS CERTAIN...

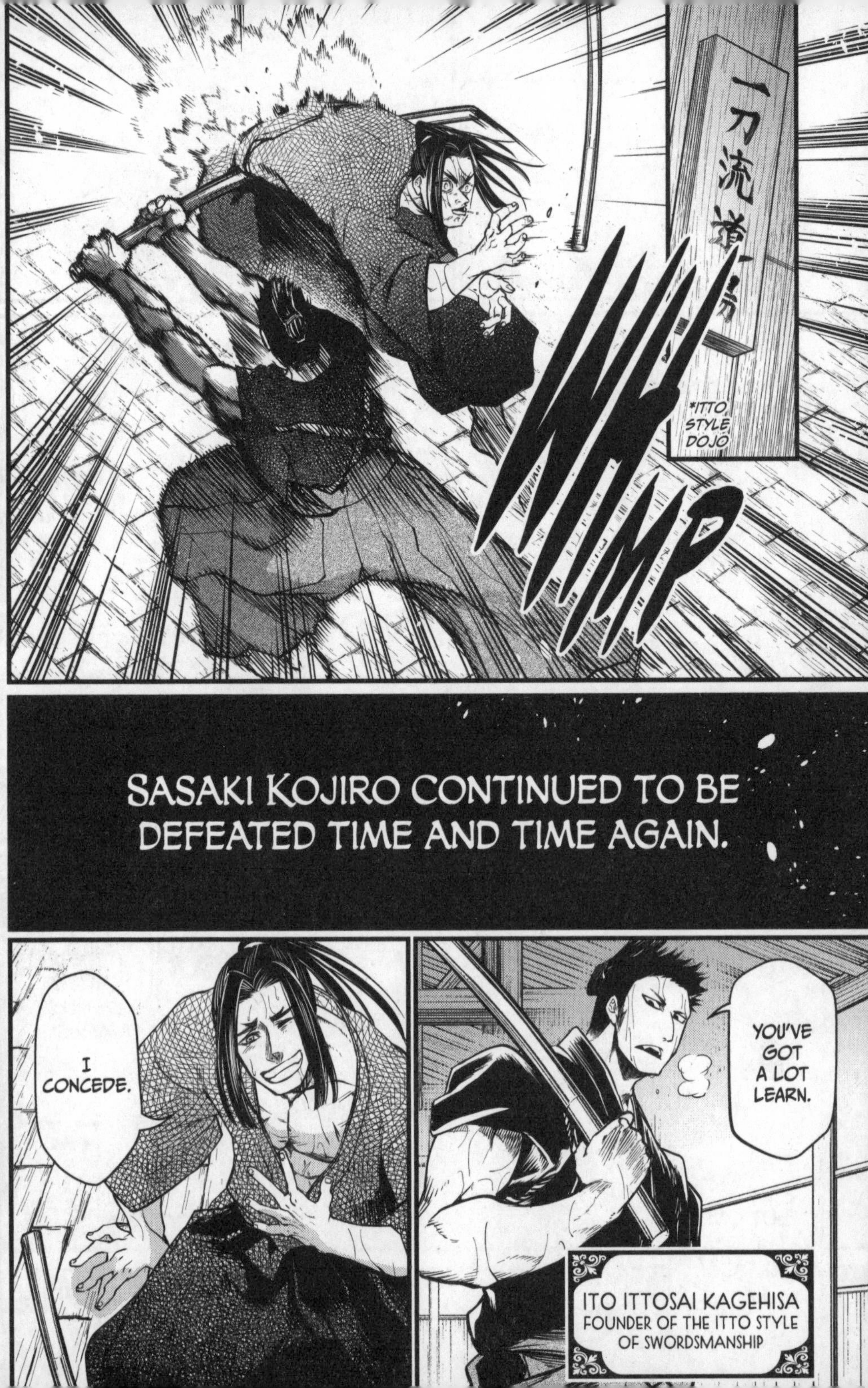
一刀流道場
*ITTO STYLE DOJO
WHUMP
SASAKI KOJIRO CONTINUED TO BE DEFEATED TIME AND TIME AGAIN.
YOU'VE GOT A LOT LEARN.
ITO ITTOSAI KAGEHISA
FOUNDER OF THE ITTO STYLE OF SWORDSMANSHIP
I CONCEDE.

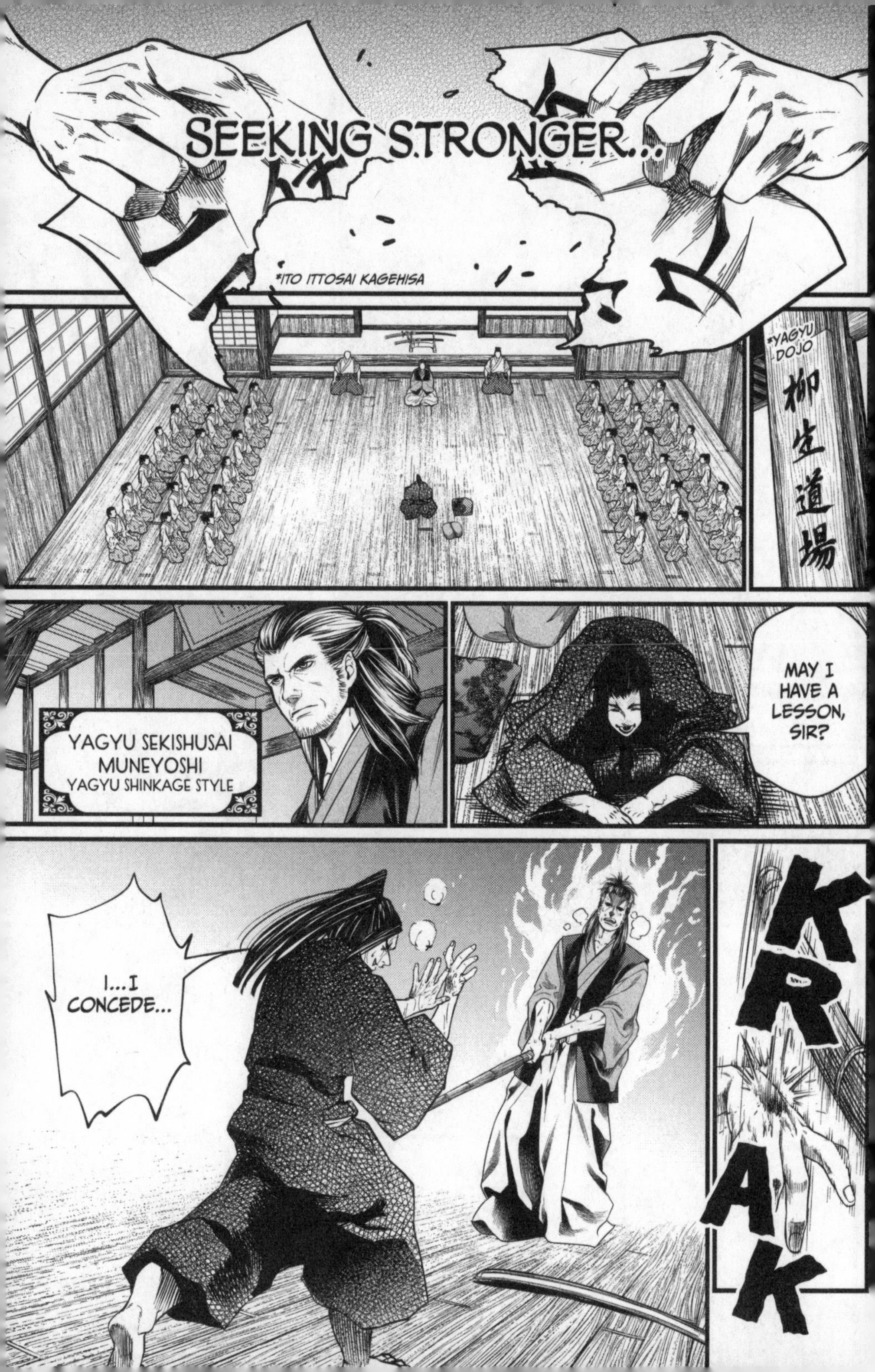
SEEKING STRONGER...
*ITO ITTOSAI KAGEHISA
*YAGYU DOJO
柳生道場
MAY I HAVE A LESSON, SIR?
YAGYU SEKISHUSAI MUNEYOSHI
YAGYU SHINKAGE STYLE
KRAK
I...I CONCEDE...

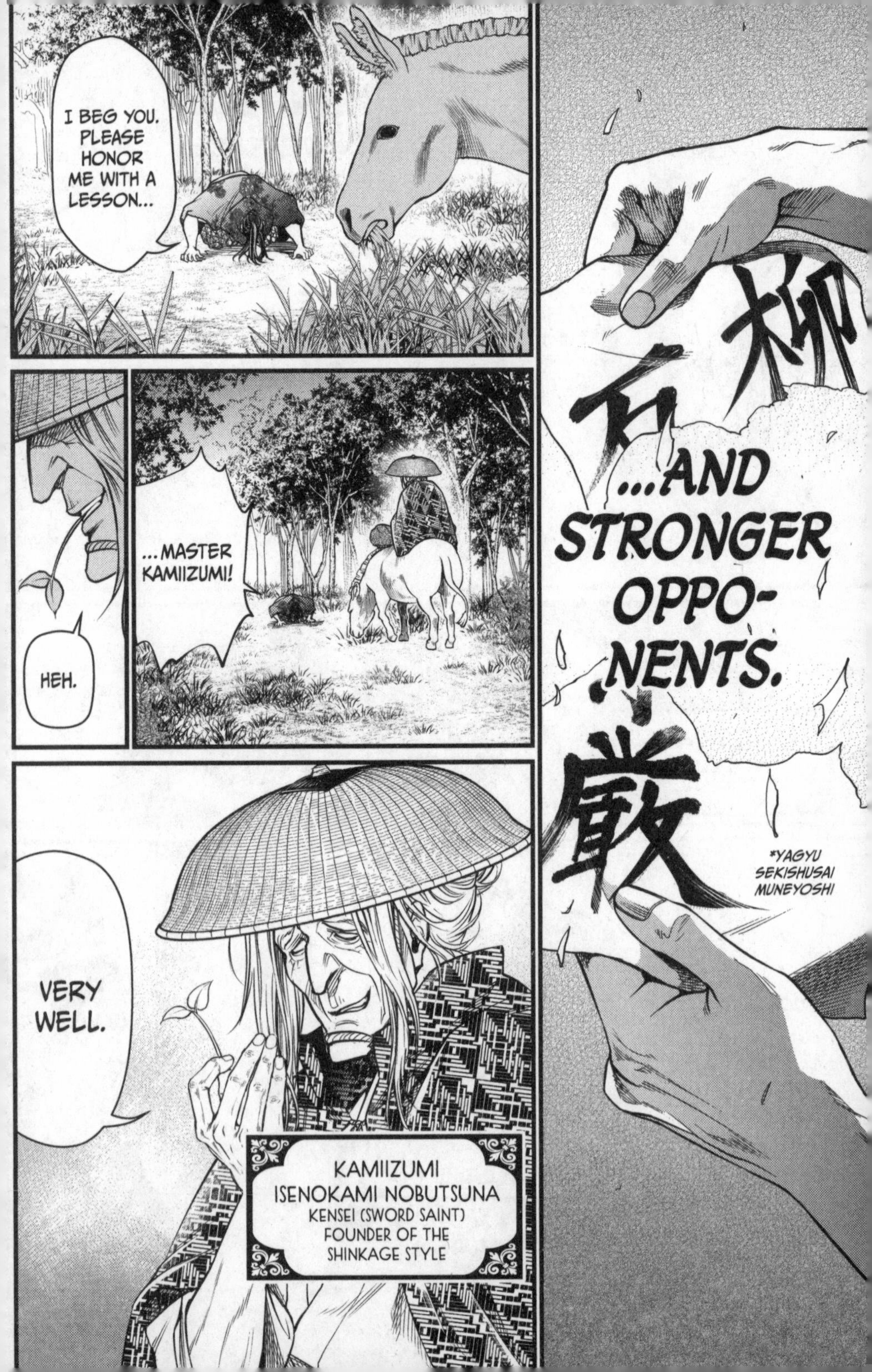
柳
石
...AND STRONGER OPPONENTS.
巌
*YAGYU SEKISHUSAI MUNEYOSHI
I BEG YOU. PLEASE HONOR ME WITH A LESSON...
...MASTER KAMIIZUMI!
HEH.
VERY WELL.
KAMIIZUMI ISENOKAMI NOBUTSUNA
KENSEI (SWORD SAINT)
FOUNDER OF THE SHINKAGE STYLE

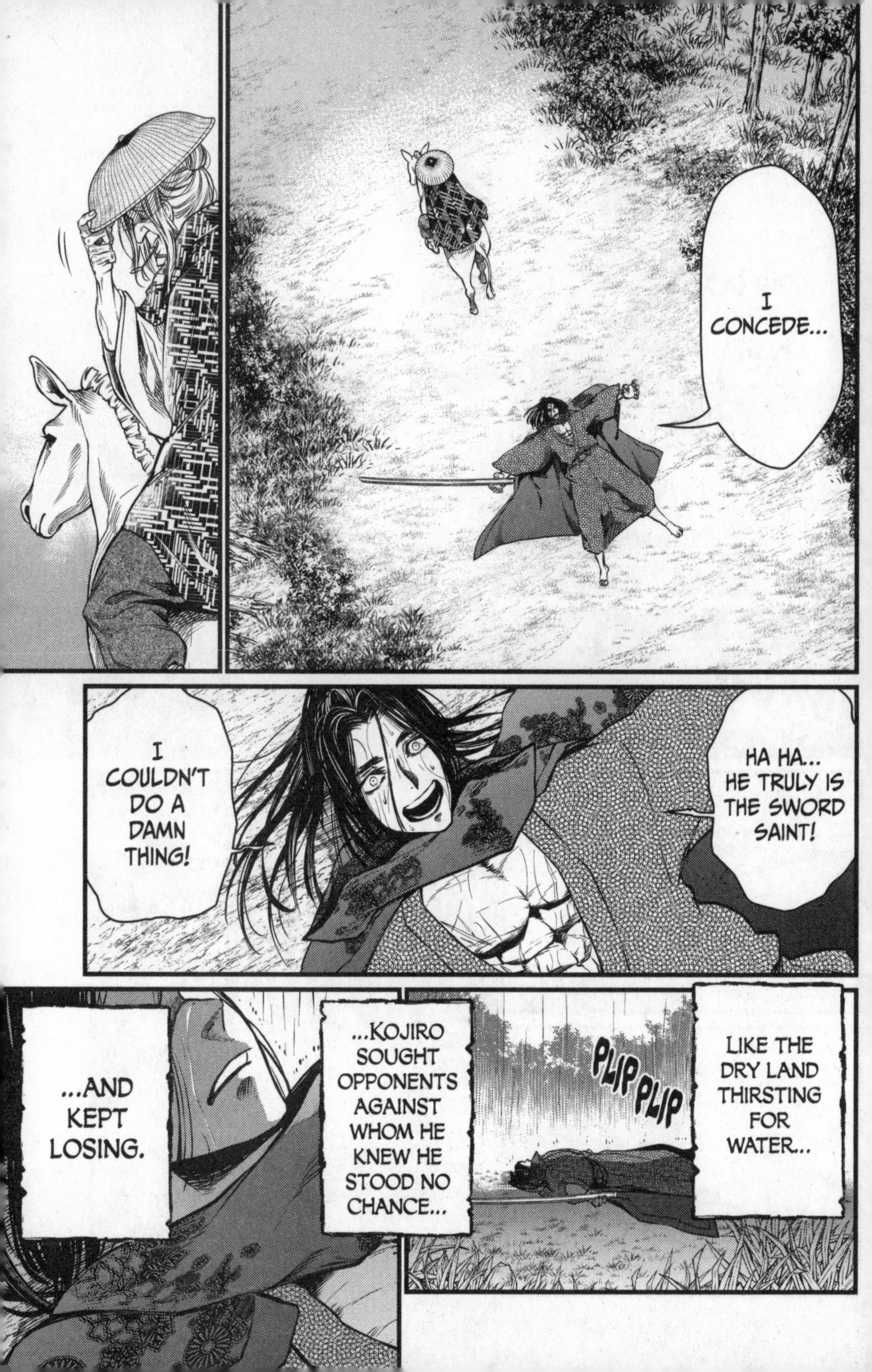
I CONCEDE...
HA HA... HE TRULY IS THE SWORD SAINT!
I COULDN'T DO A DAMN THING!
LIKE THE DRY LAND THIRSTING FOR WATER...
PLIP PLIP
...KOJIRO SOUGHT OPPONENTS AGAINST WHOM HE KNEW HE STOOD NO CHANCE...
...AND KEPT LOSING.

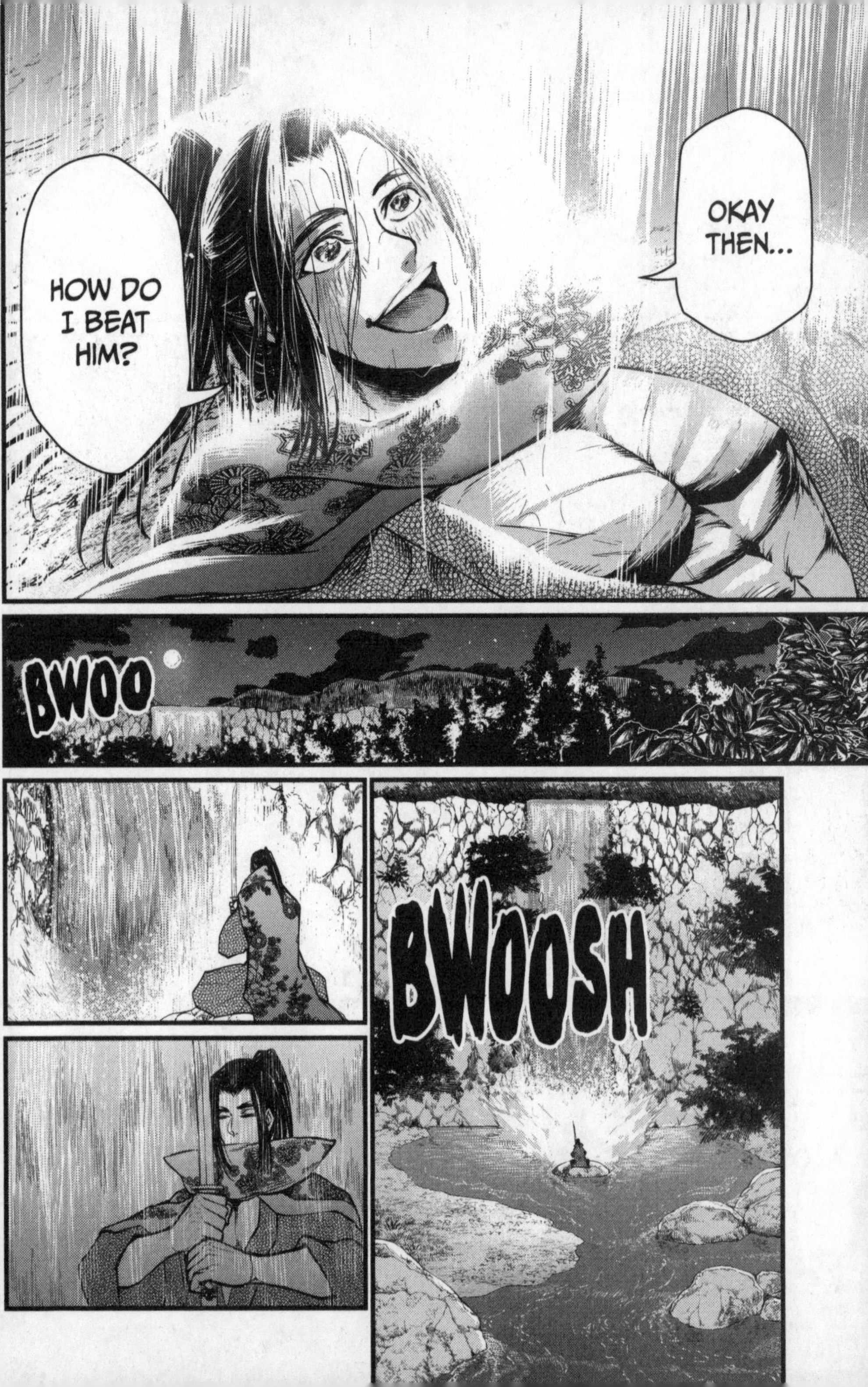
OKAY THEN...
HOW DO I BEAT HIM?
BWOO
BWOOSH

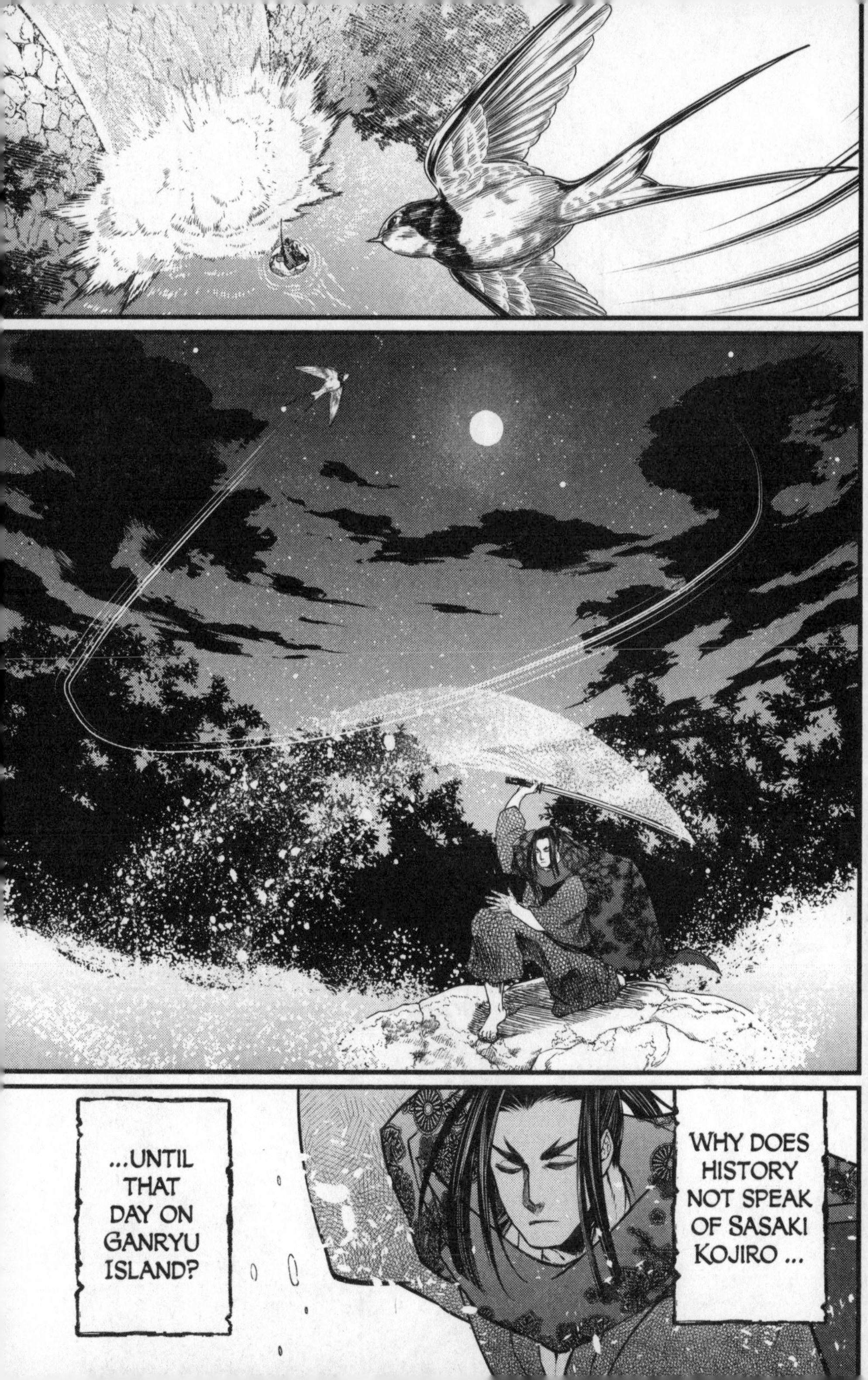
WHY DOES HISTORY NOT SPEAK OF SASAKI KOJIRO ...
...UNTIL THAT DAY ON GANRYU ISLAND?

THE ONLY
REASON
IS...

? ZWIK

...HE
KEPT
LOSING...

...AS HE
STROVE TO
BECOME THE
ULTIMATE
SWORDSMAN!

RRIP

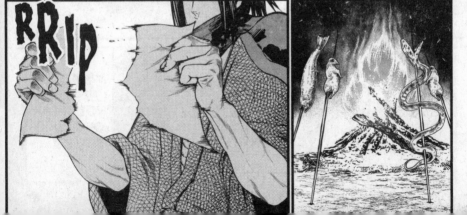

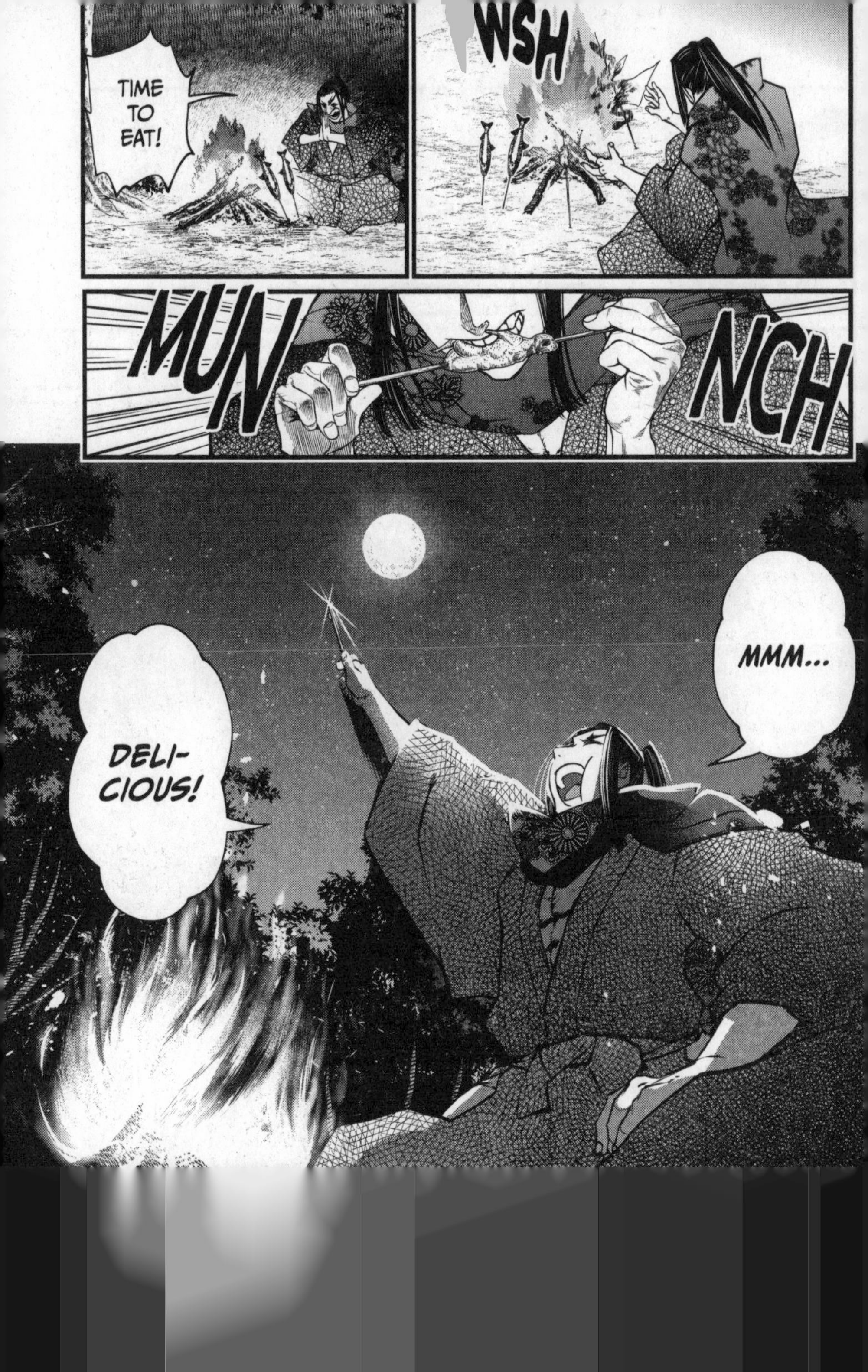
WSH
TIME TO EAT!
MUN
NCH
MMM...
DELI-CIOUS!

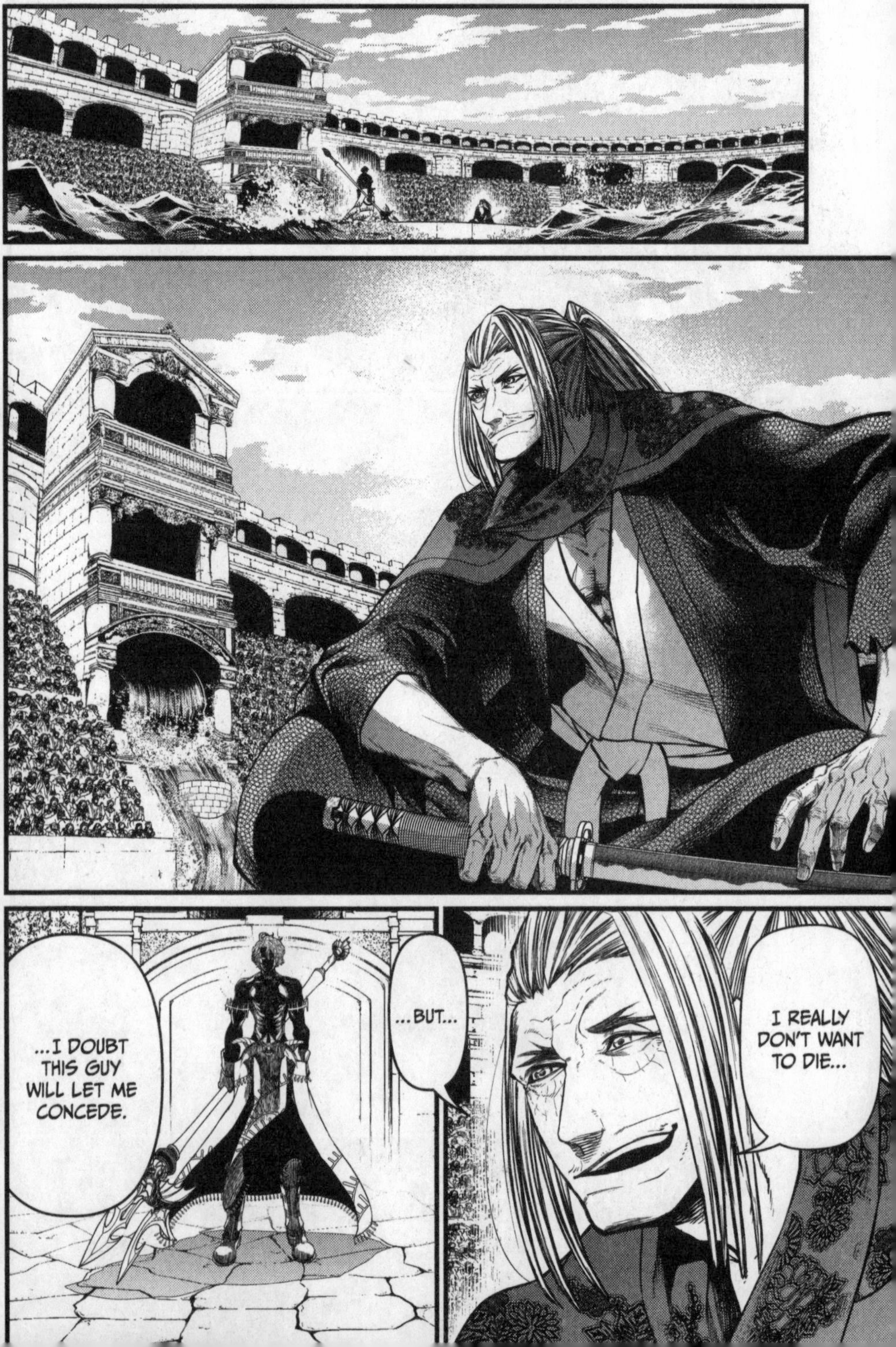
I REALLY DON'T WANT TO DIE...
...BUT...
...I DOUBT THIS GUY WILL LET ME CONCEDE.

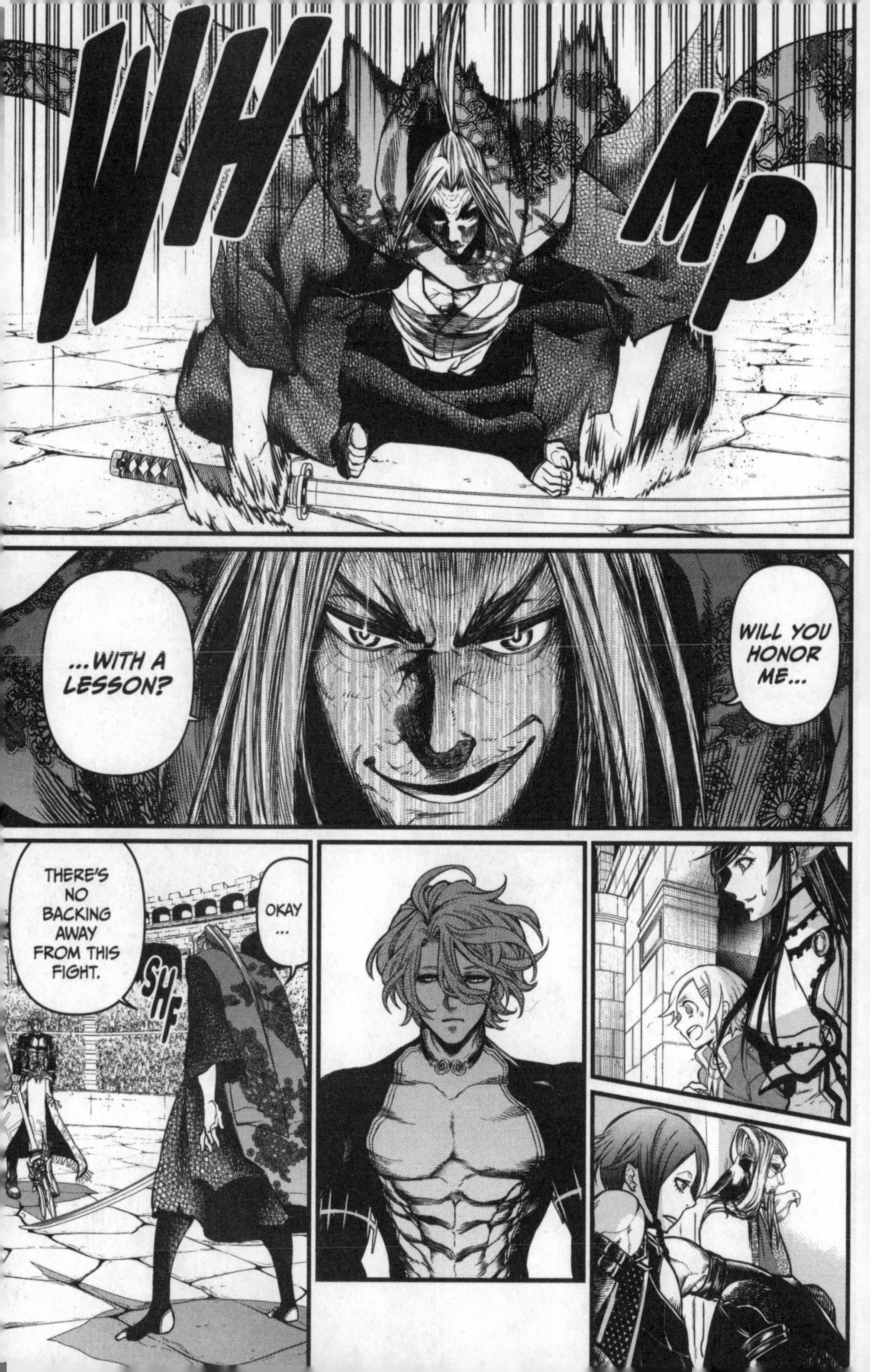
WH
MP
WILL YOU HONOR ME...
...WITH A LESSON?
OKAY ...
THERE'S NO BACKING AWAY FROM THIS FIGHT.
SHF

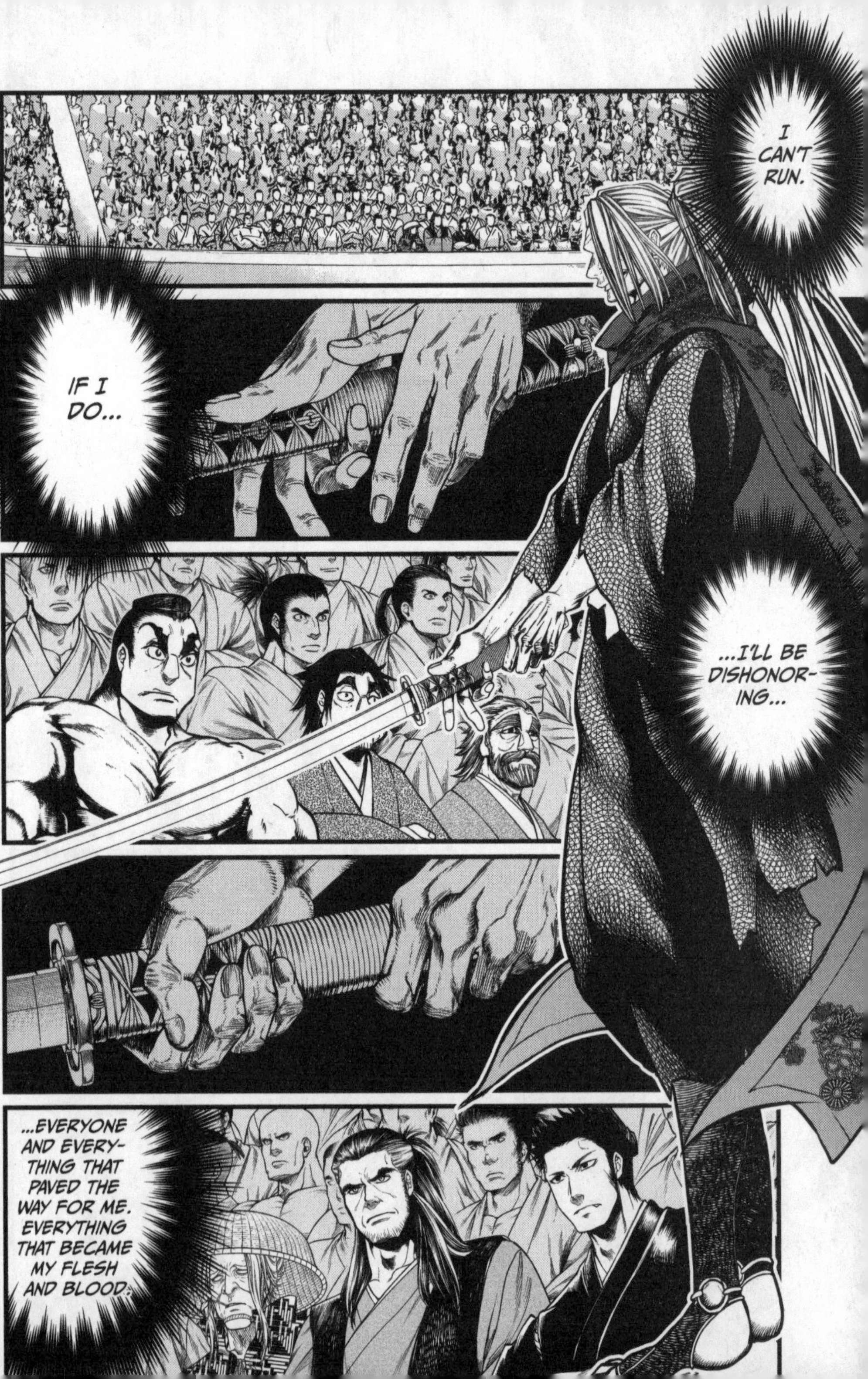
I CAN'T RUN.
IF I DO...
...I'LL BE DISHONOR-ING...
...EVERYONE AND EVERY-THING THAT PAVED THE WAY FOR ME. EVERYTHING THAT BECAME MY FLESH AND BLOOD.

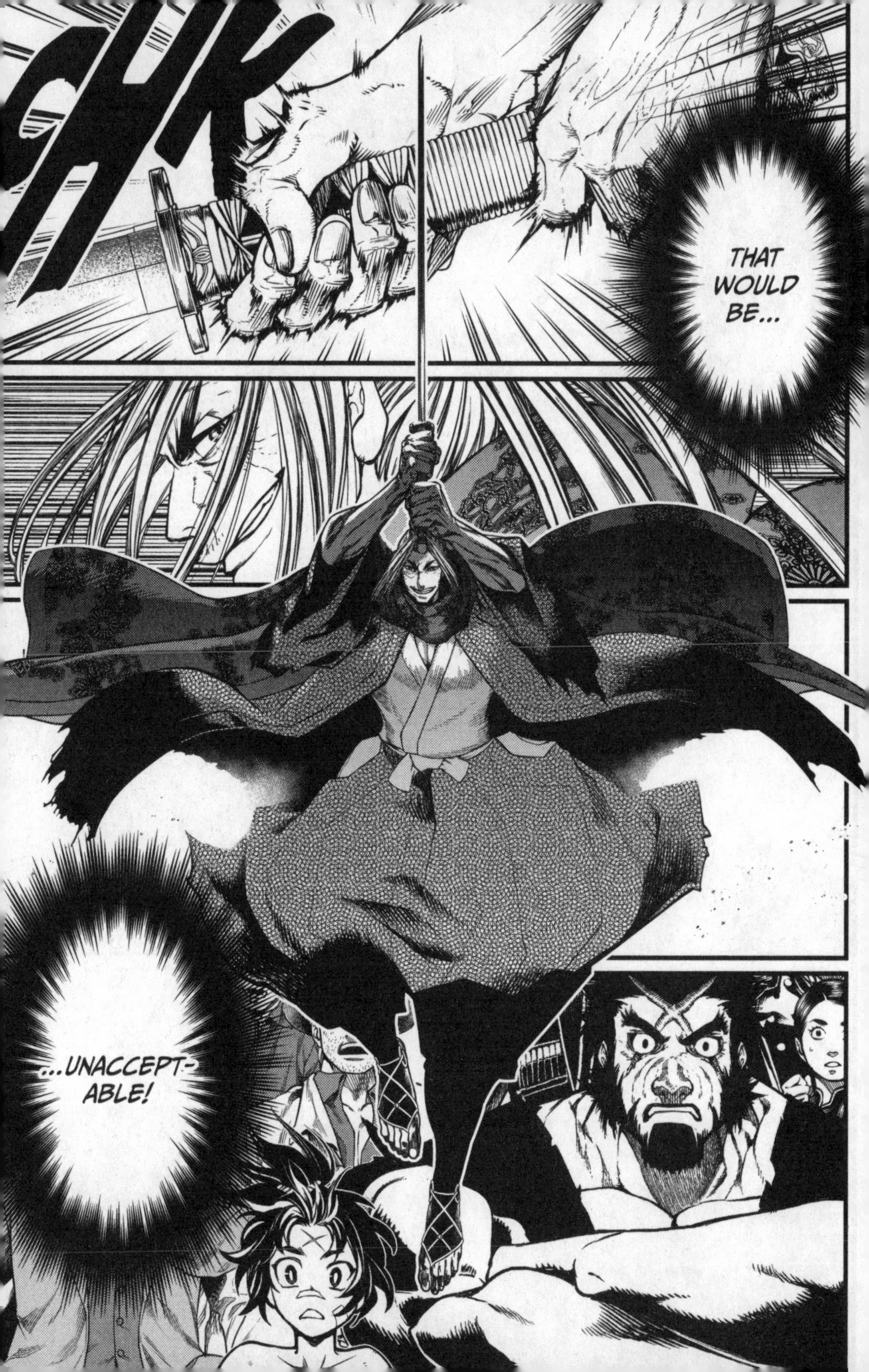
CHK
THAT WOULD BE...
...UNACCEPT-ABLE!

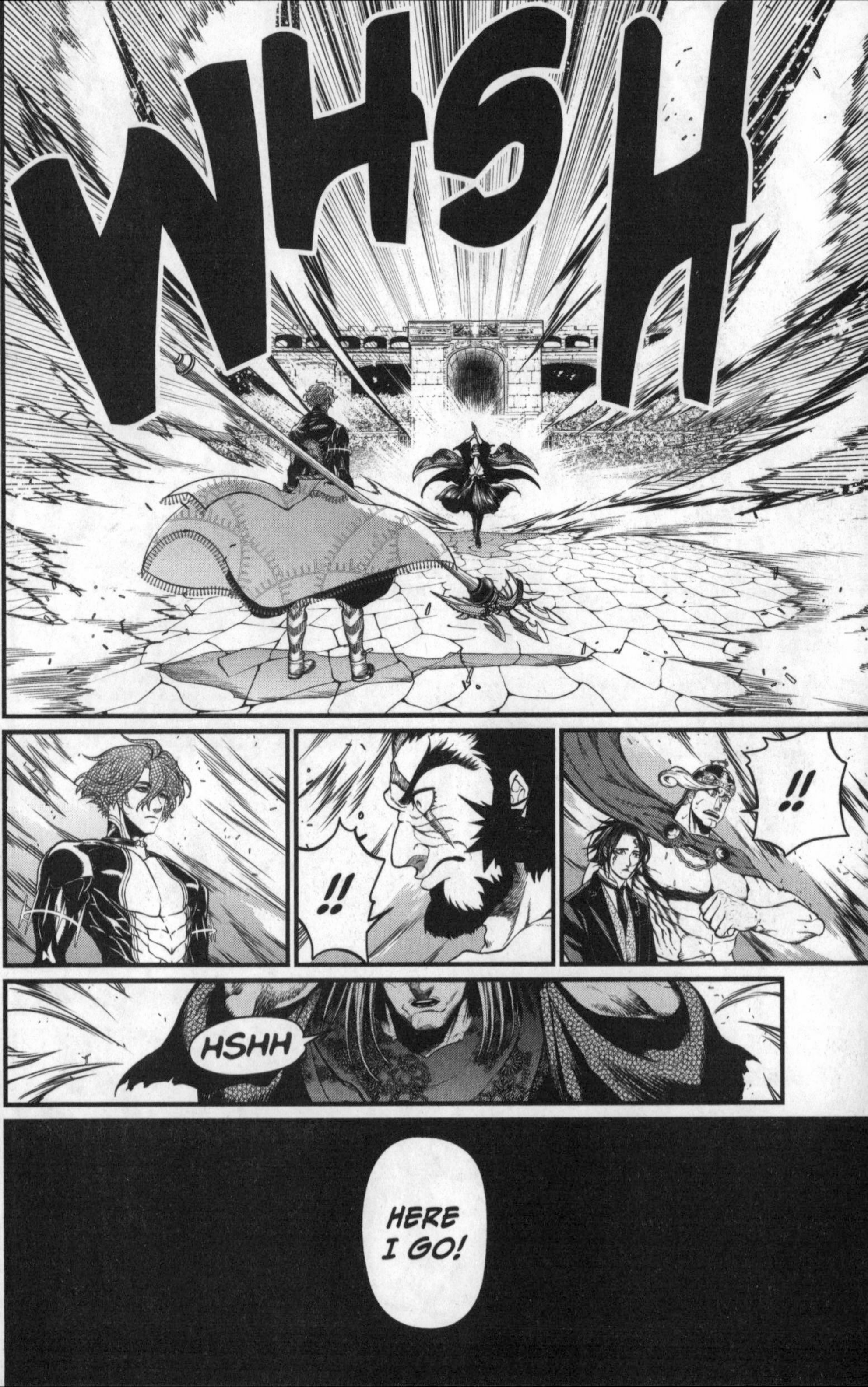
WHSH
!!
!!
HSHH
HERE I GO!

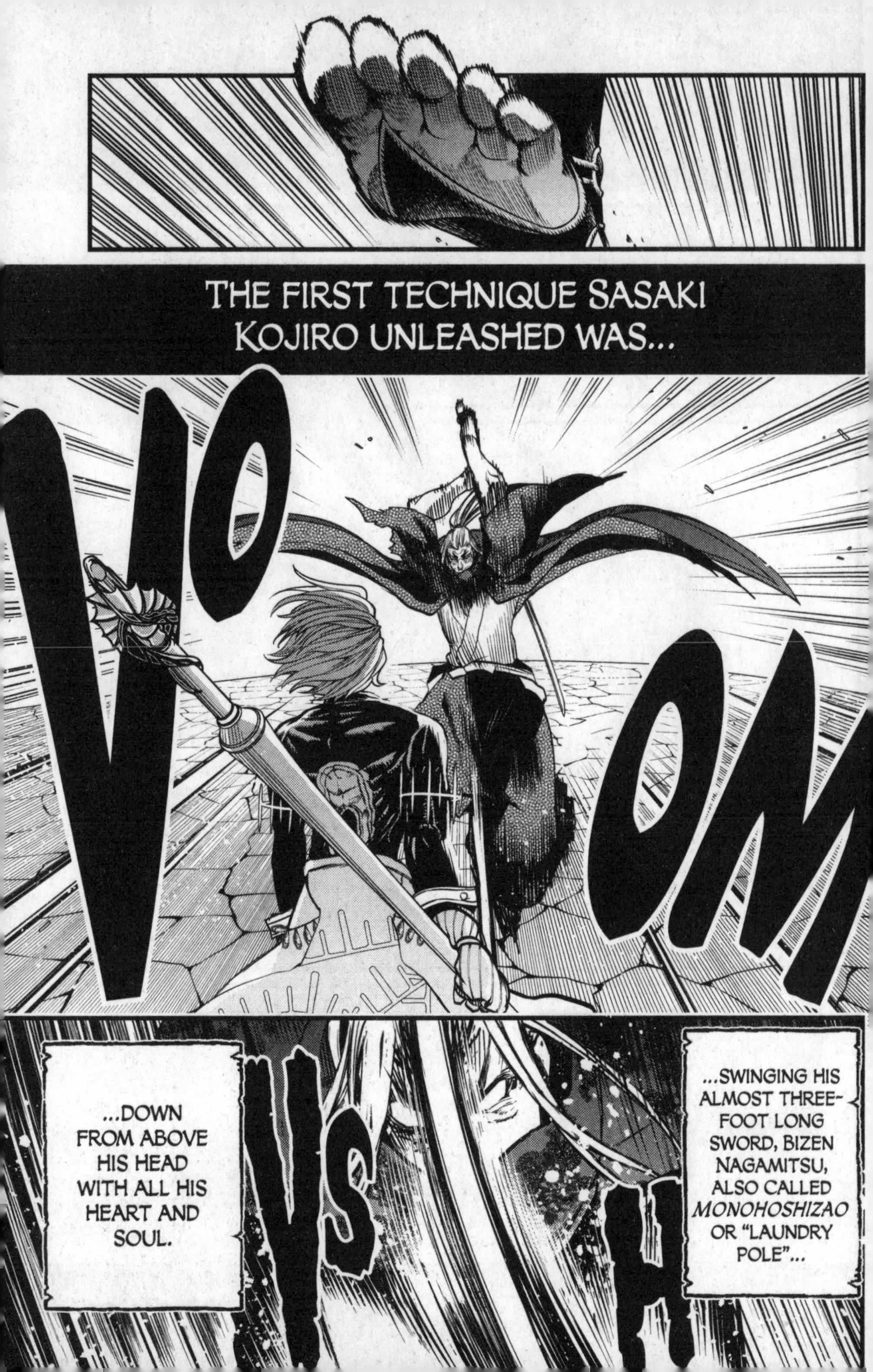
THE FIRST TECHNIQUE SASAKI KOJIRO UNLEASHED WAS...
VOOM
...SWINGING HIS ALMOST THREE-FOOT LONG SWORD, BIZEN NAGAMITSU, ALSO CALLED *MONOHOSHIZAO* OR "LAUNDRY POLE"...
...DOWN FROM ABOVE HIS HEAD WITH ALL HIS HEART AND SOUL.

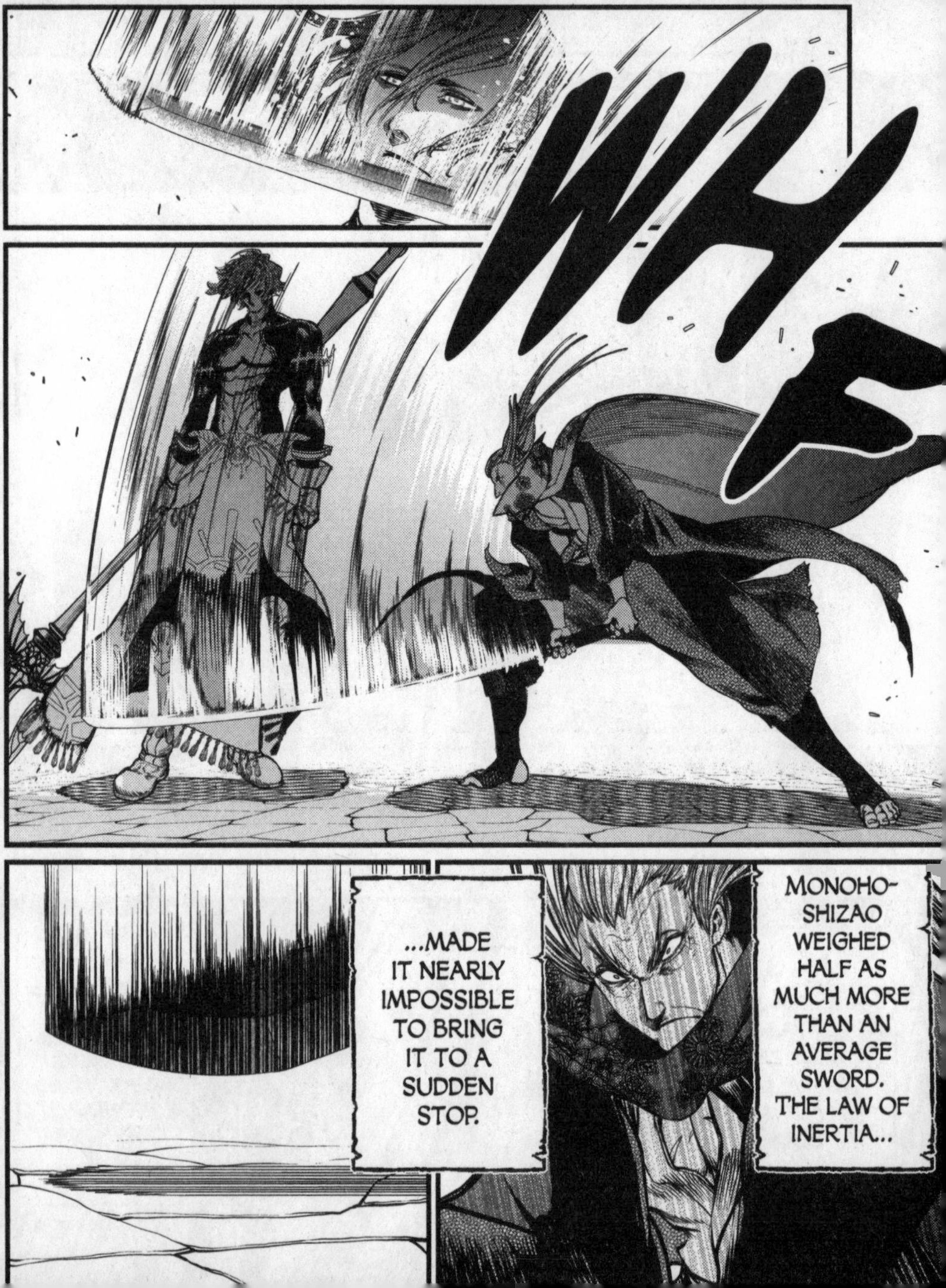
WHF
MONOHO-SHIZAO WEIGHED HALF AS MUCH MORE THAN AN AVERAGE SWORD. THE LAW OF INERTIA...
...MADE IT NEARLY IMPOSSIBLE TO BRING IT TO A SUDDEN STOP.

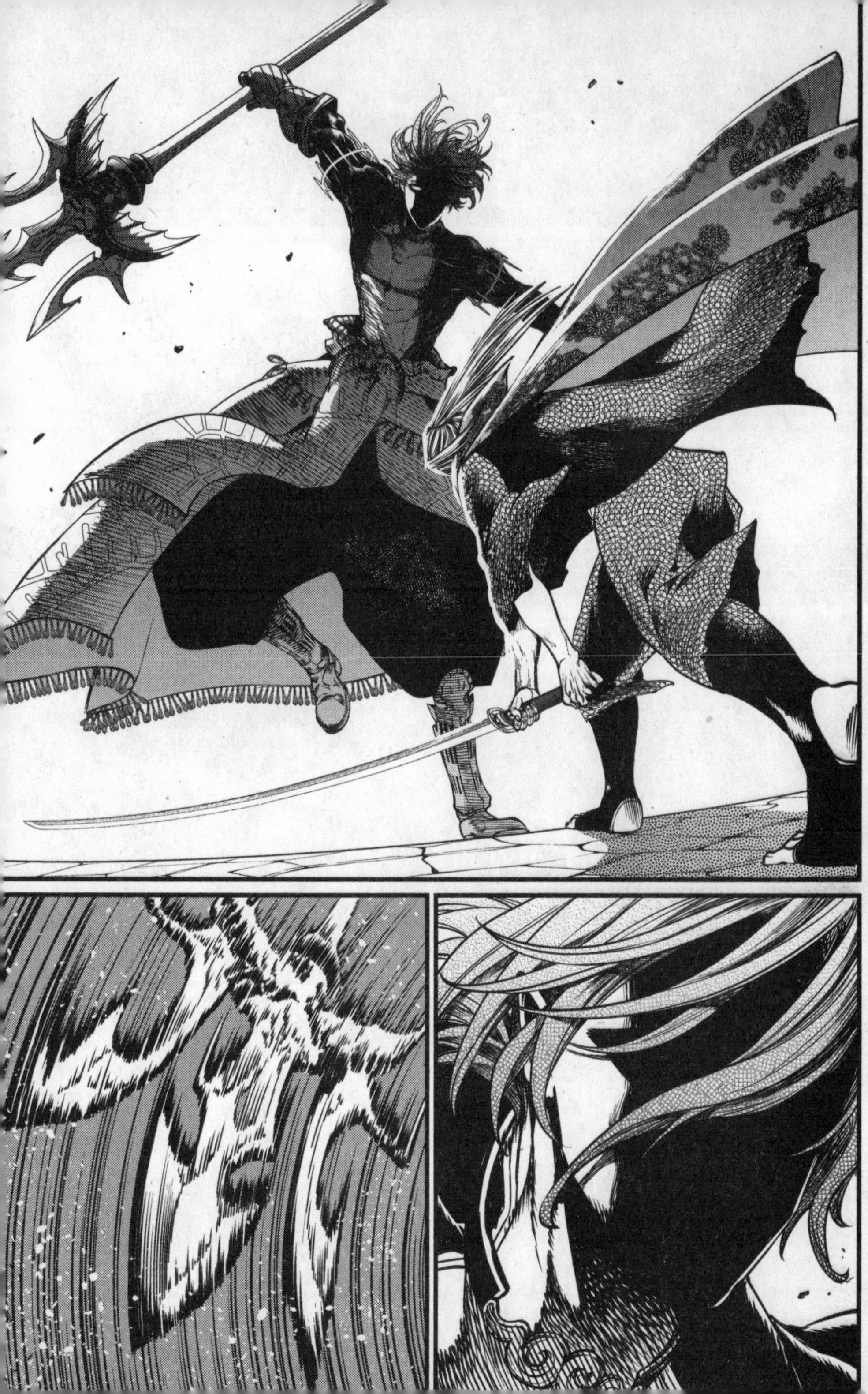

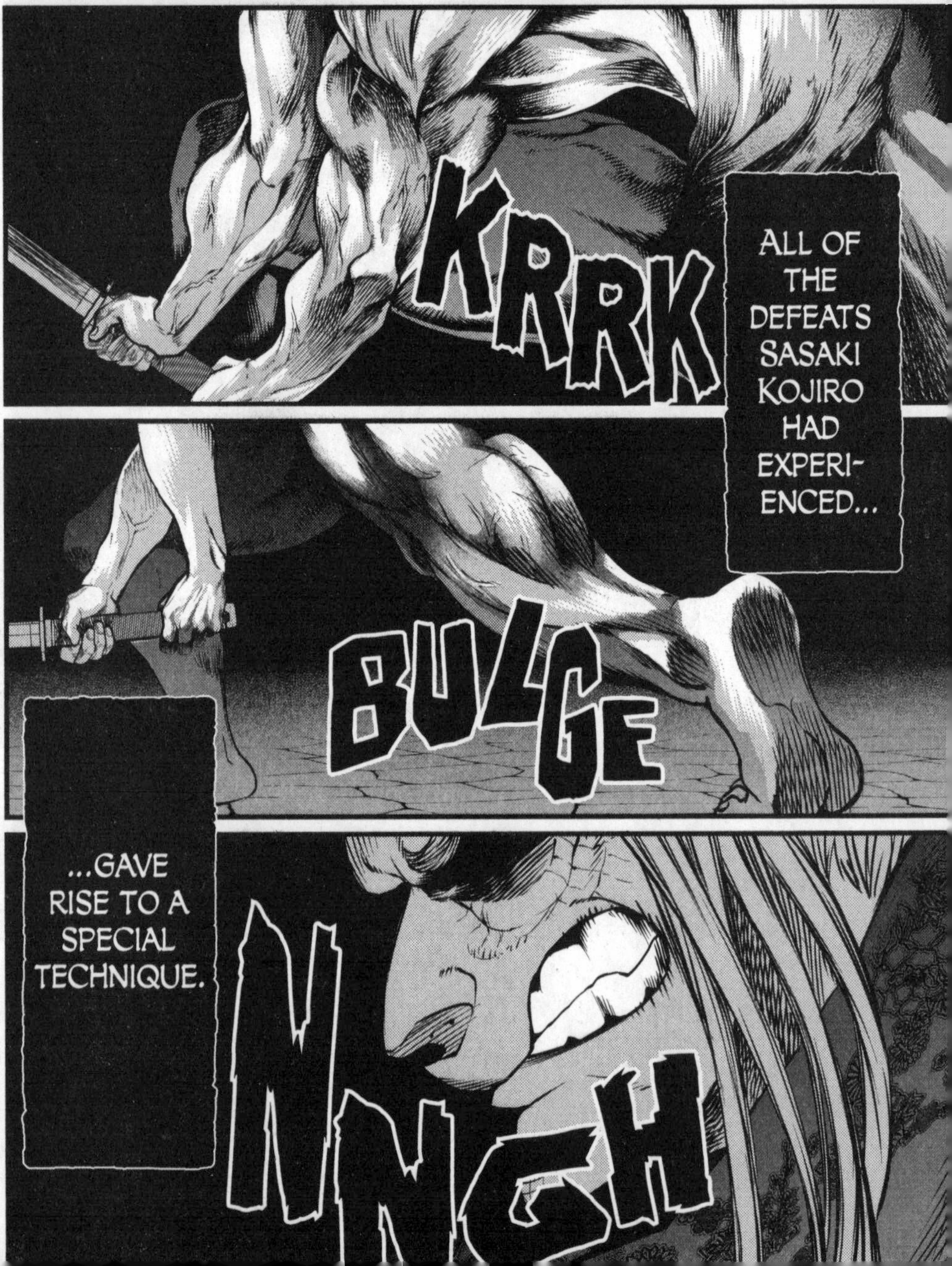
ALL OF THE DEFEATS SASAKI KOJIRO HAD EXPERI- ENCED...
KRRK
BULGE
...GAVE RISE TO A SPECIAL TECHNIQUE.
NNGH

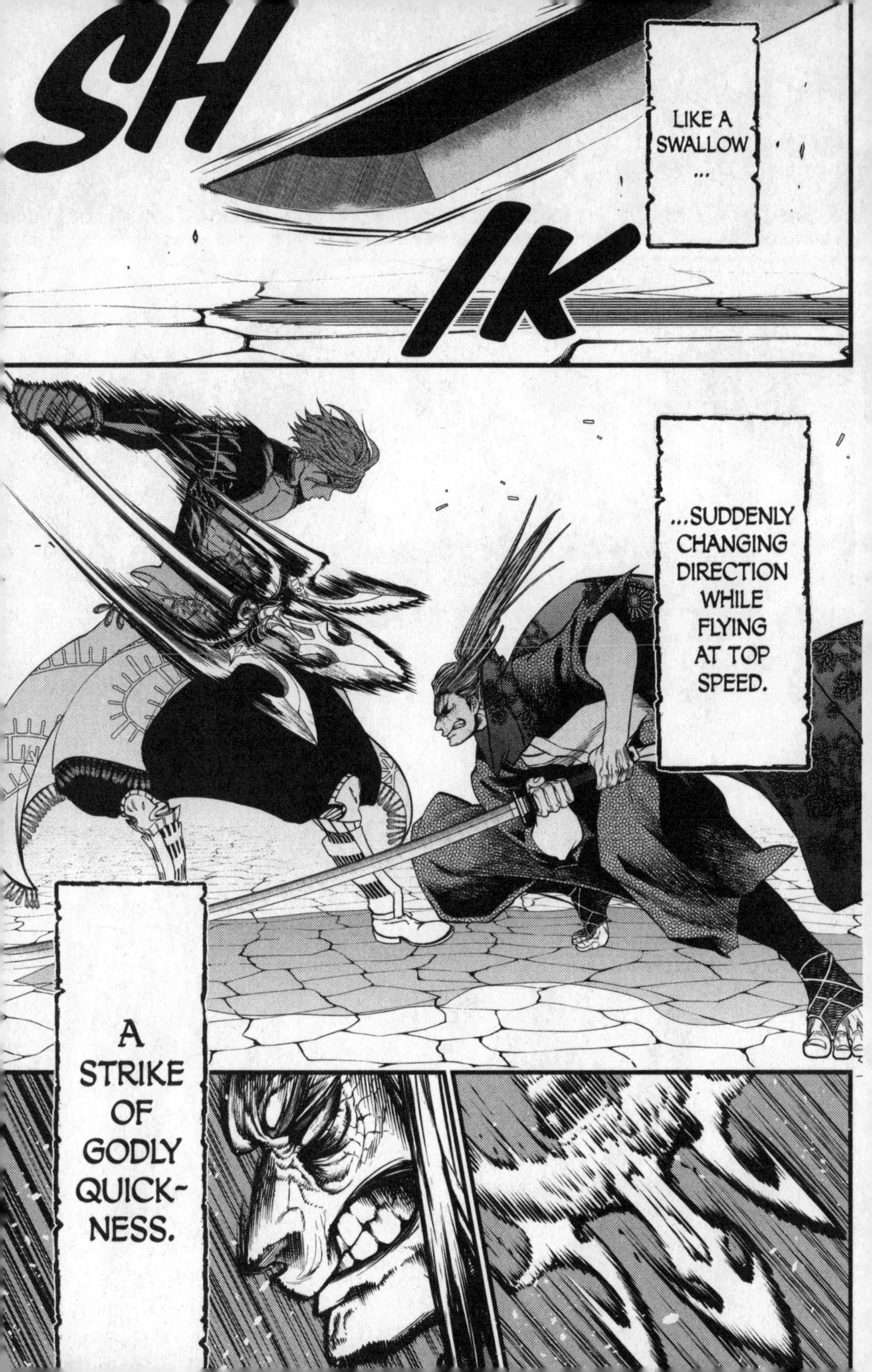
LIKE A SWALLOW ...
SH IK
...SUDDENLY CHANGING DIRECTION WHILE FLYING AT TOP SPEED.
A STRIKE OF GODLY QUICK-NESS.

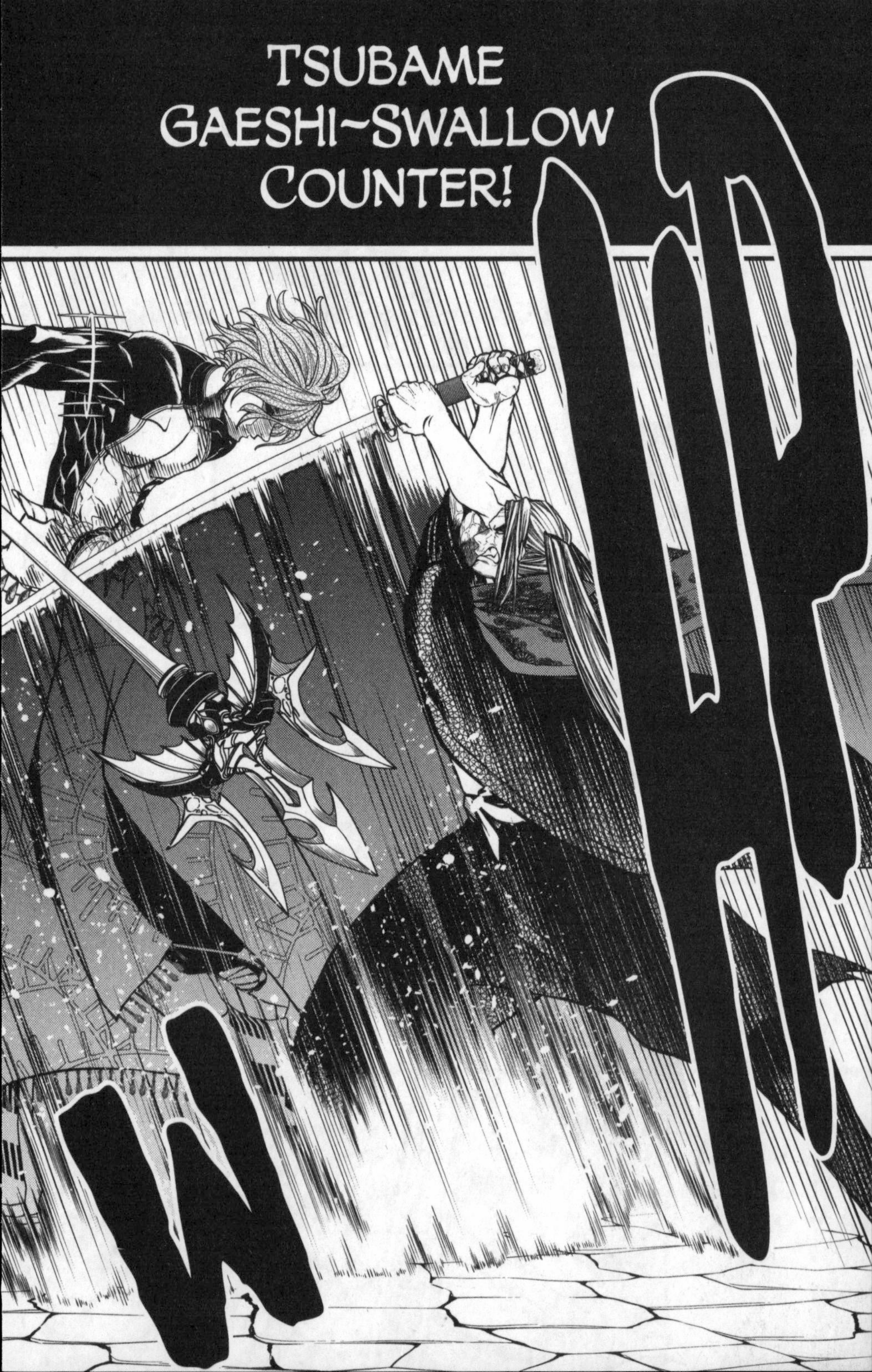
TSUBAME GAESHI-SWALLOW COUNTER!

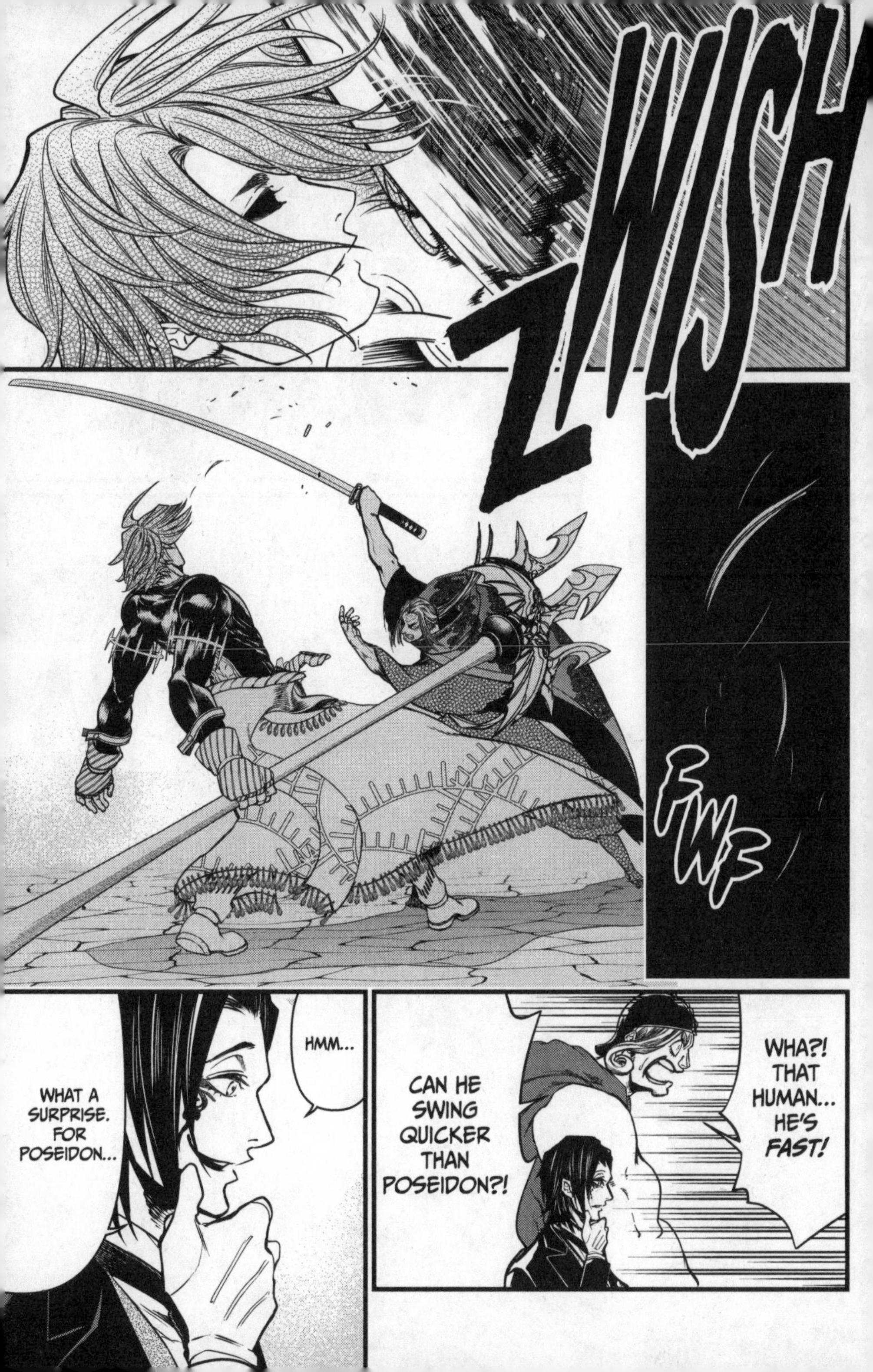
ZWISH
FWF
WHA?! THAT HUMAN... HE'S FAST!
CAN HE SWING QUICKER THAN POSEIDON?!
HMM...
WHAT A SURPRISE. FOR POSEIDON...

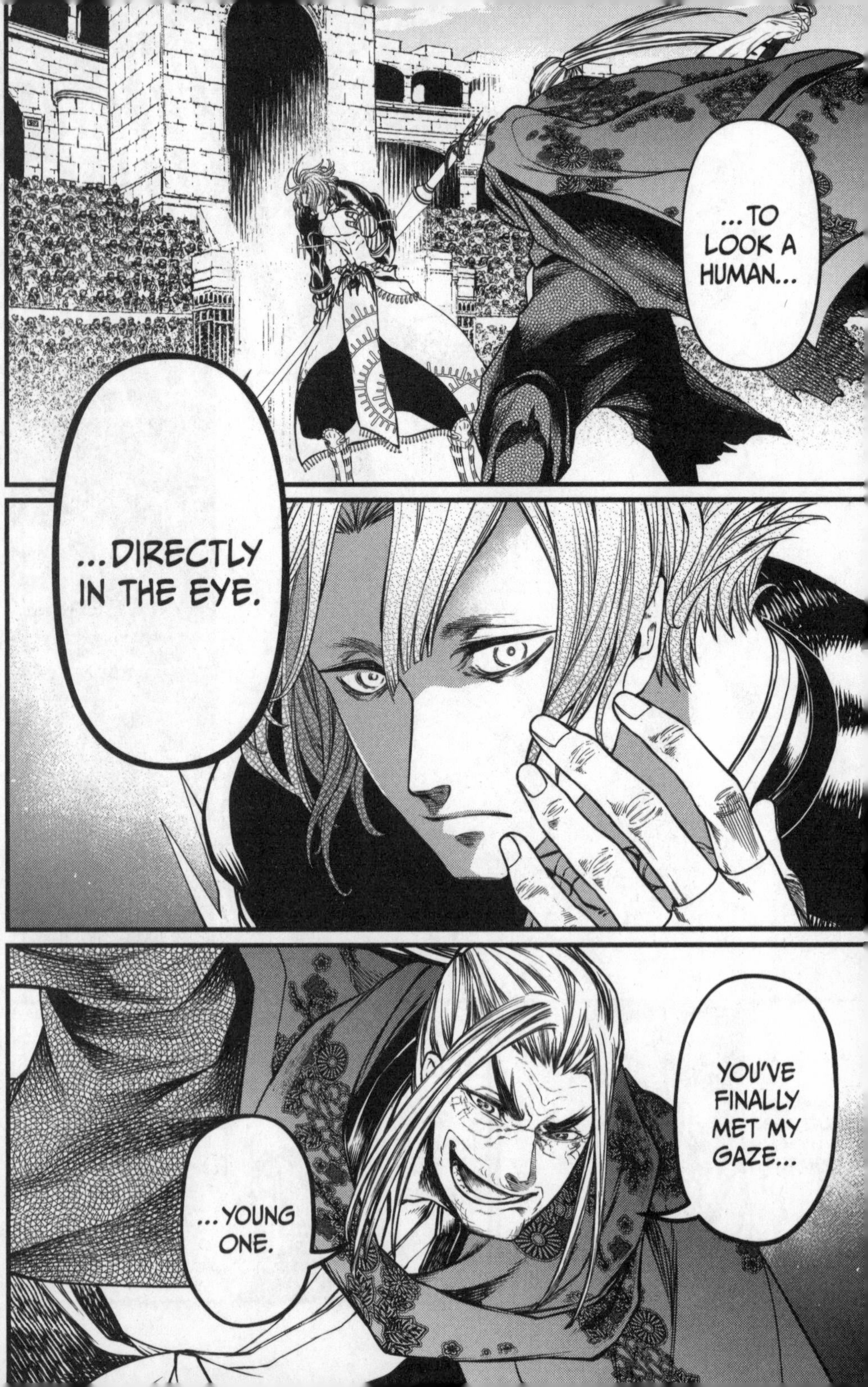
...TO LOOK A HUMAN...
...DIRECTLY IN THE EYE.
YOU'VE FINALLY MET MY GAZE...
...YOUNG ONE.

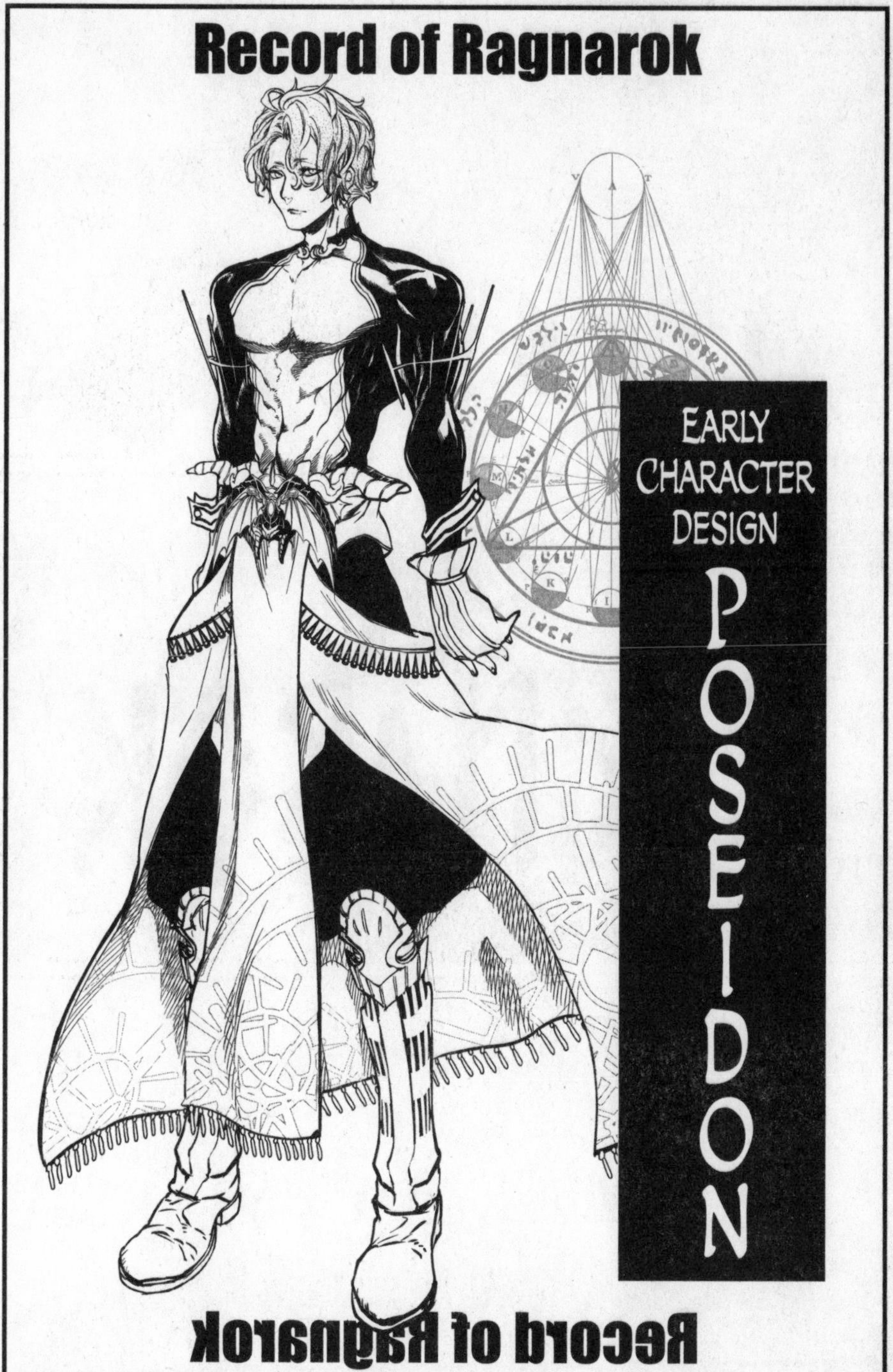
Record of Ragnarok
EARLY CHARACTER DESIGN
POSEIDON
Record of Ragnarok

RECORD OF
RAGNAROK

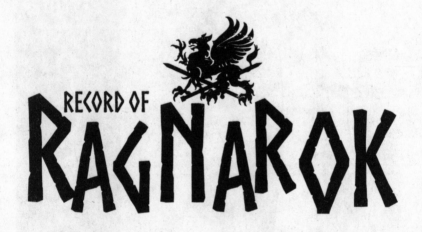

Chapter 17: Secret Technique

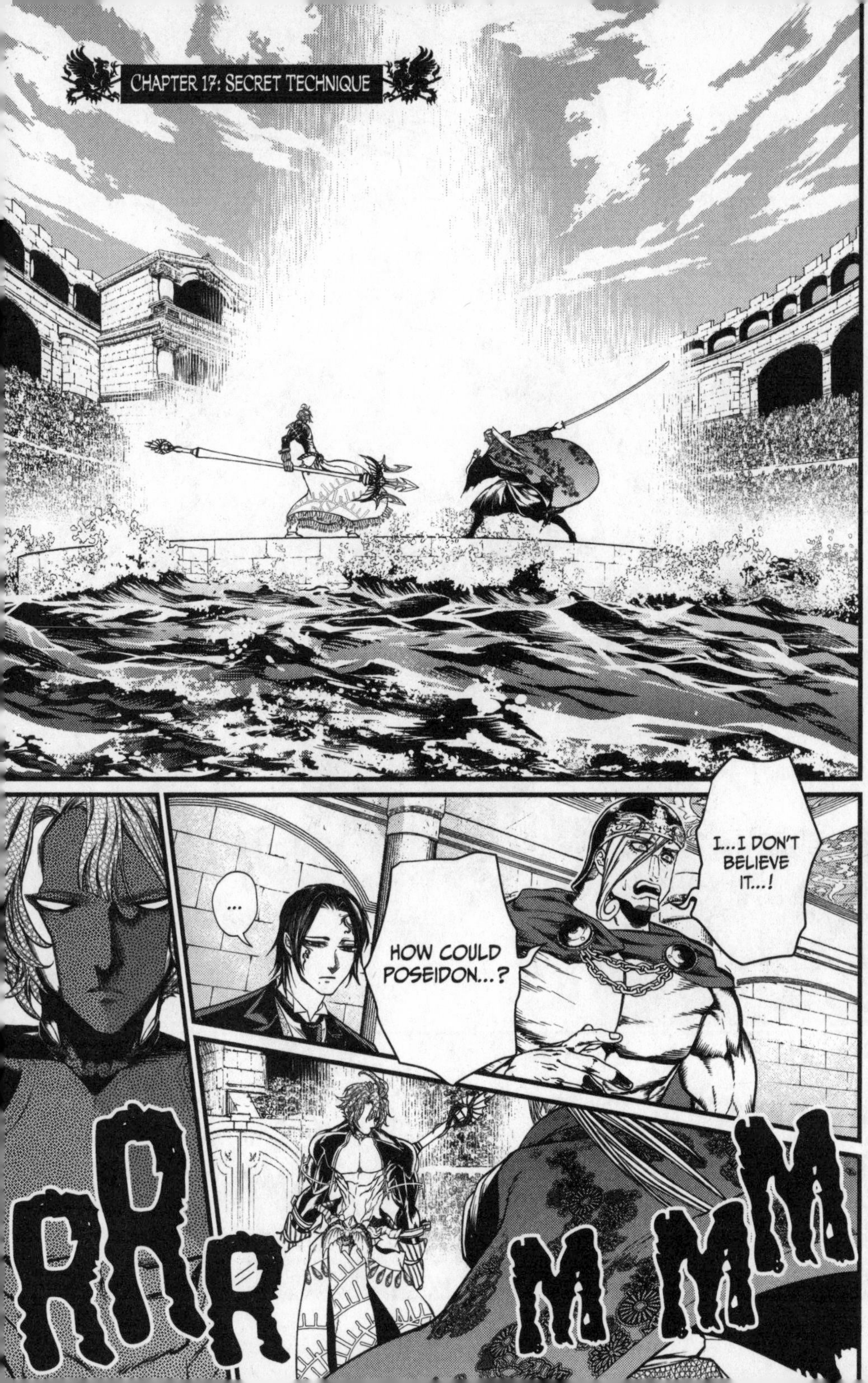
I...I DON'T BELIEVE IT...!
HOW COULD POSEIDON...?
...
RORRMMMM

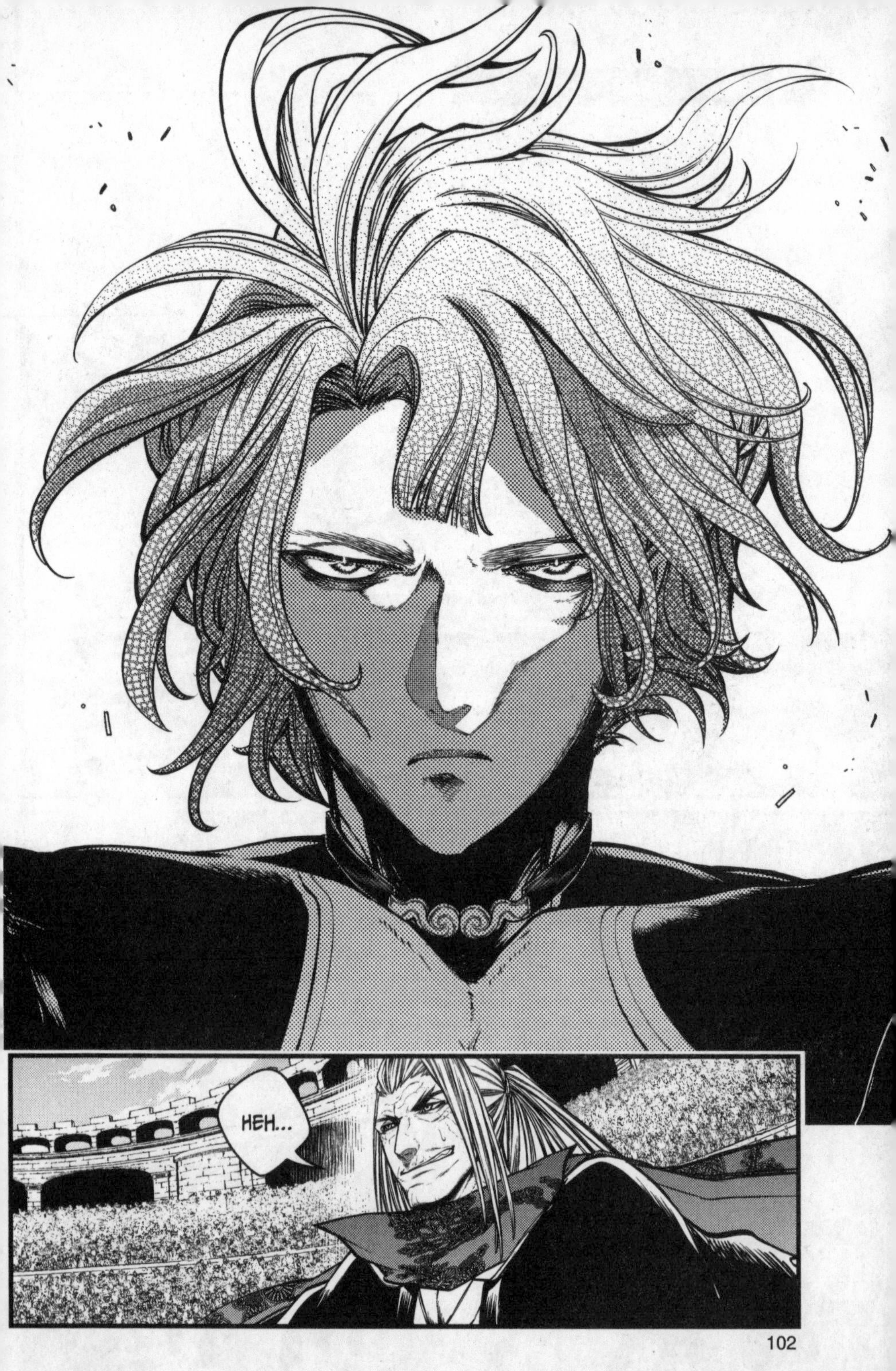
HEH...

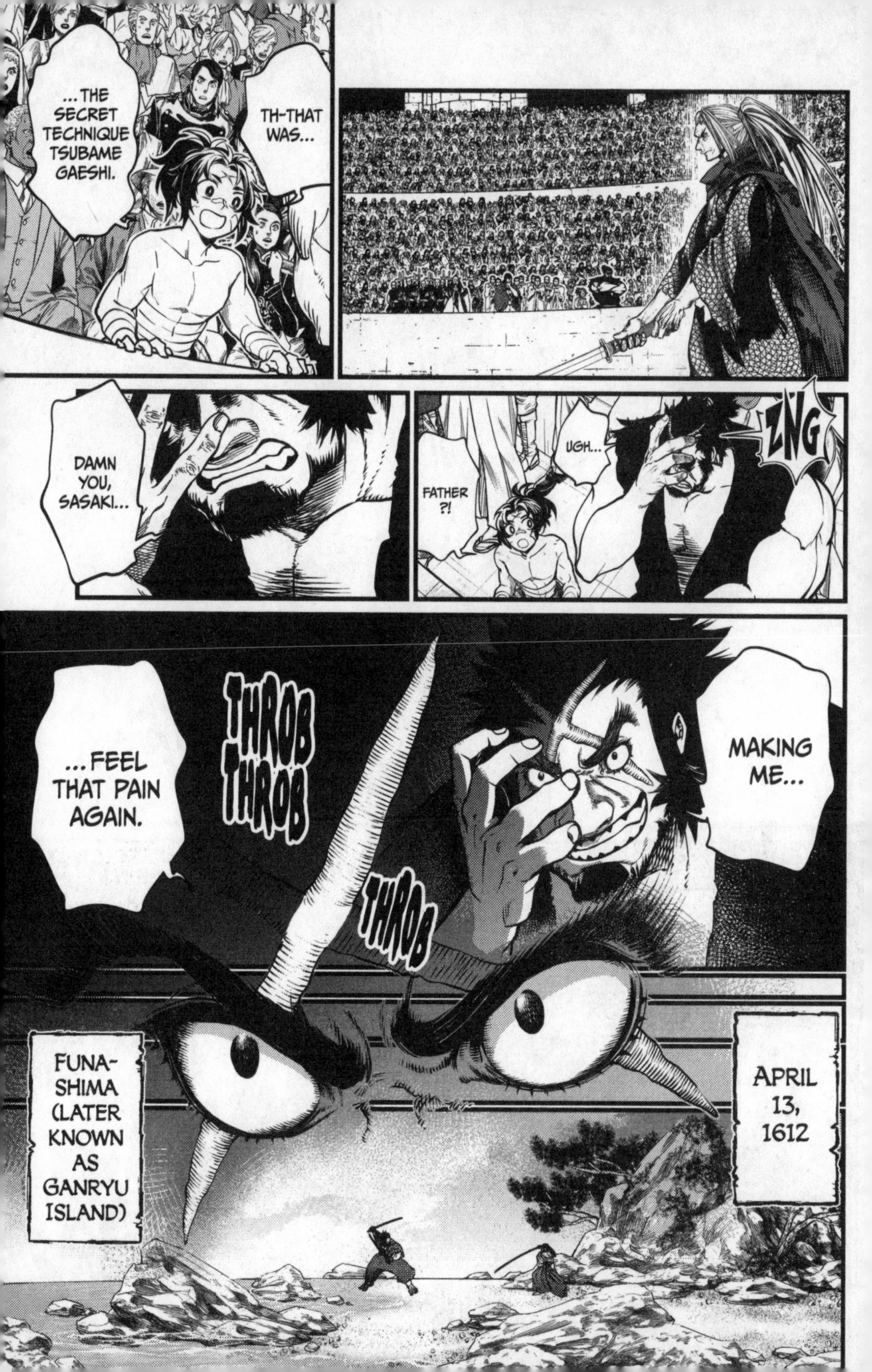
TH-THAT WAS...
...THE SECRET TECHNIQUE TSUBAME GAESHI.
ZNG
UGH...
FATHER?!
DAMN YOU, SASAKI...
MAKING ME...
THROB THROB
...FEEL THAT PAIN AGAIN.
THROB
APRIL 13, 1612
FUNA-SHIMA (LATER KNOWN AS GANRYU ISLAND)

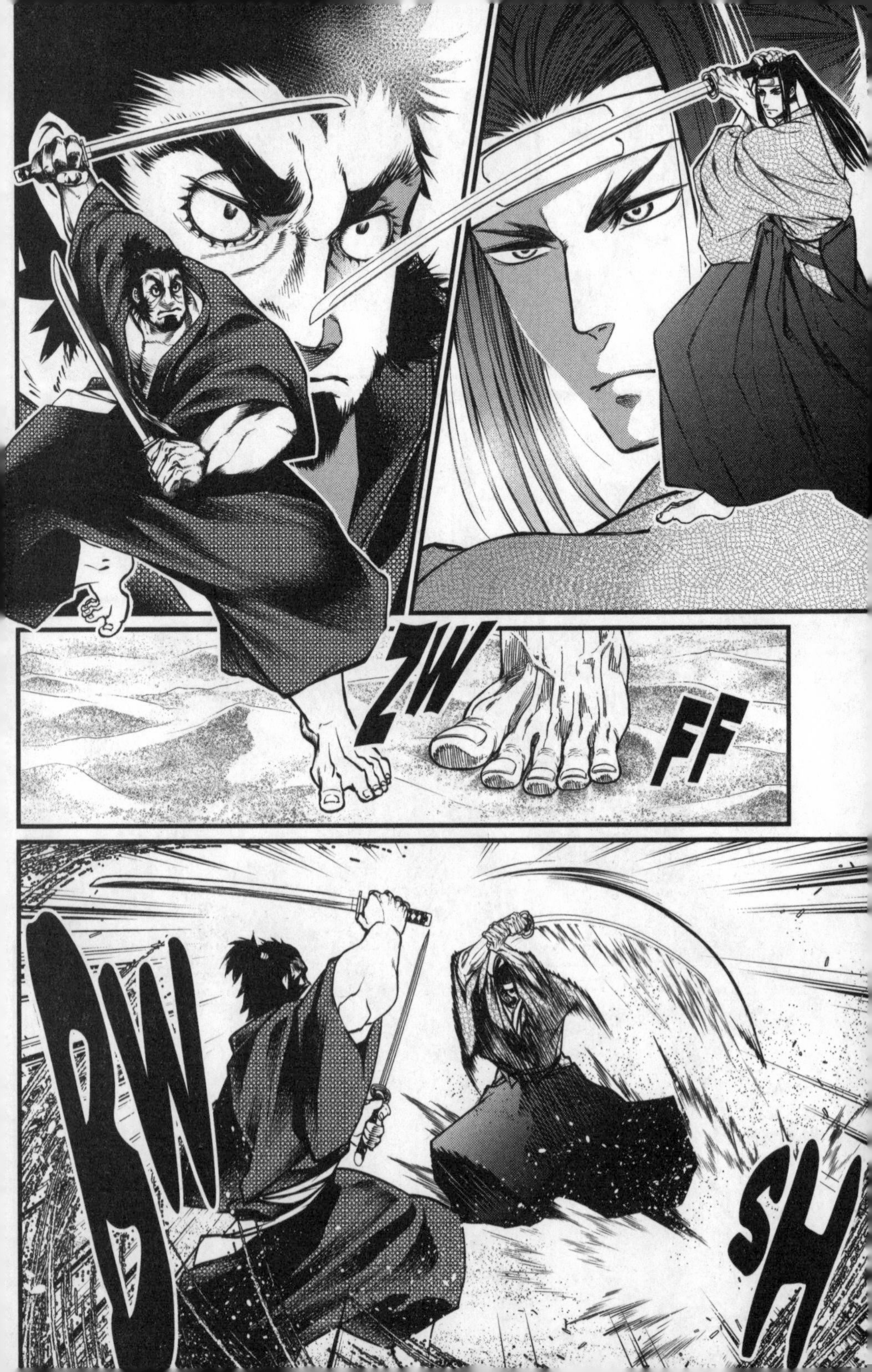
ZW
FF
SH
RW

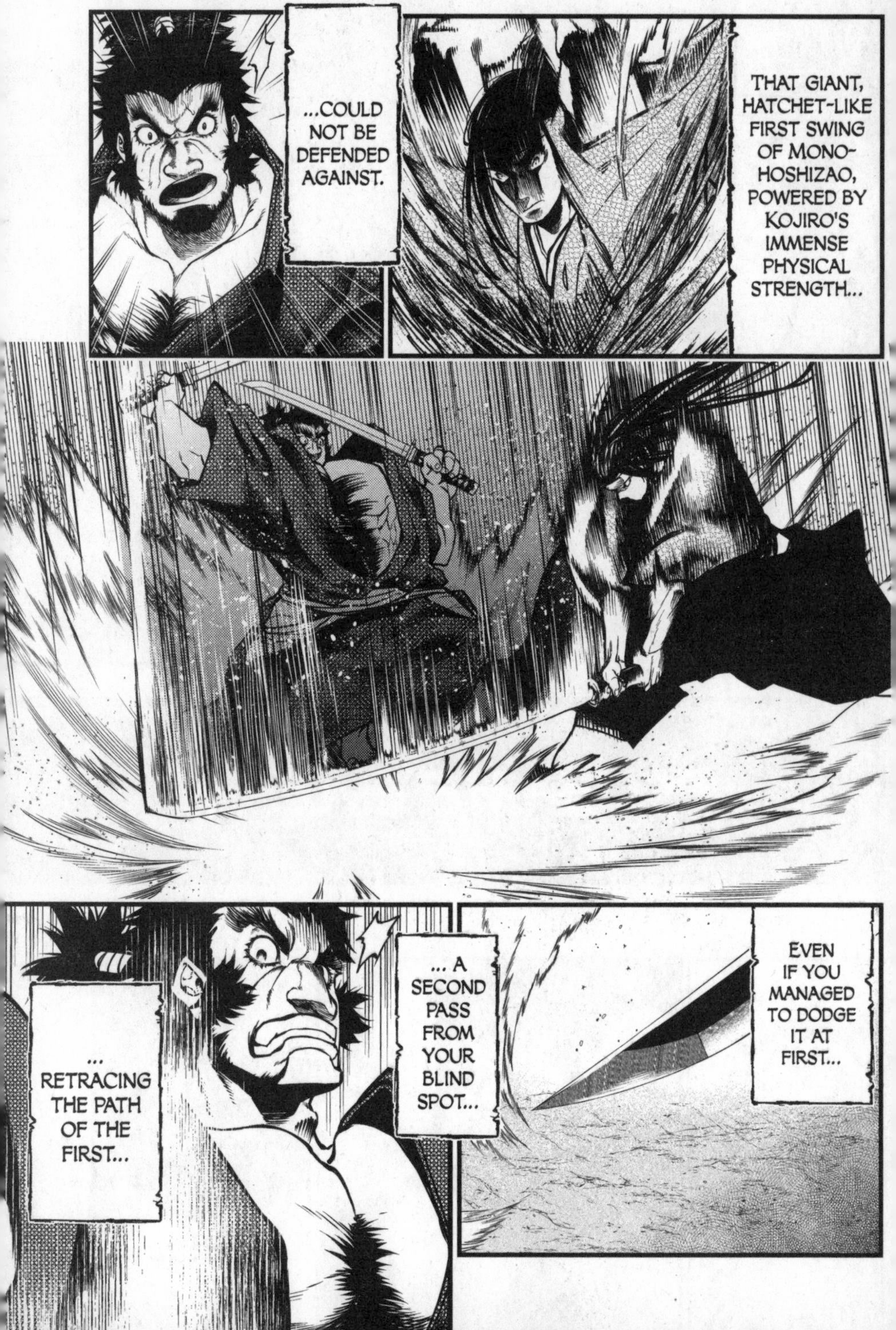
THAT GIANT, HATCHET-LIKE FIRST SWING OF MONO-HOSHIZAO, POWERED BY KOJIRO'S IMMENSE PHYSICAL STRENGTH...
...COULD NOT BE DEFENDED AGAINST.
EVEN IF YOU MANAGED TO DODGE IT AT FIRST...
... A SECOND PASS FROM YOUR BLIND SPOT...
... RETRACING THE PATH OF THE FIRST...

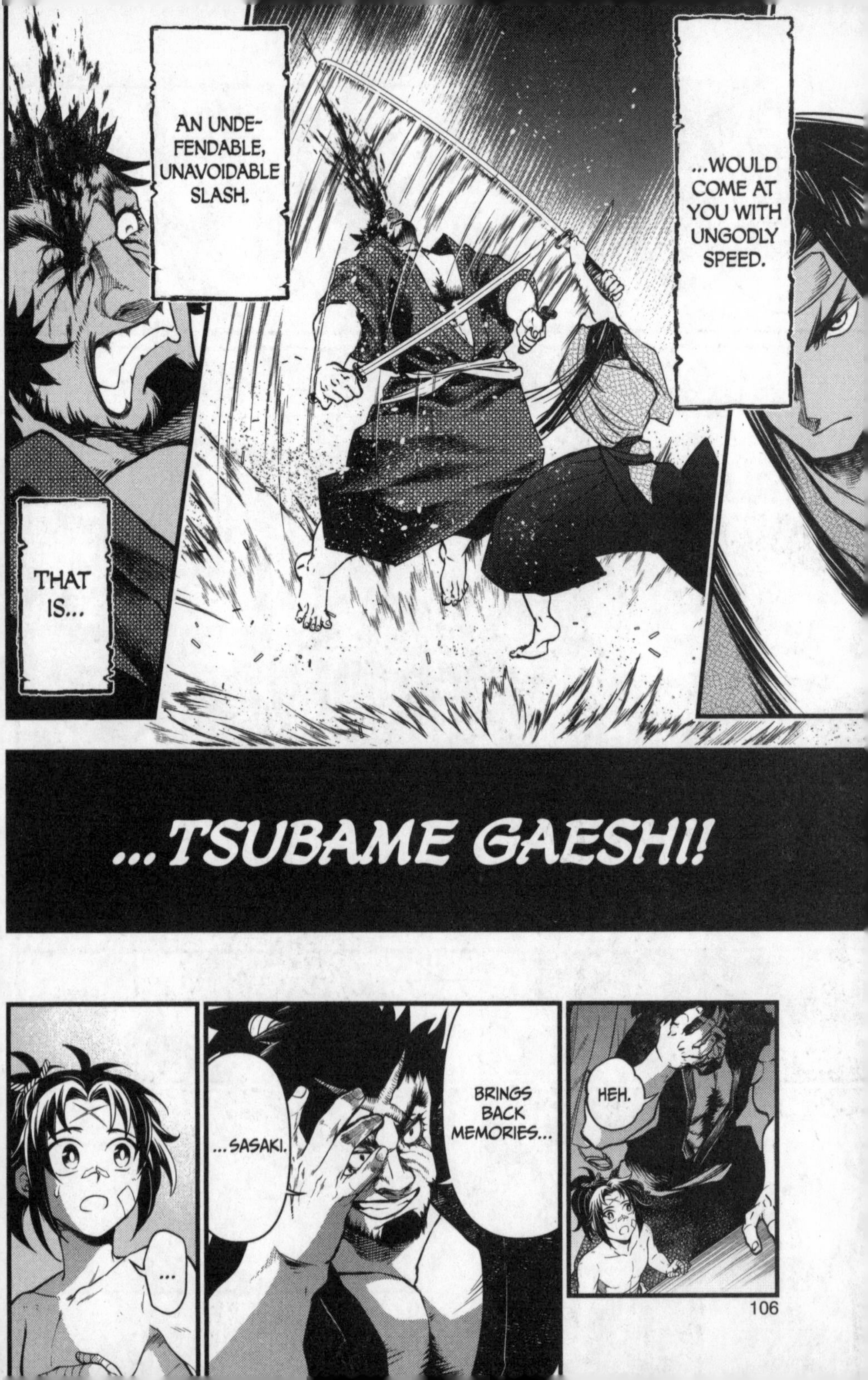
...WOULD COME AT YOU WITH UNGODLY SPEED.
AN UNDE-FENDABLE, UNAVOIDABLE SLASH.
THAT IS...
...TSUBAME GAESHI!
HEH.
BRINGS BACK MEMORIES...
...SASAKI.
...

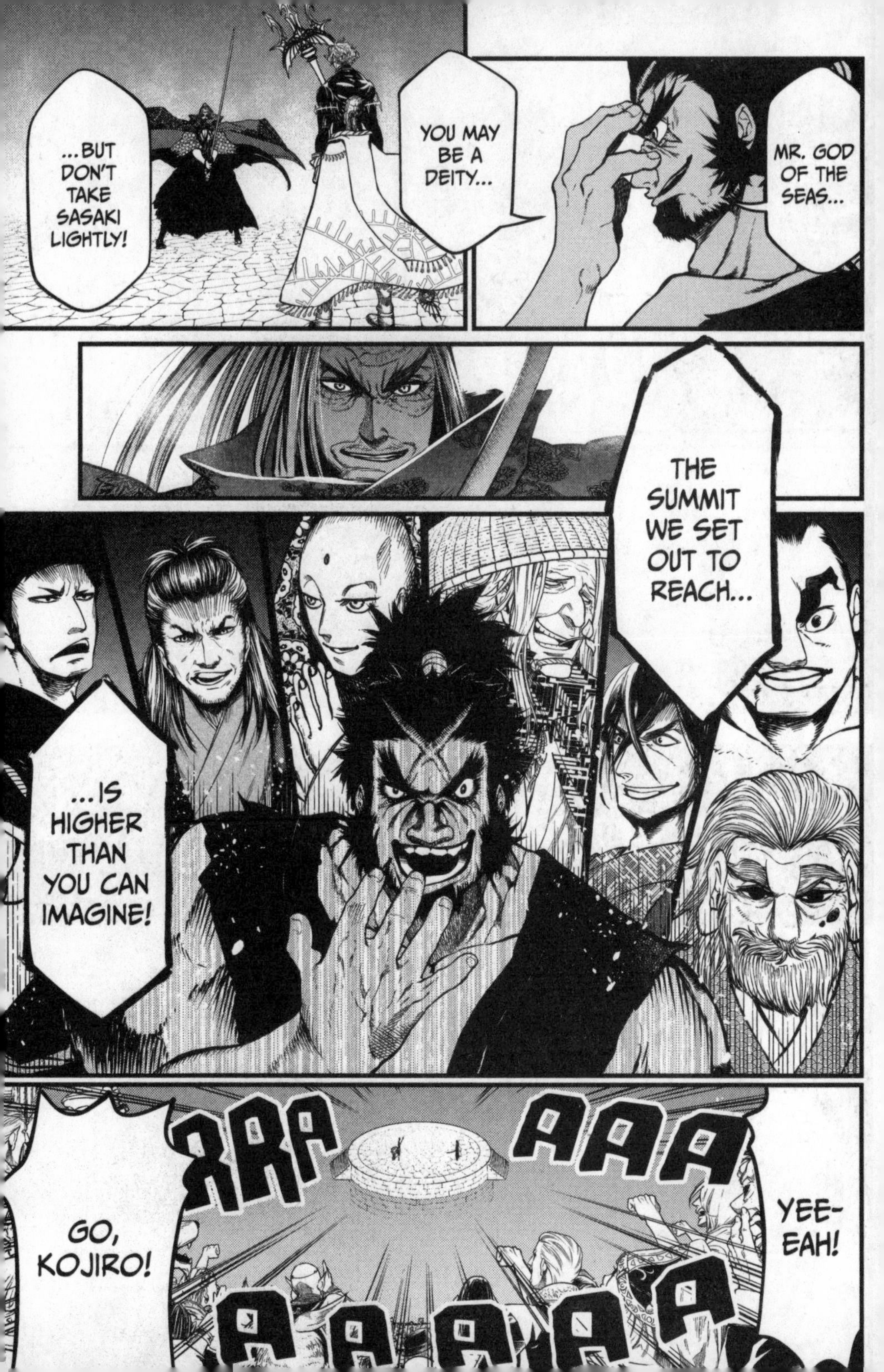
MR. GOD OF THE SEAS...
YOU MAY BE A DEITY...
...BUT DON'T TAKE SASAKI LIGHTLY!
THE SUMMIT WE SET OUT TO REACH...
...IS HIGHER THAN YOU CAN IMAGINE!
YEE-EAH!
RRA AAA
AAAAA
GO, KOJIRO!

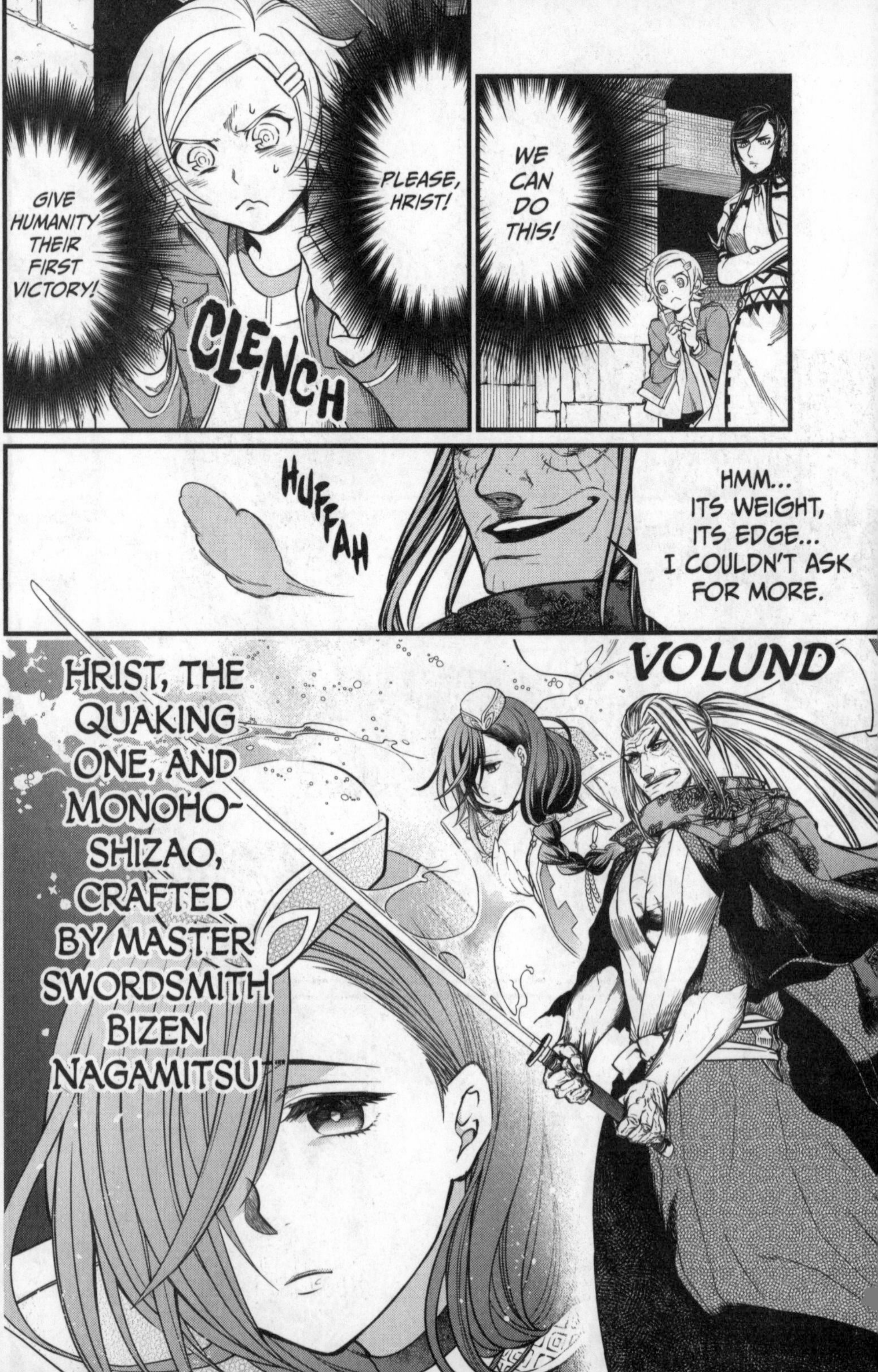
WE CAN DO THIS!
PLEASE, HRIST!
GIVE HUMANITY THEIR FIRST VICTORY!
CLENCH
HMM... ITS WEIGHT, ITS EDGE... I COULDN'T ASK FOR MORE.
HUFFAH
VOLUND
HRIST, THE QUAKING ONE, AND MONOHOSHIZAO, CRAFTED BY MASTER SWORDSMITH BIZEN NAGAMITSU

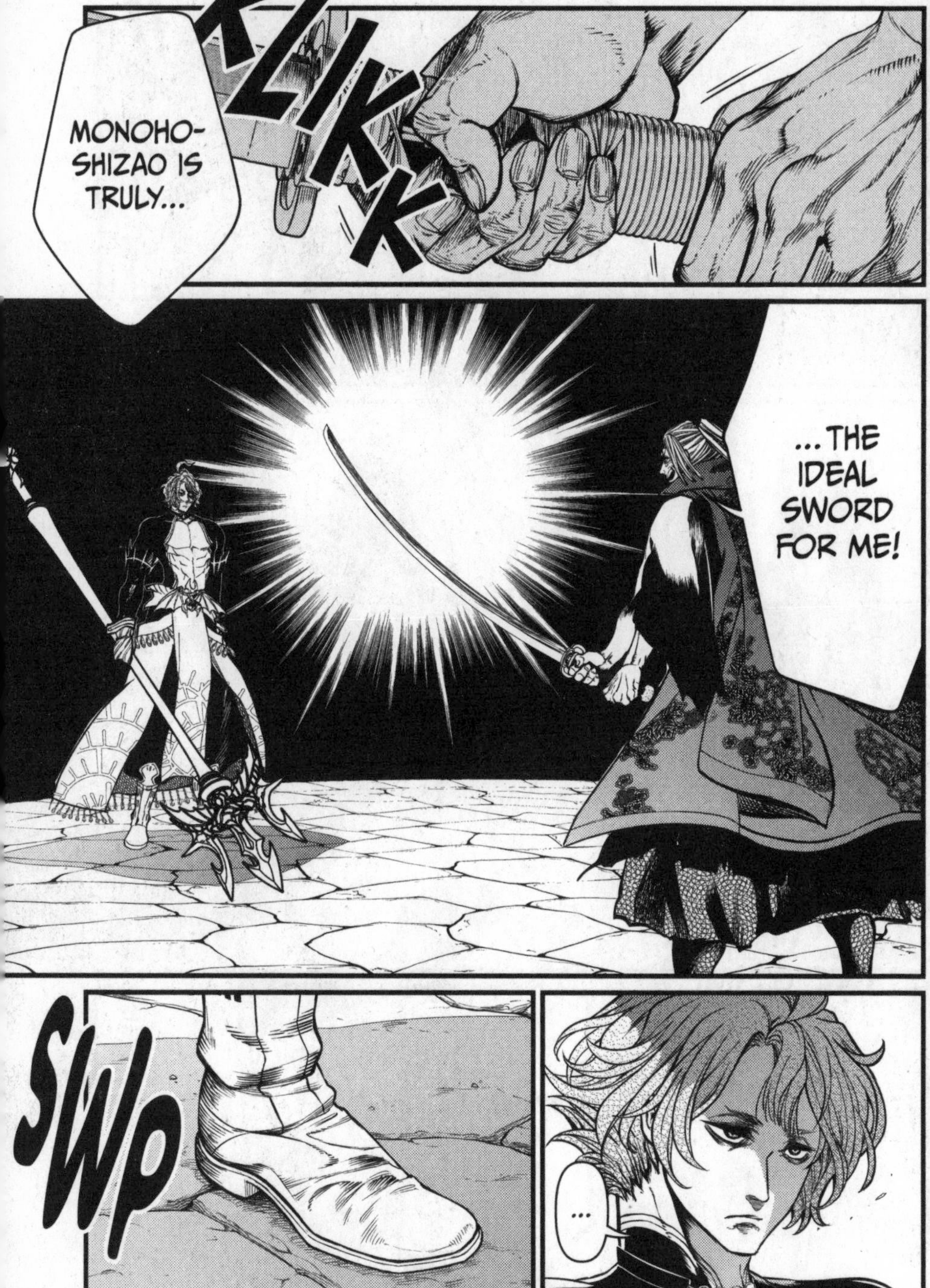
KLIKK
MONOHO-SHIZAO IS TRULY...
...THE IDEAL SWORD FOR ME!
...
SWP

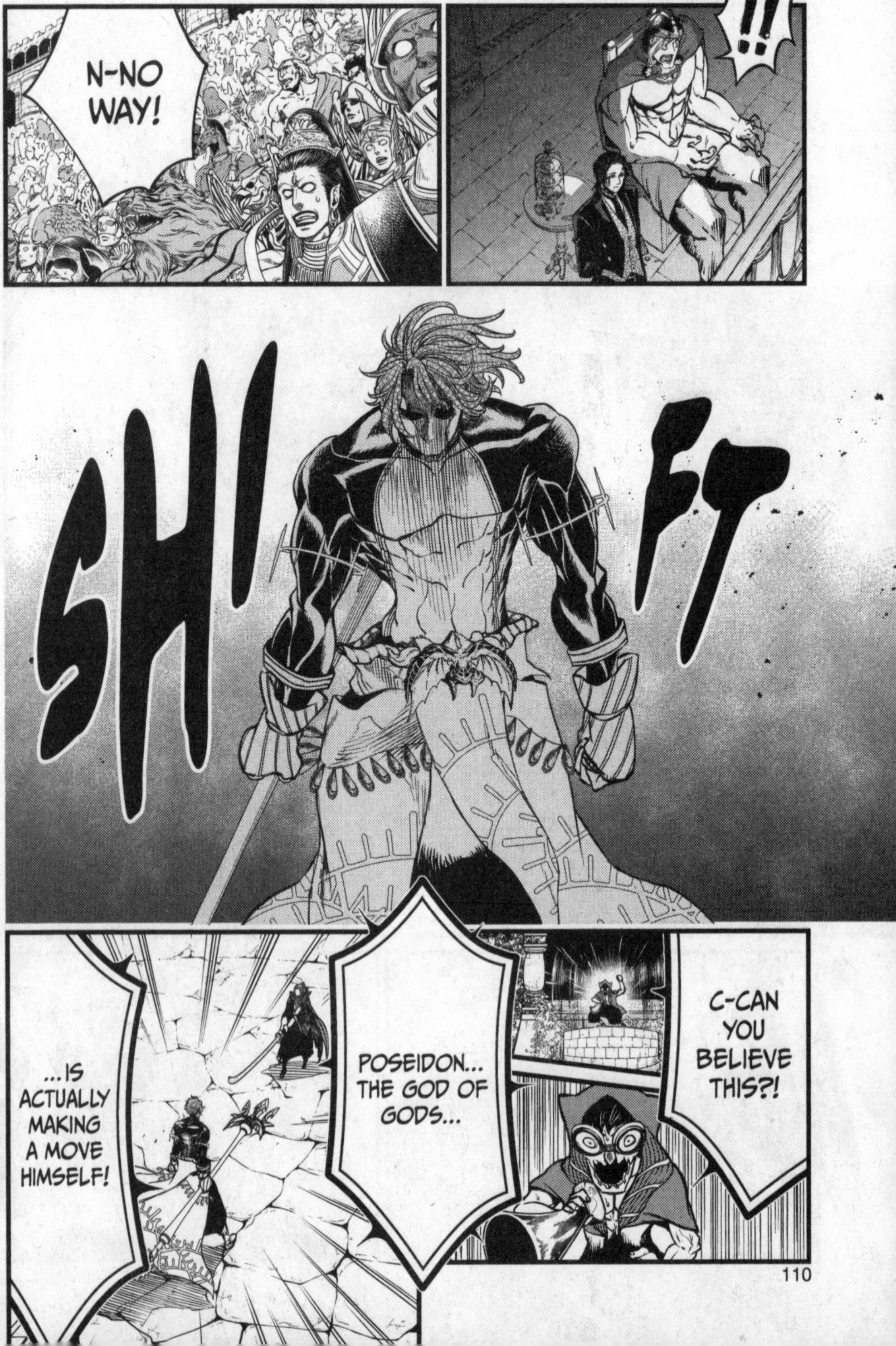
!!
N-NO WAY!
SHIFT
C-CAN YOU BELIEVE THIS?!
POSEIDON... THE GOD OF GODS...
...IS ACTUALLY MAKING A MOVE HIMSELF!

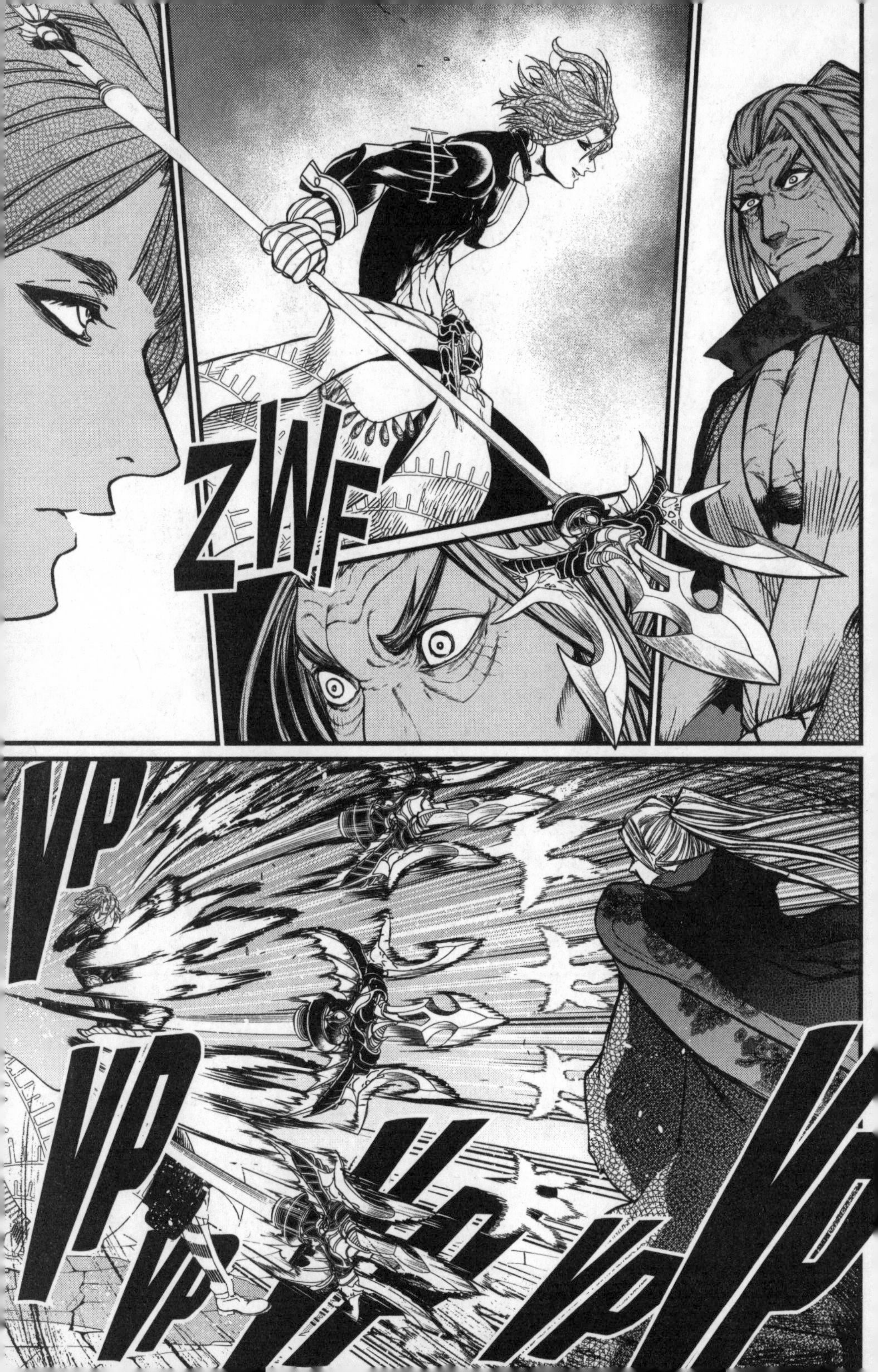
ZWF
VP
VP
VP
VP
VP

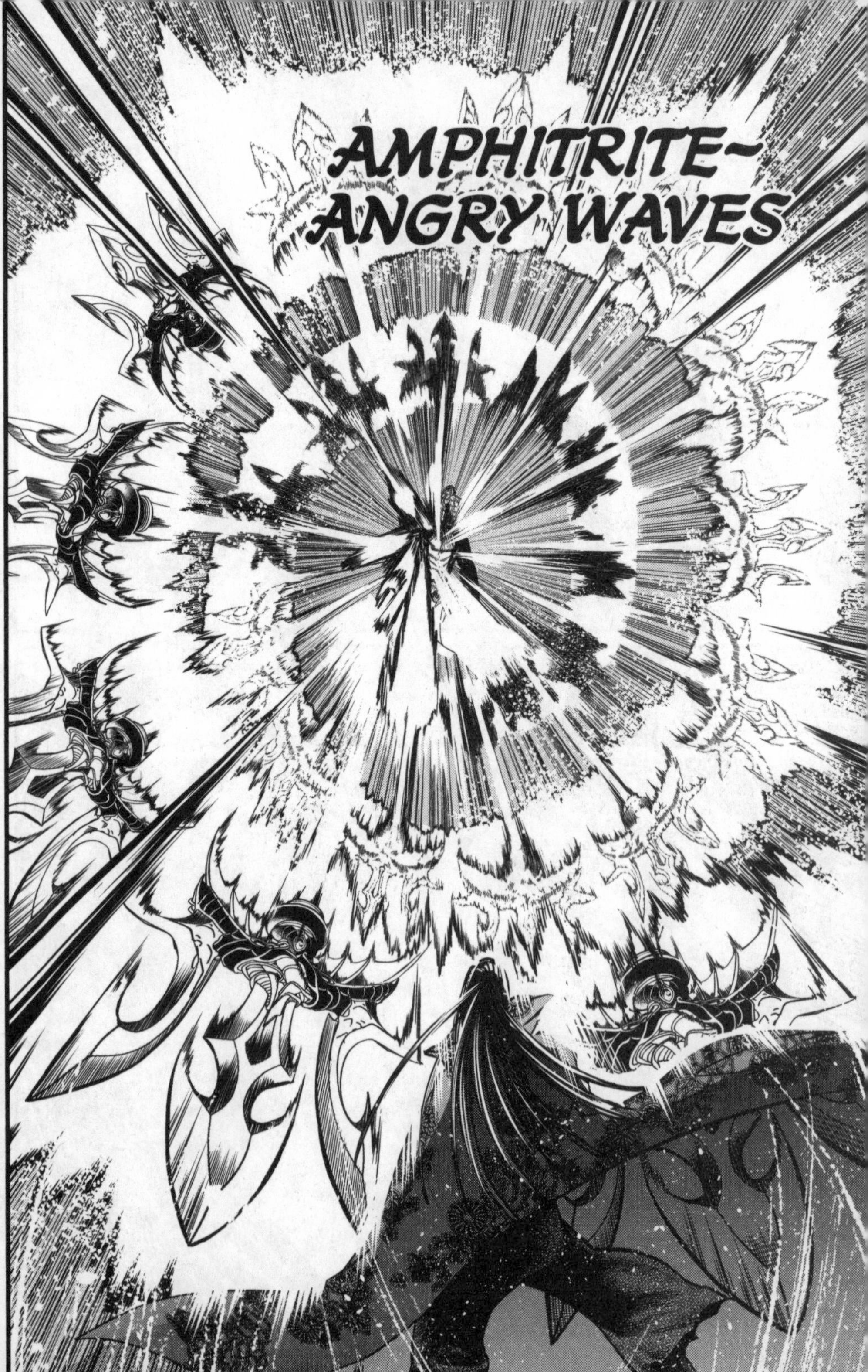
AMPHITRITE-
ANGRY WAVES

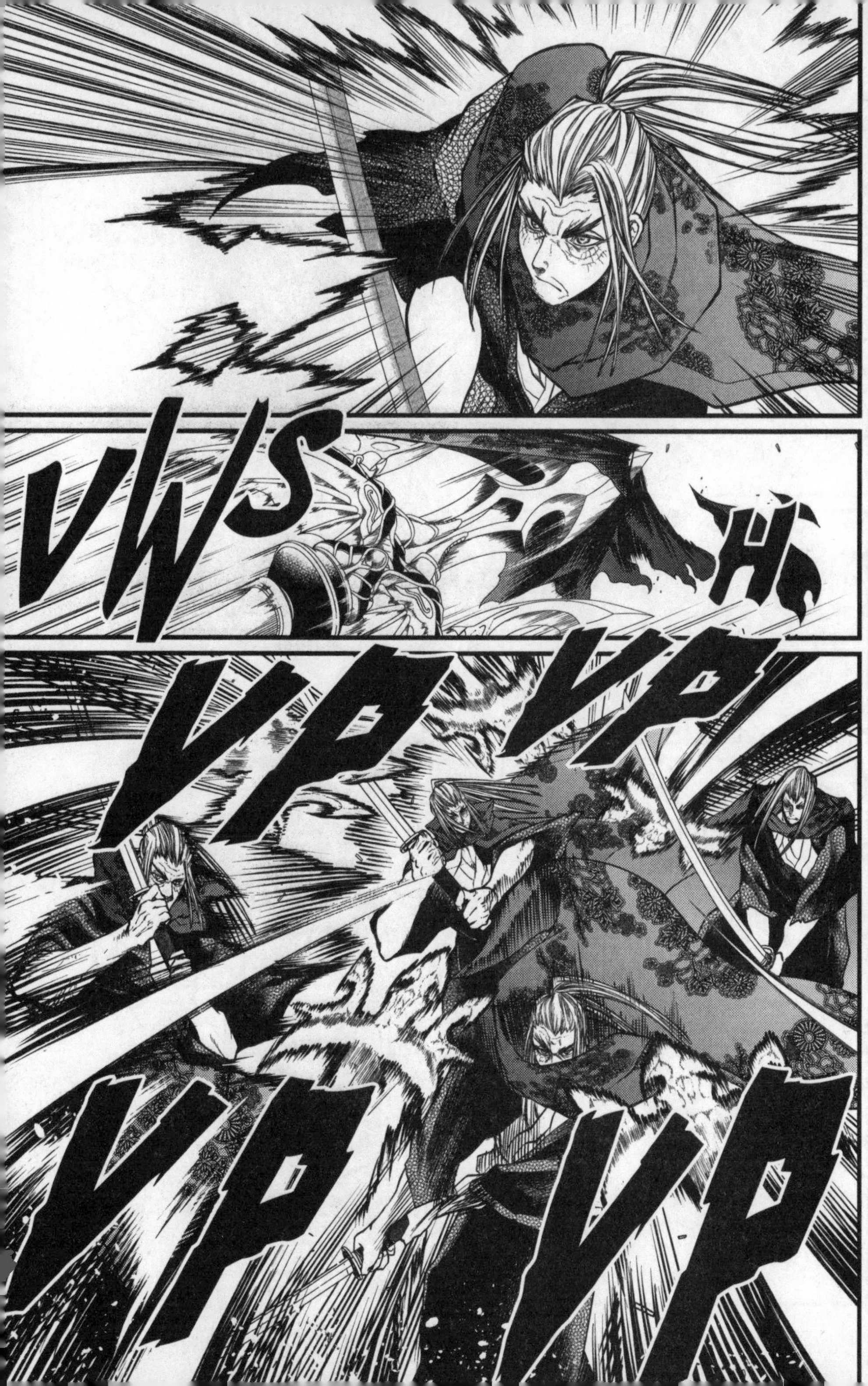
VWSH

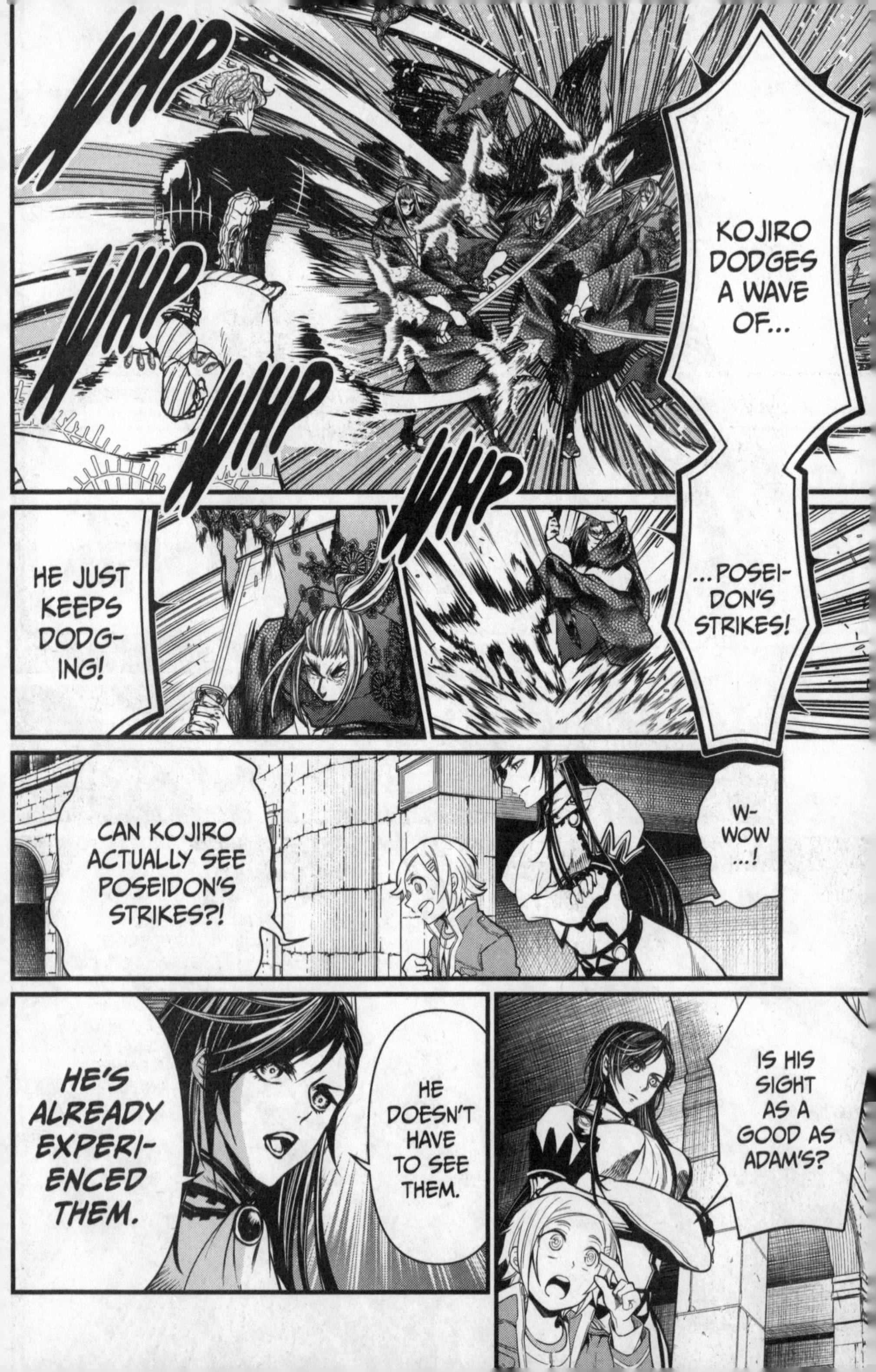
KOJIRO DODGES A WAVE OF...
WHIP
WHIP
WHIP
WHIP
...POSEI-DON'S STRIKES!
HE JUST KEEPS DODG-ING!
W-WOW ...!
CAN KOJIRO ACTUALLY SEE POSEIDON'S STRIKES?!
IS HIS SIGHT AS A GOOD AS ADAM'S?
HE DOESN'T HAVE TO SEE THEM.
HE'S ALREADY EXPERI-ENCED THEM.

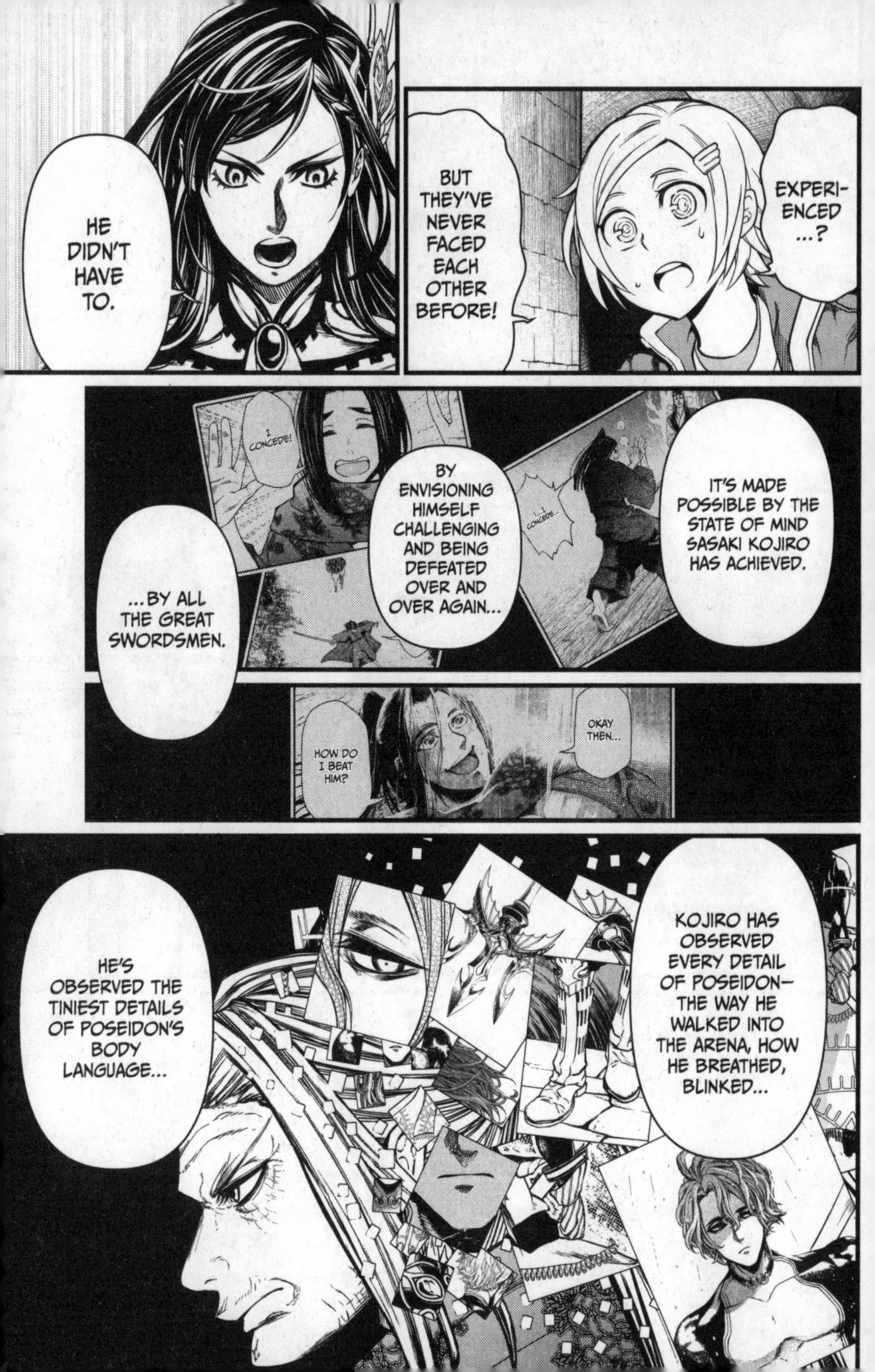
EXPERI-ENCED ...?
BUT THEY'VE NEVER FACED EACH OTHER BEFORE!
HE DIDN'T HAVE TO.
IT'S MADE POSSIBLE BY THE STATE OF MIND SASAKI KOJIRO HAS ACHIEVED.
I... I CONCEDE...
BY ENVISIONING HIMSELF CHALLENGING AND BEING DEFEATED OVER AND OVER AGAIN...
I CONCEDE!
...BY ALL THE GREAT SWORDSMEN.
OKAY THEN...
HOW DO I BEAT HIM?
KOJIRO HAS OBSERVED EVERY DETAIL OF POSEIDON—THE WAY HE WALKED INTO THE ARENA, HOW HE BREATHED, BLINKED...
HE'S OBSERVED THE TINIEST DETAILS OF POSEIDON'S BODY LANGUAGE...

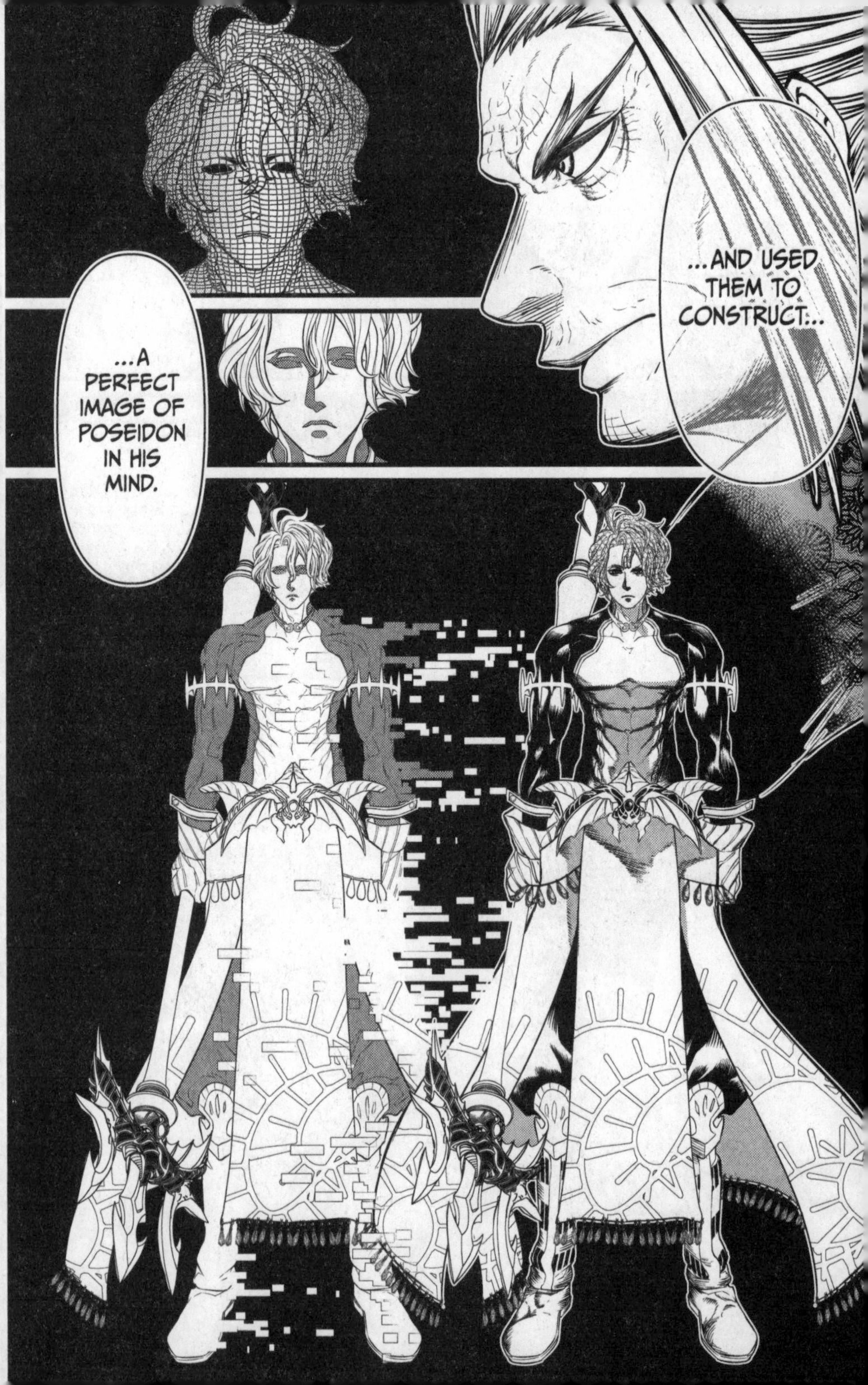
...AND USED THEM TO CONSTRUCT...
...A PERFECT IMAGE OF POSEIDON IN HIS MIND.

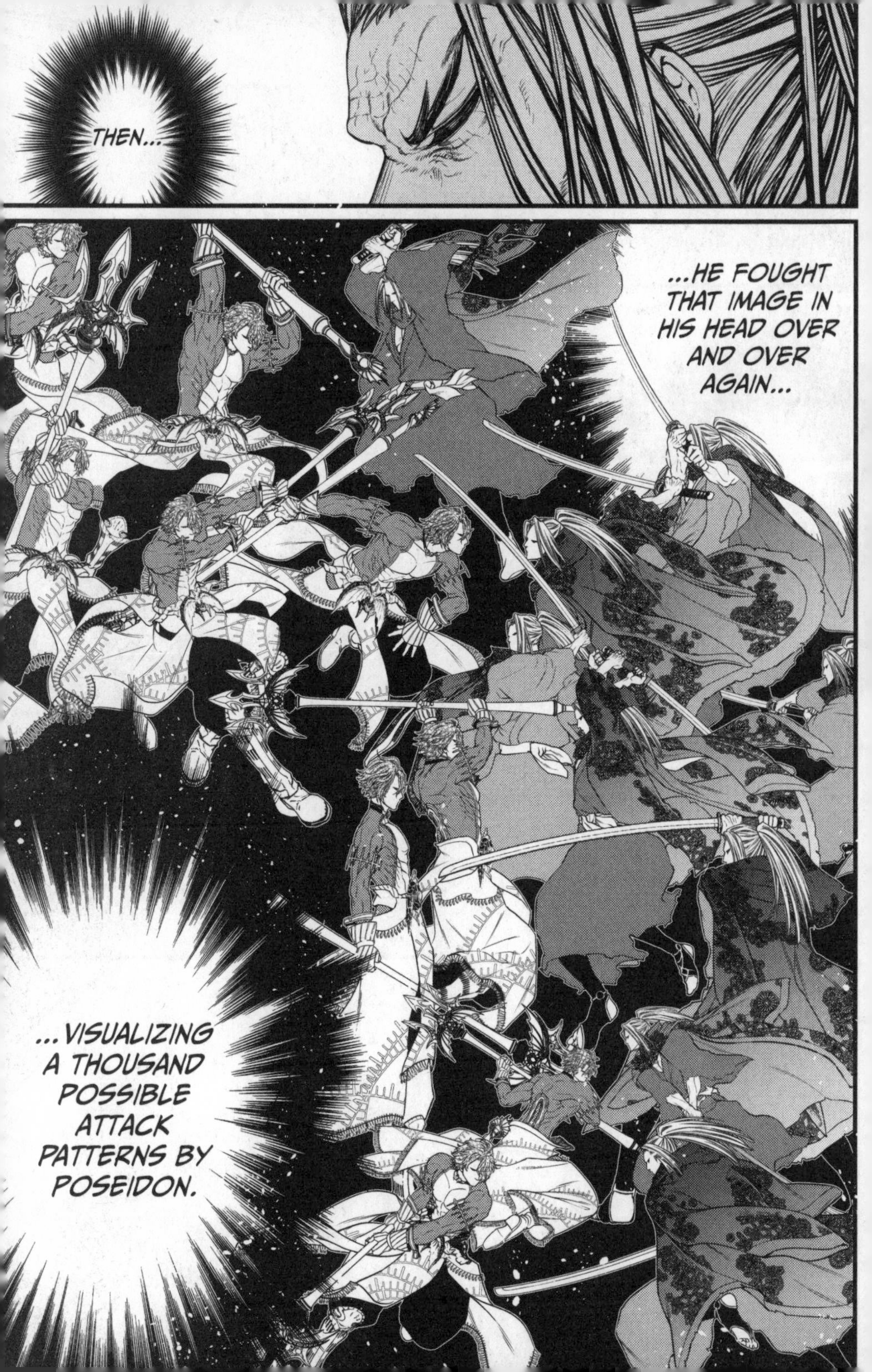
THEN...
...HE FOUGHT THAT IMAGE IN HIS HEAD OVER AND OVER AGAIN...
...VISUALIZING A THOUSAND POSSIBLE ATTACK PATTERNS BY POSEIDON.

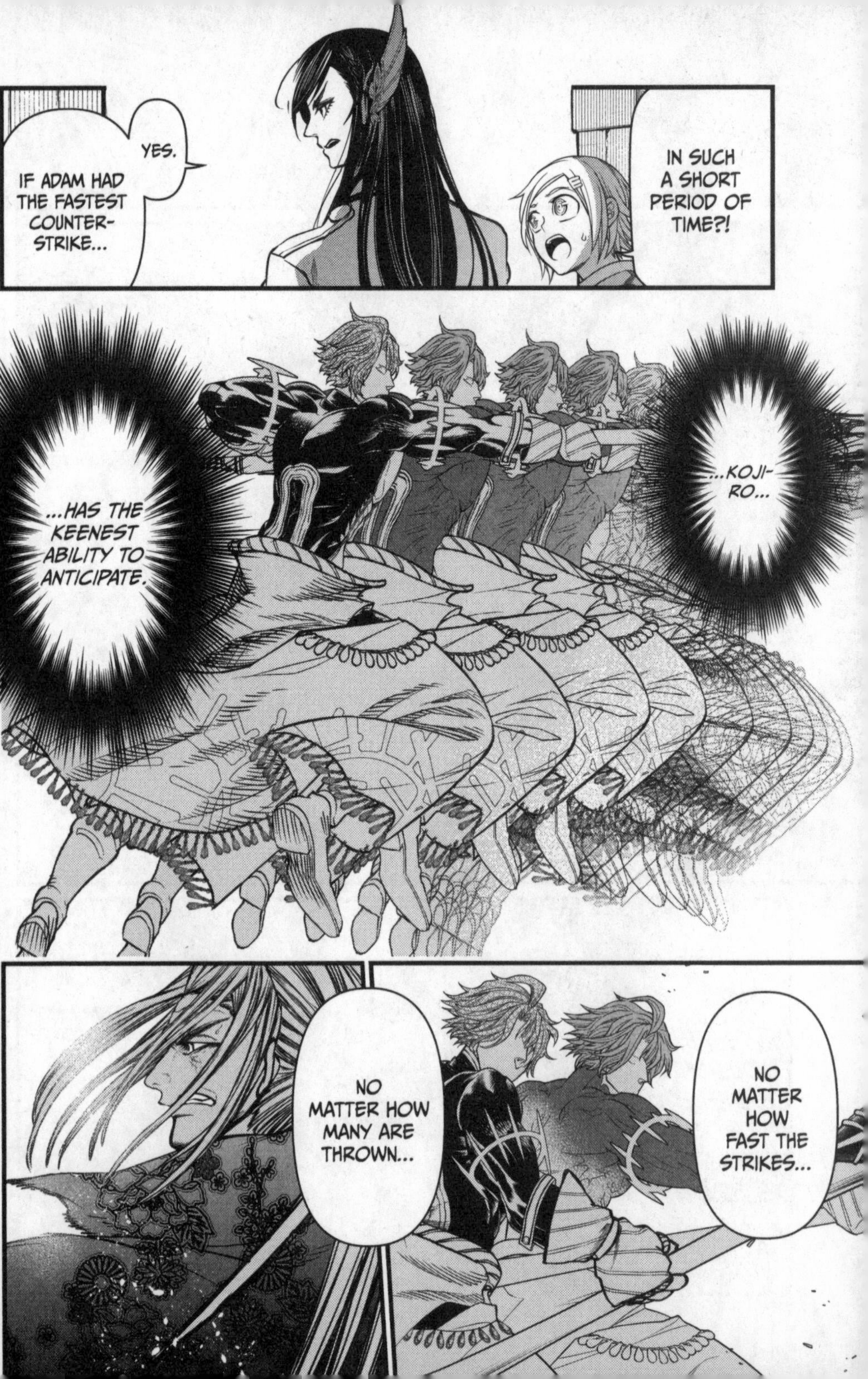
IN SUCH A SHORT PERIOD OF TIME?!
YES.
IF ADAM HAD THE FASTEST COUNTER-STRIKE...
...KOJI-RO...
...HAS THE KEENEST ABILITY TO ANTICIPATE.
NO MATTER HOW FAST THE STRIKES...
NO MATTER HOW MANY ARE THROWN...

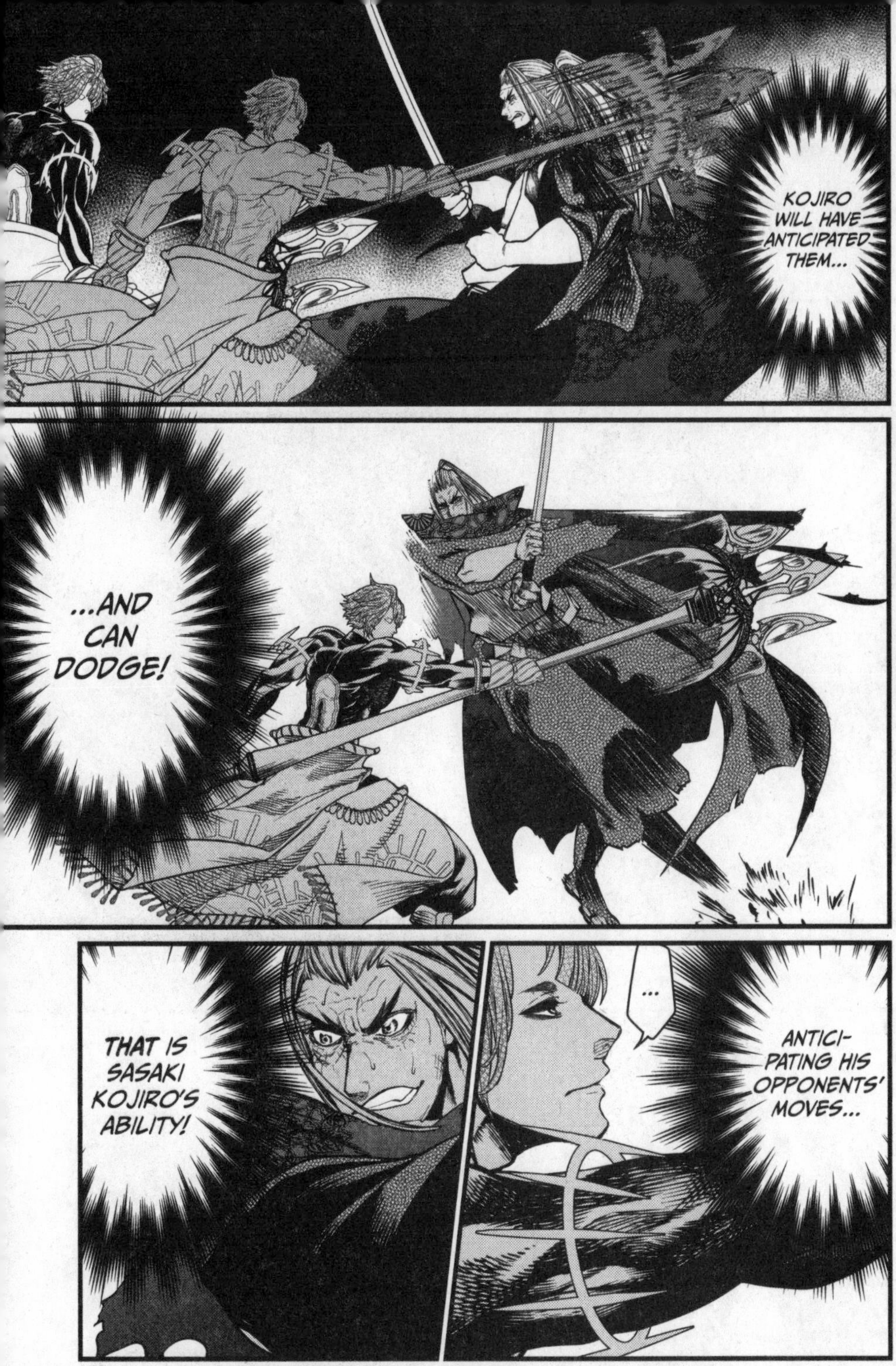
KOJIRO WILL HAVE ANTICIPATED THEM...
...AND CAN DODGE!
...
ANTICI-PATING HIS OPPONENTS' MOVES...
THAT IS SASAKI KOJIRO'S ABILITY!

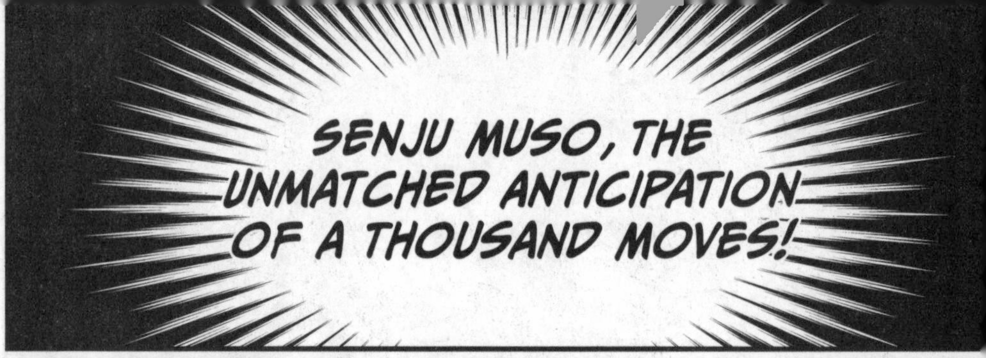
SENJU MUSO, THE UNMATCHED ANTICIPATION OF A THOUSAND MOVES!

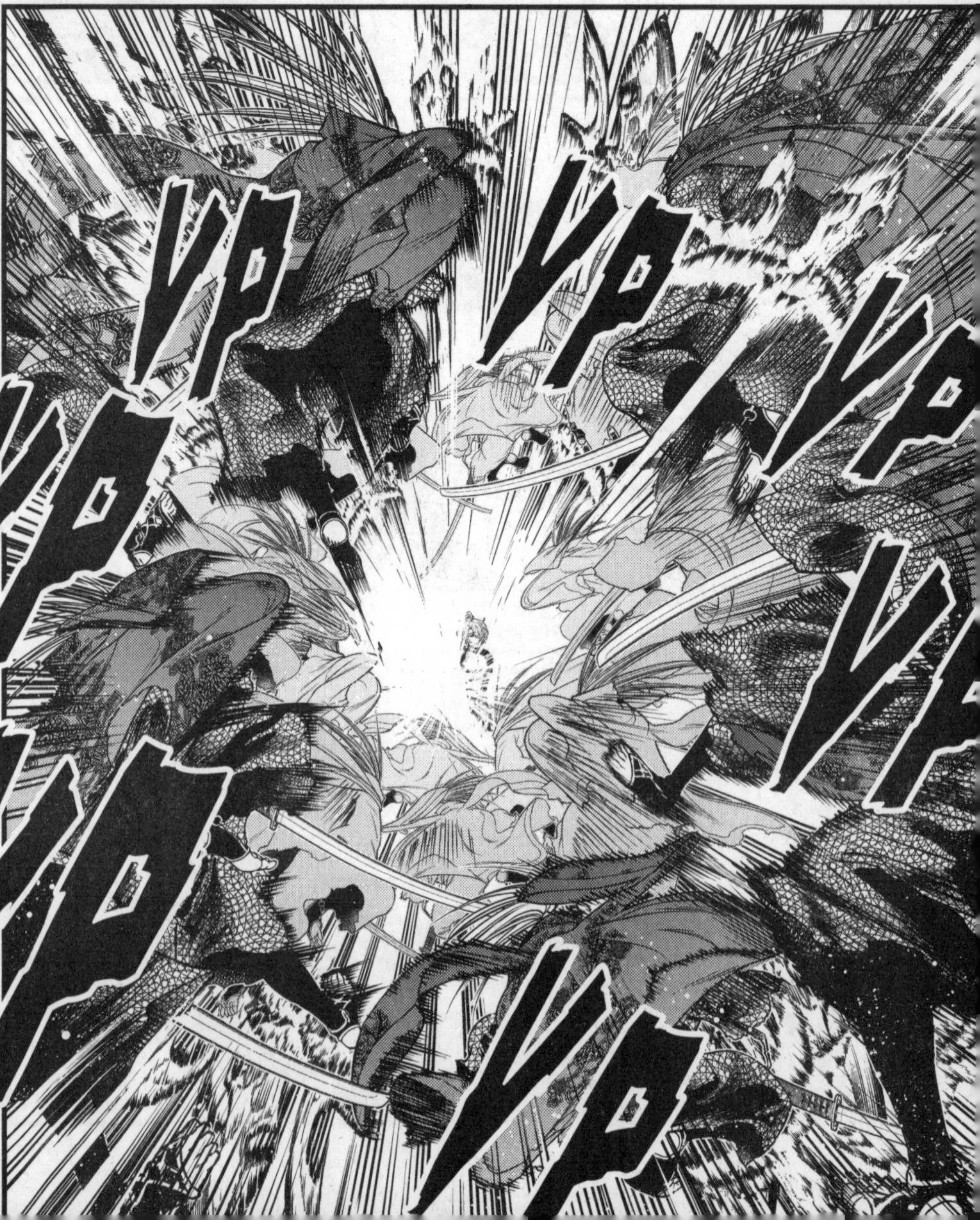
VP
VP
VP
VP
VP
VP
VP

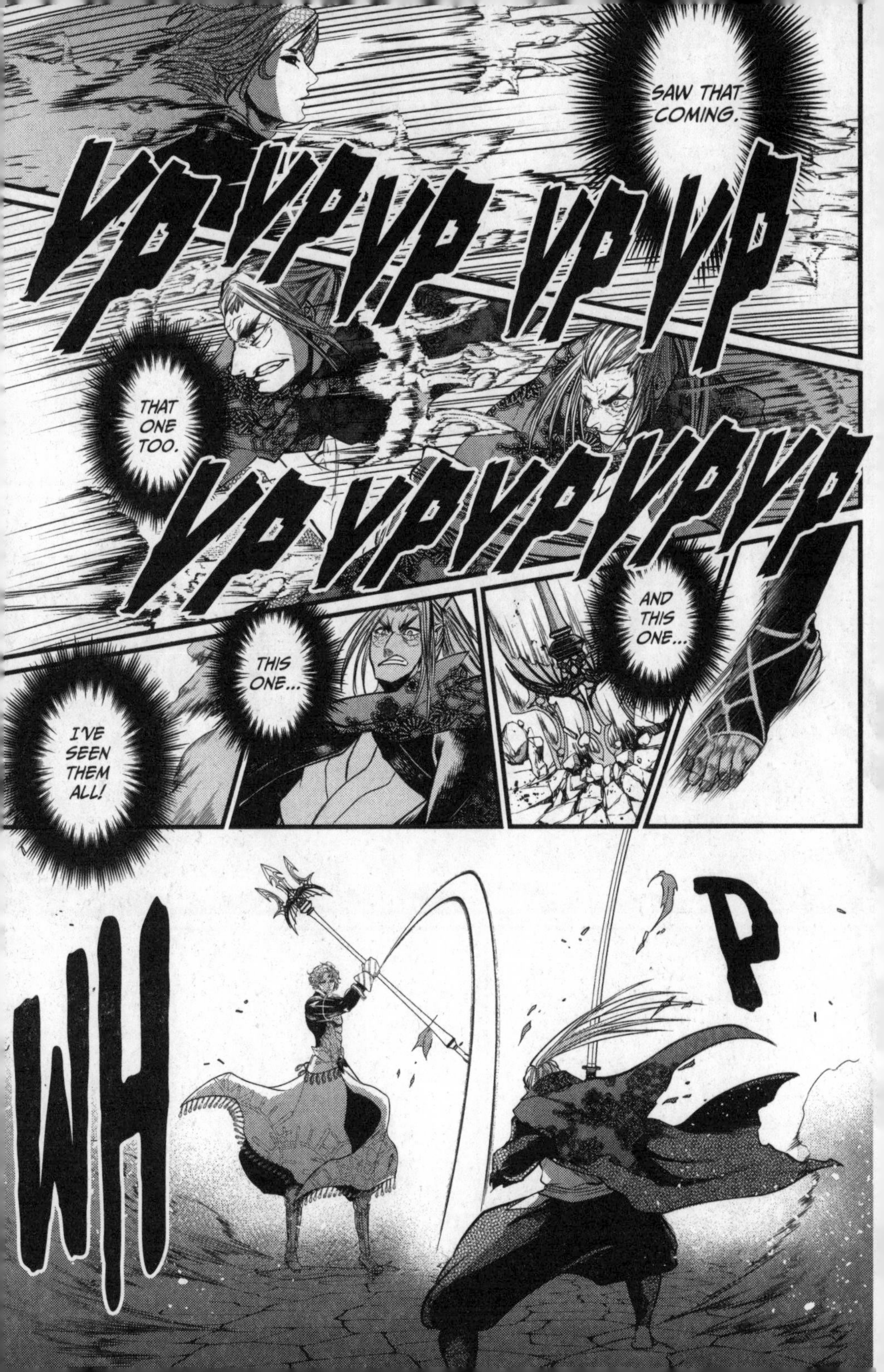
SAW THAT COMING.
THAT ONE TOO.
AND THIS ONE...
THIS ONE...
I'VE SEEN THEM ALL!
P
WH

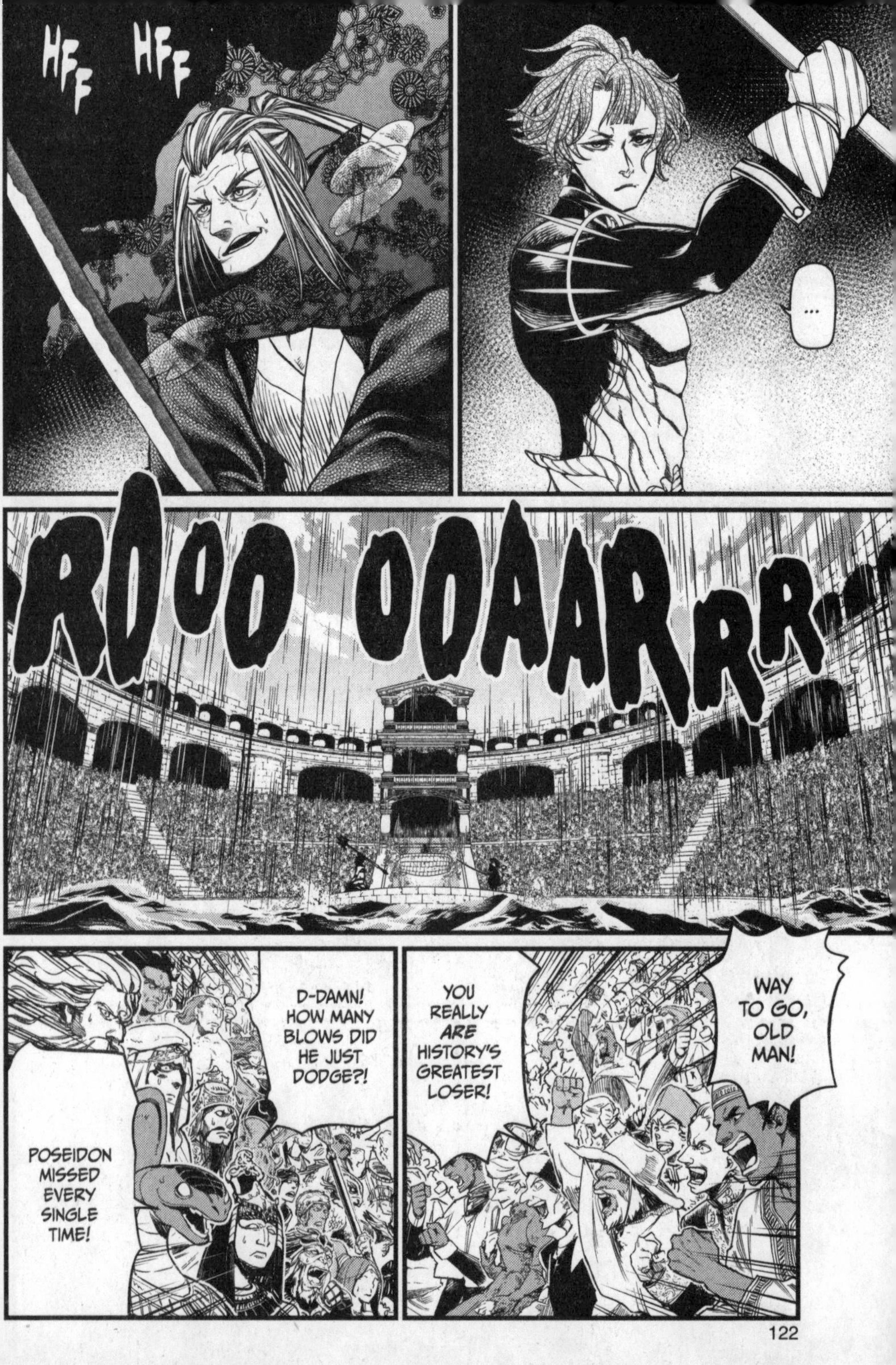
...
HFF HFF
ROOO ODAARRR...
WAY TO GO, OLD MAN!
YOU REALLY ARE HISTORY'S GREATEST LOSER!
D-DAMN! HOW MANY BLOWS DID HE JUST DODGE?!
POSEIDON MISSED EVERY SINGLE TIME!

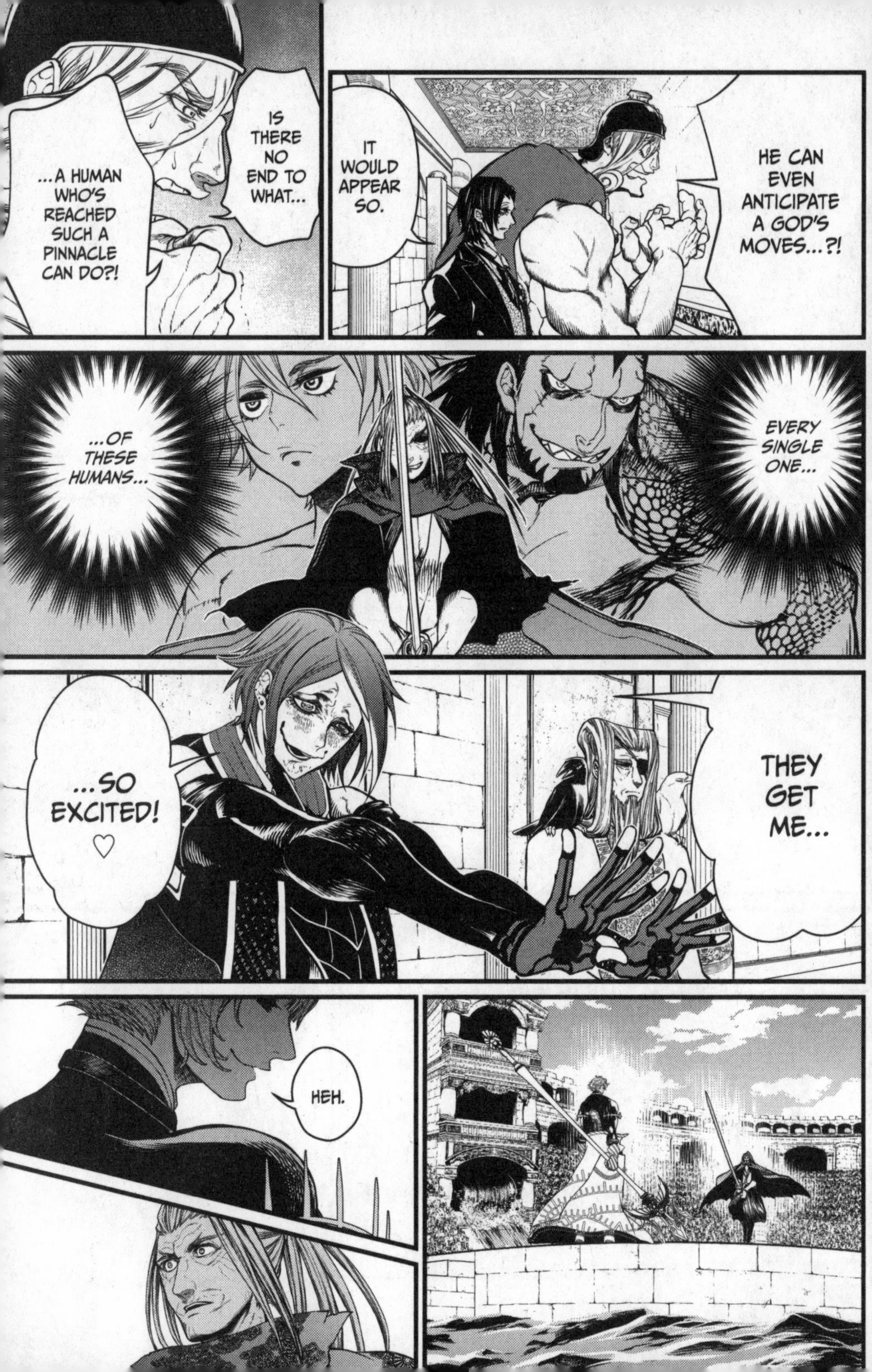
HE CAN EVEN ANTICIPATE A GOD'S MOVES...?!
IT WOULD APPEAR SO.
IS THERE NO END TO WHAT...
...A HUMAN WHO'S REACHED SUCH A PINNACLE CAN DO?!
EVERY SINGLE ONE...
...OF THESE HUMANS...
THEY GET ME...
...SO EXCITED! ♡
HEH.

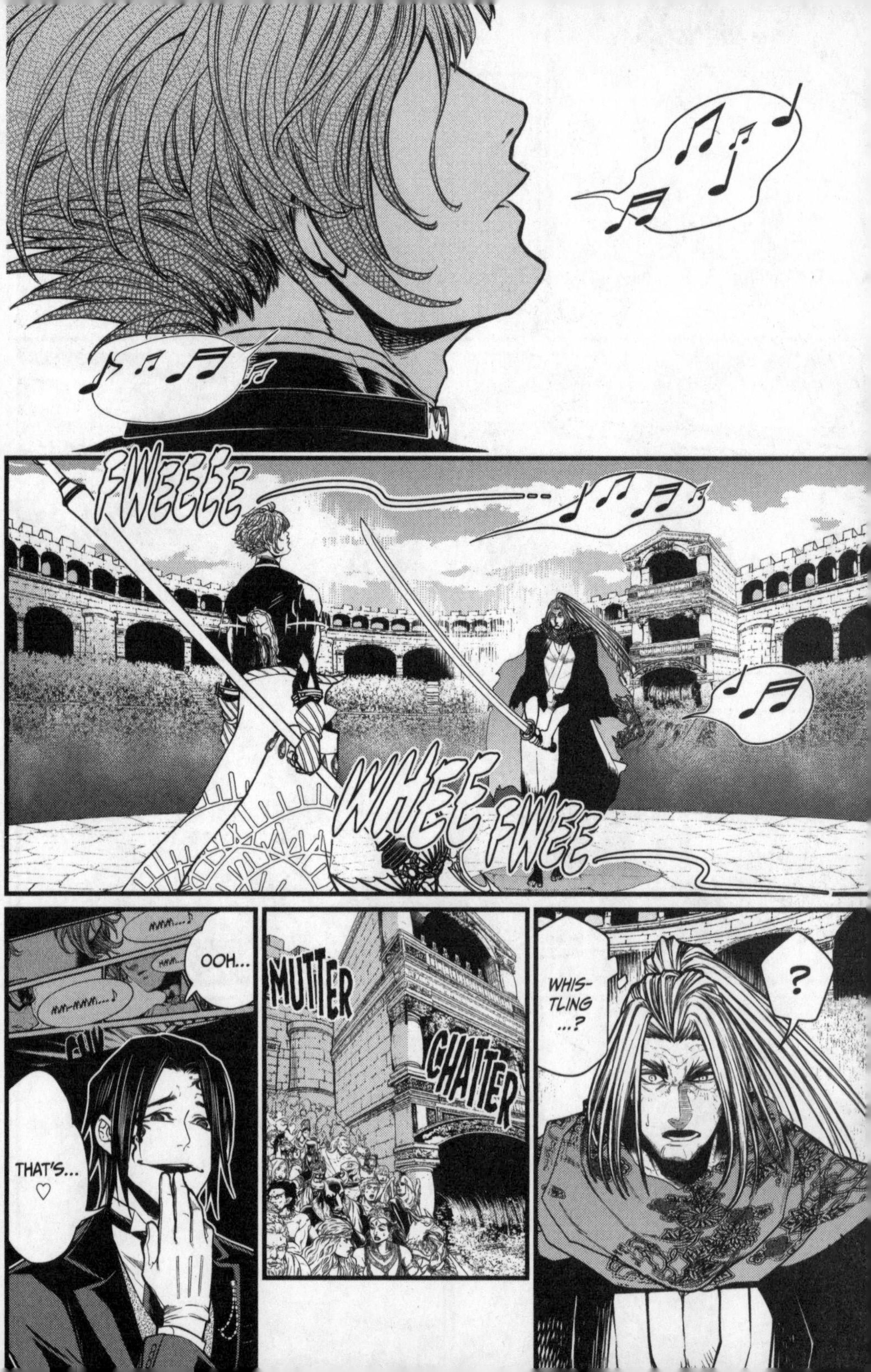
FWEEEE
WHEE FWEE
?
WHIS-TLING ...?
MUTTER
CHATTER
MMM...♪
OOH...
MM-MMM...♪
THAT'S... ♡

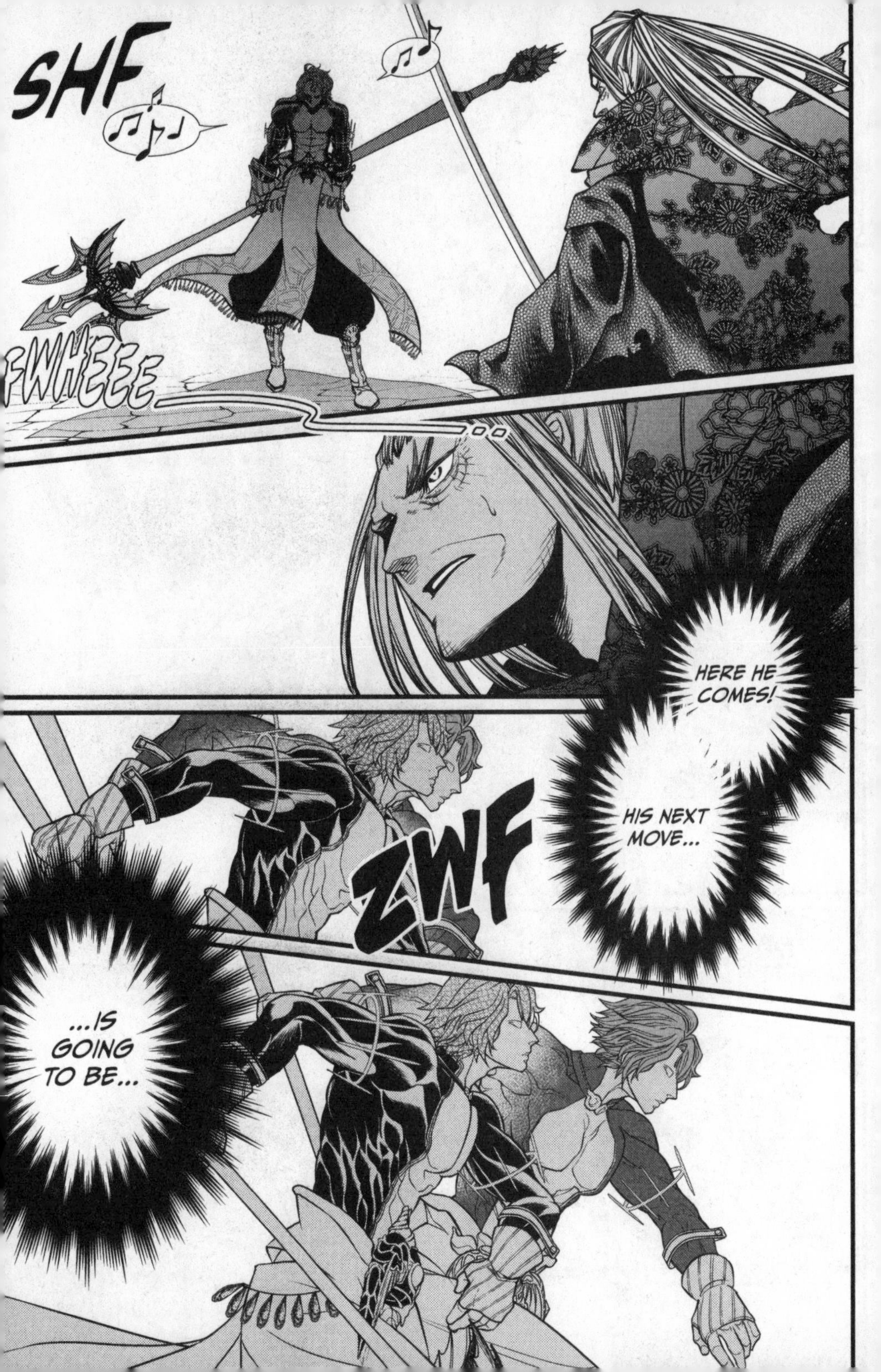
SHF
FWHEEE
...
HERE HE COMES!
HIS NEXT MOVE...
ZWF
...IS GOING TO BE...

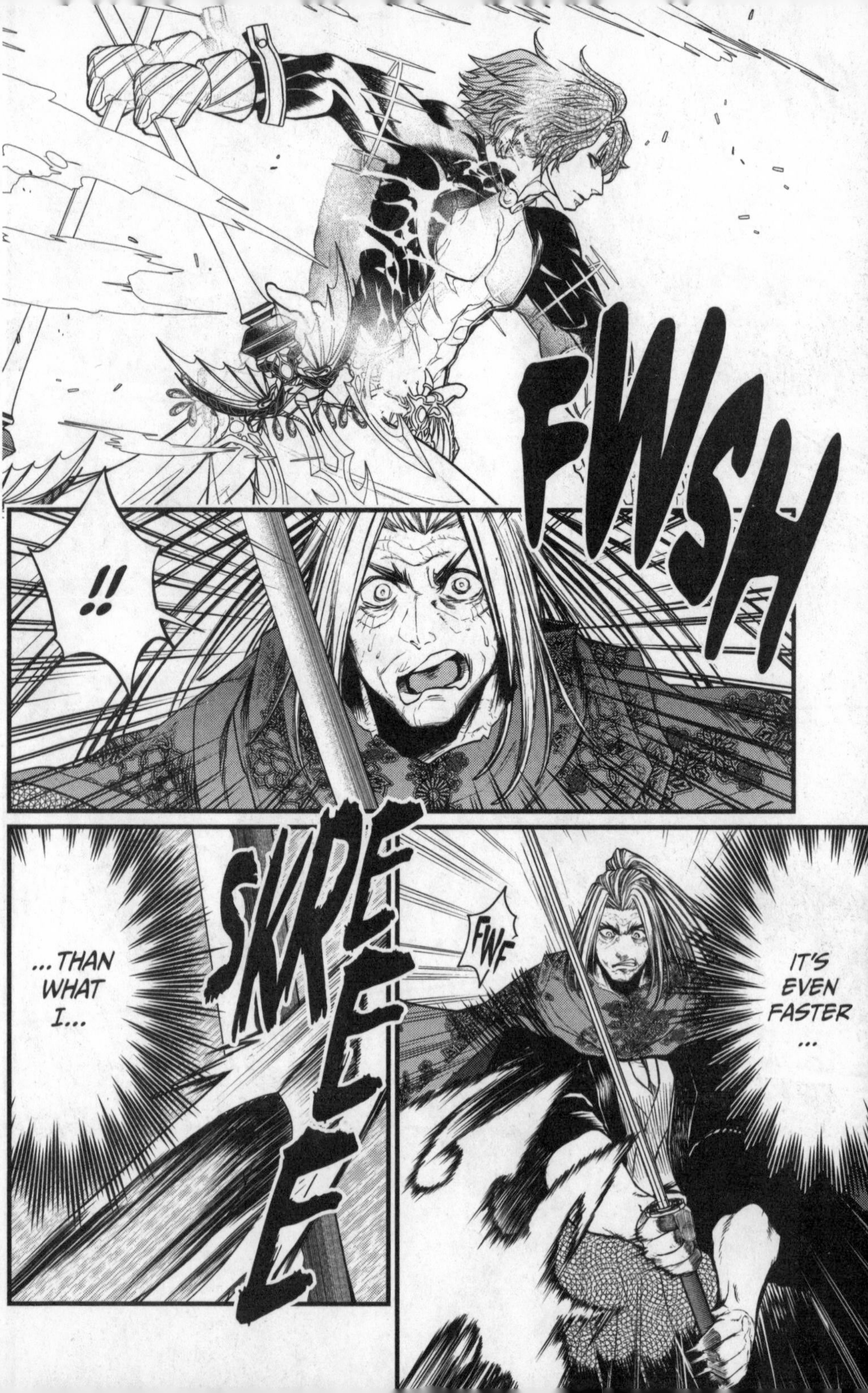
FWSH
!!
FWF
IT'S EVEN FASTER ...
...THAN WHAT I...
SKREEE

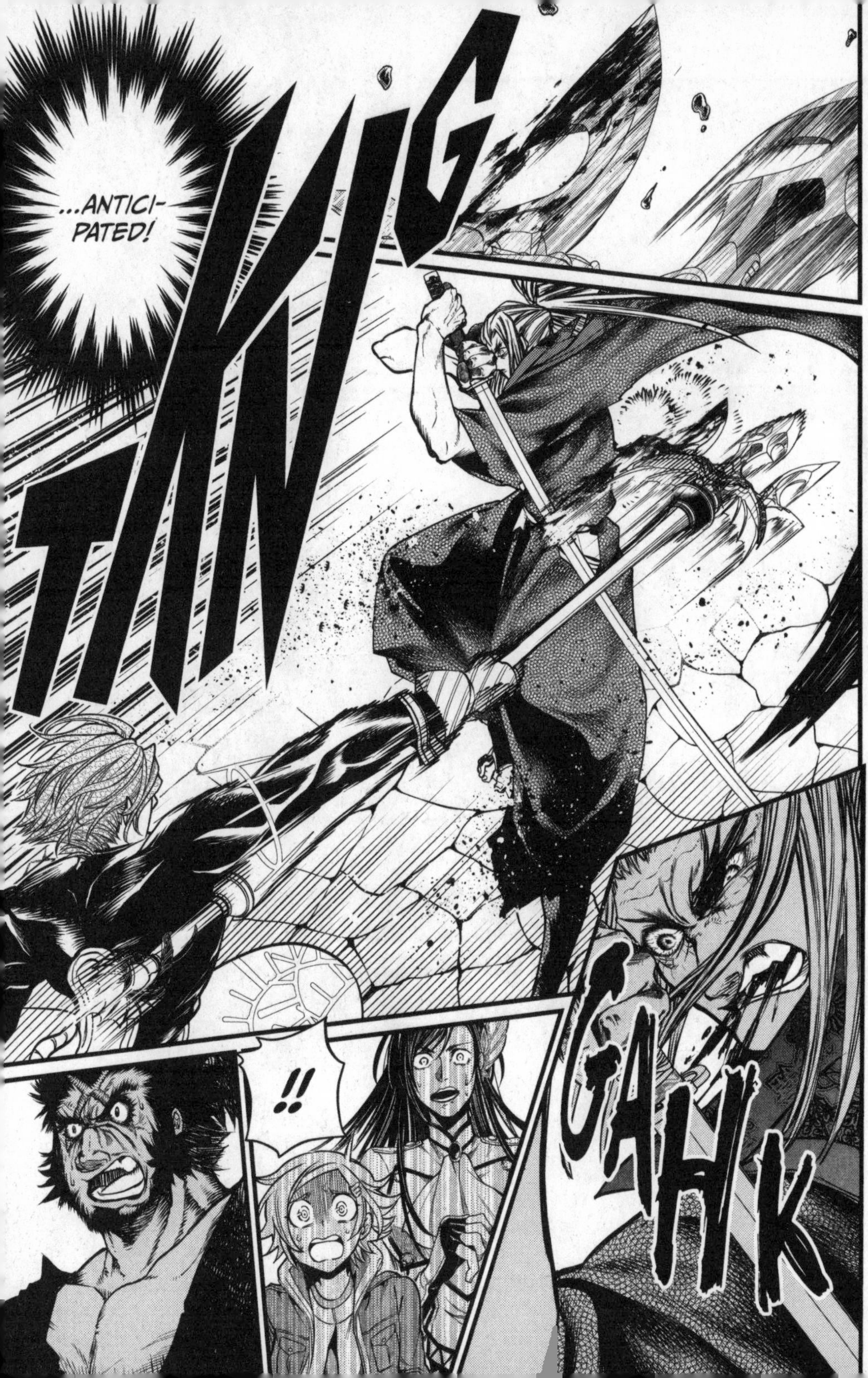
...ANTICI-
PATED!
GAHK
!!

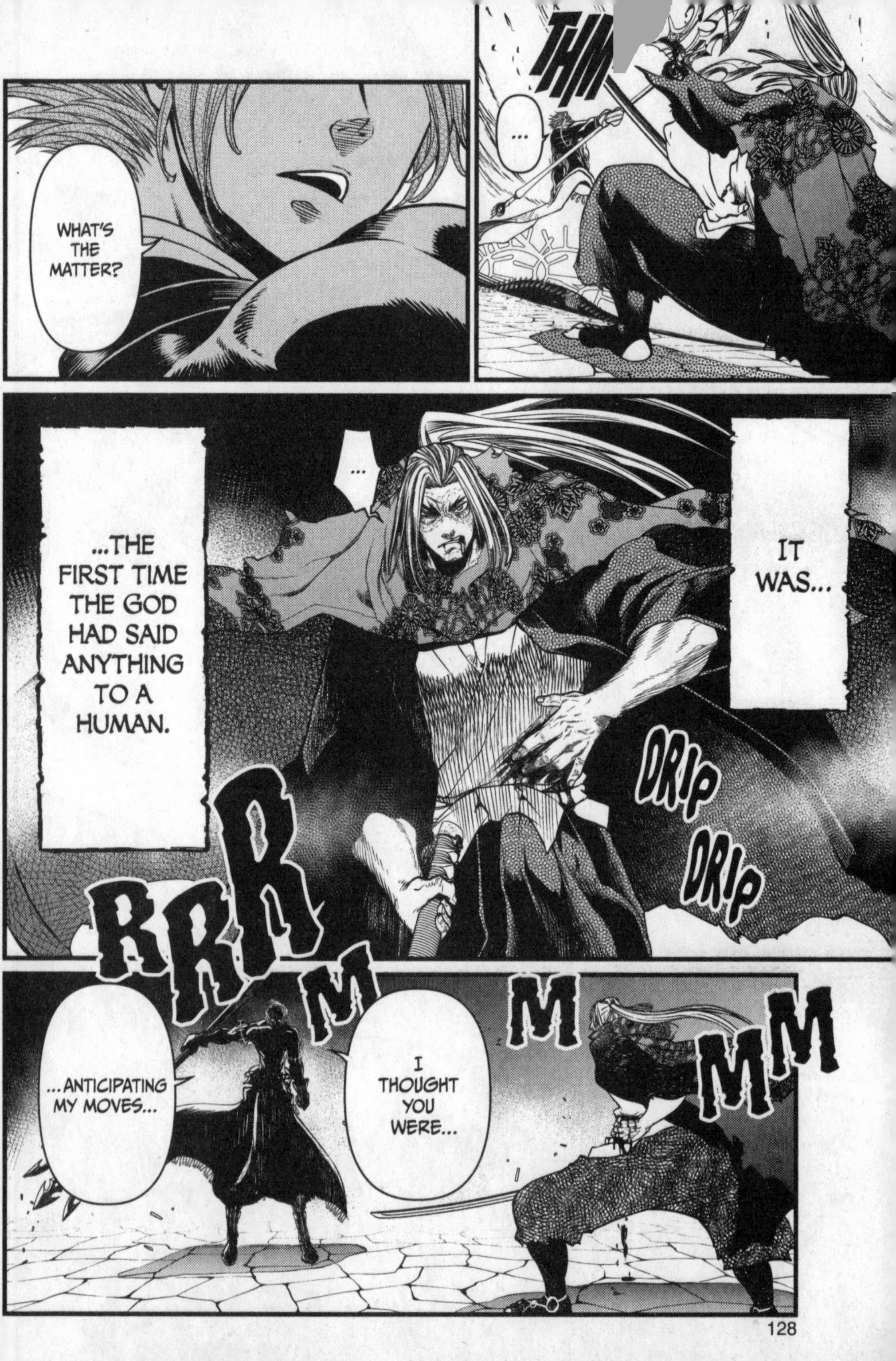
THM
...
WHAT'S THE MATTER?
IT WAS...
...
...THE FIRST TIME THE GOD HAD SAID ANYTHING TO A HUMAN.
DRIP DRIP
RRRMMMMM
I THOUGHT YOU WERE...
...ANTICIPATING MY MOVES...

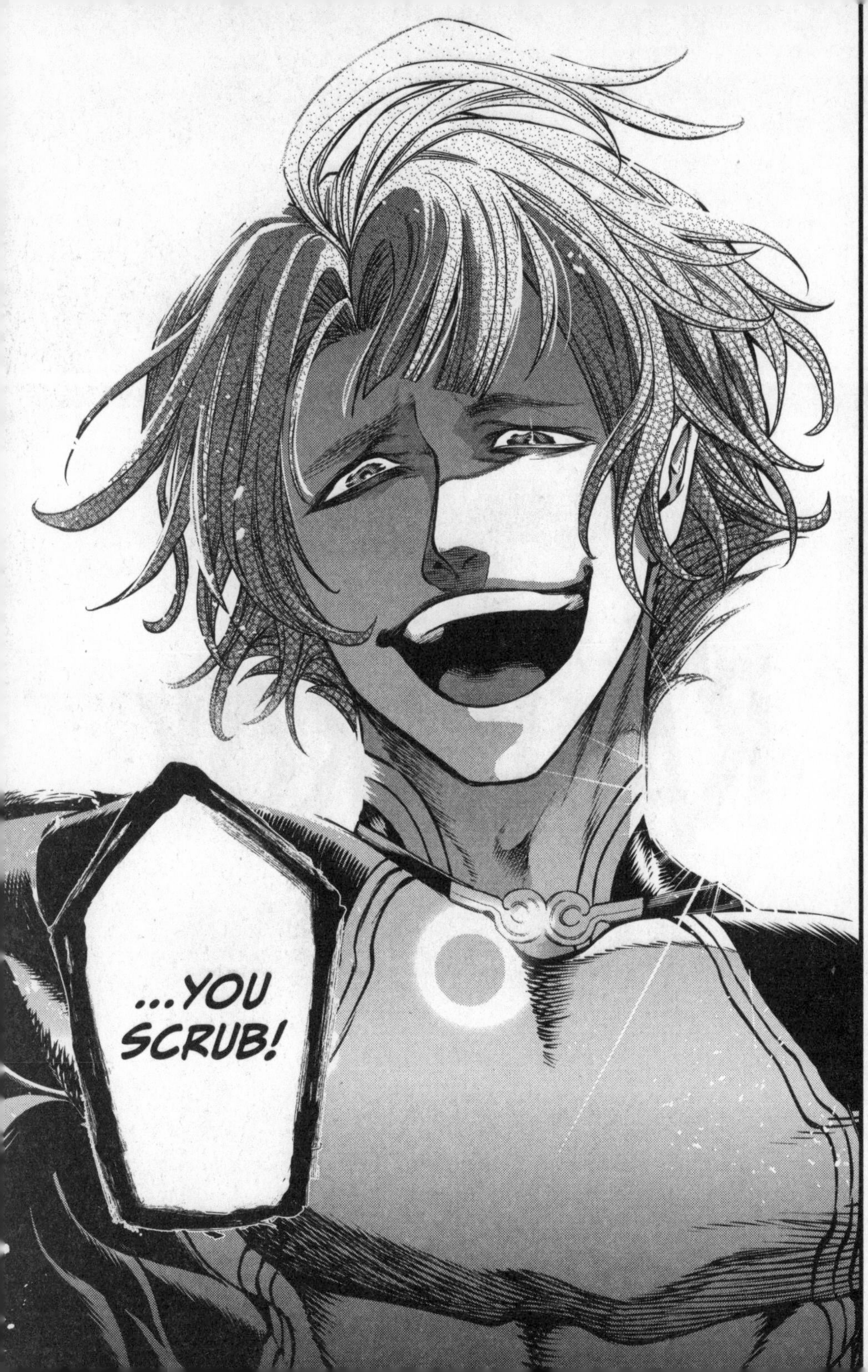
...YOU SCRUB!

RECORD OF

RAGNAROK

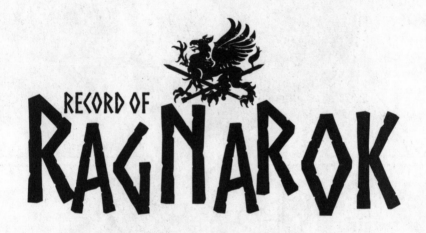

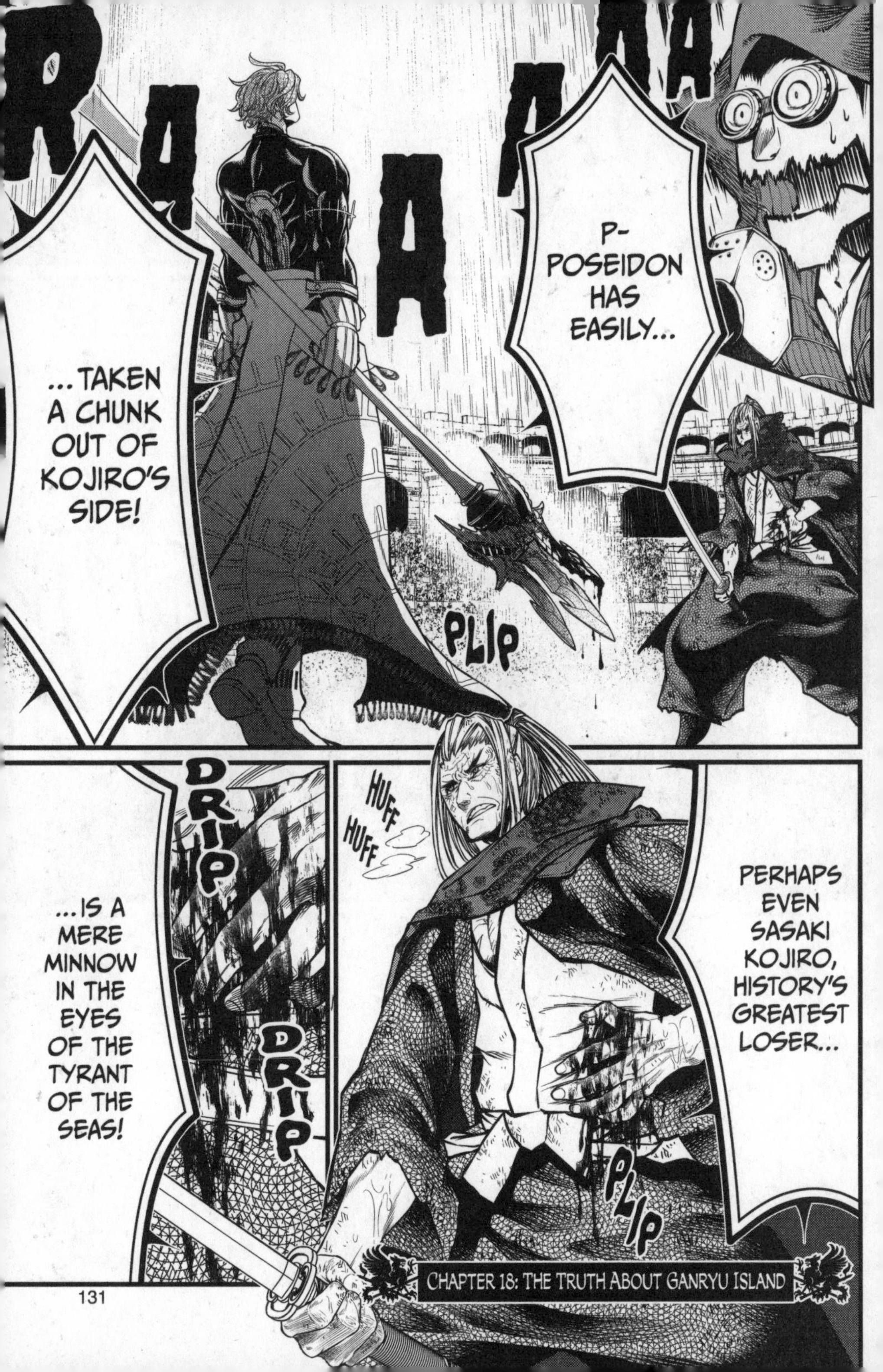
RAAAAA
P-POSEIDON HAS EASILY...
...TAKEN A CHUNK OUT OF KOJIRO'S SIDE!
PLIP
PERHAPS EVEN SASAKI KOJIRO, HISTORY'S GREATEST LOSER...
HUFF HUFF
PLIP
...IS A MERE MINNOW IN THE EYES OF THE TYRANT OF THE SEAS!
DRIP DRIP

Chapter 18: The Truth About Ganryu Island

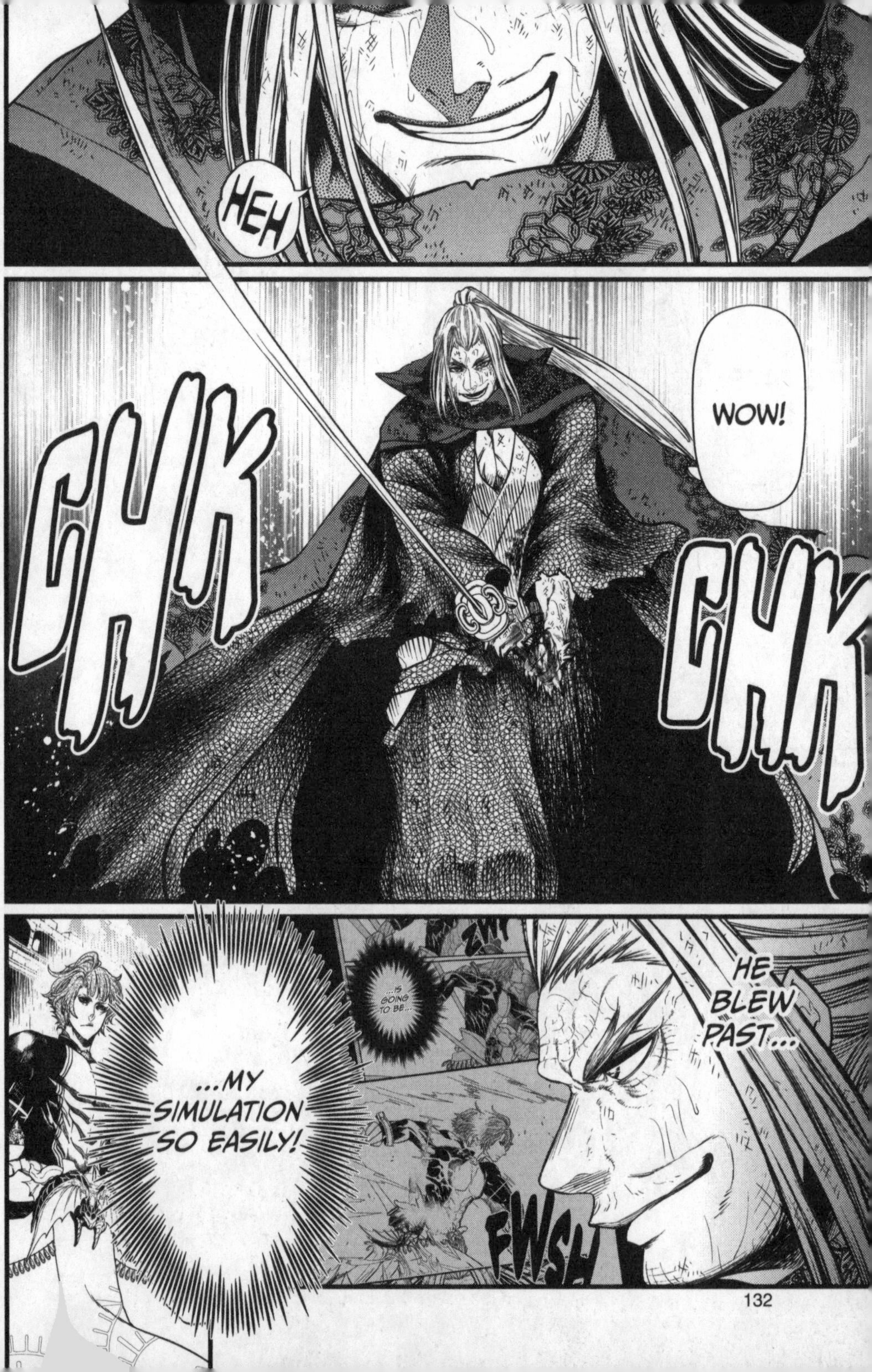
HEH
WOW!
CHK
CHK
HE BLEW PAST...
FWSH
...IS GOING TO BE...
...MY SIMULATION SO EASILY!

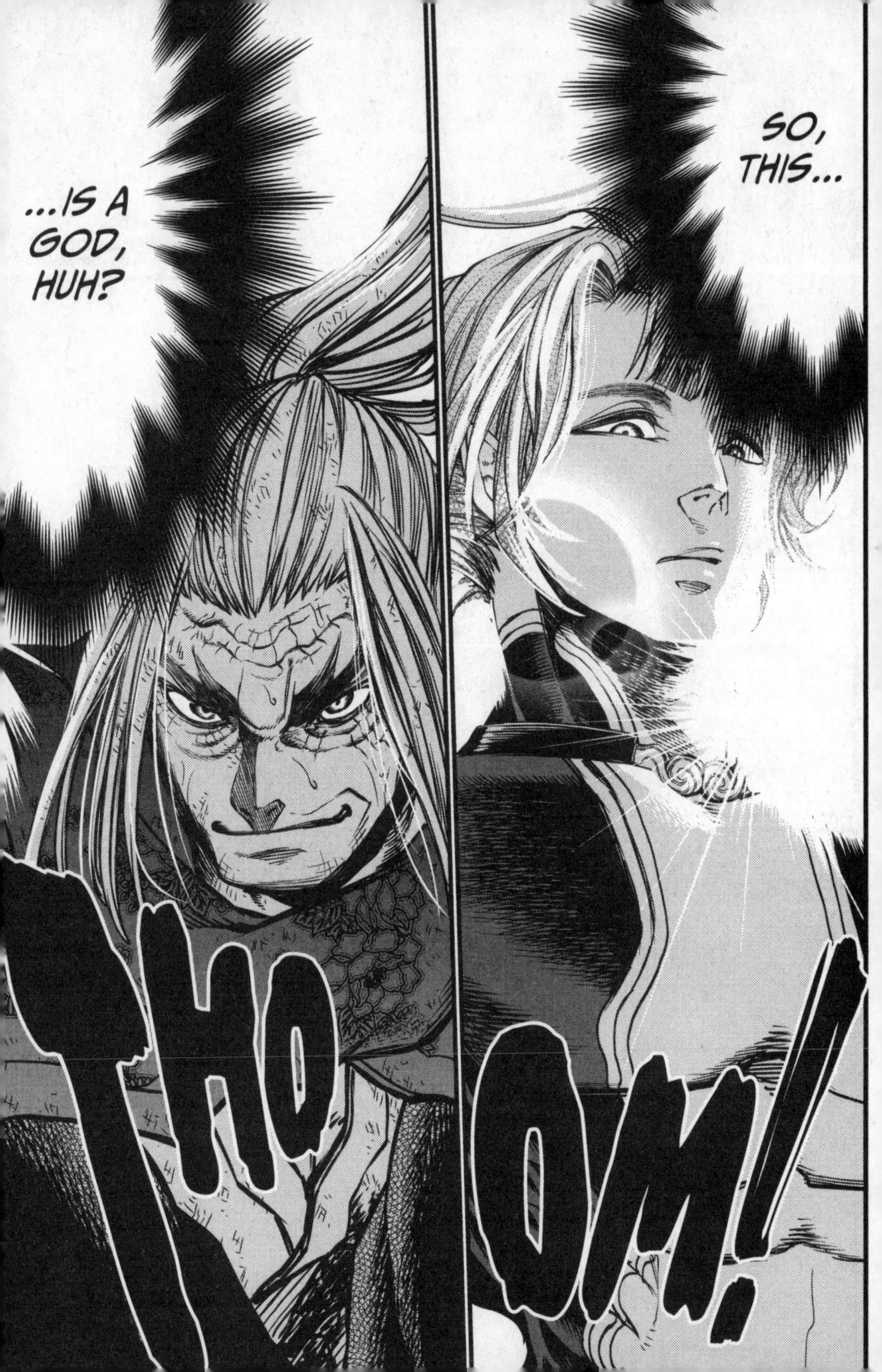
SO, THIS...
...IS A GOD, HUH?
THOOM!

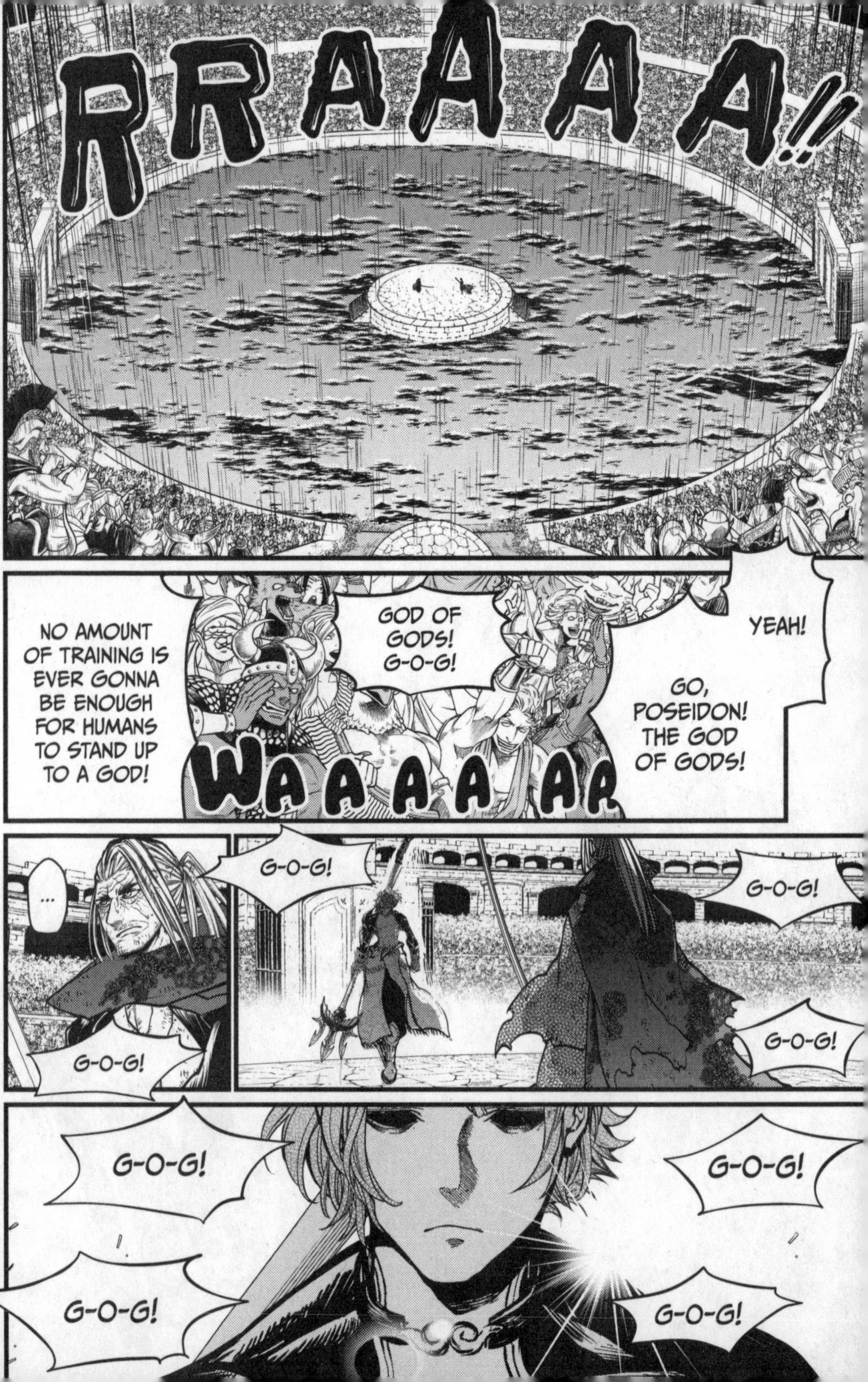
RRAAAA!!
YEAH!
GO, POSEIDON! THE GOD OF GODS!
GOD OF GODS! G-O-G!
WAAAAAR
NO AMOUNT OF TRAINING IS EVER GONNA BE ENOUGH FOR HUMANS TO STAND UP TO A GOD!
G-O-G!
G-O-G!
G-O-G!
...
G-O-G!
G-O-G!
G-O-G!
G-O-G!
G-O-G!

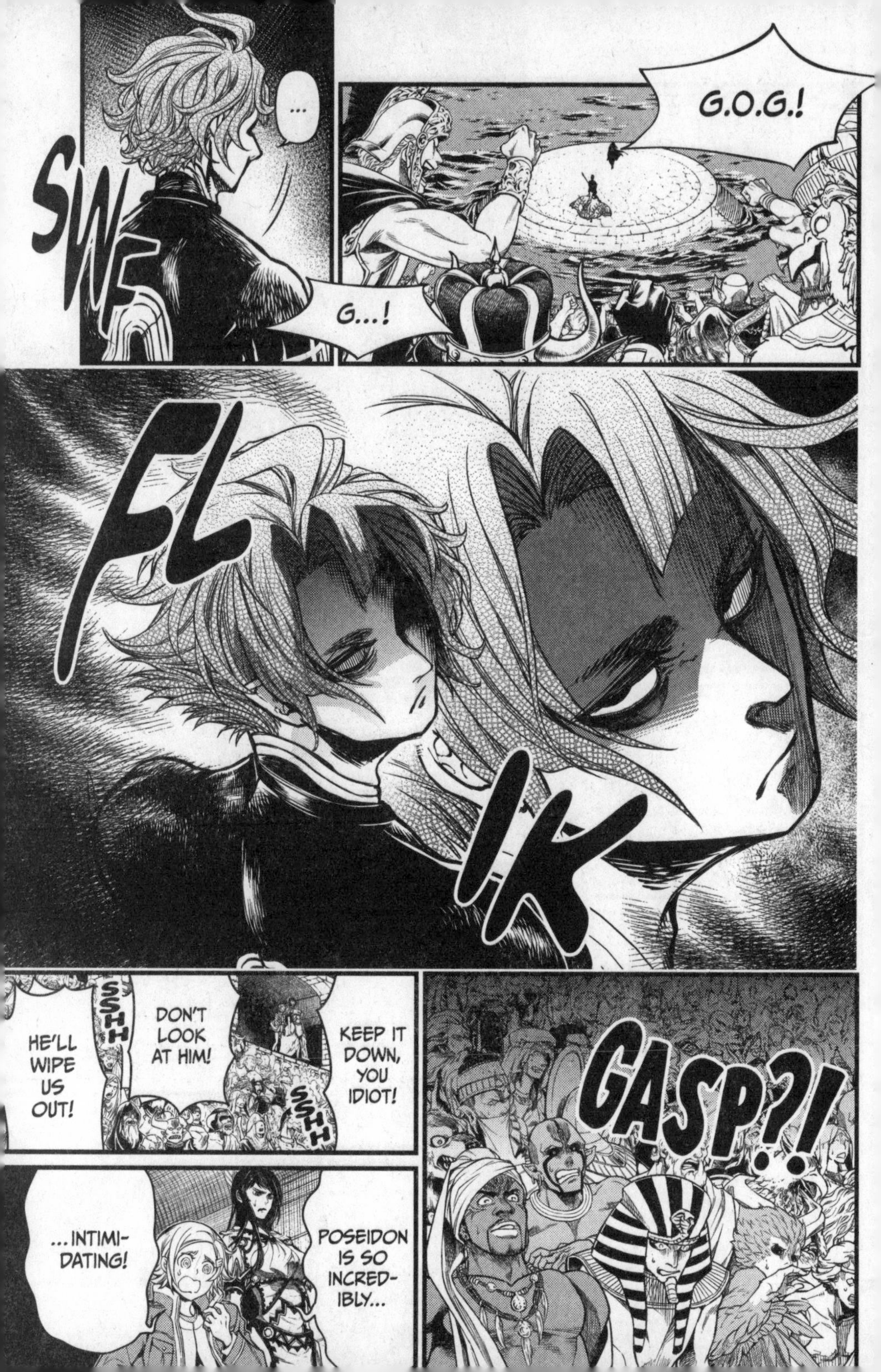
G.O.G.!
G...!
...
FLIK
GASP?!
KEEP IT DOWN, YOU IDIOT!
SSHH
DON'T LOOK AT HIM!
SSHH
HE'LL WIPE US OUT!
POSEIDON IS SO INCRED-IBLY...
...INTIMI-DATING!

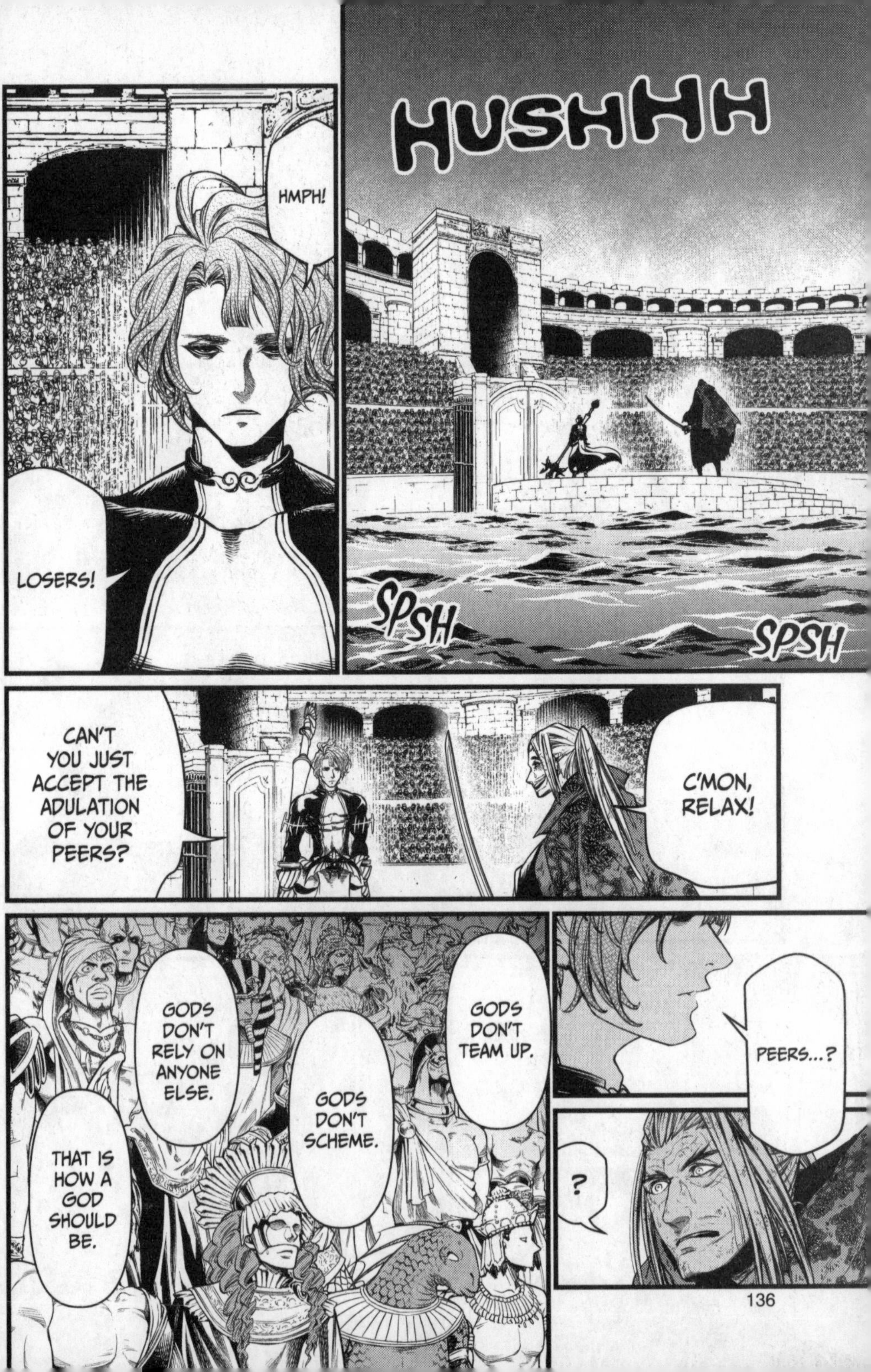
HUSHHH
SPSH
SPSH
HMPH!
LOSERS!
C'MON, RELAX!
CAN'T YOU JUST ACCEPT THE ADULATION OF YOUR PEERS?
PEERS...?
?
GODS DON'T TEAM UP.
GODS DON'T RELY ON ANYONE ELSE.
GODS DON'T SCHEME.
THAT IS HOW A GOD SHOULD BE.

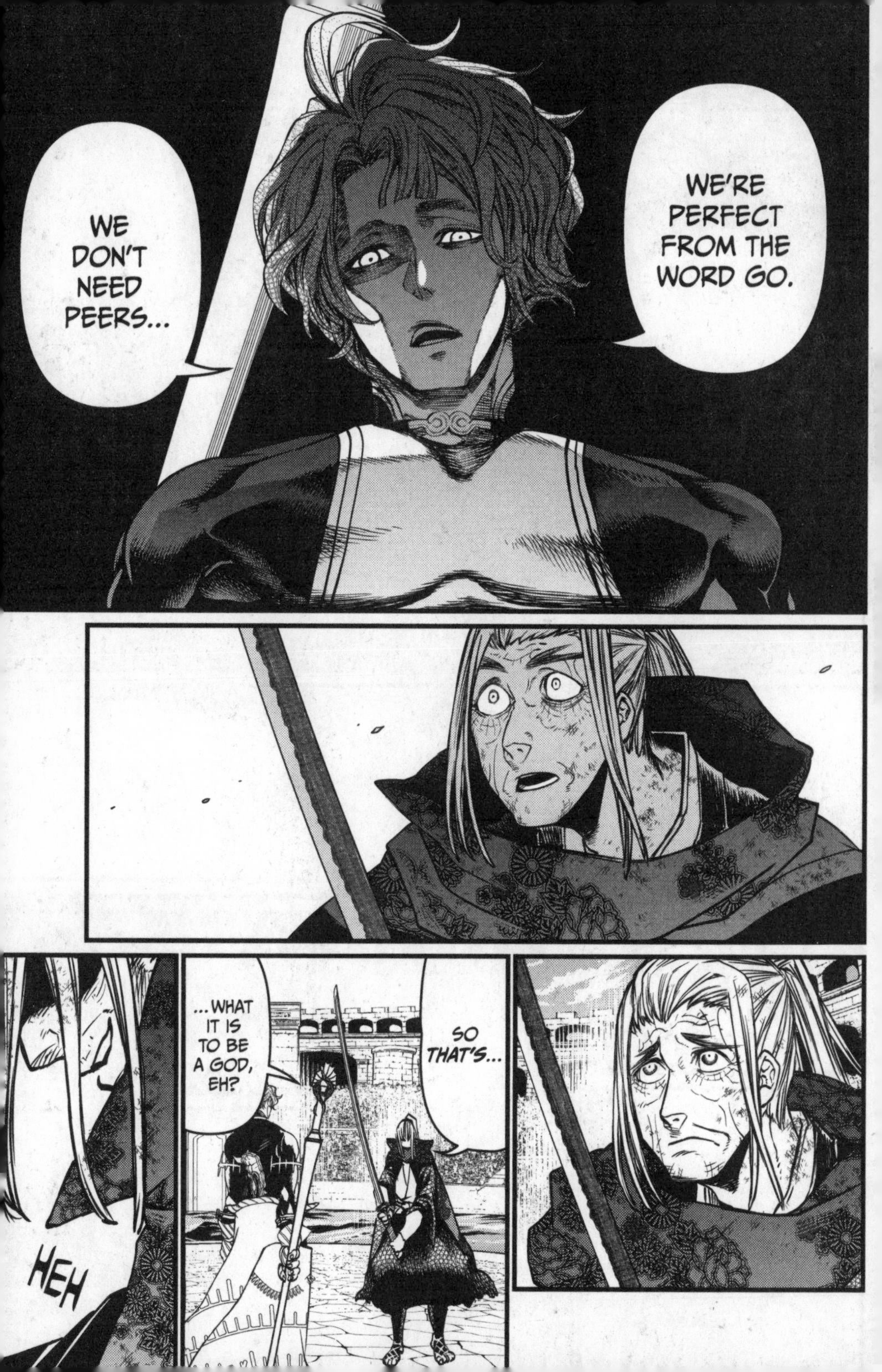
WE'RE PERFECT FROM THE WORD GO.
WE DON'T NEED PEERS...
SO THAT'S...
...WHAT IT IS TO BE A GOD, EH?
HEH

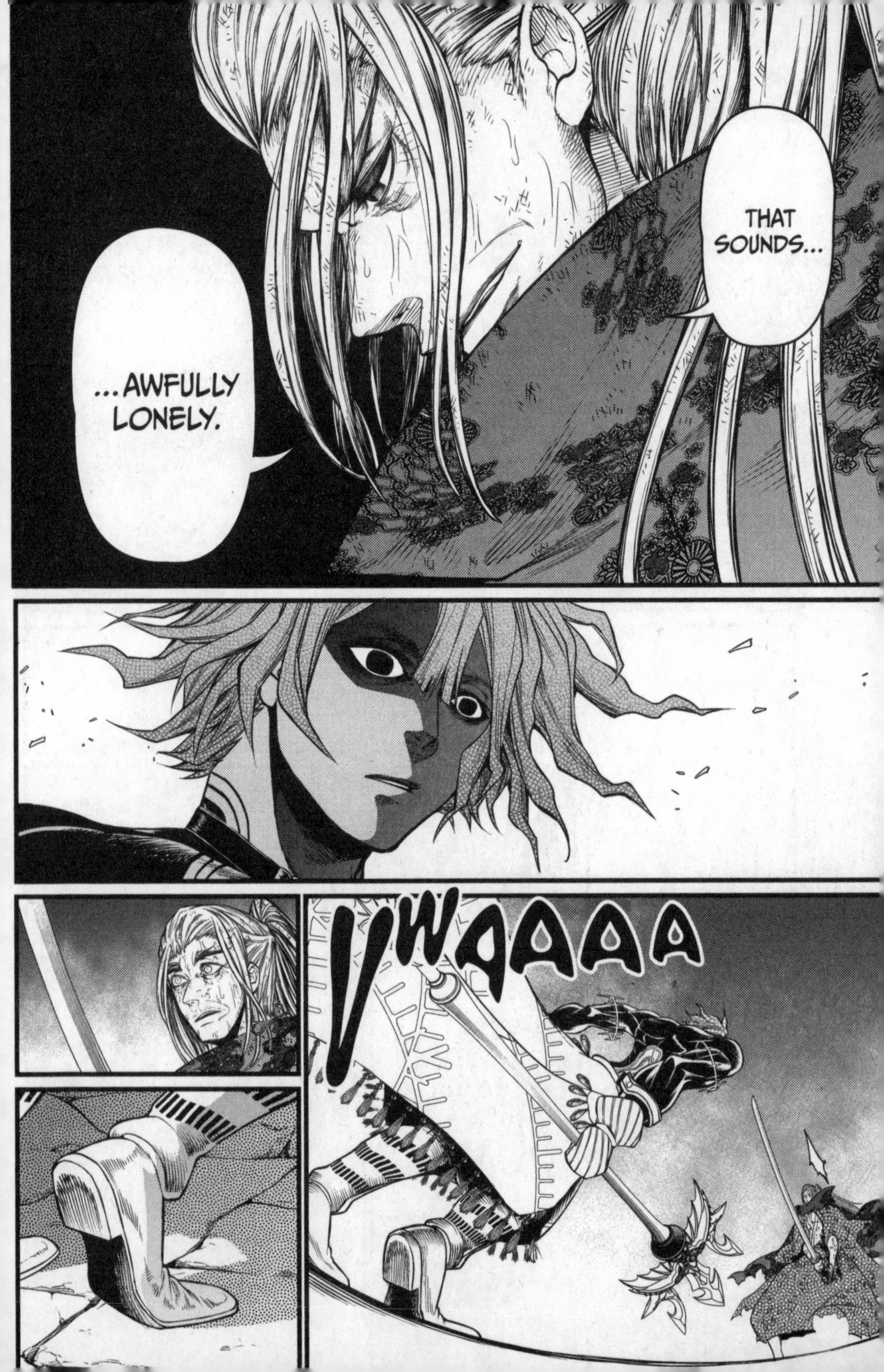
THAT SOUNDS...
...AWFULLY LONELY.
VWAAAA

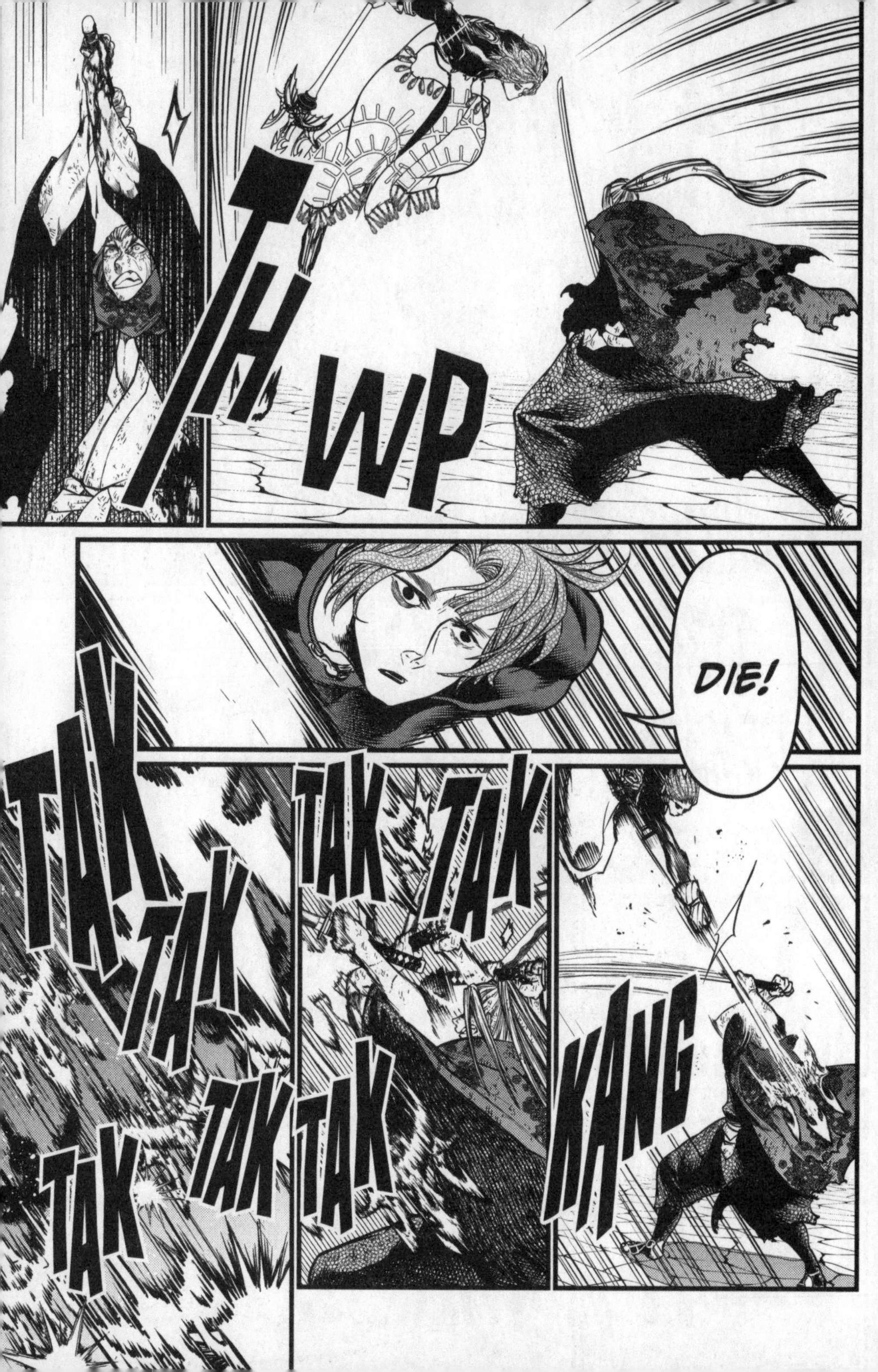
THWP
DIE!
KANG
TAK TAK
TAK TAK
TAK TAK TAK
TAK TAK

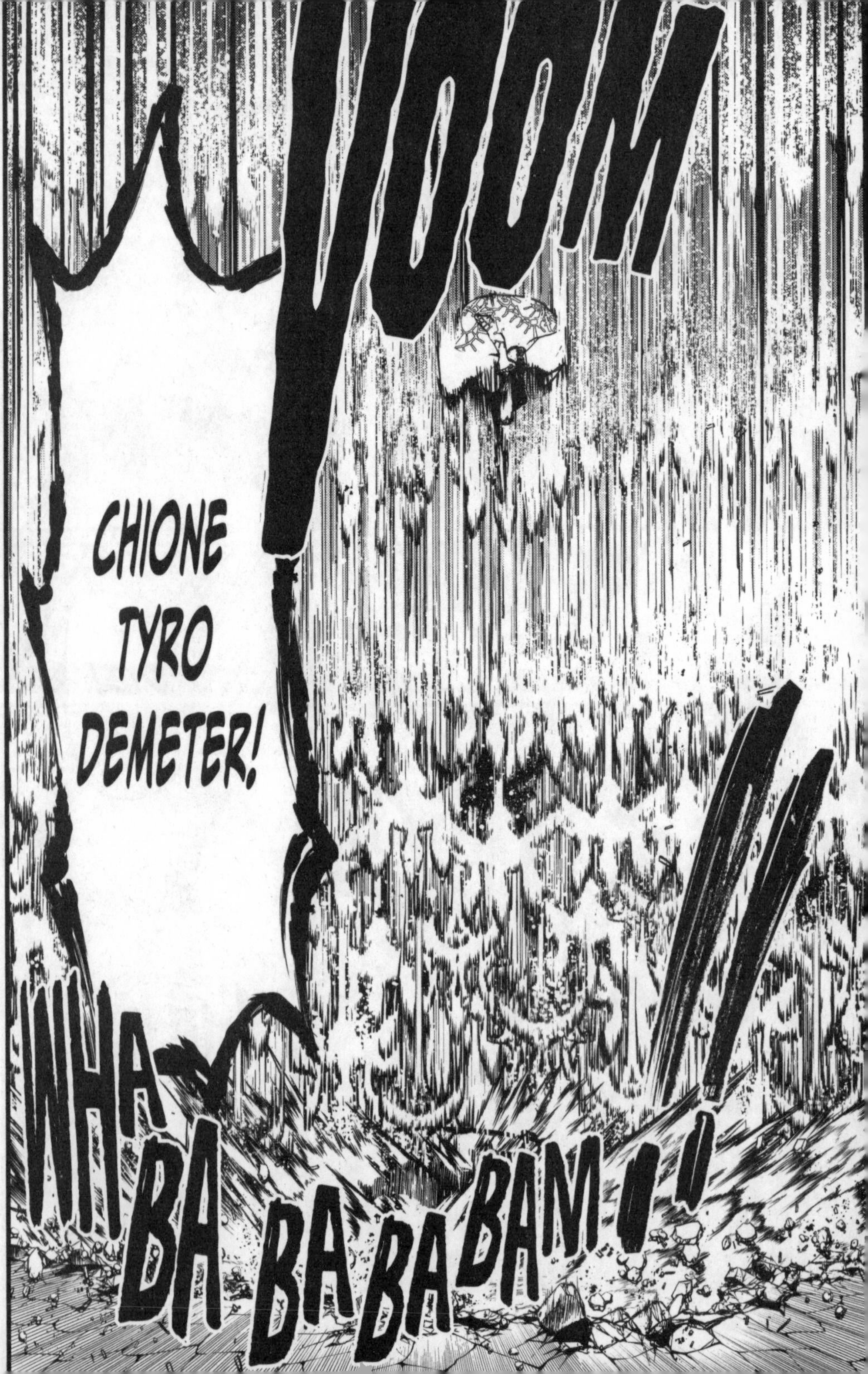
VOOM
CHIONE TYRO DEMETER!
WHA-BA BA BA BAM!!

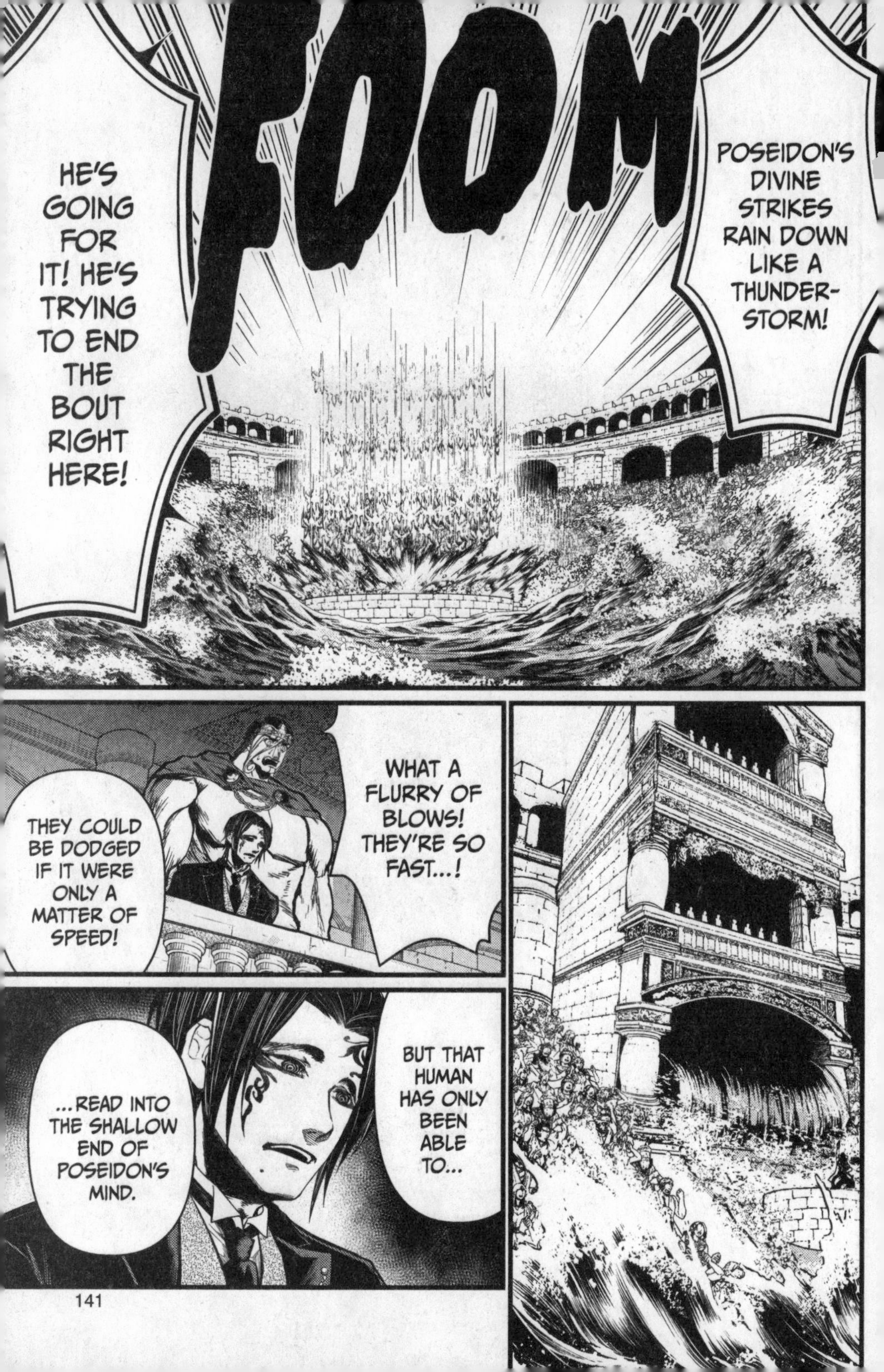
POSEIDON'S DIVINE STRIKES RAIN DOWN LIKE A THUNDER-STORM!
FOOM
HE'S GOING FOR IT! HE'S TRYING TO END THE BOUT RIGHT HERE!
WHAT A FLURRY OF BLOWS! THEY'RE SO FAST...!
THEY COULD BE DODGED IF IT WERE ONLY A MATTER OF SPEED!
BUT THAT HUMAN HAS ONLY BEEN ABLE TO...
...READ INTO THE SHALLOW END OF POSEIDON'S MIND.

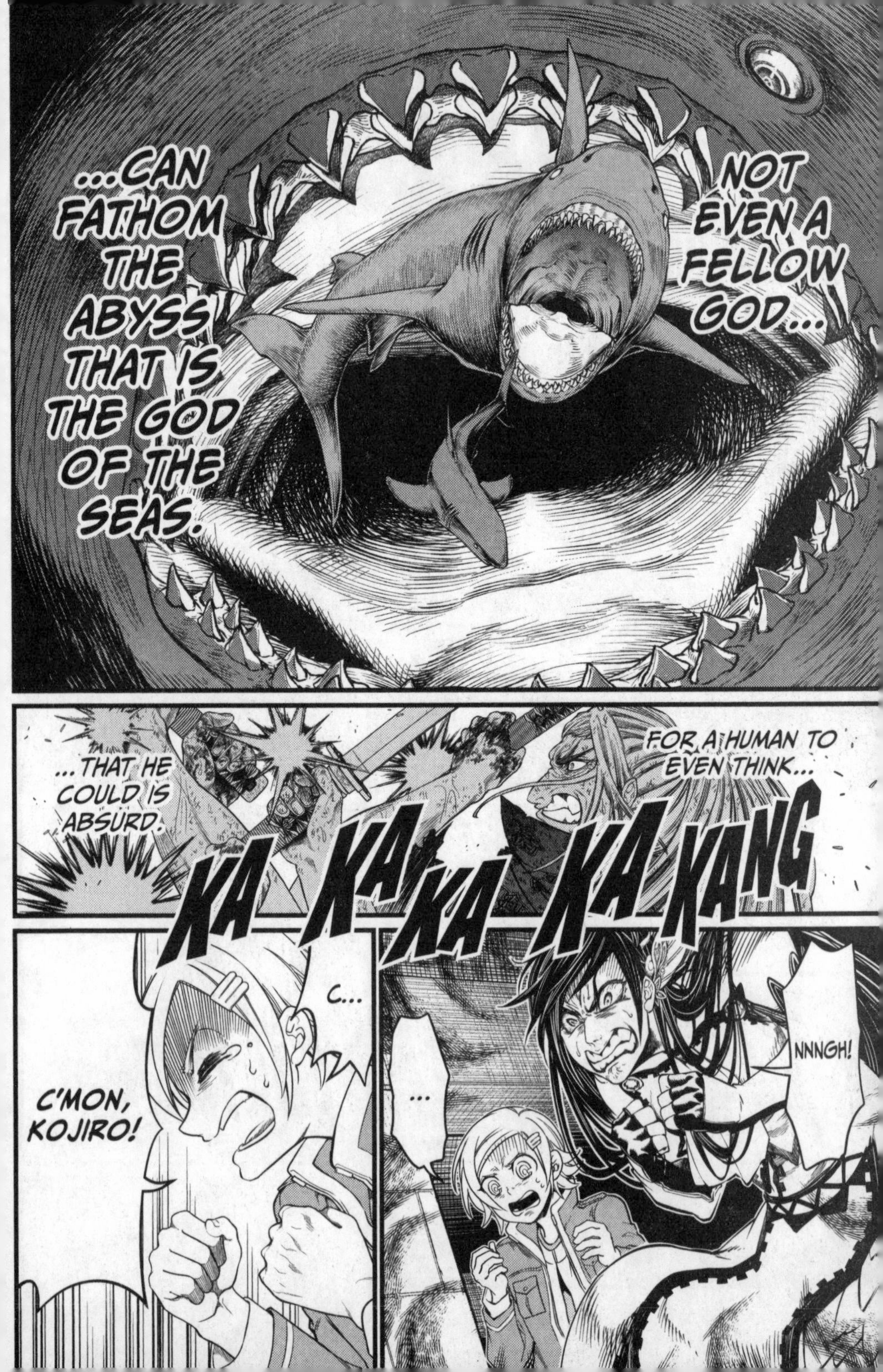
NOT EVEN A FELLOW GOD...
...CAN FATHOM THE ABYSS THAT IS THE GOD OF THE SEAS.
FOR A HUMAN TO EVEN THINK...
...THAT HE COULD IS ABSURD.
KA KA KA KA KA KANG
NNNGH!
...
C...
C'MON, KOJIRO!

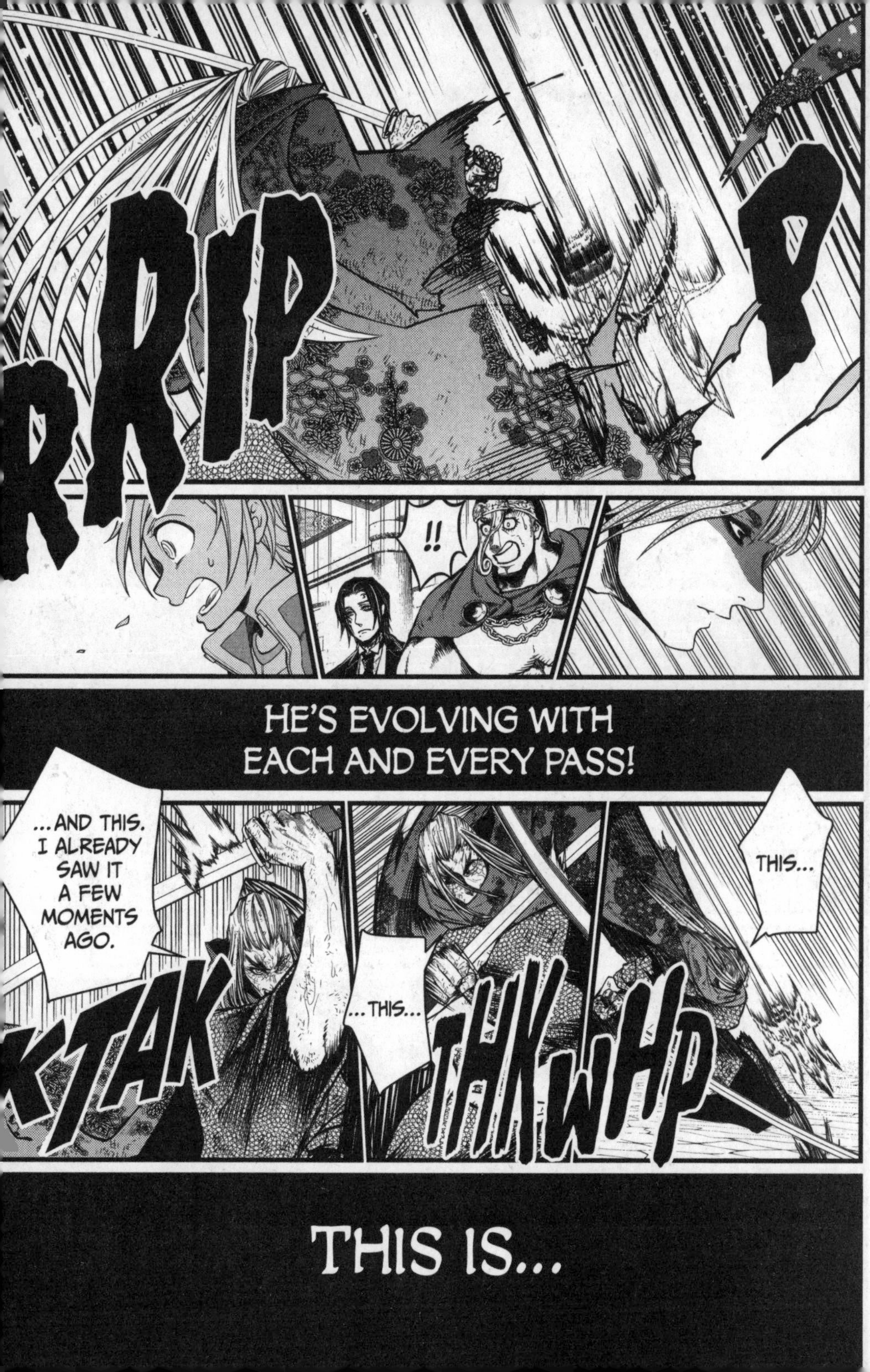
RRIP
!!
HE'S EVOLVING WITH EACH AND EVERY PASS!
THIS...
...THIS...
THKWHP
...AND THIS. I ALREADY SAW IT A FEW MOMENTS AGO.
KTAK
THIS IS...

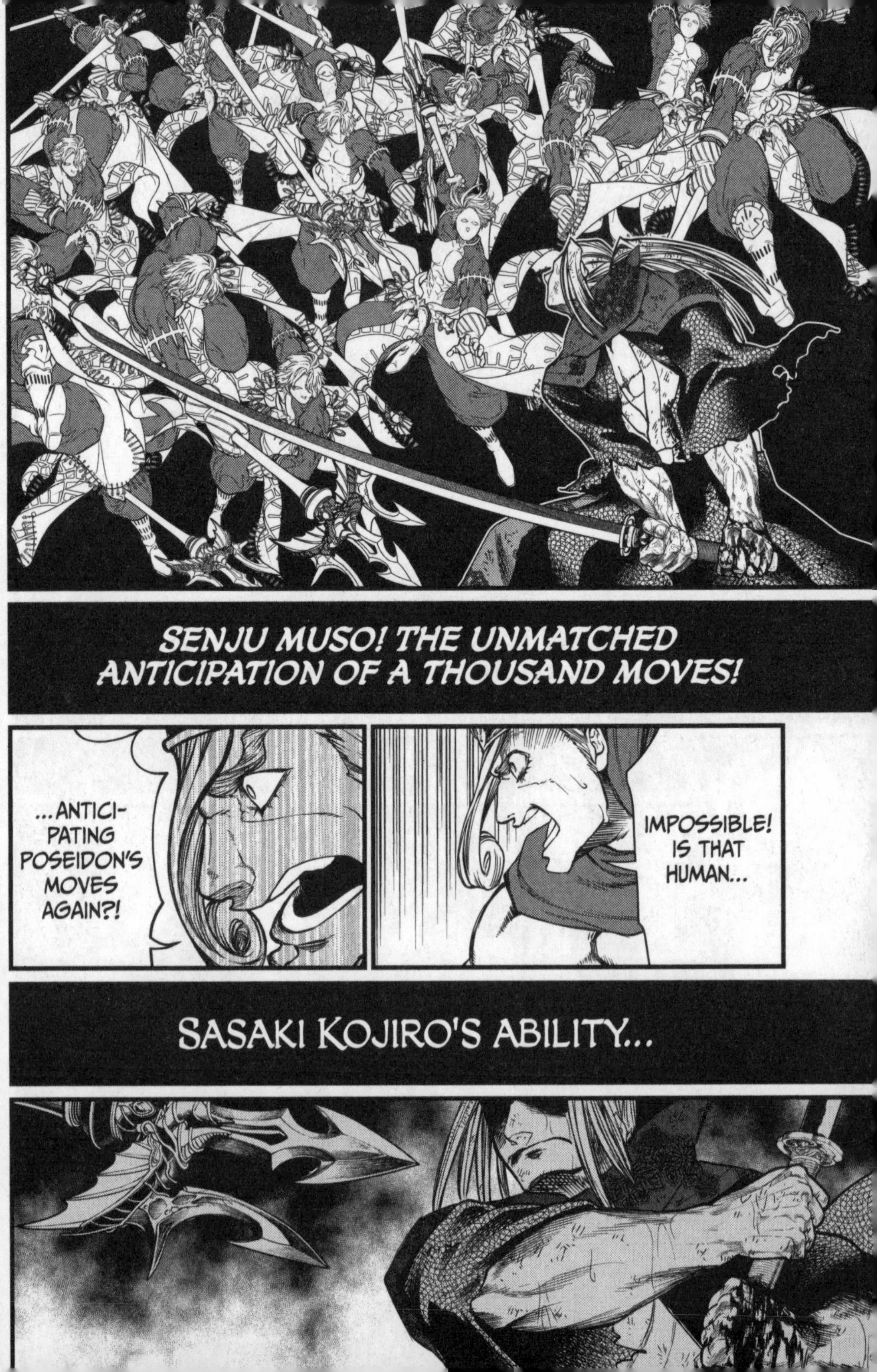
SENJU MUSO! THE UNMATCHED ANTICIPATION OF A THOUSAND MOVES!
IMPOSSIBLE! IS THAT HUMAN...
...ANTICIPATING POSEIDON'S MOVES AGAIN?!
SASAKI KOJIRO'S ABILITY...

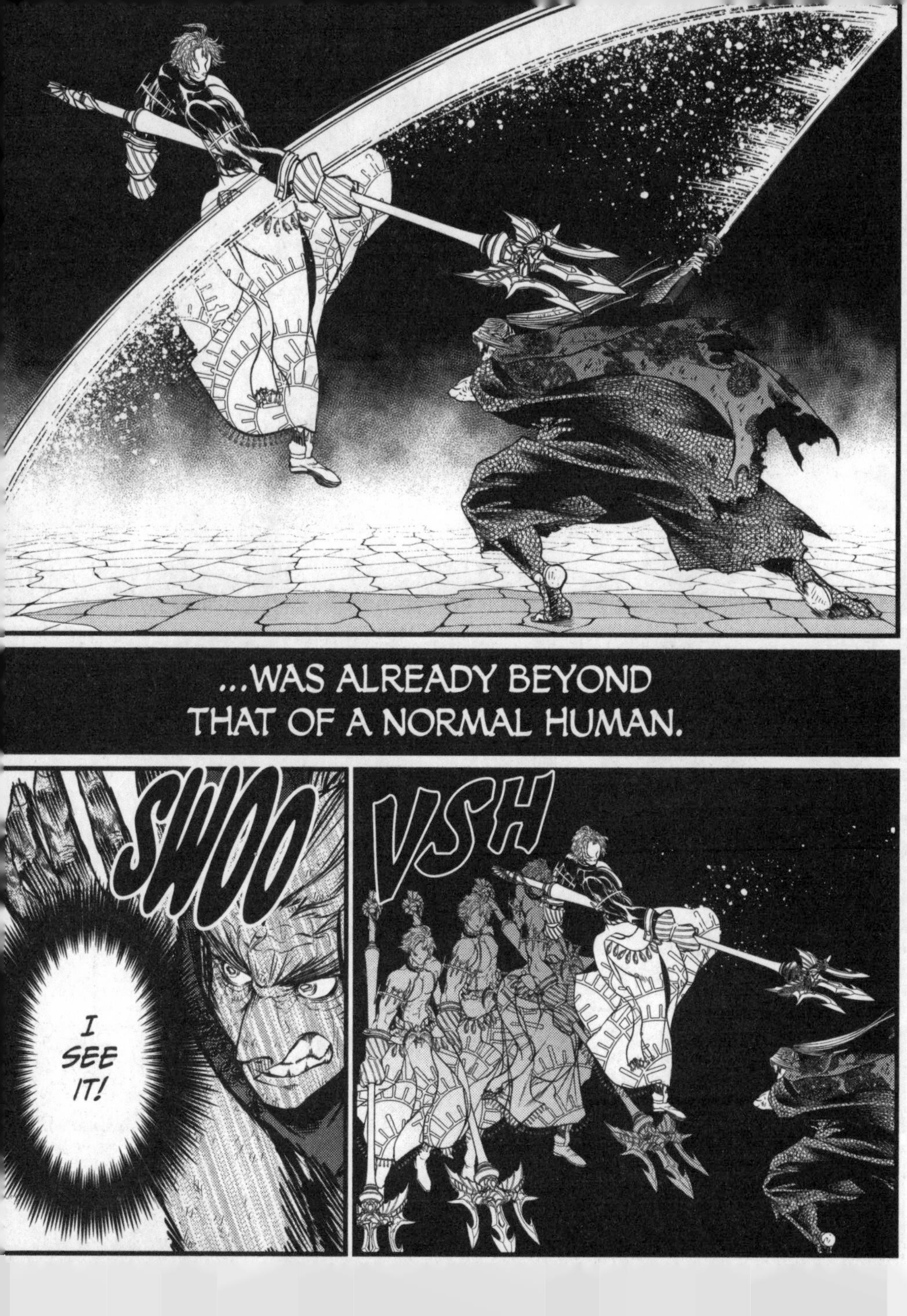
...WAS ALREADY BEYOND THAT OF A NORMAL HUMAN.
VSH
SWOO
I SEE IT!

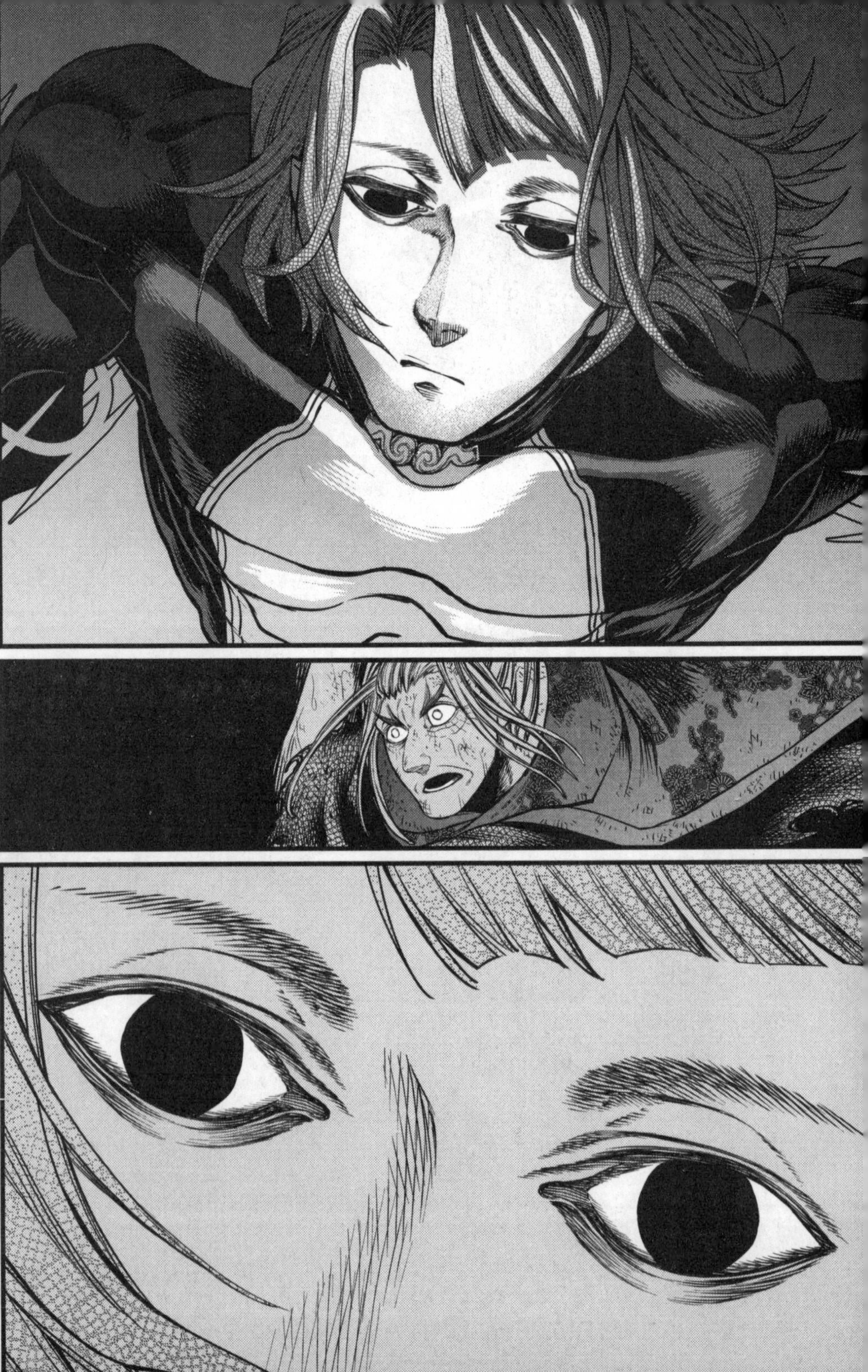

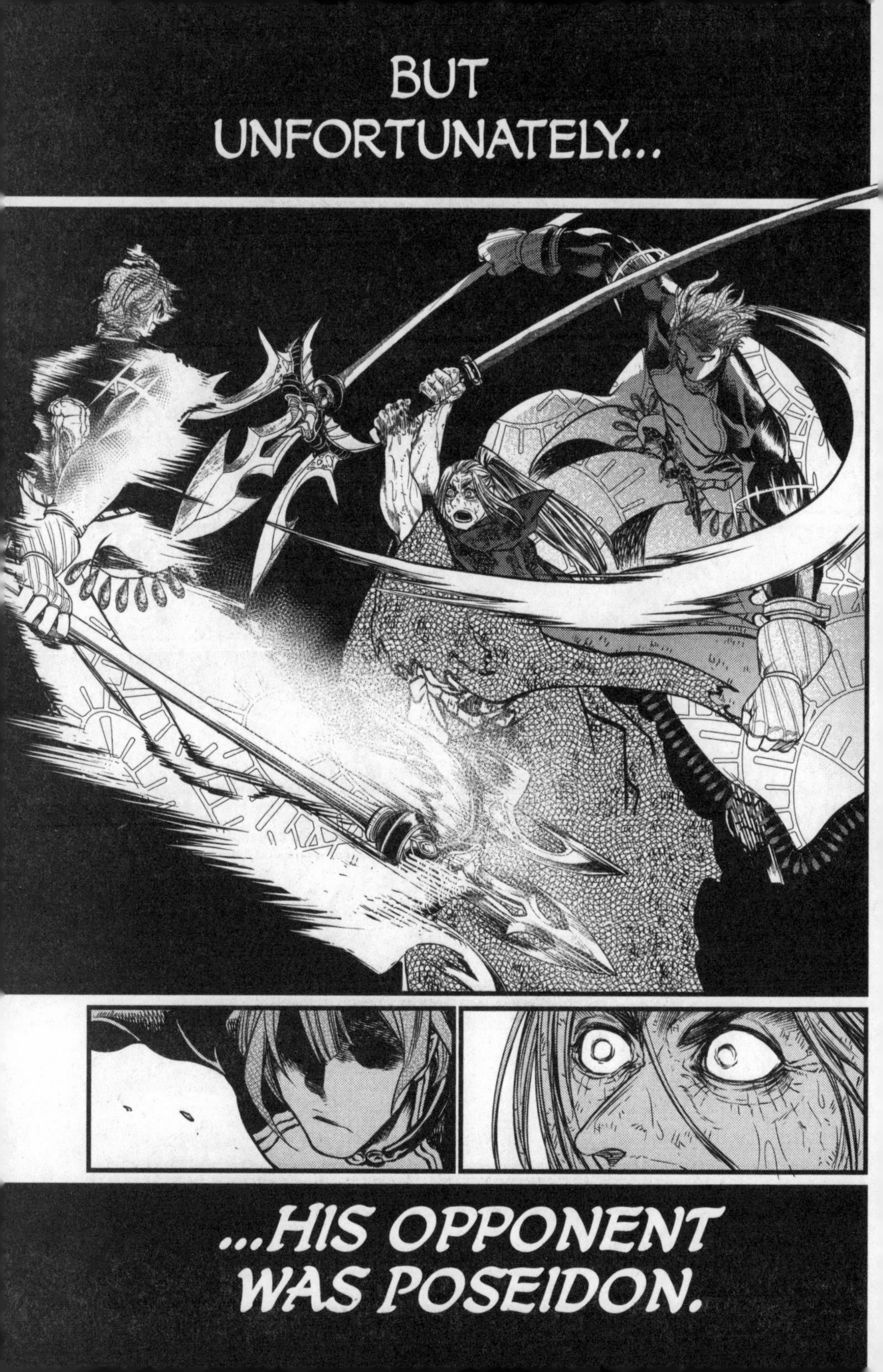
BUT UNFORTUNATELY...
...HIS OPPONENT WAS POSEIDON.

WHAT
...?!

FWSH

SH

...CAME FROM A BLIND SPOT I DIDN'T ANTICIPATE!

THAT STRIKE...

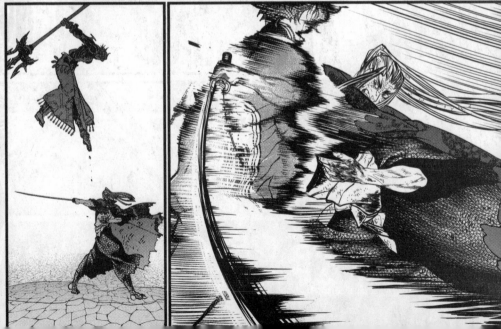

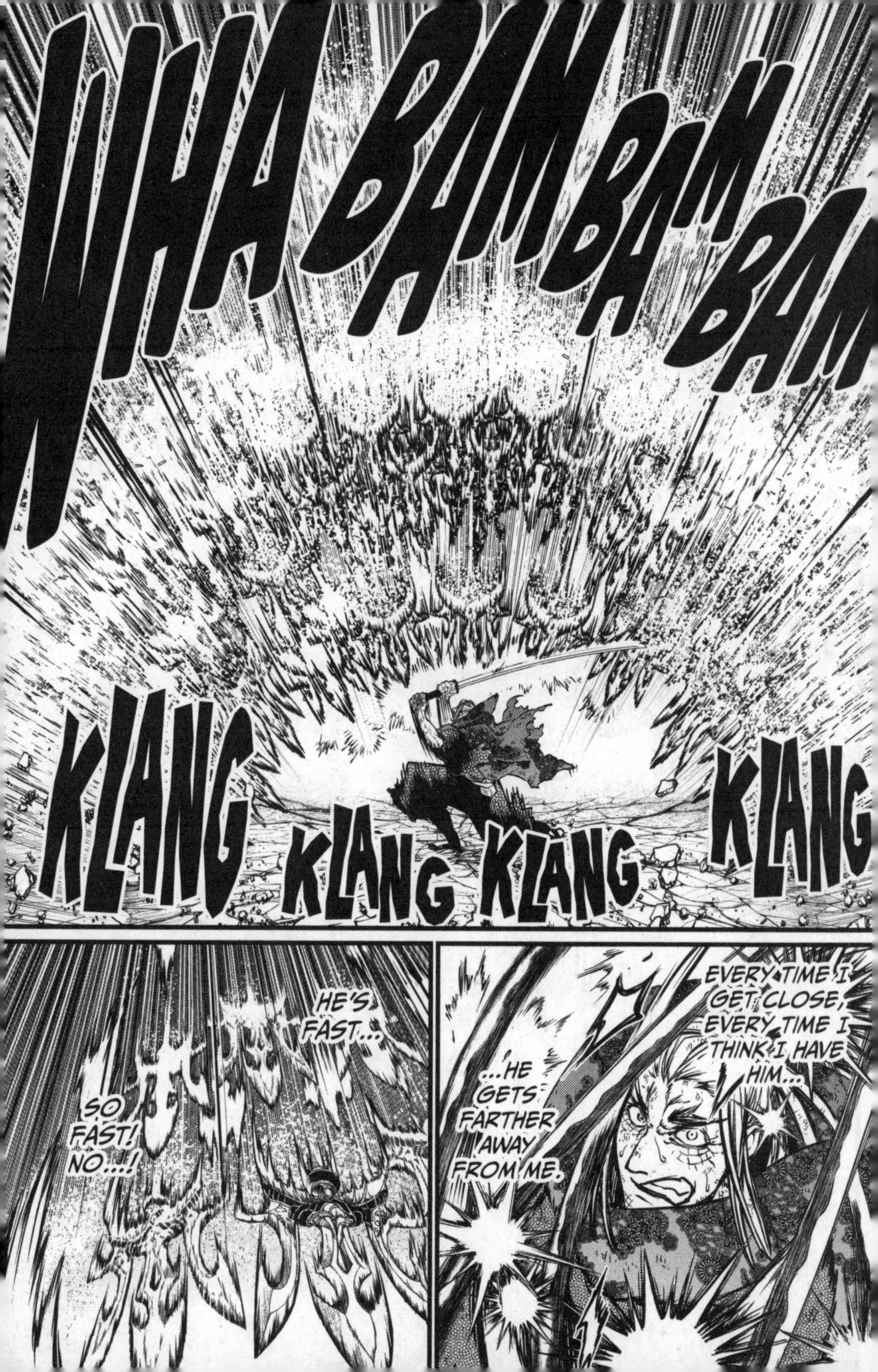
WHABAMBAMBAM
KLANG
KLANG
KLANG
KLANG
EVERY TIME I GET CLOSE, EVERY TIME I THINK I HAVE HIM...
...HE GETS FARTHER AWAY FROM ME.
HE'S FAST...
SO FAST! NO...!

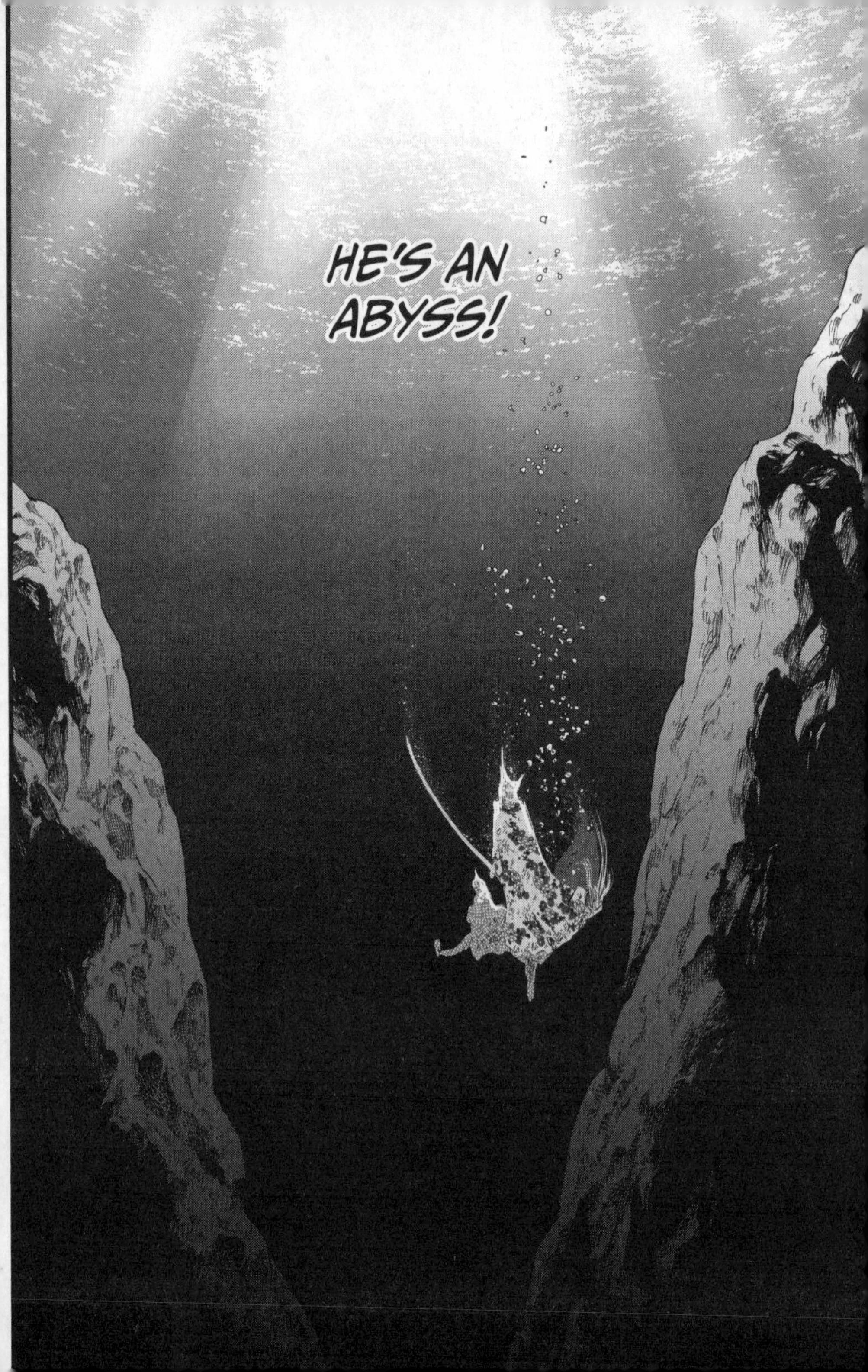
HE'S AN ABYSS!

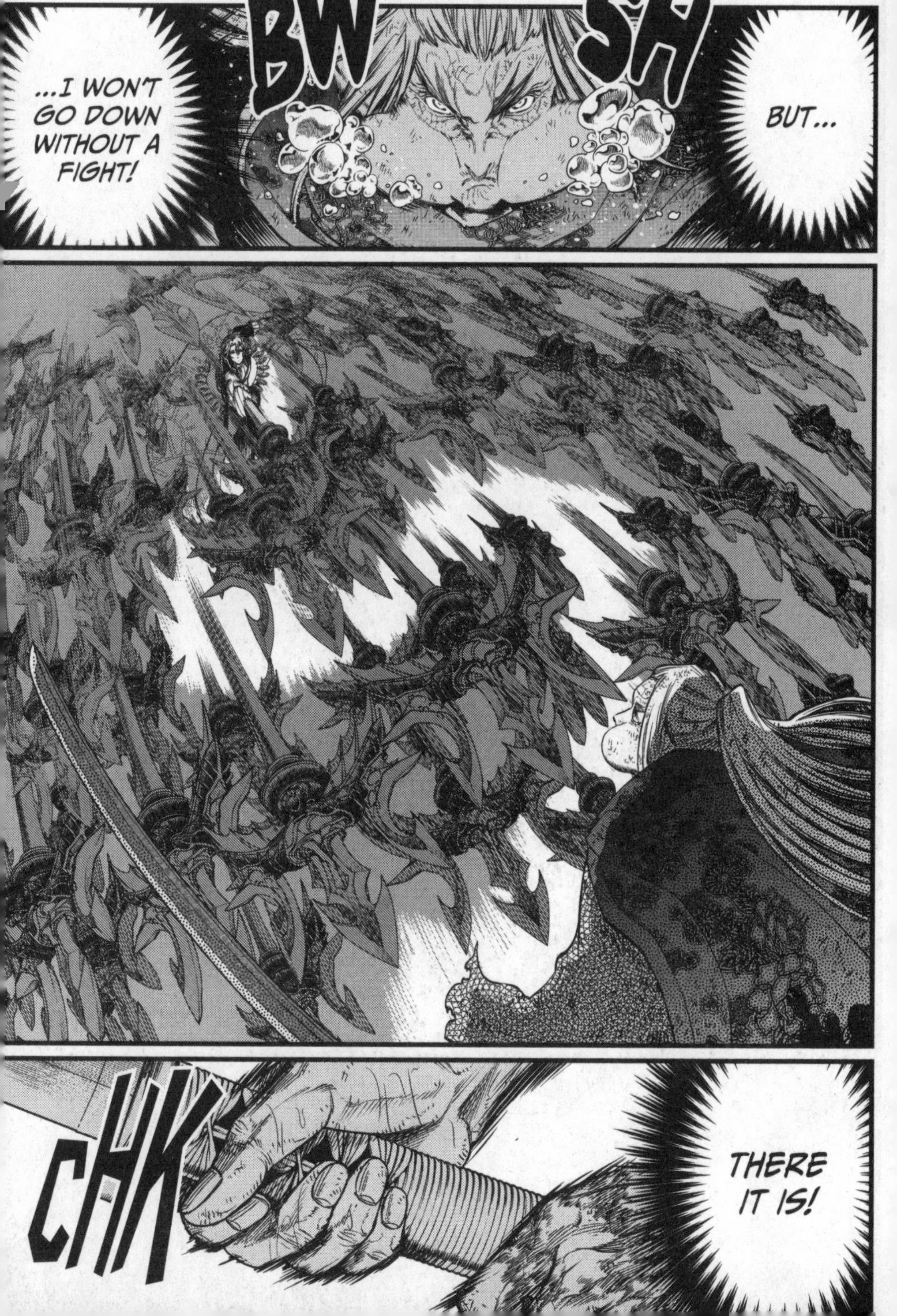
BUT...
BWSH
...I WON'T GO DOWN WITHOUT A FIGHT!
THERE IT IS!
CHK

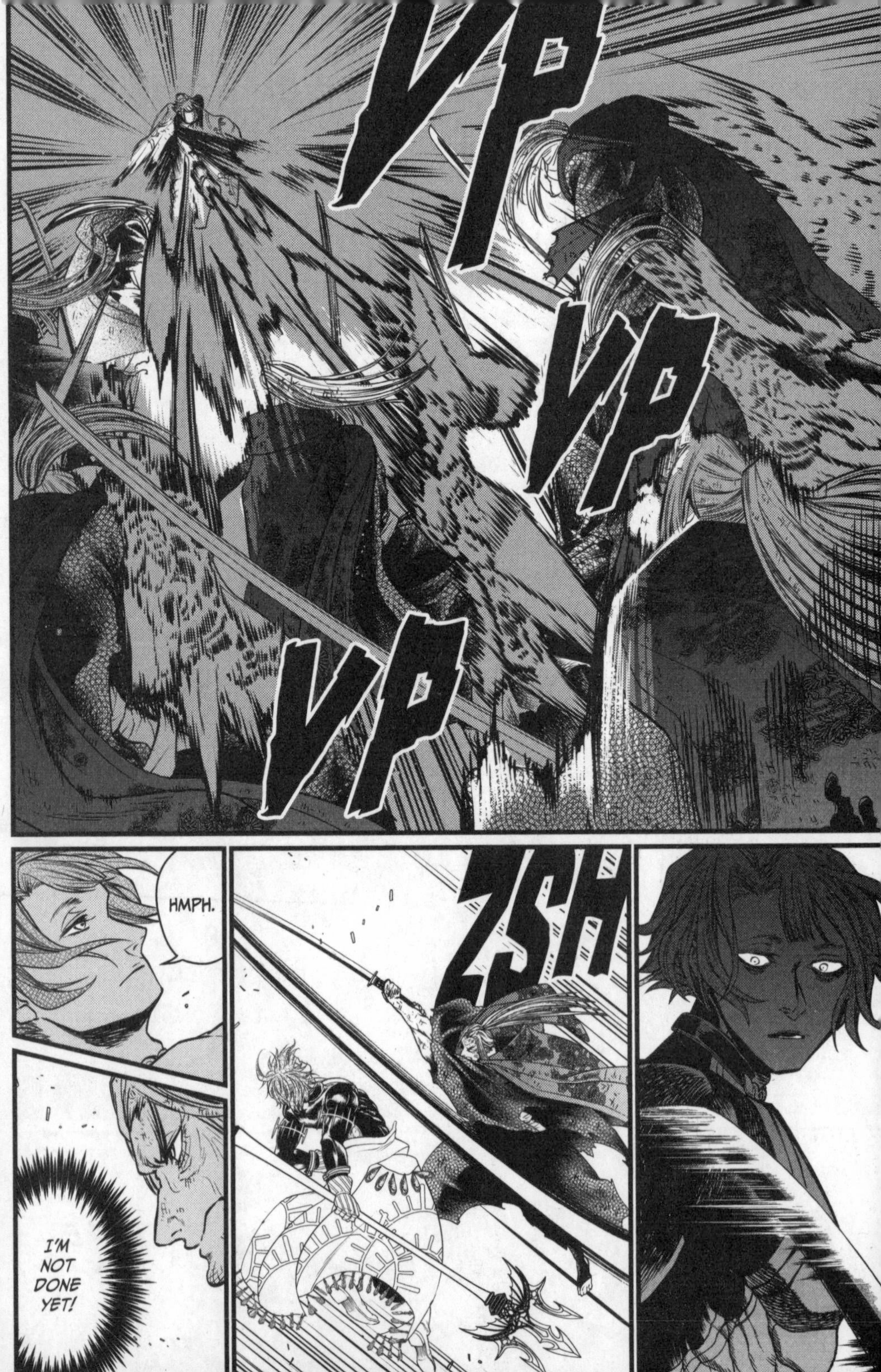
VP
VP
VP
ZSH
HMPH.
I'M NOT DONE YET!

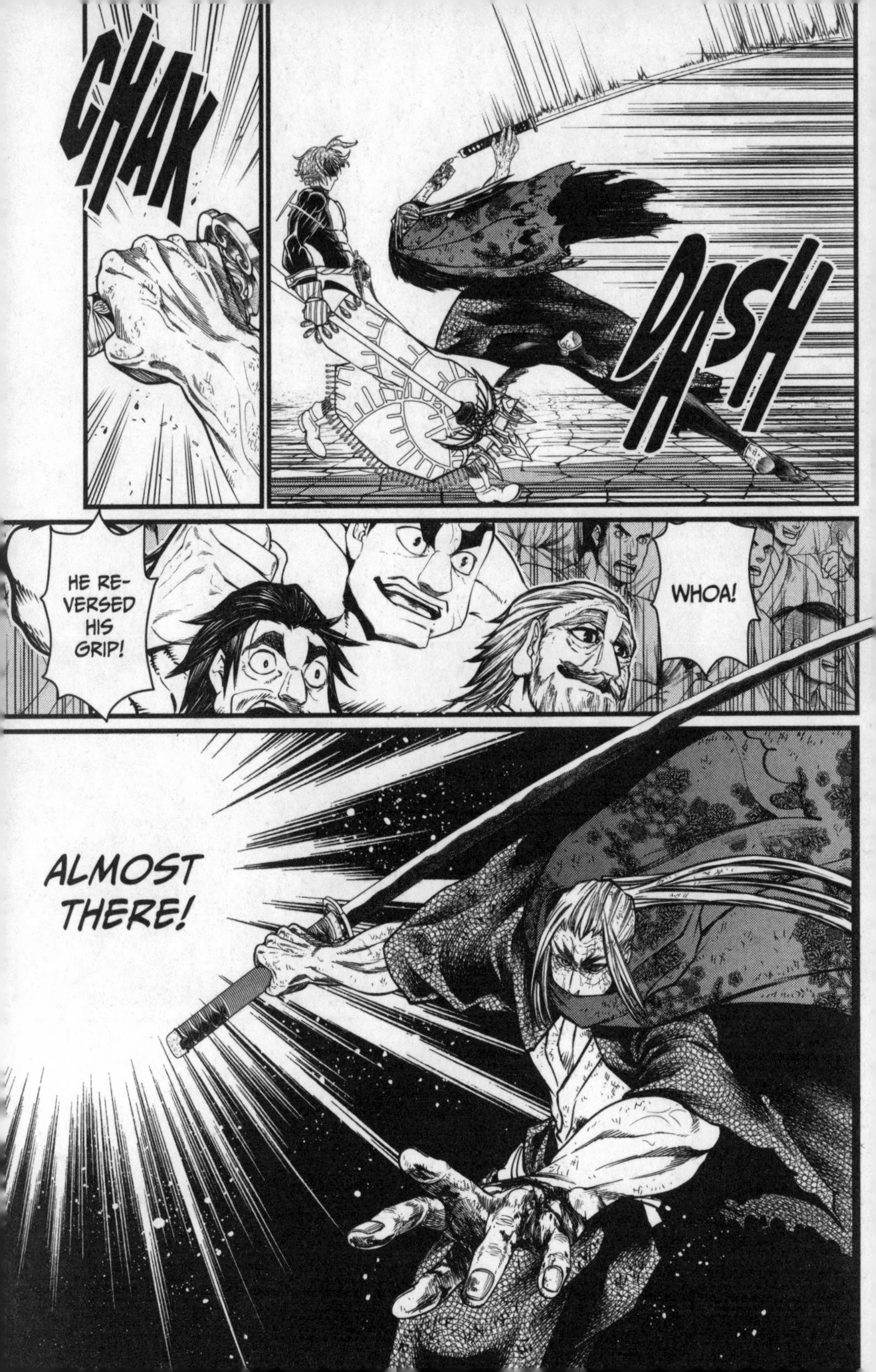
DASH
CHAK
WHOA!
HE RE-VERSED HIS GRIP!
ALMOST THERE!

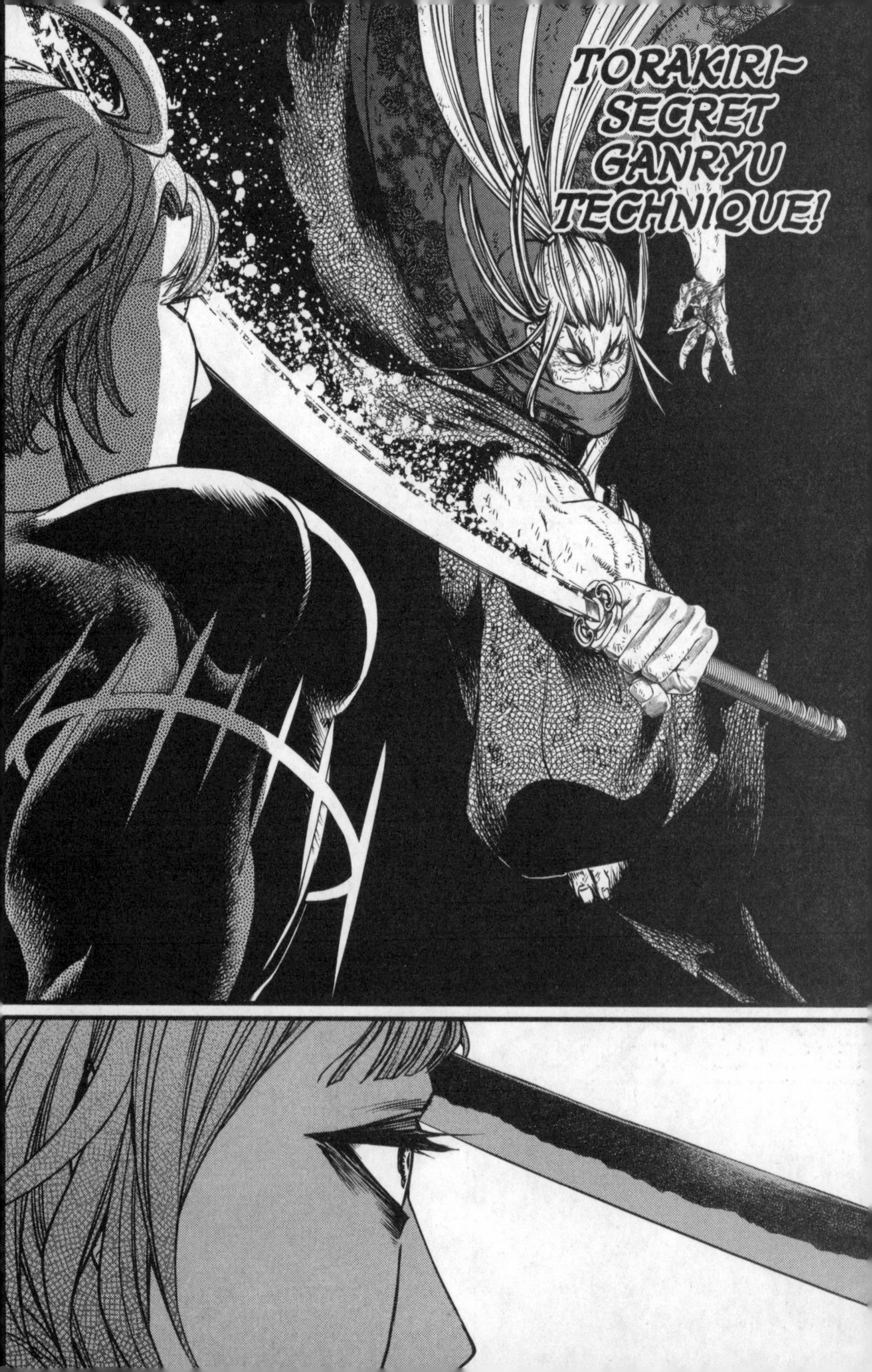
TORAKIRI-
SECRET
GANRYU
TECHNIQUE!

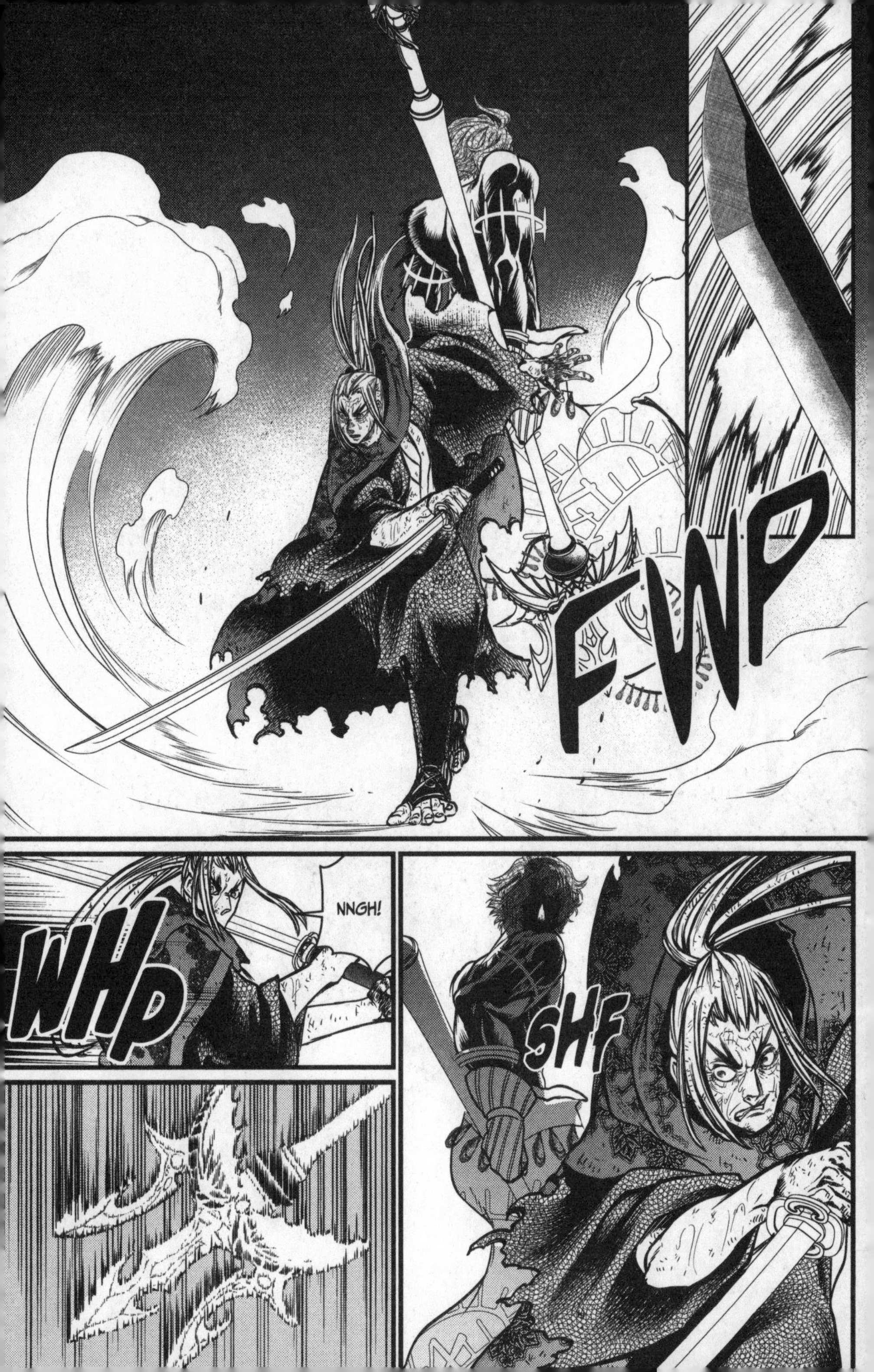
FWP
SHF
NNGH!
WHP

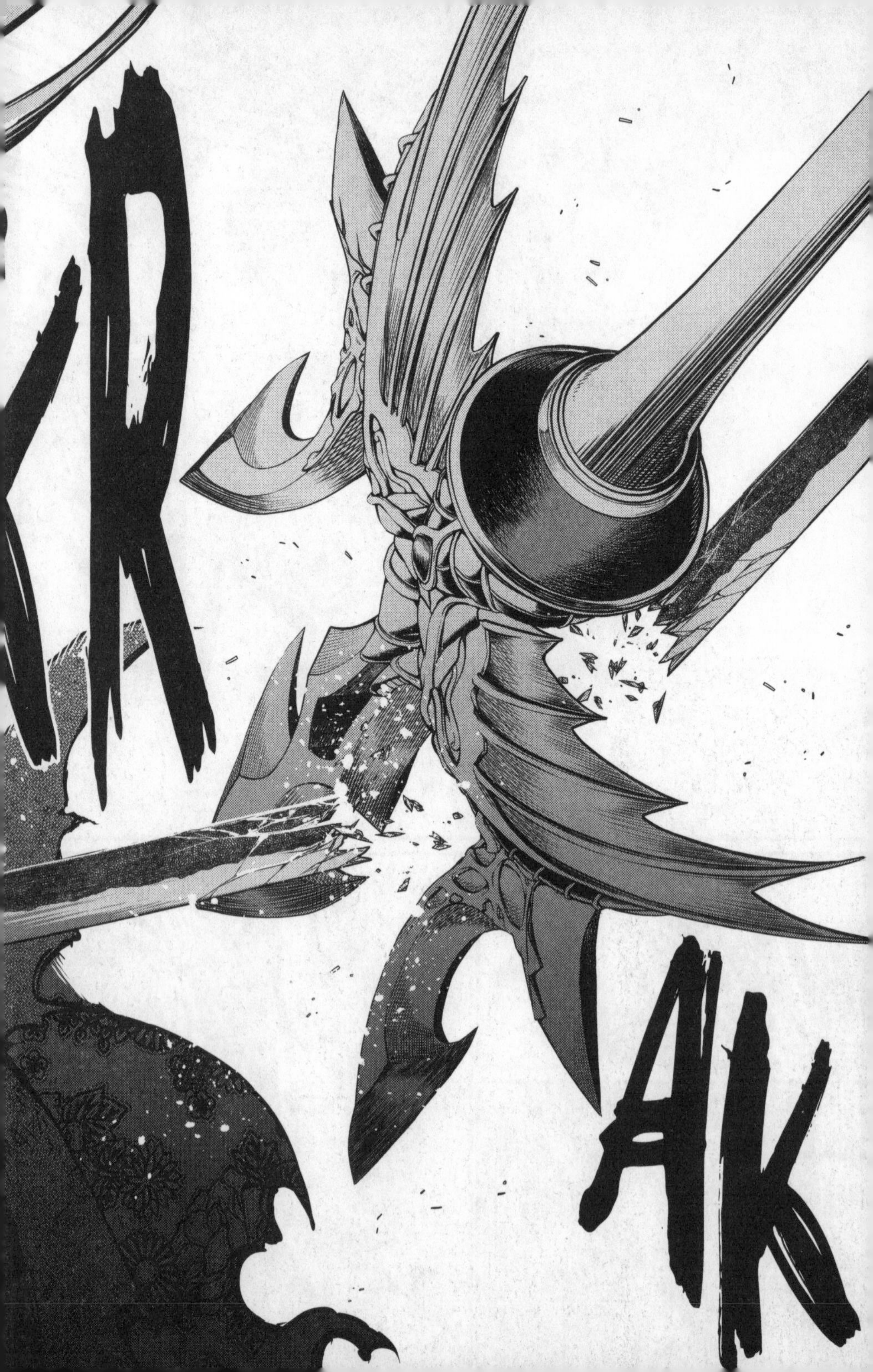
R
AK

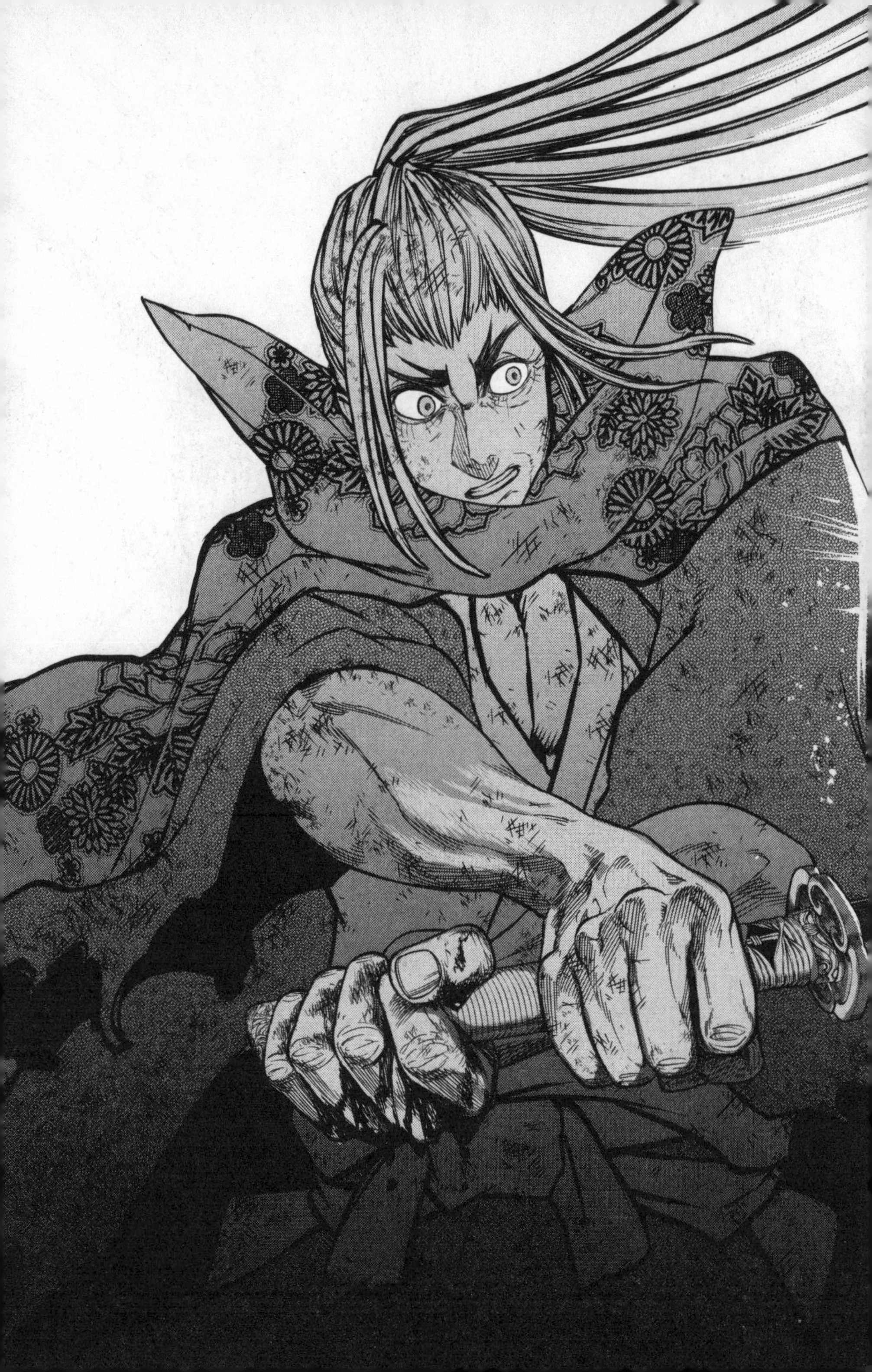

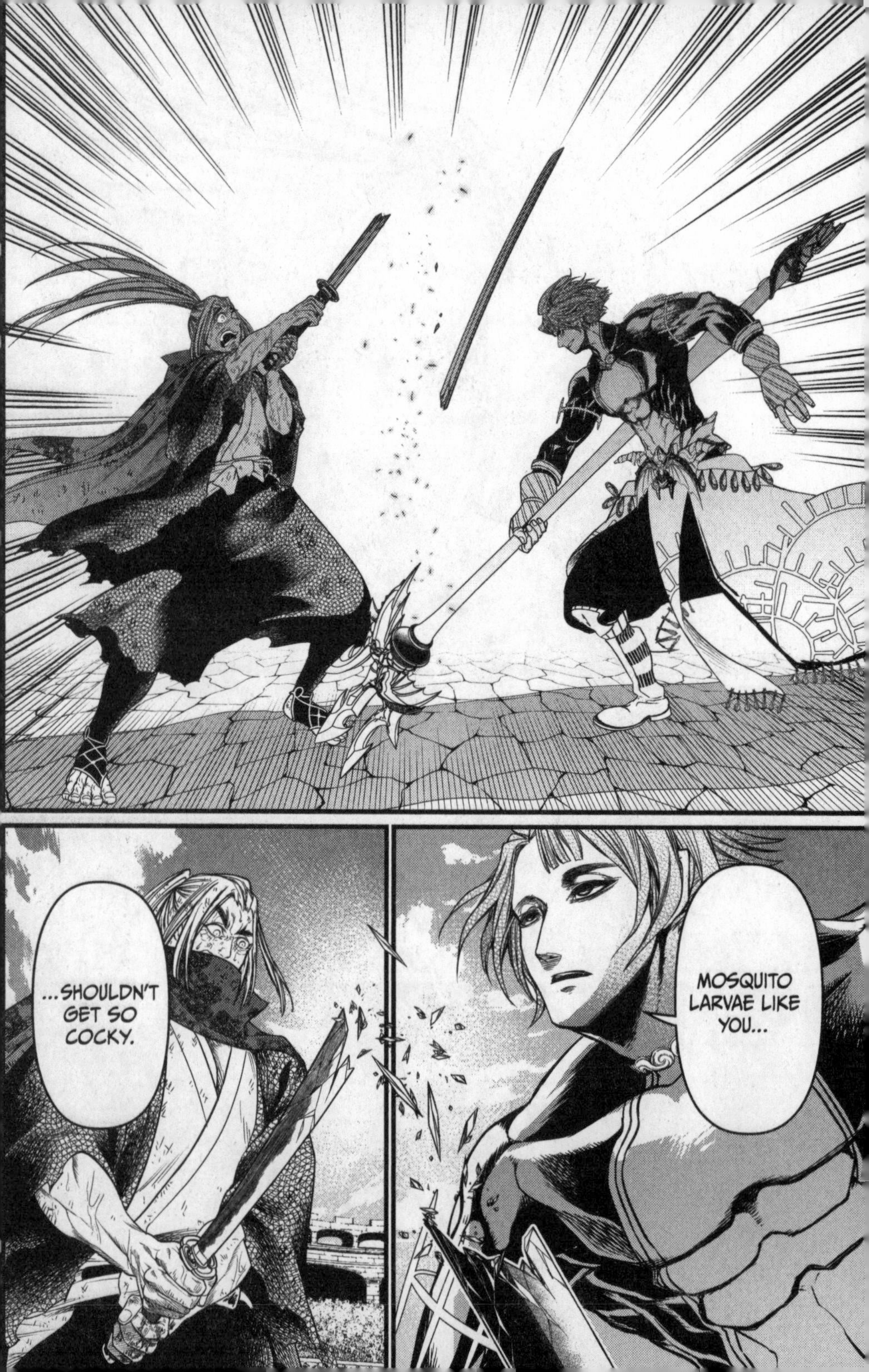
MOSQUITO LARVAE LIKE YOU...
...SHOULDN'T GET SO COCKY.

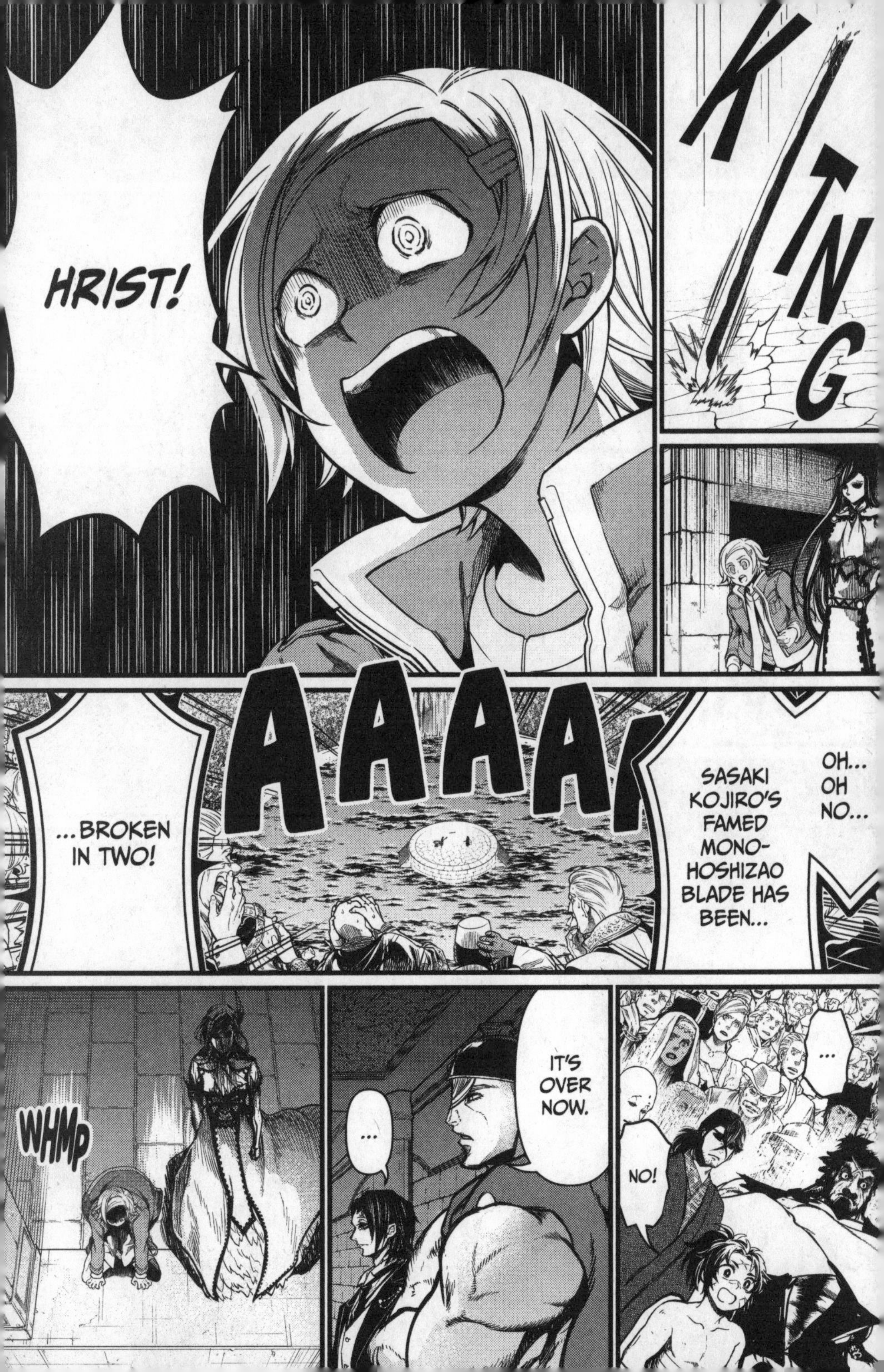
KTING
HRIST!
OH... OH NO...
SASAKI KOJIRO'S FAMED MONO-HOSHIZAO BLADE HAS BEEN...
AAAA
...BROKEN IN TWO!
...
NO!
IT'S OVER NOW.
...
WHMP

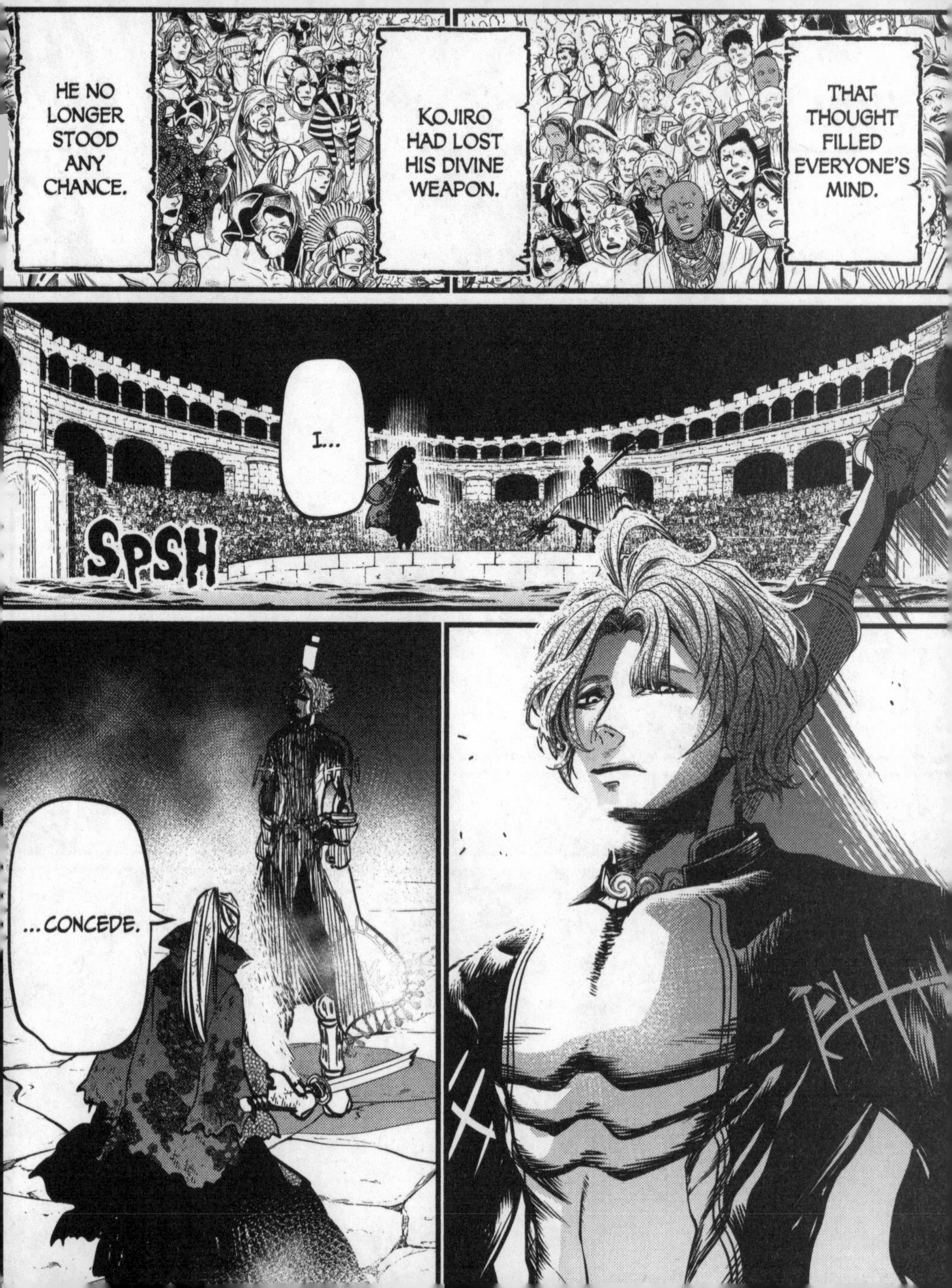
THAT THOUGHT FILLED EVERYONE'S MIND.
KOJIRO HAD LOST HIS DIVINE WEAPON.
HE NO LONGER STOOD ANY CHANCE.
I...
SPSH
...CONCEDE.

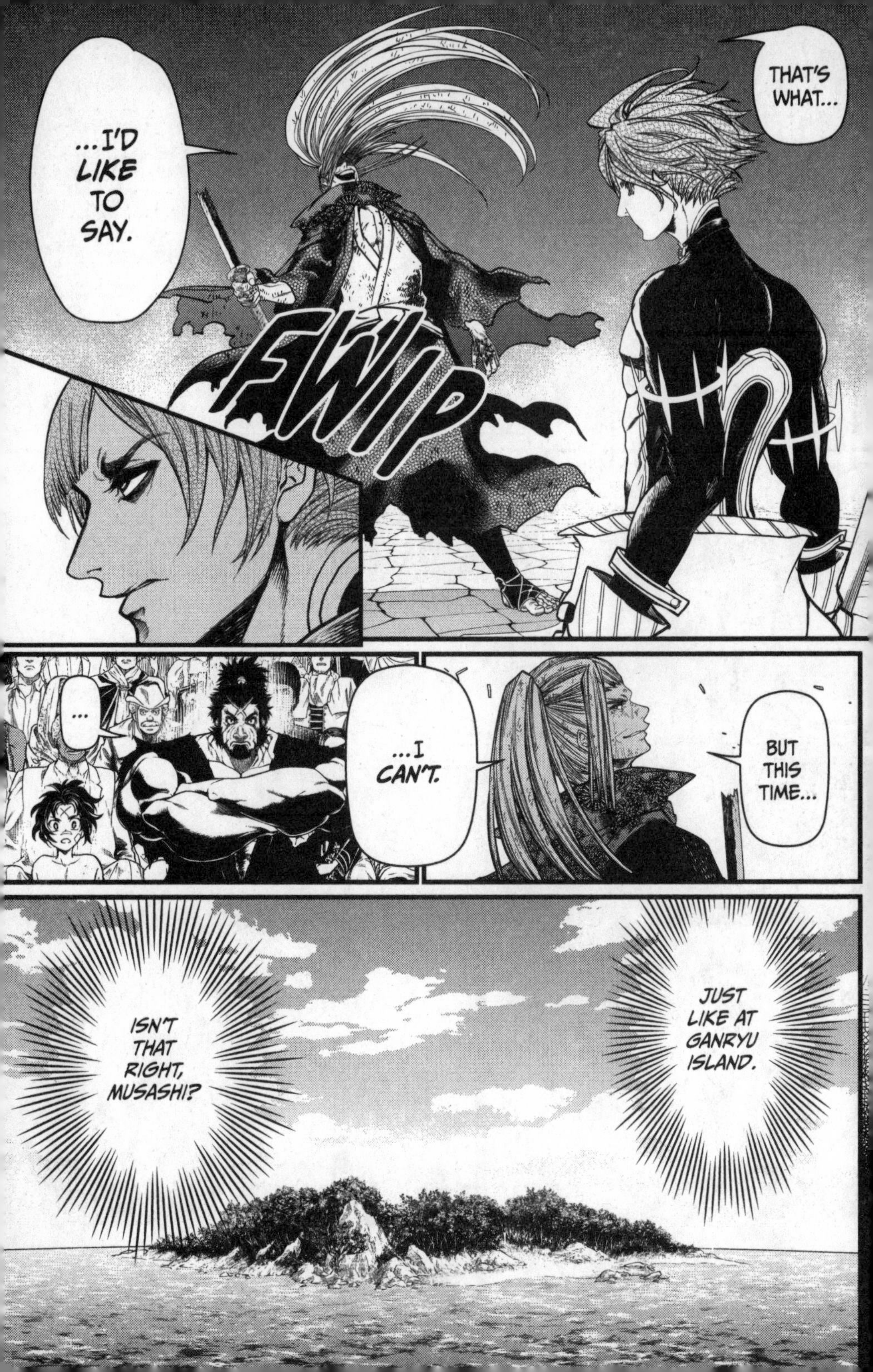
THAT'S WHAT...
...I'D LIKE TO SAY.
FWIP
BUT THIS TIME...
...I CAN'T.
...
JUST LIKE AT GANRYU ISLAND.
ISN'T THAT RIGHT, MUSASHI?

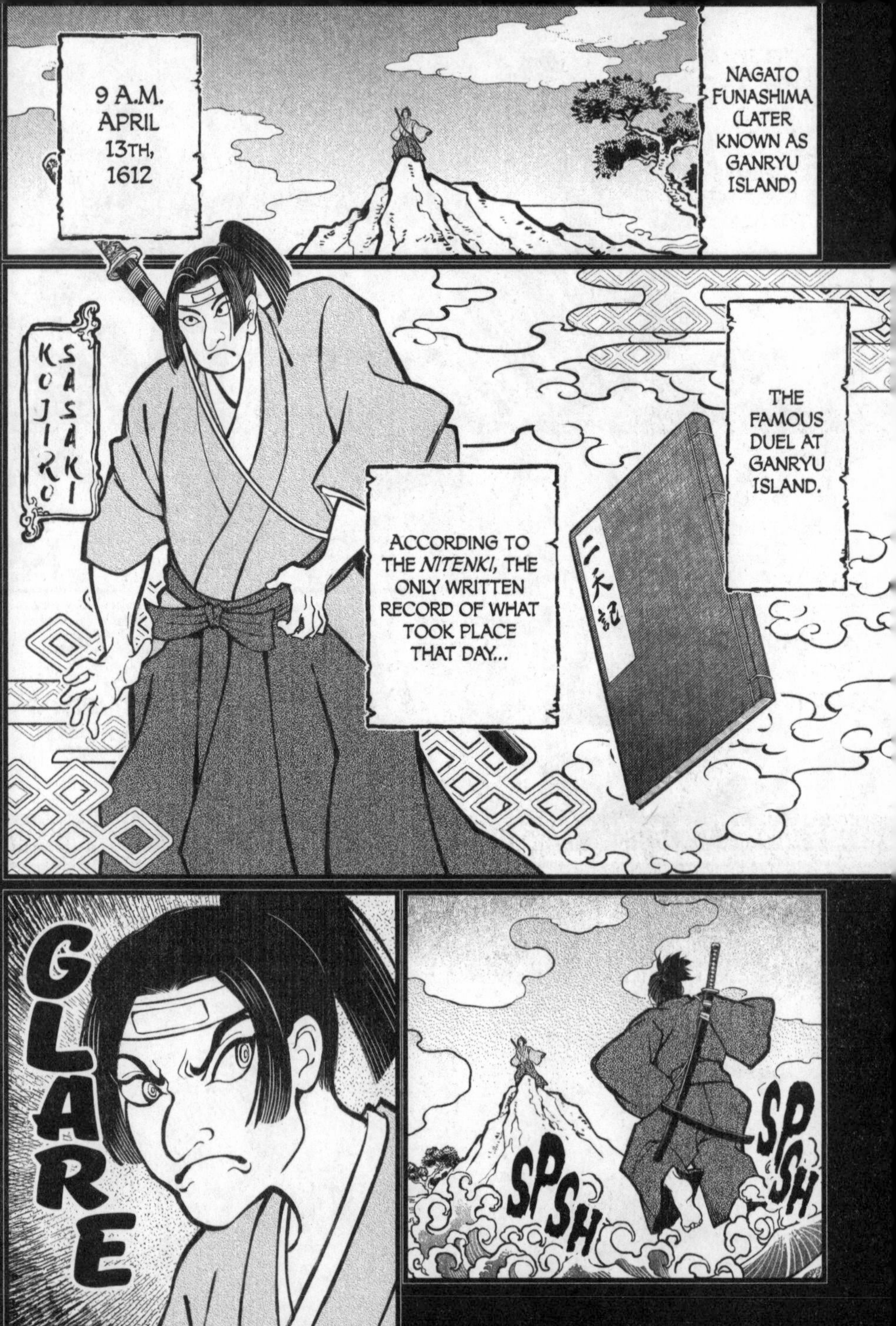
NAGATO FUNASHIMA (LATER KNOWN AS GANRYU ISLAND)
9 A.M. APRIL 13TH, 1612
THE FAMOUS DUEL AT GANRYU ISLAND.
ACCORDING TO THE *NITENKI*, THE ONLY WRITTEN RECORD OF WHAT TOOK PLACE THAT DAY...
二天記
KOJIRO SASAKI
SPSH
SPSH
GLARE

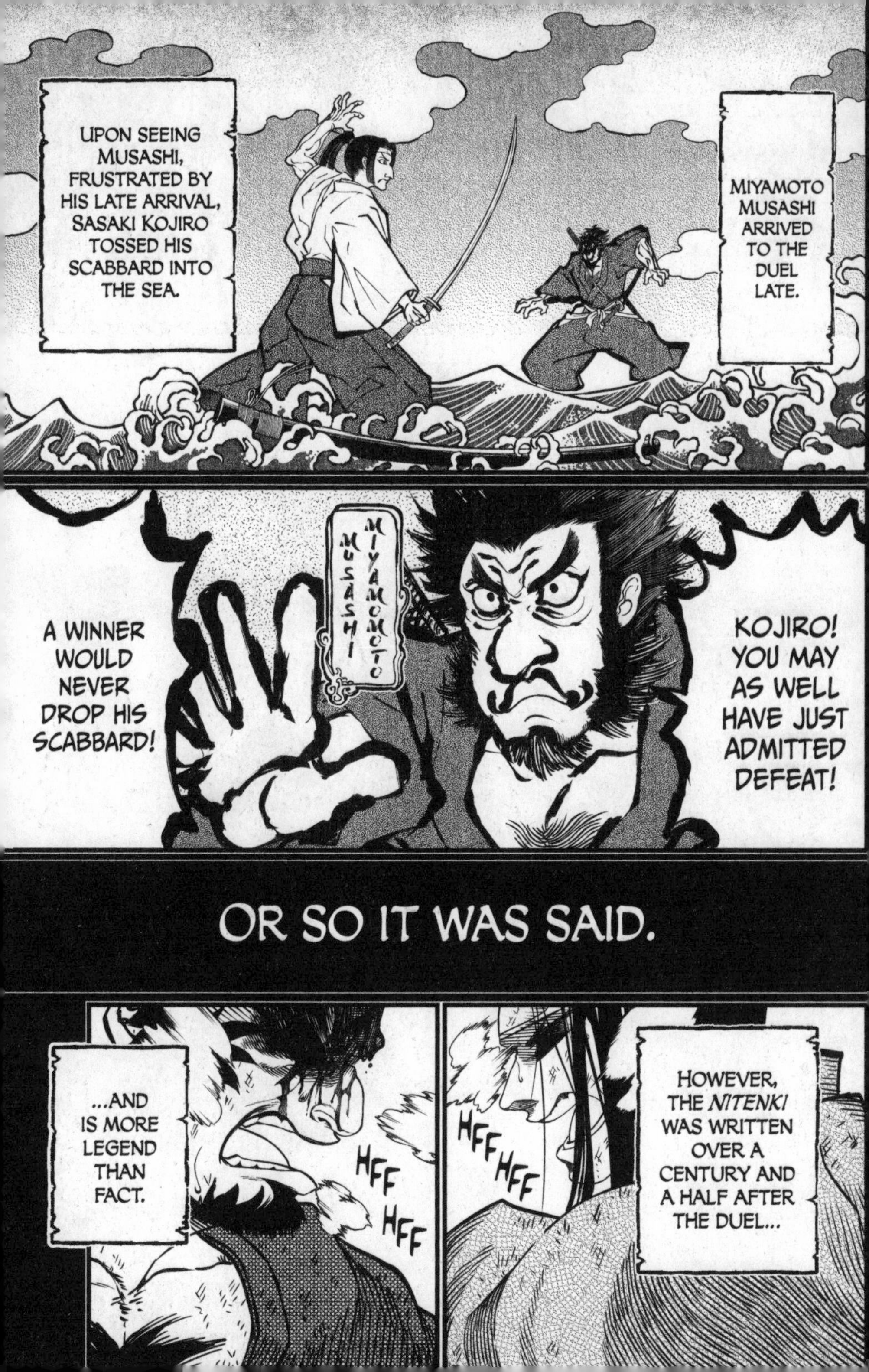
MIYAMOTO MUSASHI ARRIVED TO THE DUEL LATE.
UPON SEEING MUSASHI, FRUSTRATED BY HIS LATE ARRIVAL, SASAKI KOJIRO TOSSED HIS SCABBARD INTO THE SEA.
MIYAMOTO MUSASHI
KOJIRO! YOU MAY AS WELL HAVE JUST ADMITTED DEFEAT!
A WINNER WOULD NEVER DROP HIS SCABBARD!
OR SO IT WAS SAID.
HOWEVER, THE *NITENKI* WAS WRITTEN OVER A CENTURY AND A HALF AFTER THE DUEL...
HFF HFF
...AND IS MORE LEGEND THAN FACT.
HFF HFF

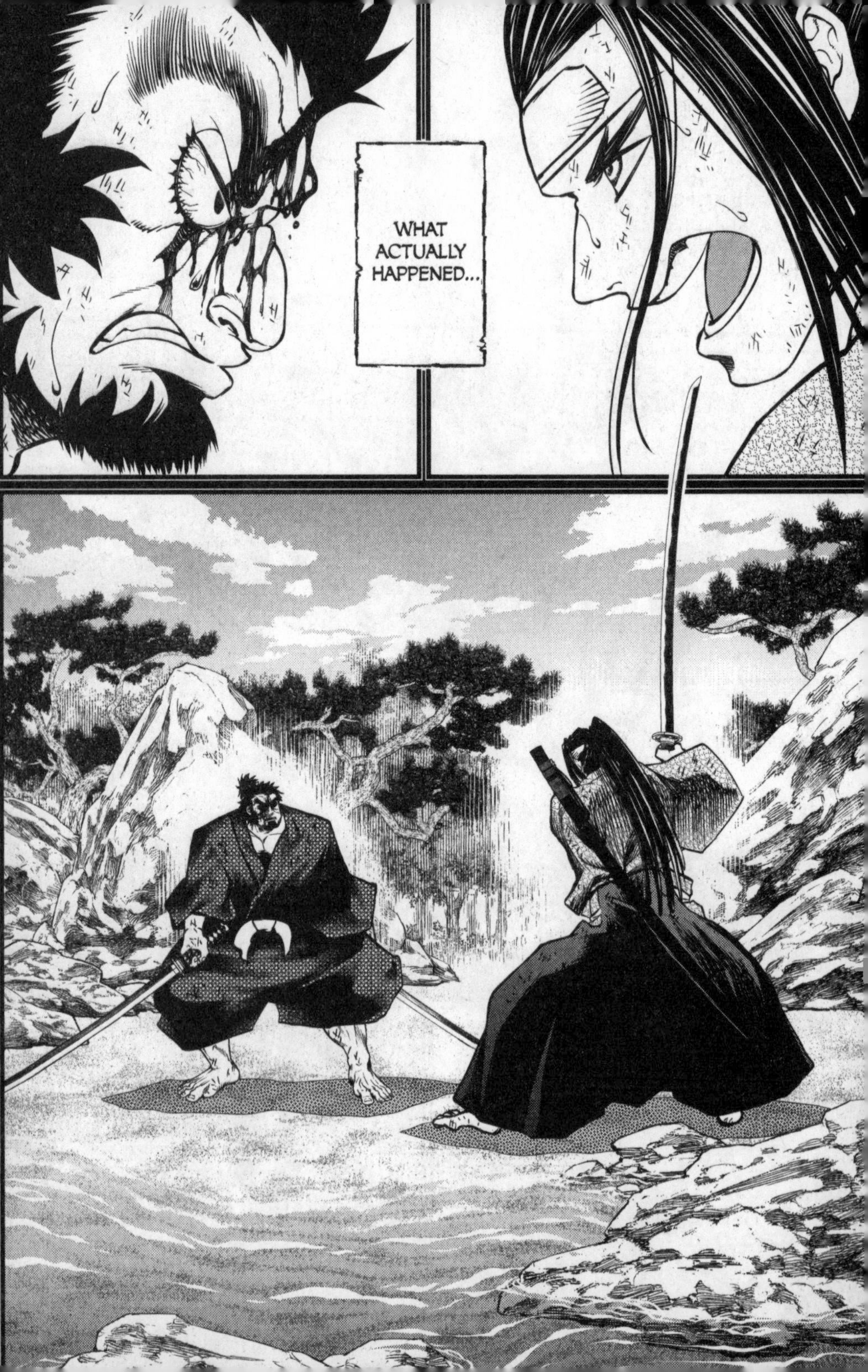
WHAT ACTUALLY HAPPENED...

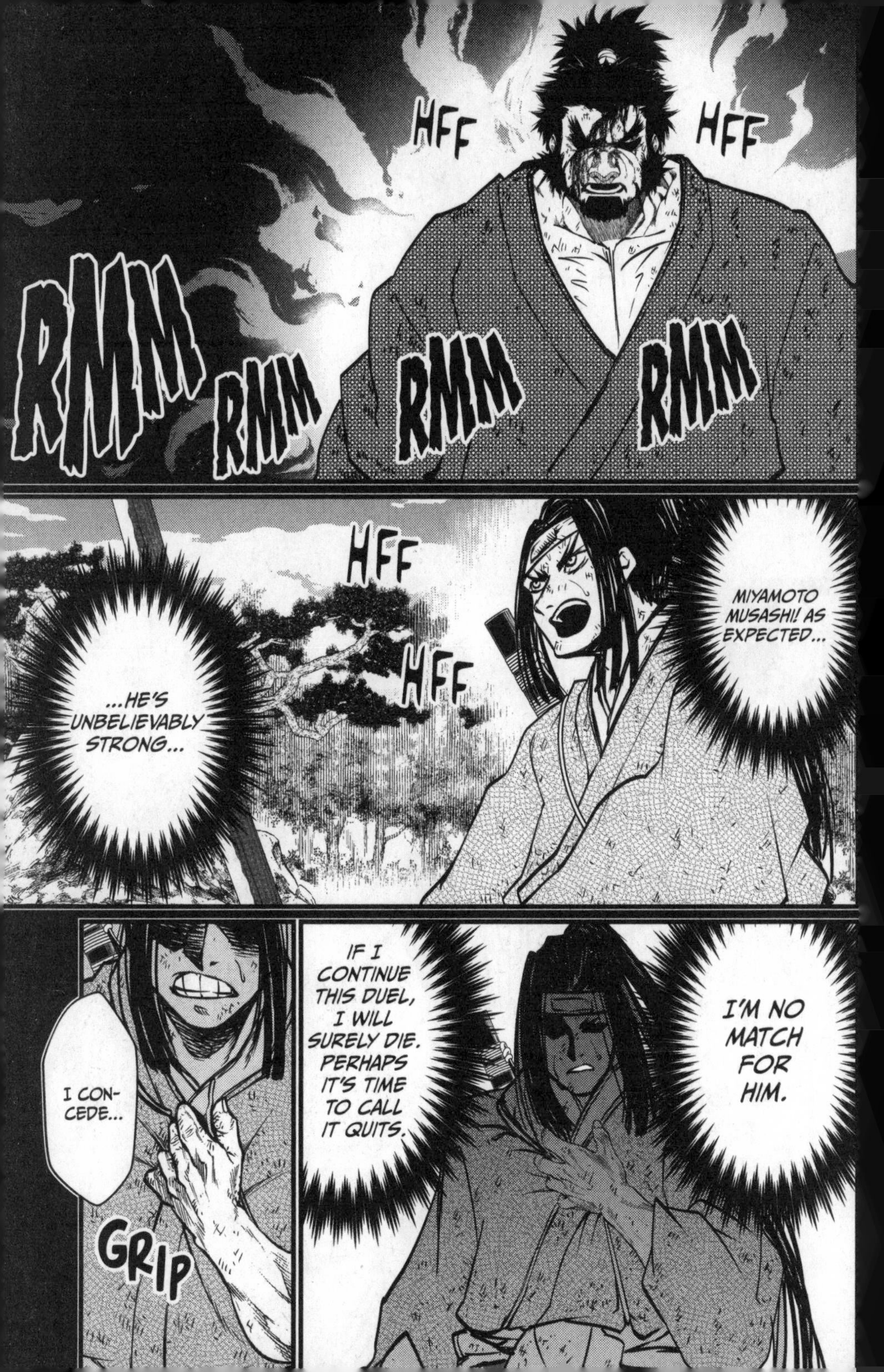
HFF
HFF
RMM
RMM
RMM
RMM
MIYAMOTO MUSASHI! AS EXPECTED...
HFF
HFF
...HE'S UNBELIEVABLY STRONG...
I'M NO MATCH FOR HIM.
IF I CONTINUE THIS DUEL, I WILL SURELY DIE. PERHAPS IT'S TIME TO CALL IT QUITS.
I CON-CEDE...
GRIP

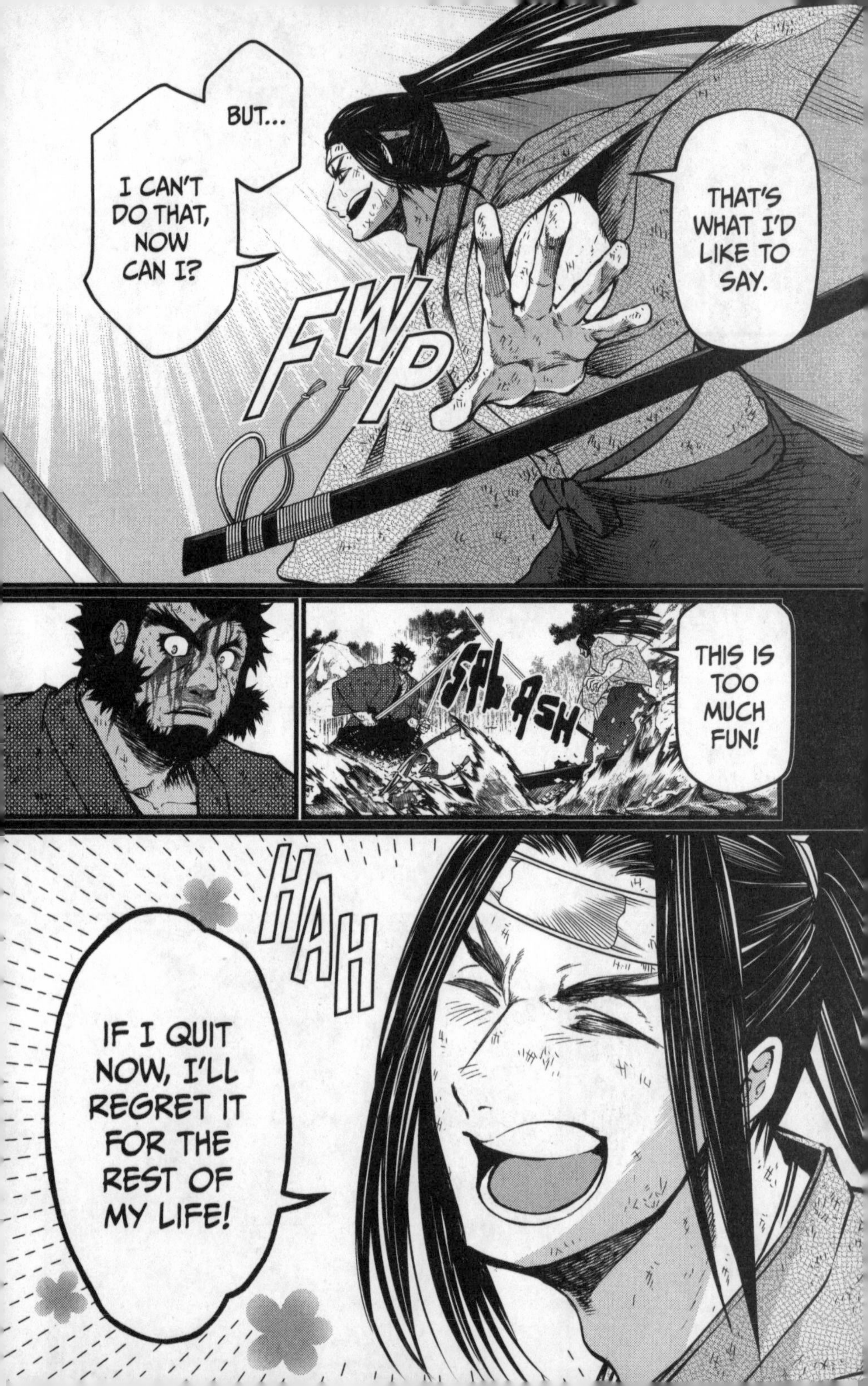
THAT'S WHAT I'D LIKE TO SAY.
BUT...
I CAN'T DO THAT, NOW CAN I?
FWP
THIS IS TOO MUCH FUN!
SPLASH
HAH HAH
IF I QUIT NOW, I'LL REGRET IT FOR THE REST OF MY LIFE!

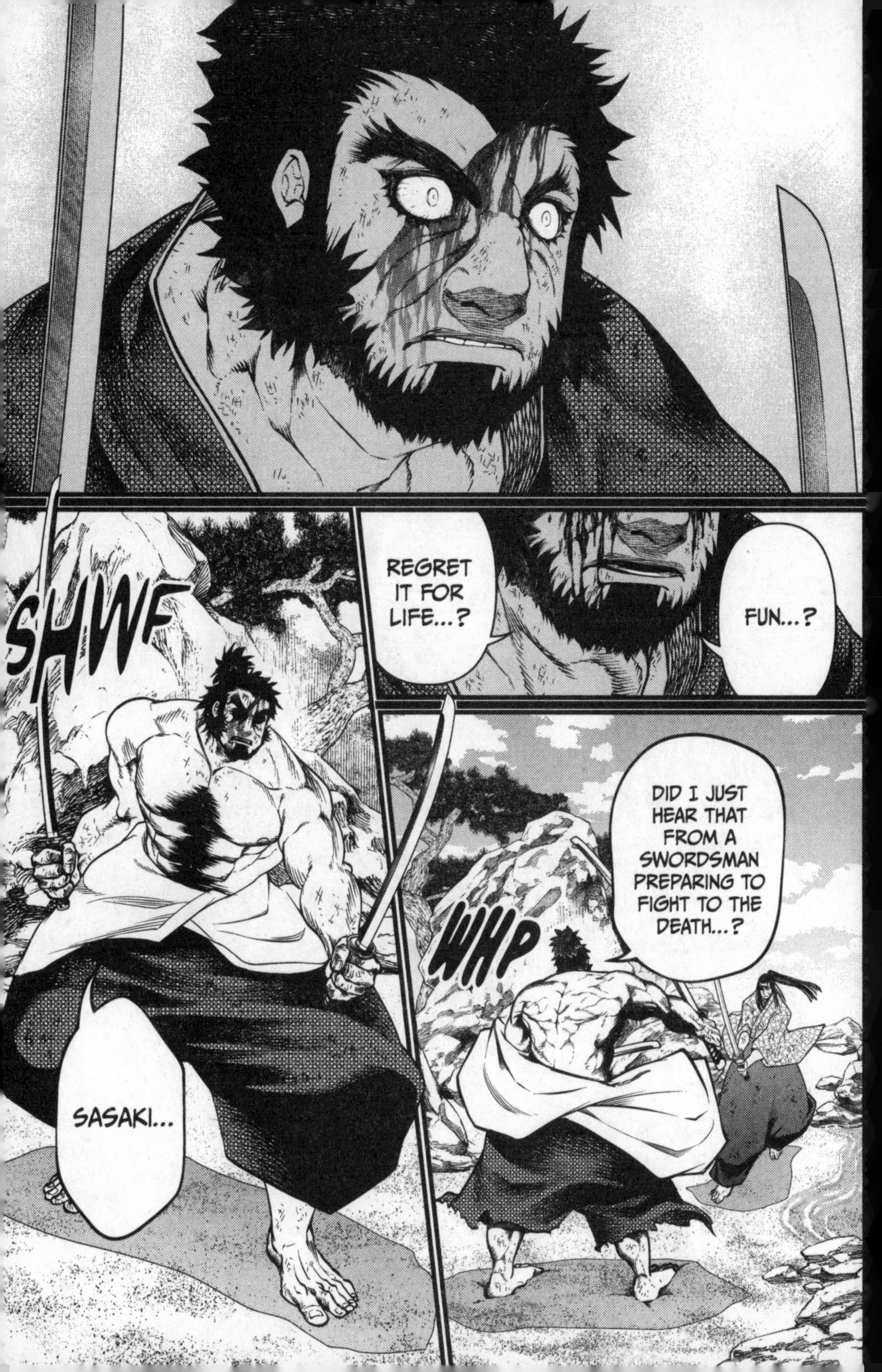
FUN...?
REGRET IT FOR LIFE...?
DID I JUST HEAR THAT FROM A SWORDSMAN PREPARING TO FIGHT TO THE DEATH...?
WHP
SHWF
SASAKI...

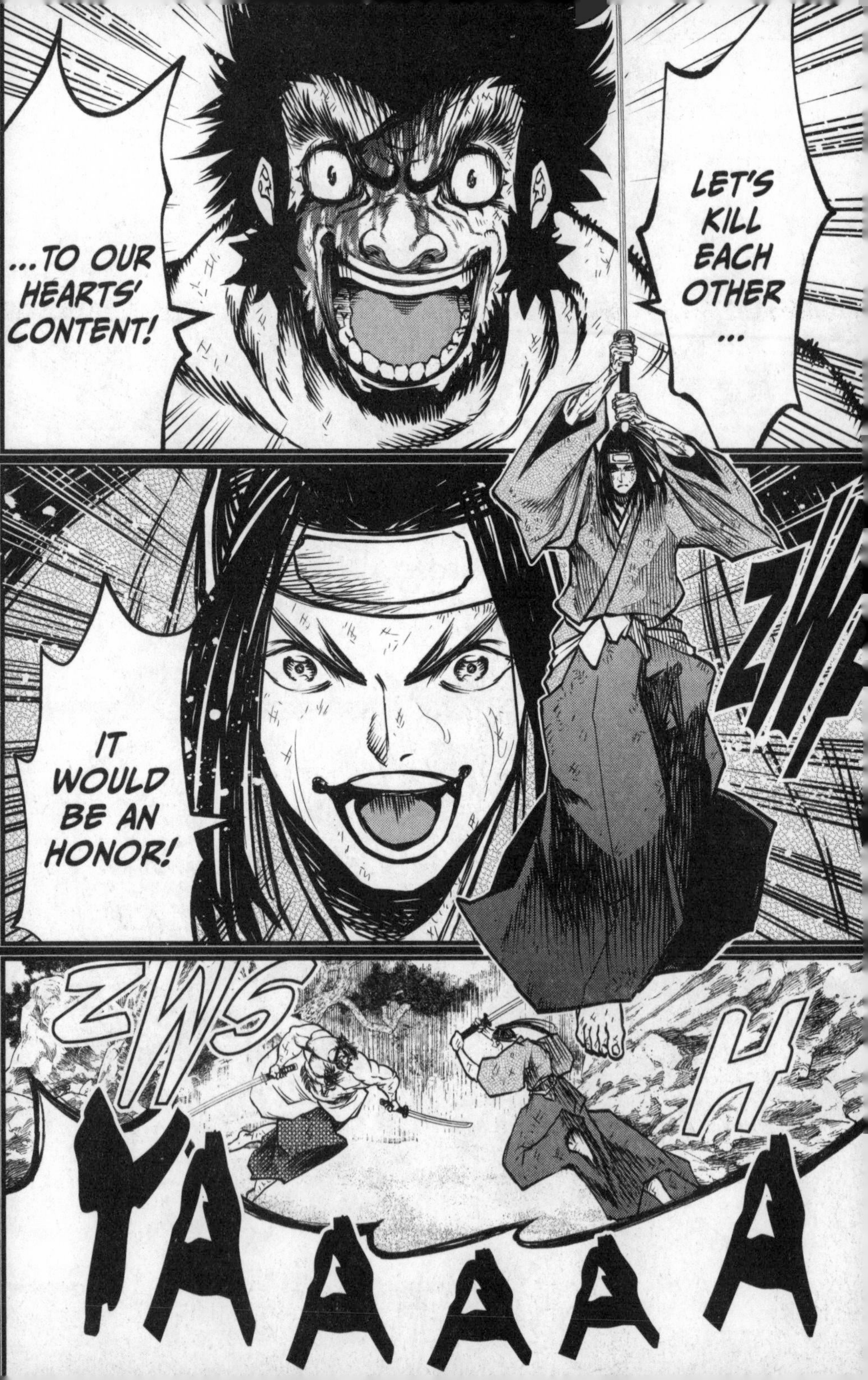
LET'S KILL EACH OTHER ...
...TO OUR HEARTS' CONTENT!
IT WOULD BE AN HONOR!
ZWSH
YAAAAA

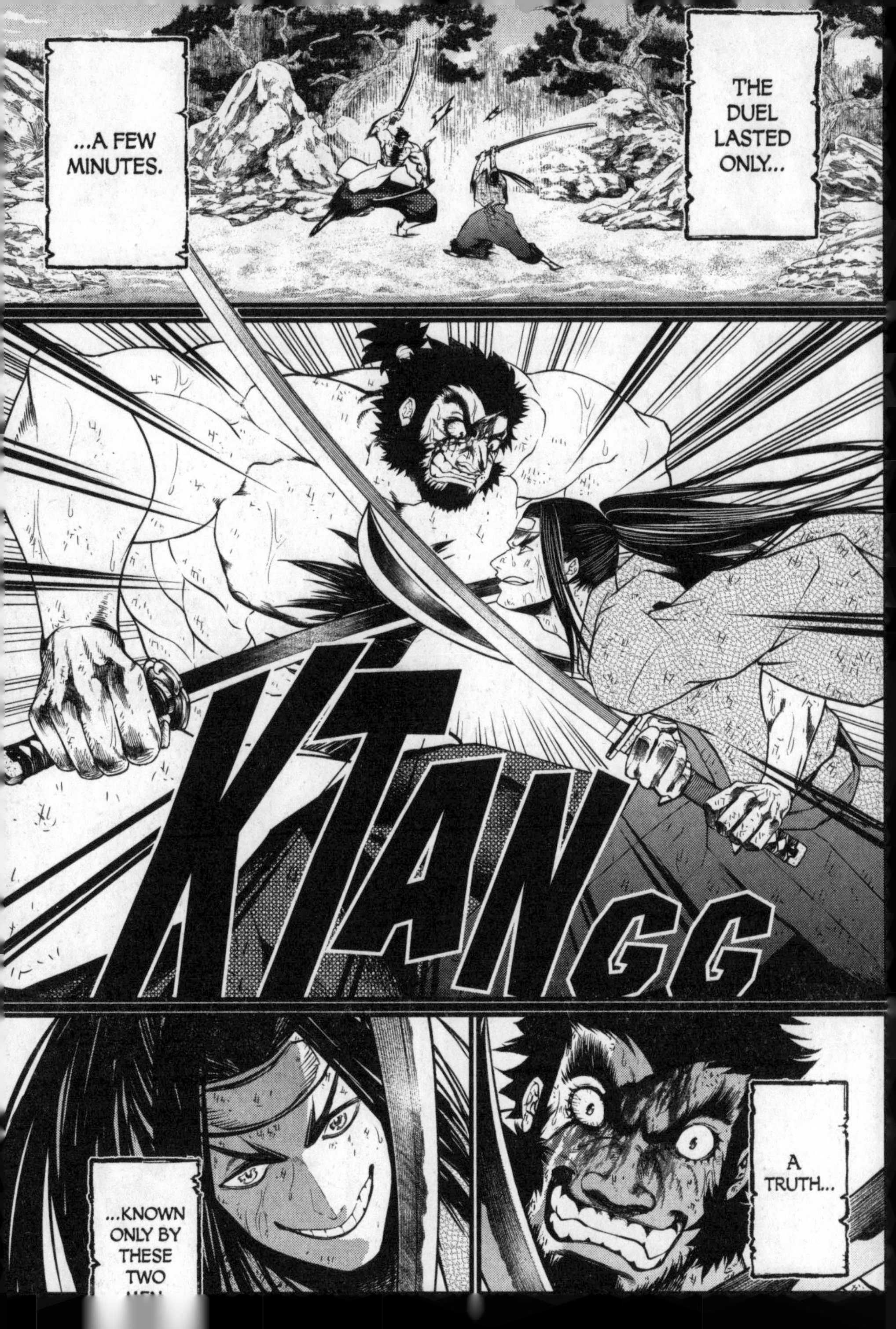
THE DUEL LASTED ONLY...
...A FEW MINUTES.
KLANGG
A TRUTH...
...KNOWN ONLY BY THESE TWO

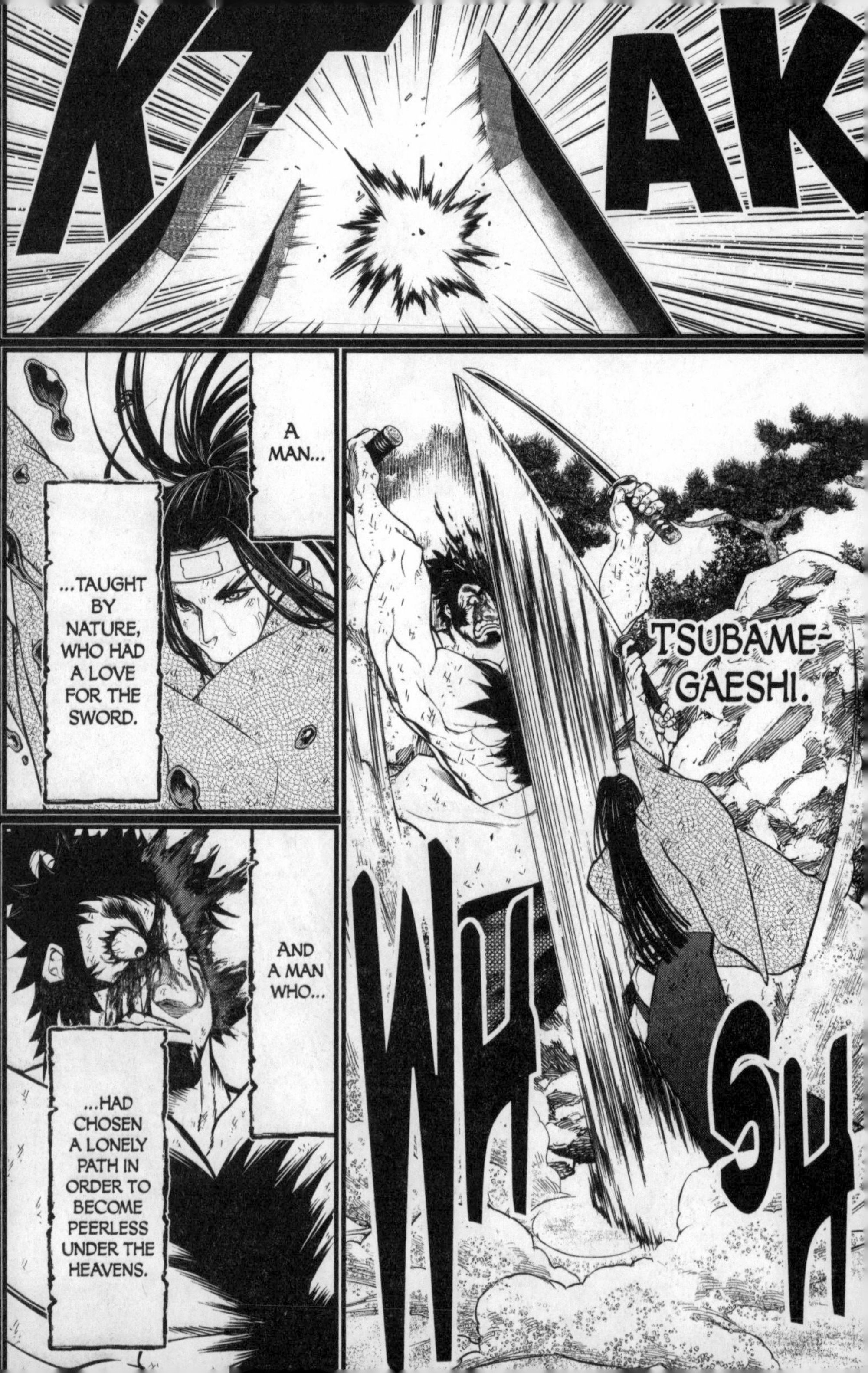
K AK
TSUBAME-GAESHI.
WH SH
A MAN...
...TAUGHT BY NATURE, WHO HAD A LOVE FOR THE SWORD.
AND A MAN WHO...
...HAD CHOSEN A LONELY PATH IN ORDER TO BECOME PEERLESS UNDER THE HEAVENS.

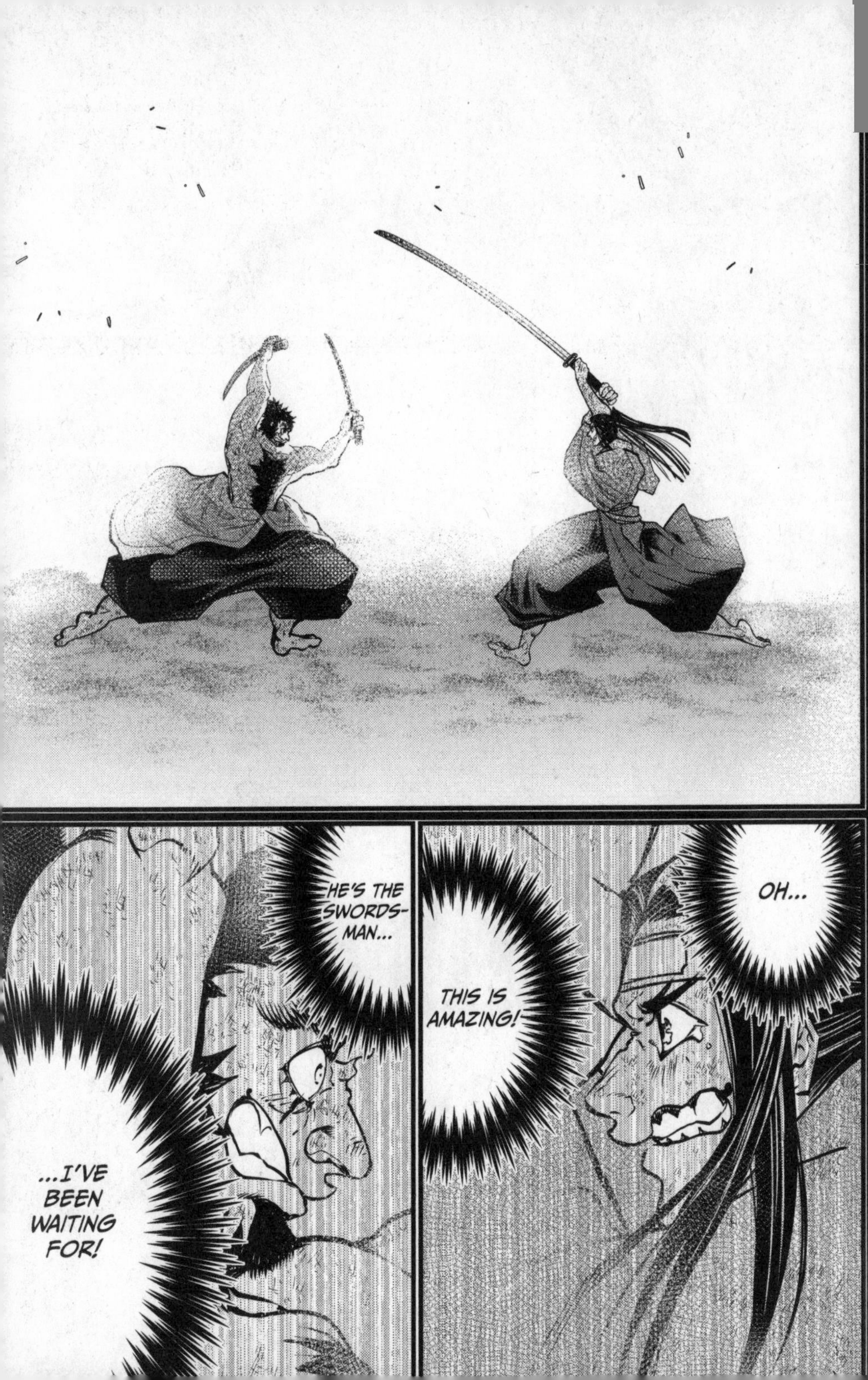
OH...
THIS IS AMAZING!
HE'S THE SWORDS-MAN...
...I'VE BEEN WAITING FOR!

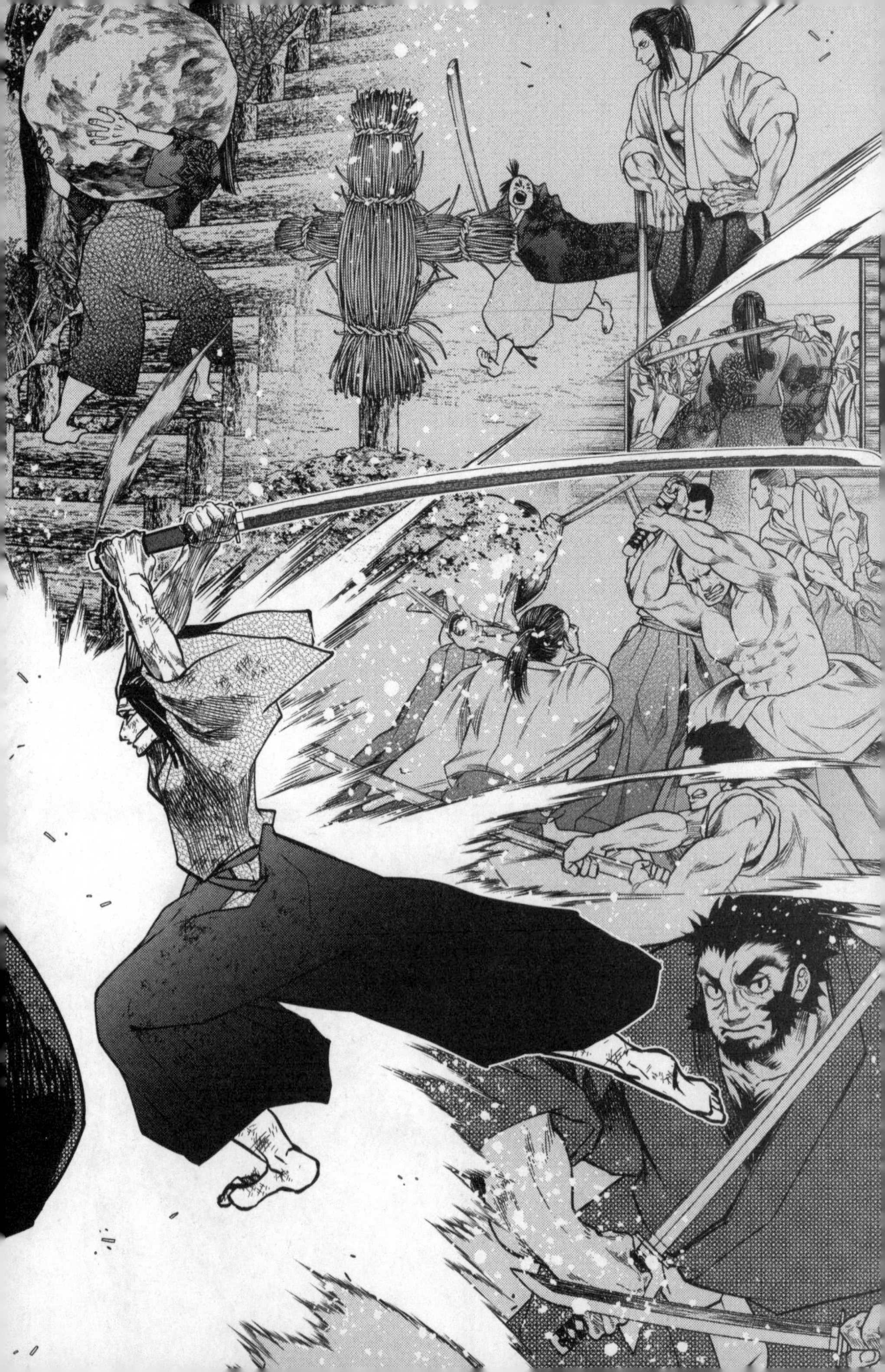

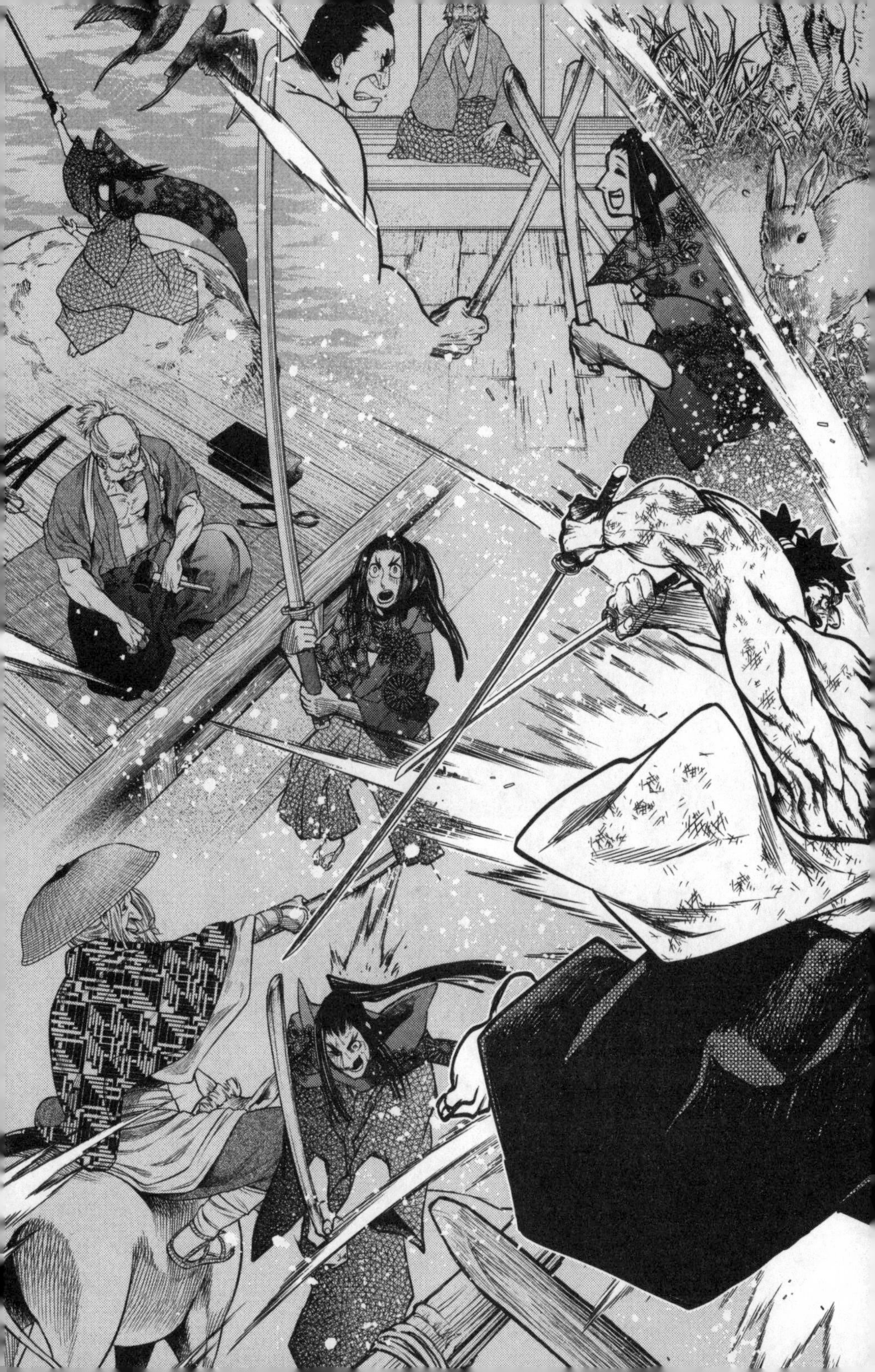

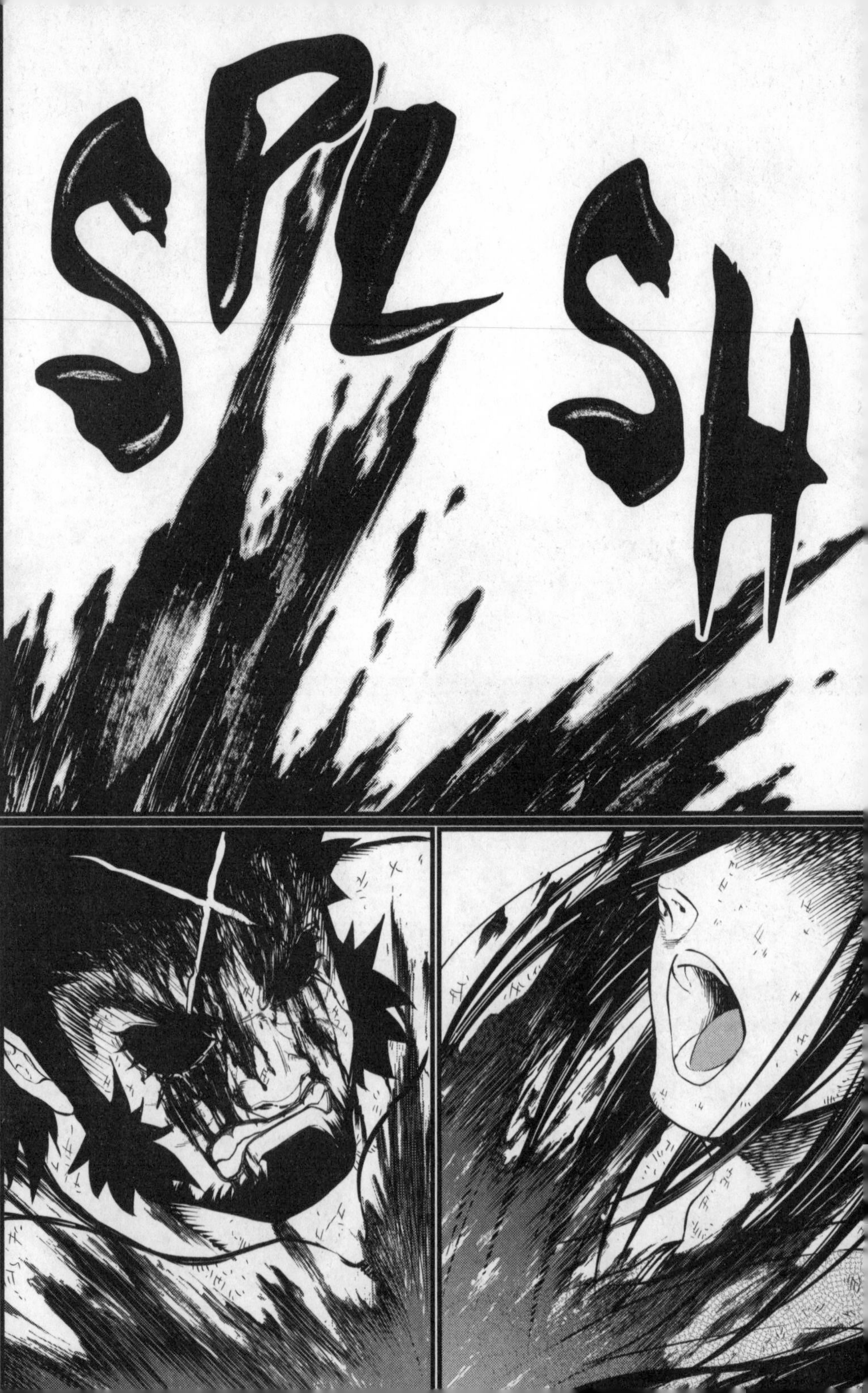
SPLSH

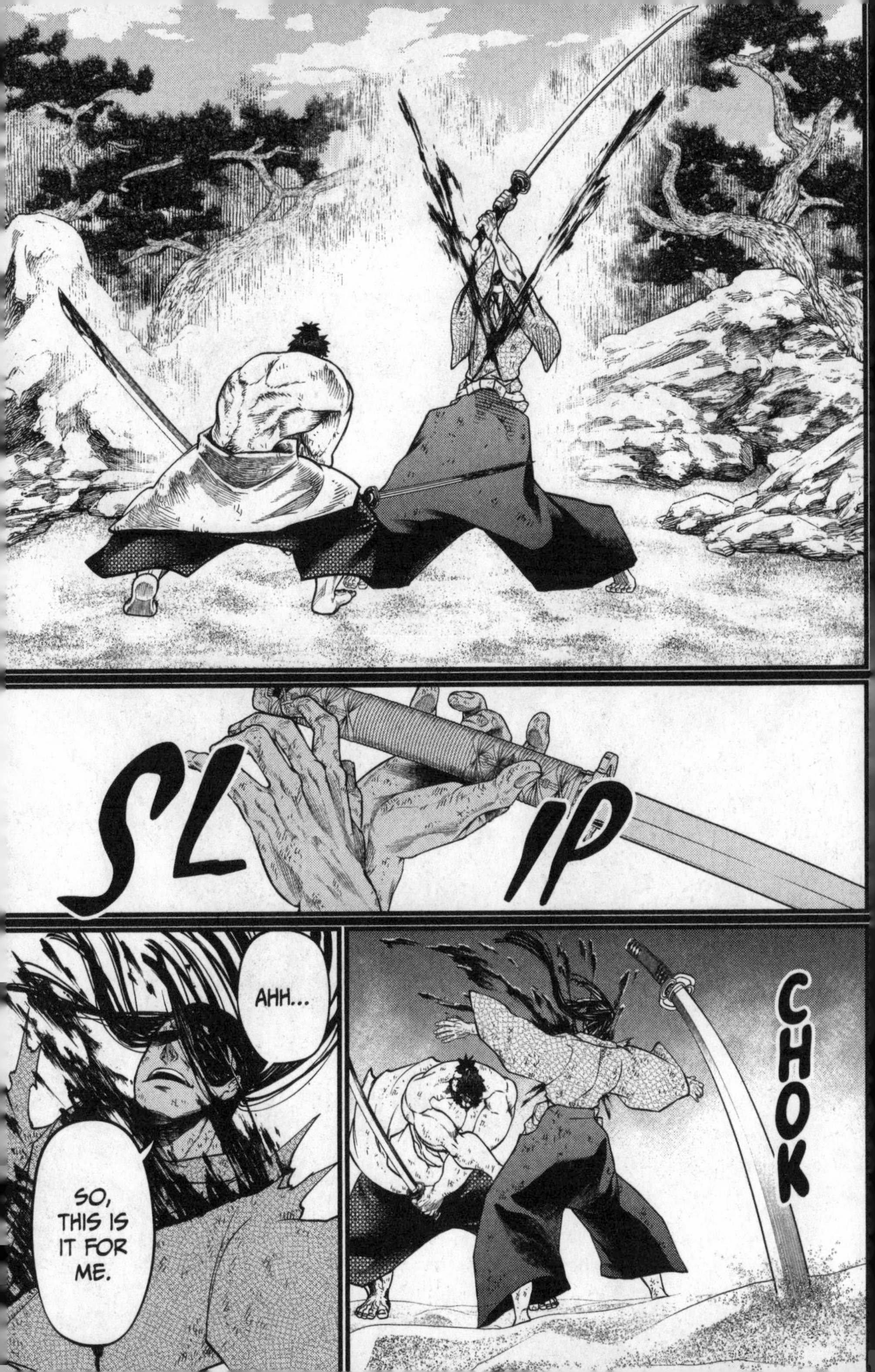
SLIP
CHOK
AHH...
SO, THIS IS IT FOR ME.

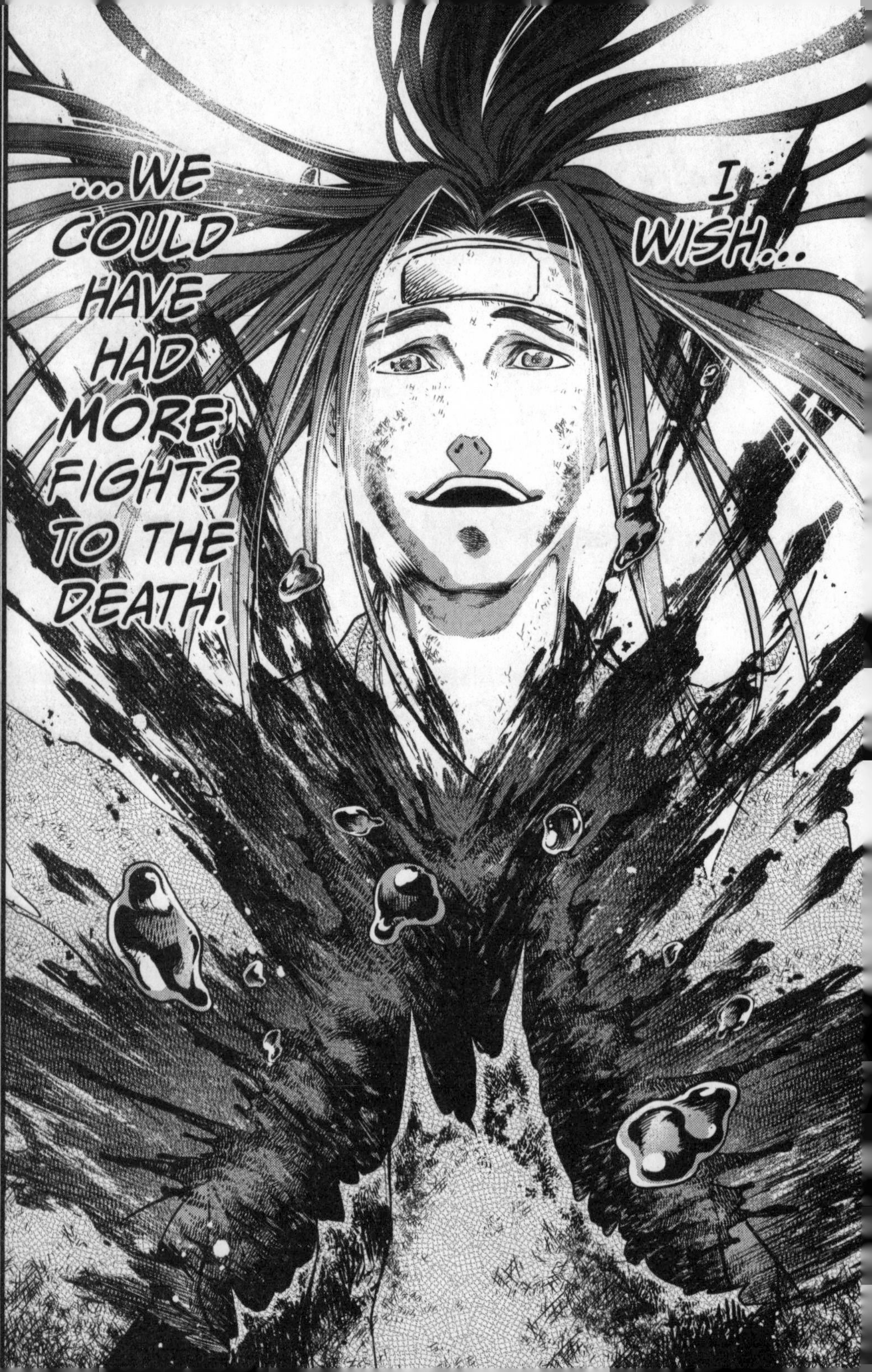
I WISH...
...WE COULD HAVE HAD MORE FIGHTS TO THE DEATH.

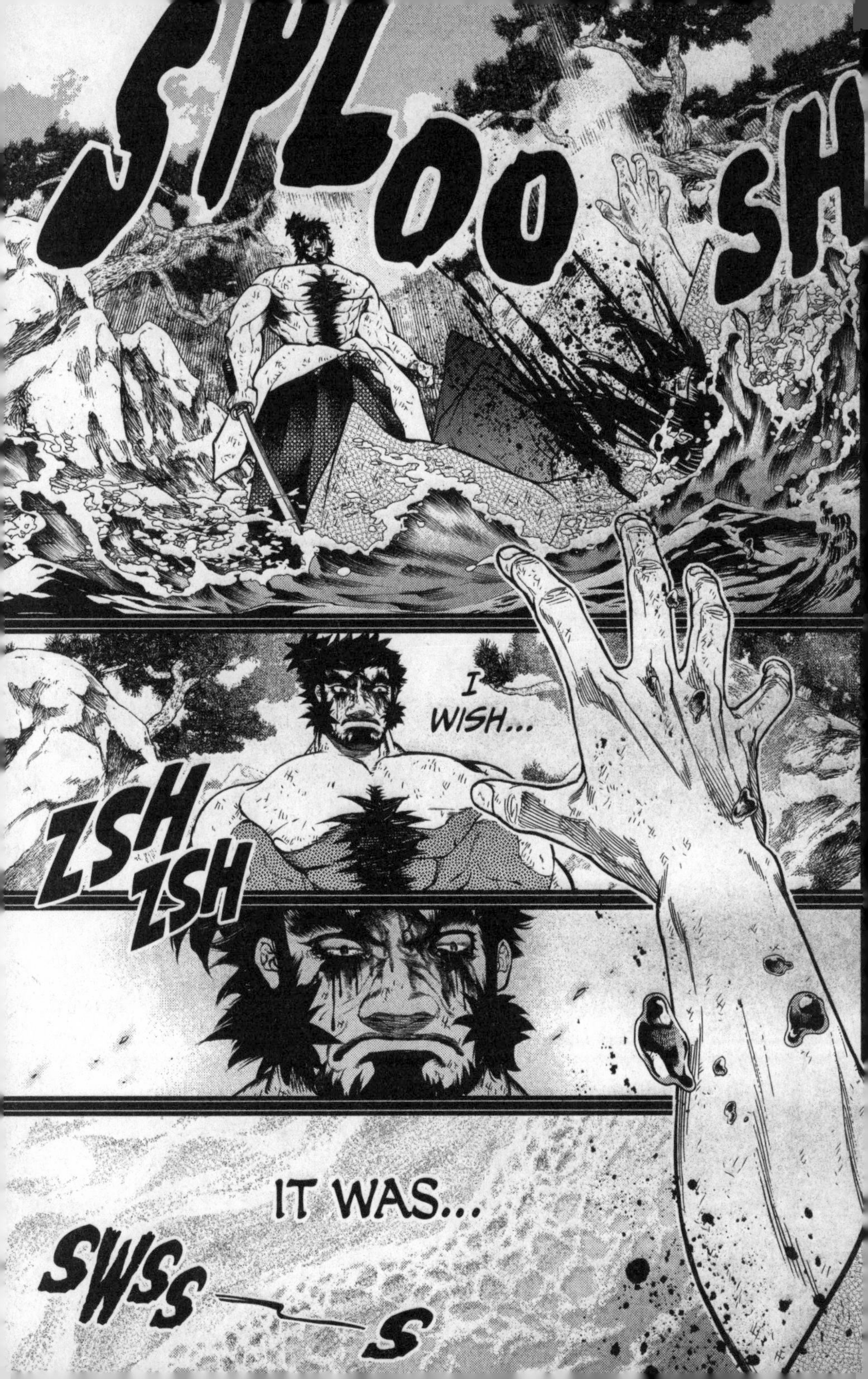
SPLOOSH
I WISH...
ZSH ZSH
IT WAS...
SWSS—S

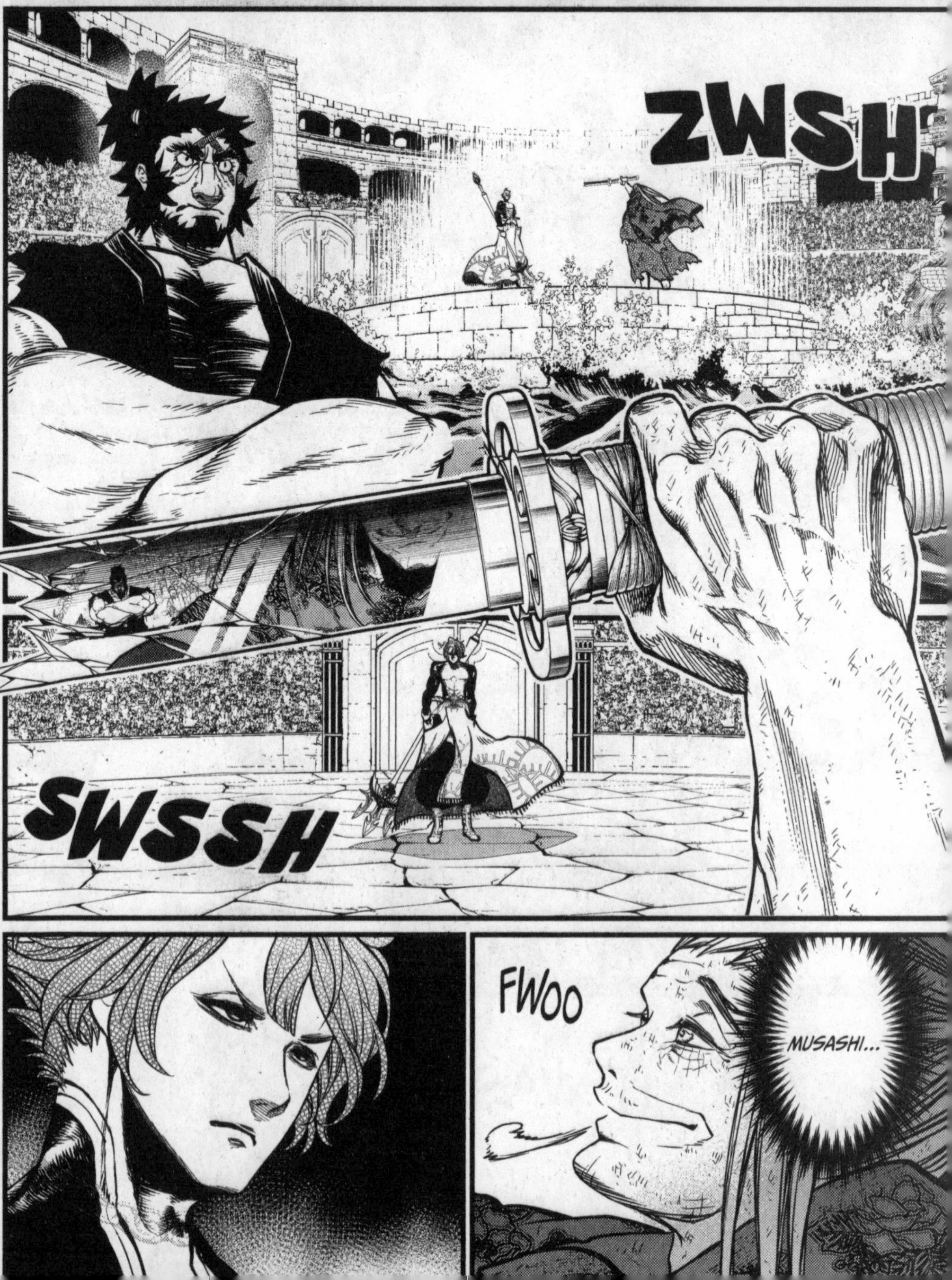
ZWSH
SWSSH
FWOO
MUSASHI...

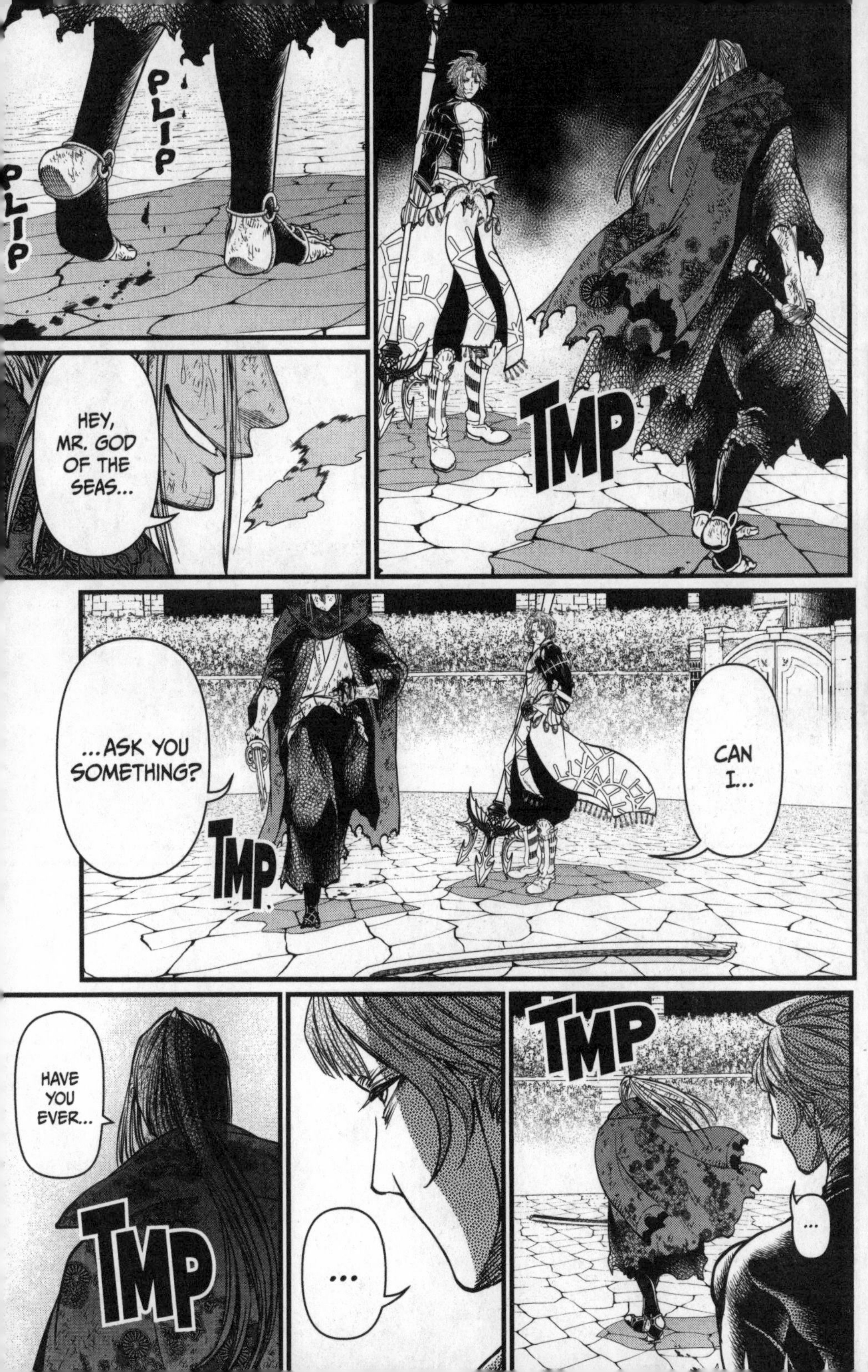
TMP
PLIP
PLIP
HEY, MR. GOD OF THE SEAS...
CAN I...
...ASK YOU SOMETHING?
TMP
TMP
...
...
HAVE YOU EVER...
TMP

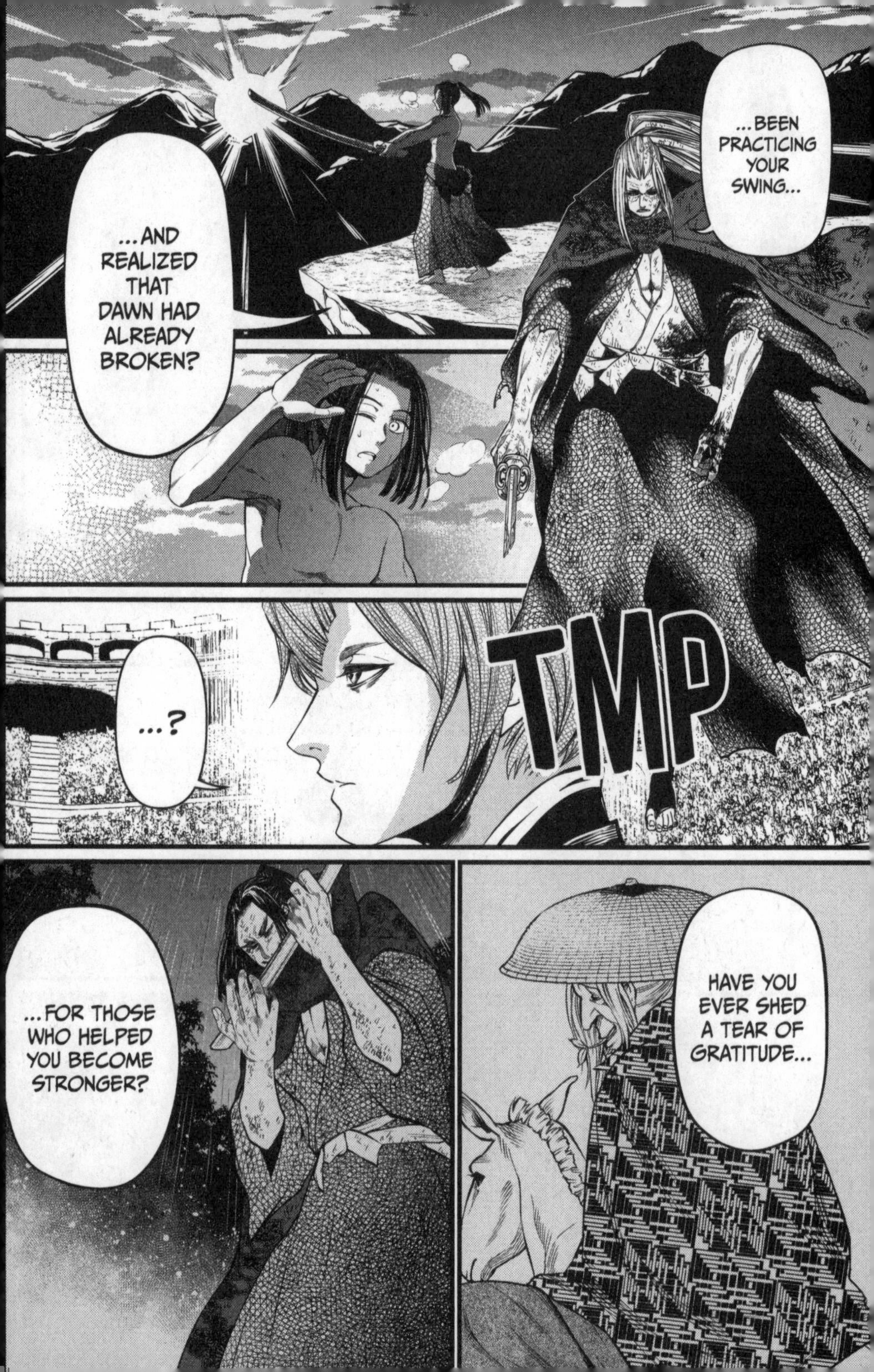
...BEEN PRACTICING YOUR SWING...
...AND REALIZED THAT DAWN HAD ALREADY BROKEN?
TMP
...?
HAVE YOU EVER SHED A TEAR OF GRATITUDE...
...FOR THOSE WHO HELPED YOU BECOME STRONGER?

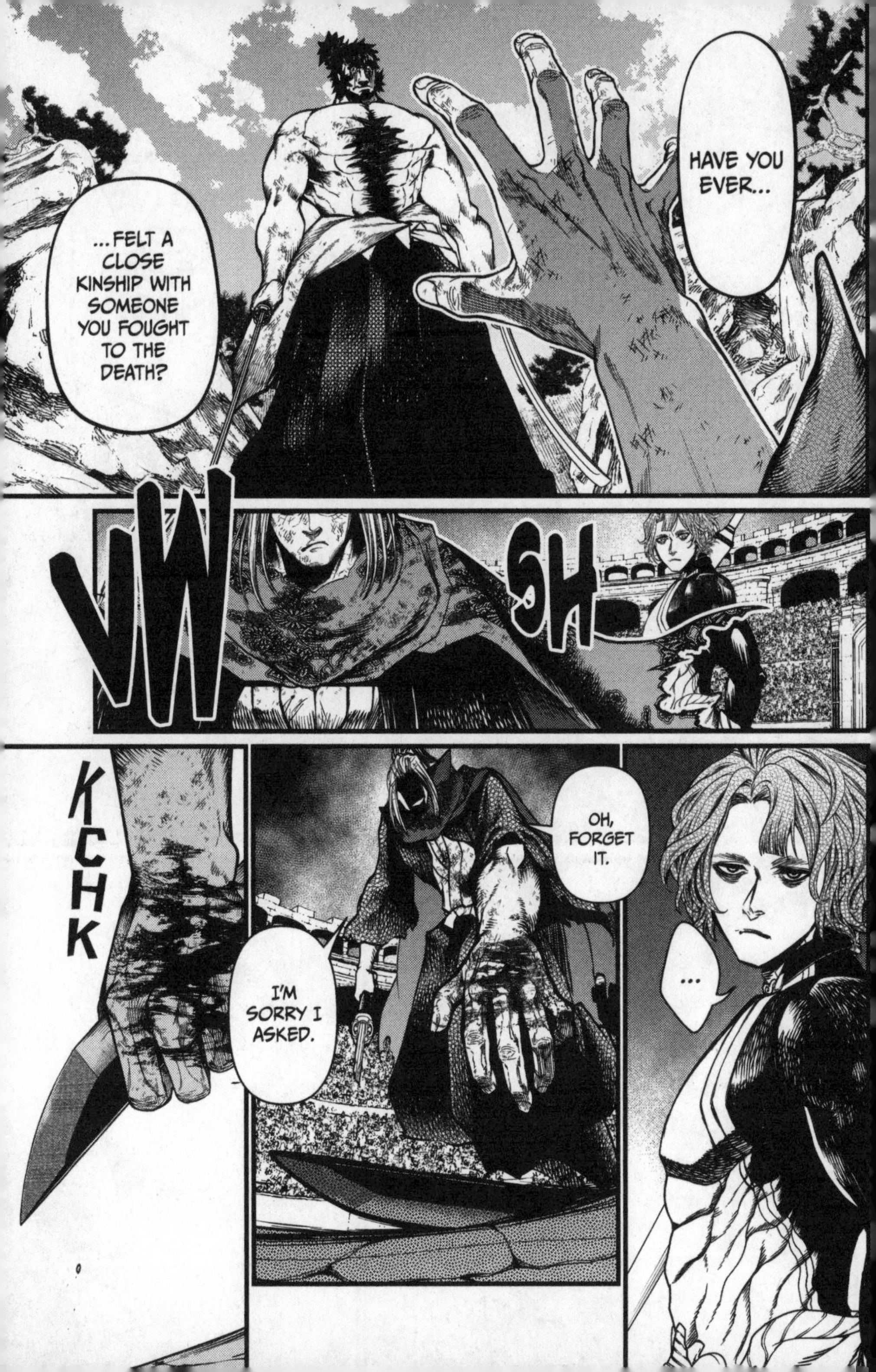
HAVE YOU EVER...
...FELT A CLOSE KINSHIP WITH SOMEONE YOU FOUGHT TO THE DEATH?
VWSH
...
OH, FORGET IT.
I'M SORRY I ASKED.
KCHK

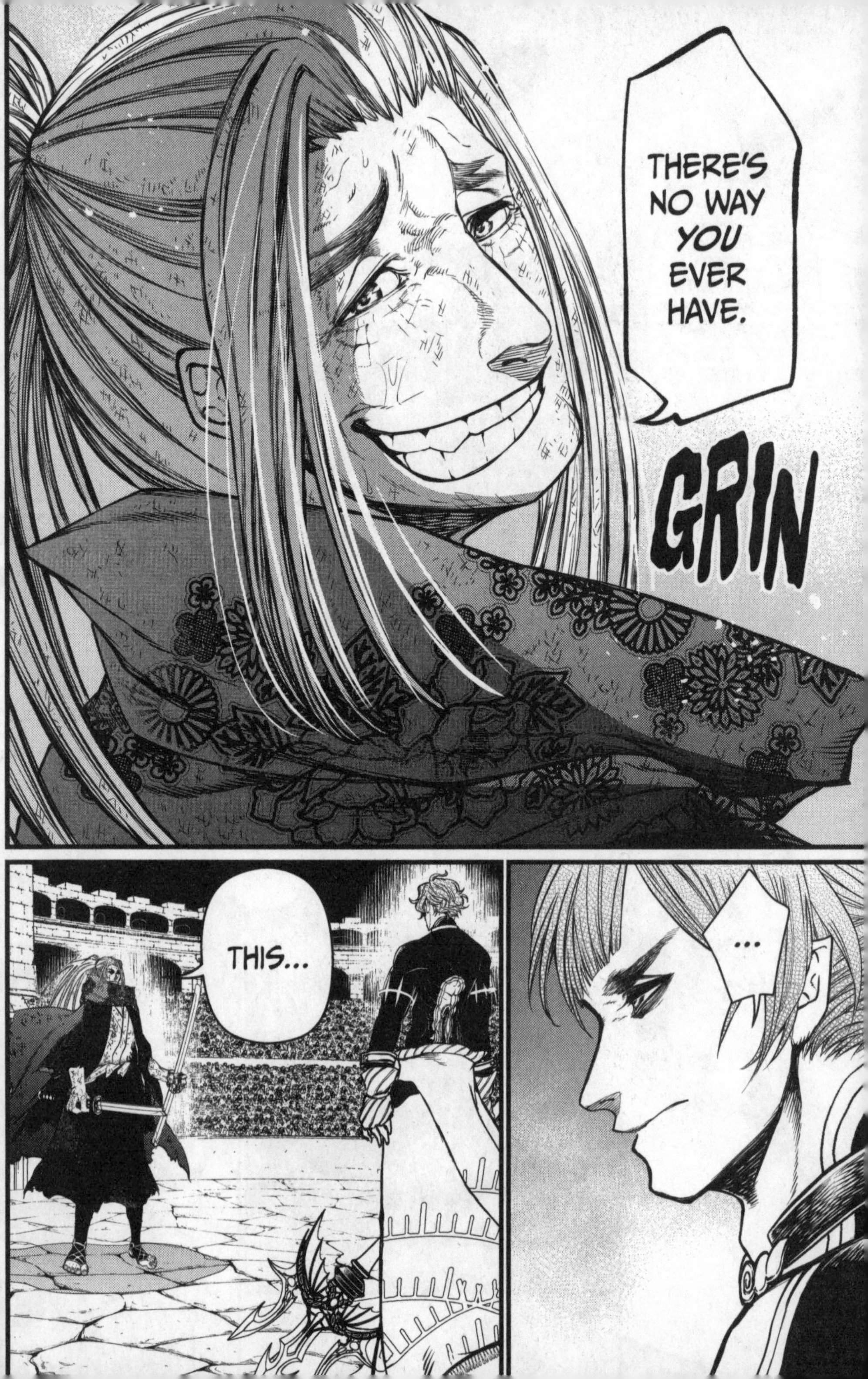
THERE'S NO WAY YOU EVER HAVE.
GRIN
...
THIS...

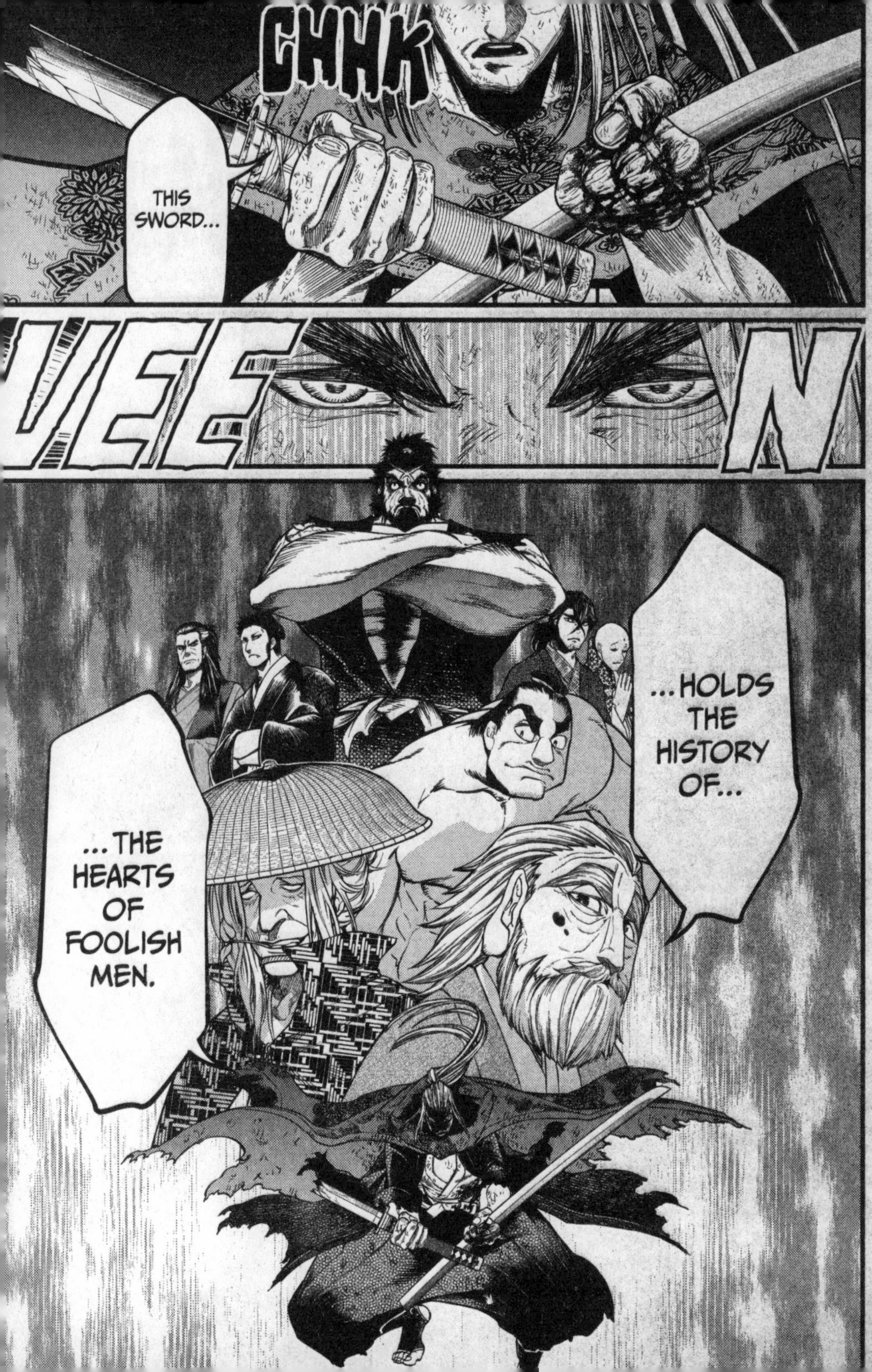
CHHK
THIS SWORD...
VEEN
...HOLDS THE HISTORY OF...
...THE HEARTS OF FOOLISH MEN.

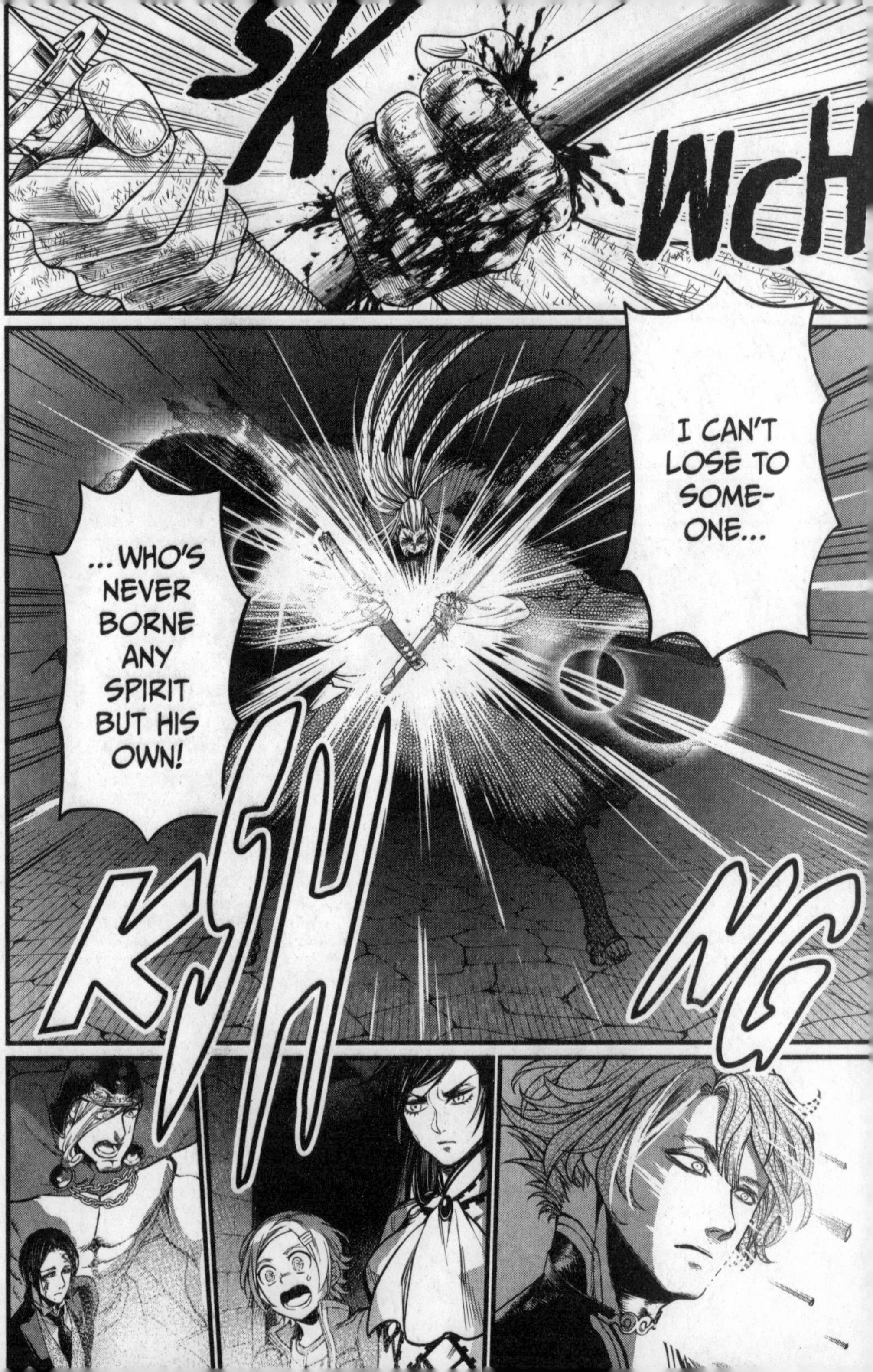
SKWCH
I CAN'T LOSE TO SOME-ONE...
...WHO'S NEVER BORNE ANY SPIRIT BUT HIS OWN!

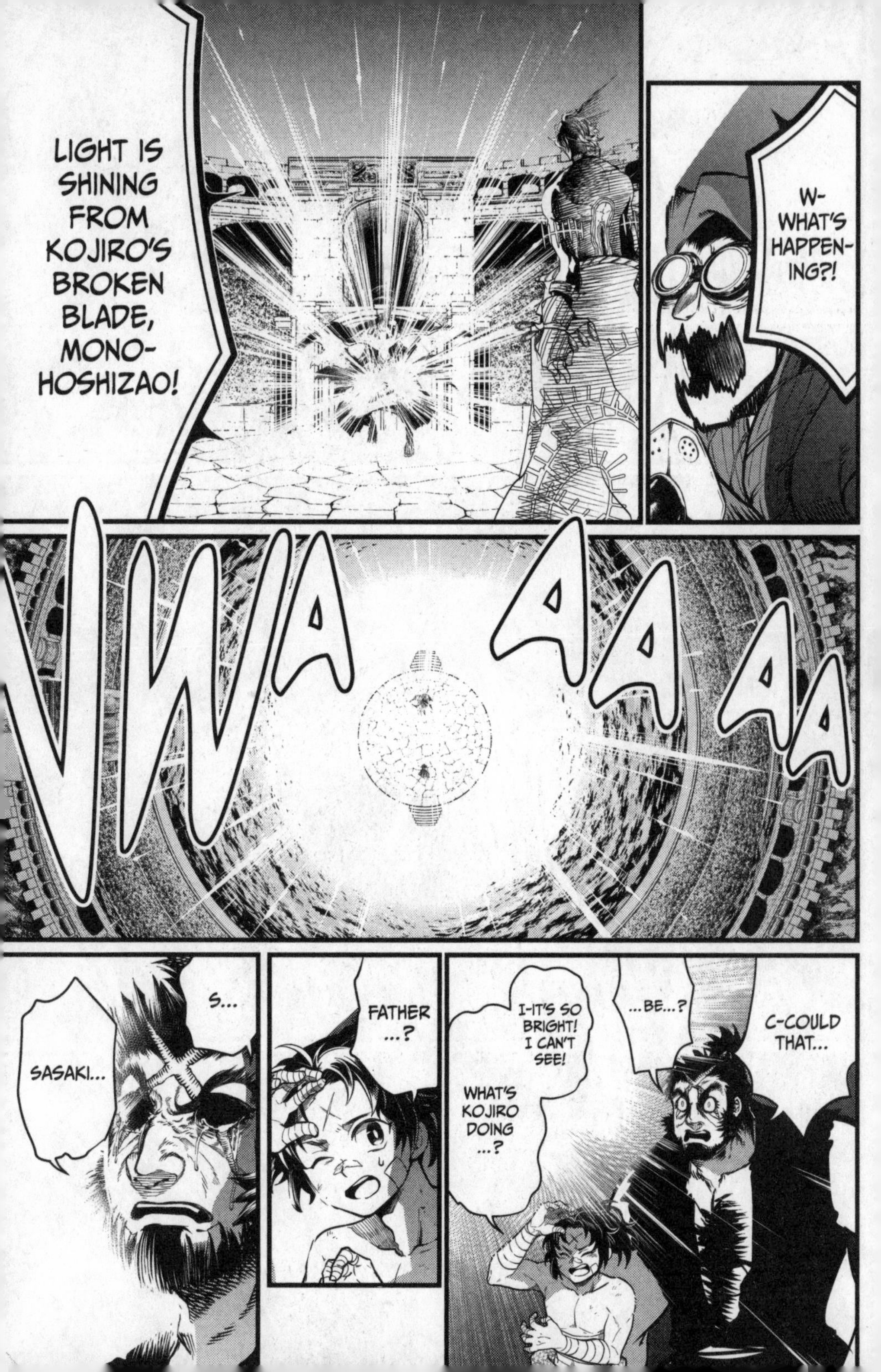
W-WHAT'S HAPPEN-ING?!
LIGHT IS SHINING FROM KOJIRO'S BROKEN BLADE, MONO-HOSHIZAO!
WAAAAAA
C-COULD THAT...
...BE...?
I-IT'S SO BRIGHT! I CAN'T SEE!
WHAT'S KOJIRO DOING...?
FATHER...?
S...
SASAKI...

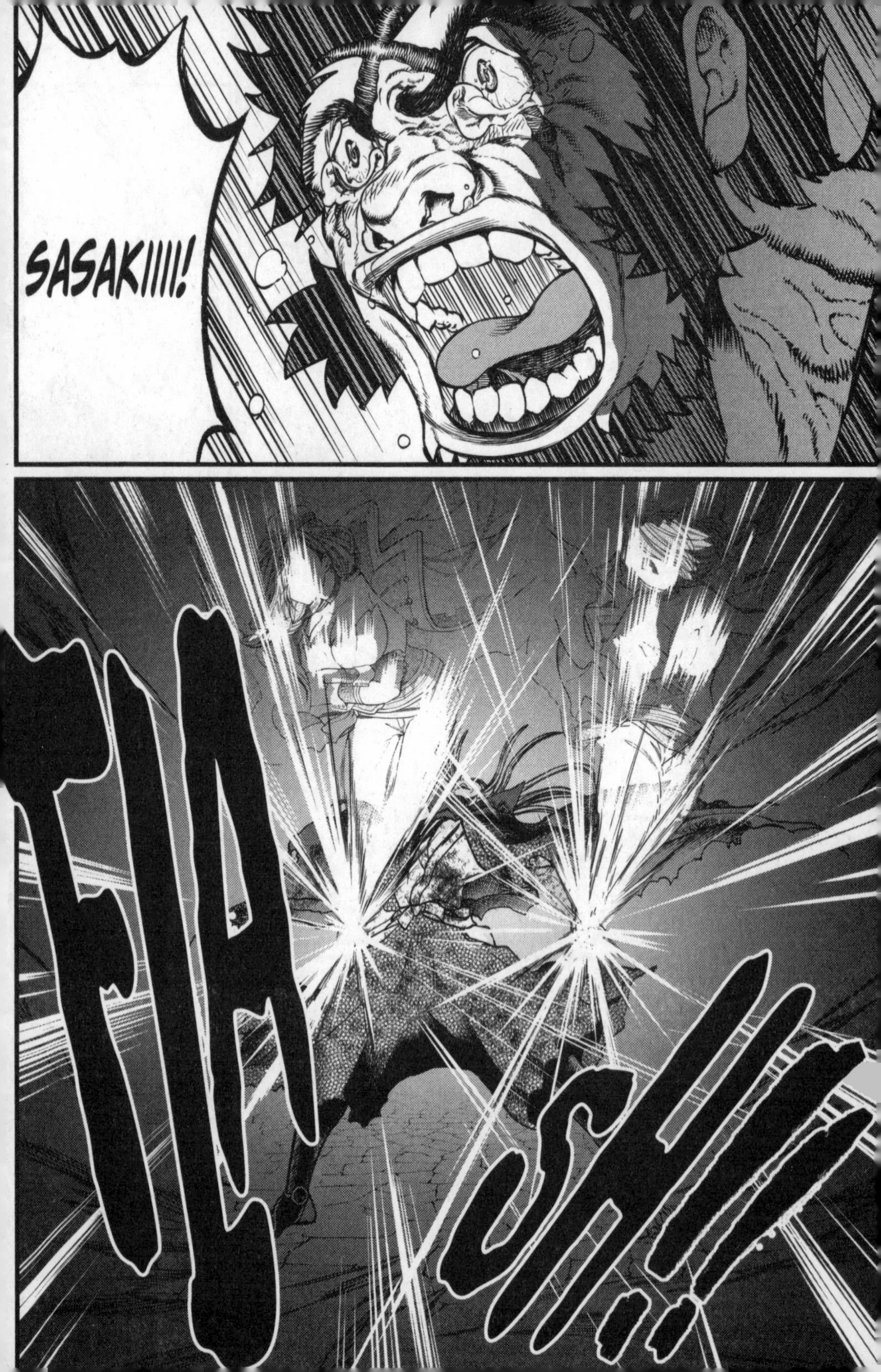
SASAKIIII!
FLASH..

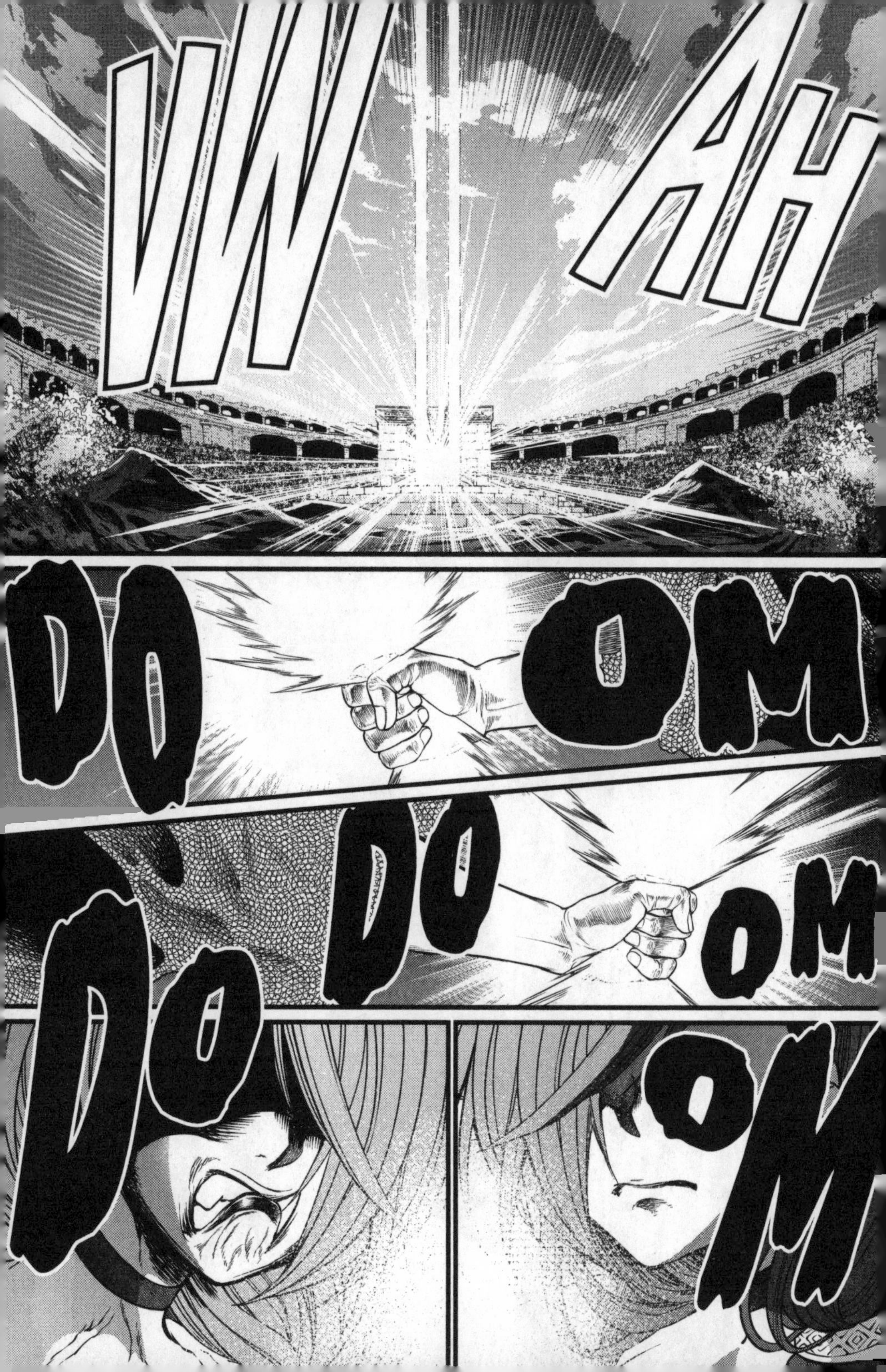
VWAH
DOOM
DOOM
DOOM

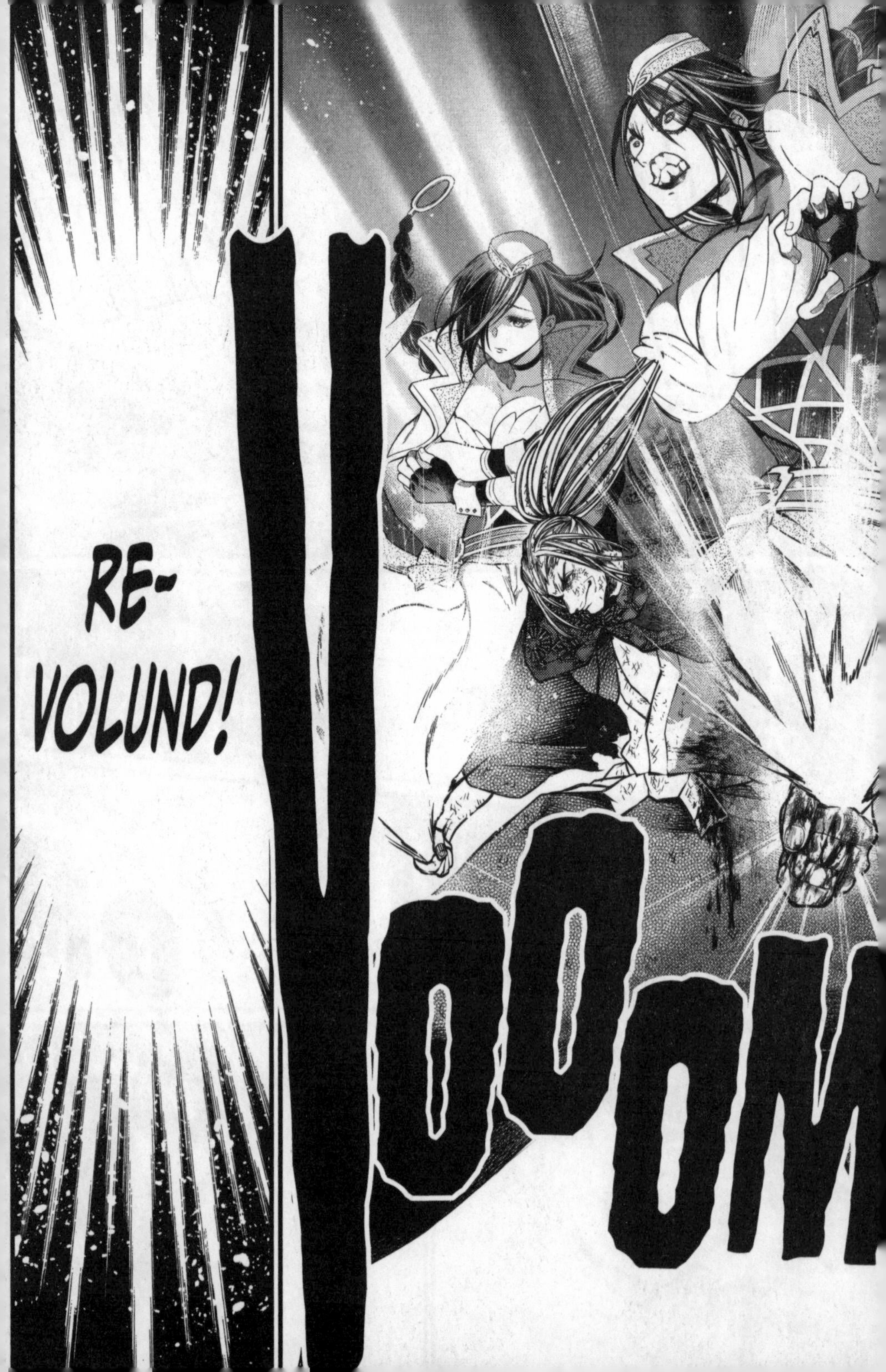
RE-
VOLUND!
VOOOM

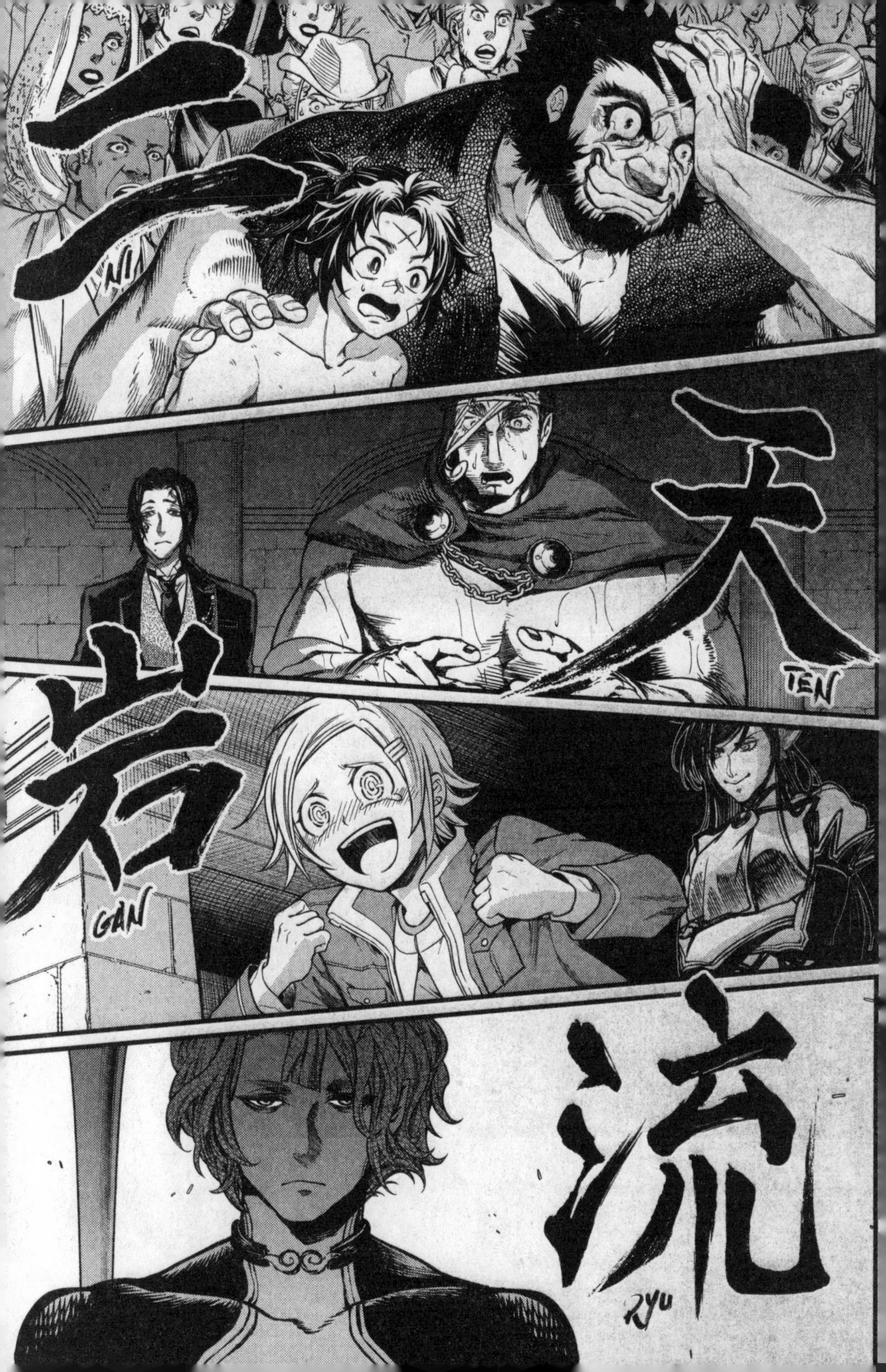
二
NI
天
TEN
岩
GAN
流
RYU

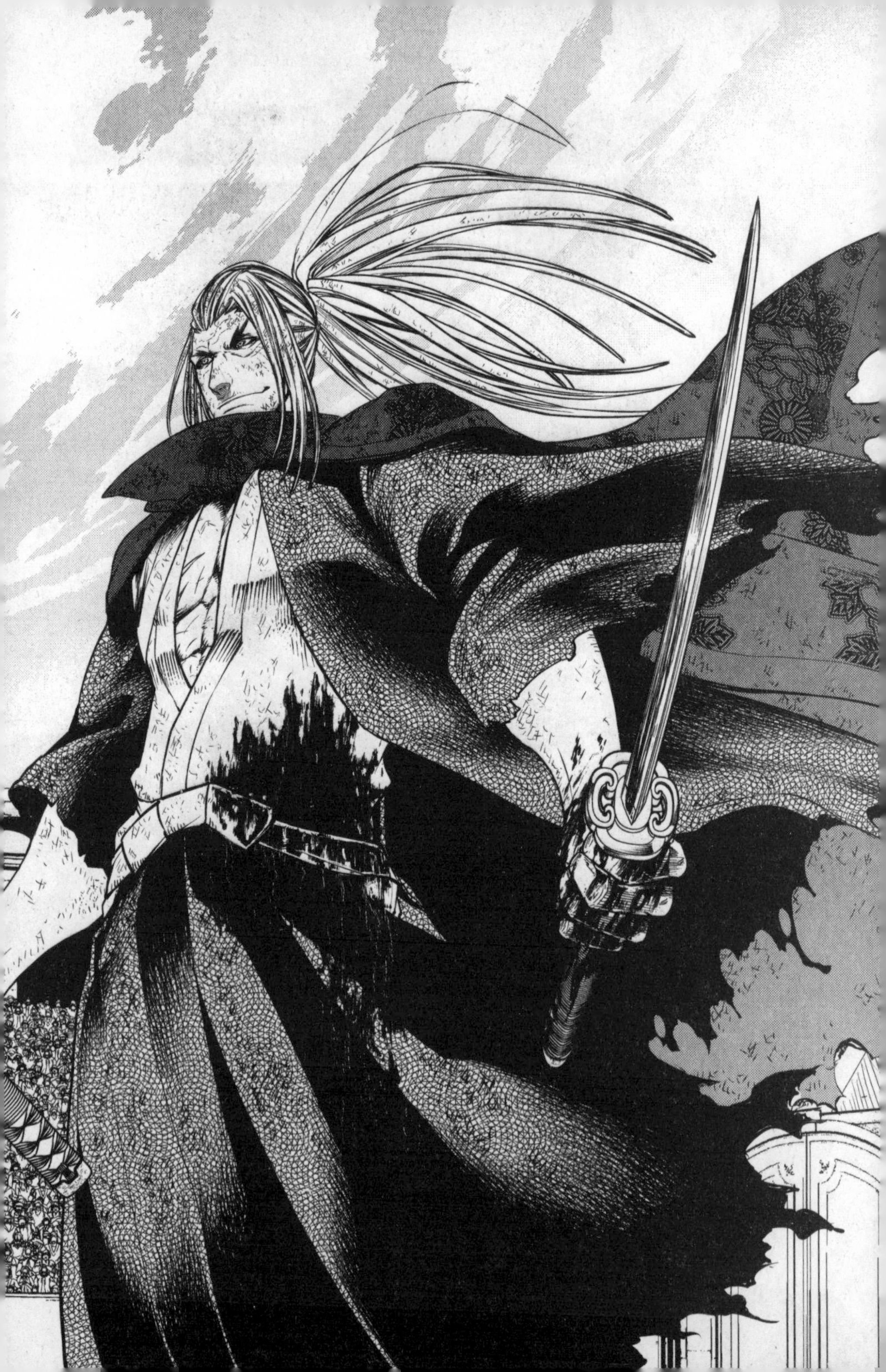

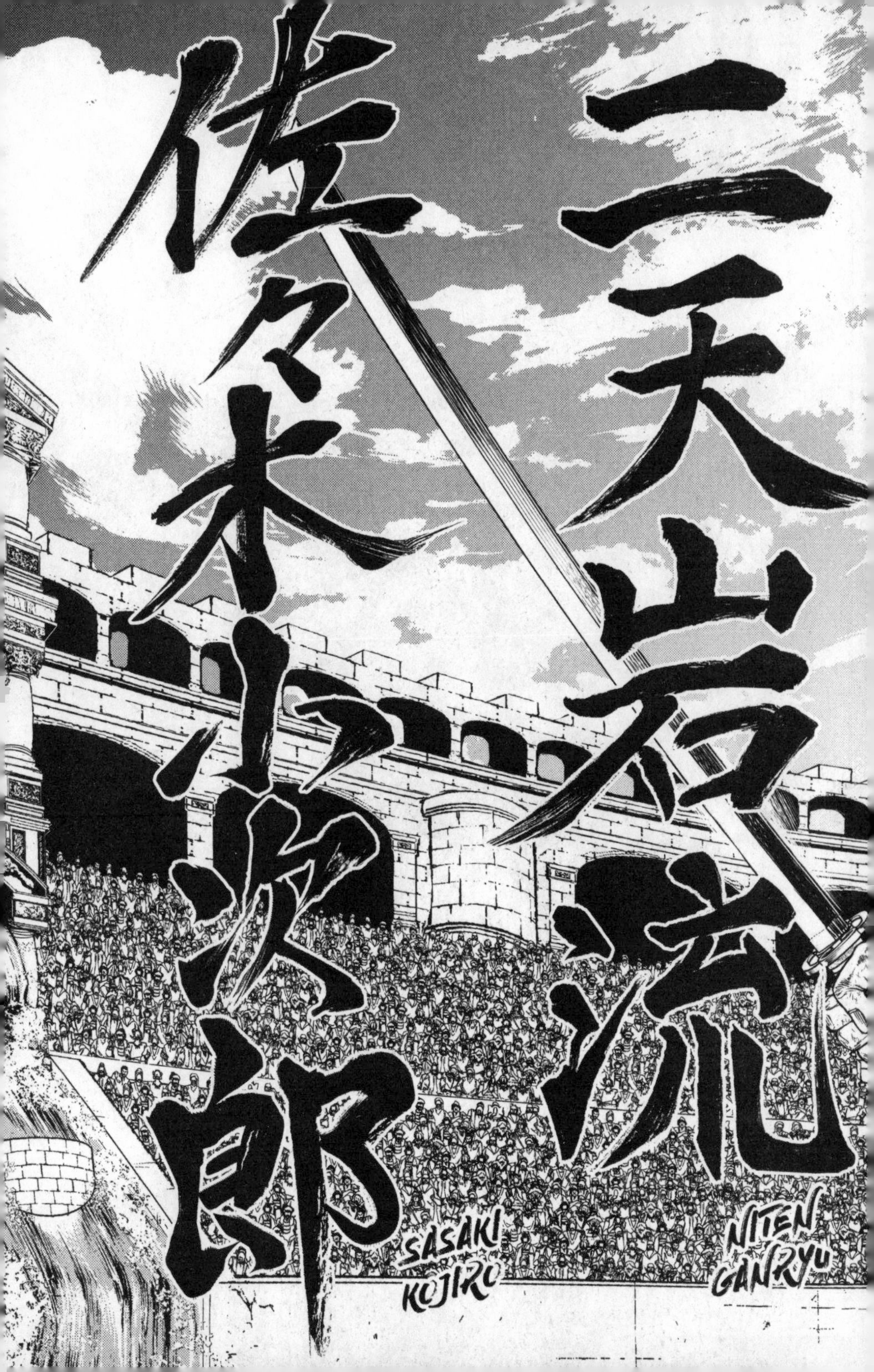
二天岩流
NITEN GANRYU
佐々木小次郎
SASAKI KOJIRO

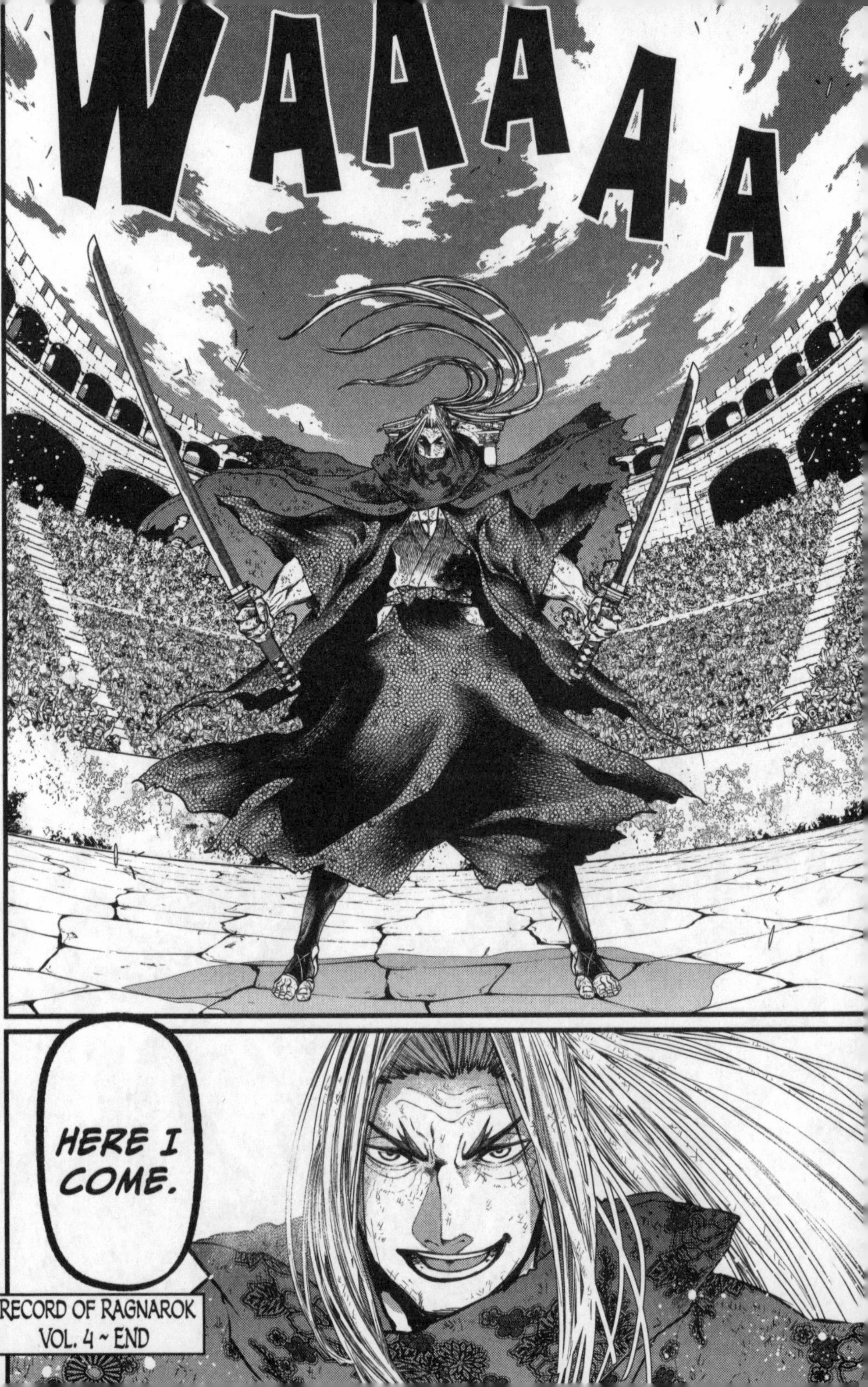
WAAAAA
HERE I COME.
RECORD OF RAGNAROK
VOL. 4 ~ END

RECORD OF

RAGNAROK

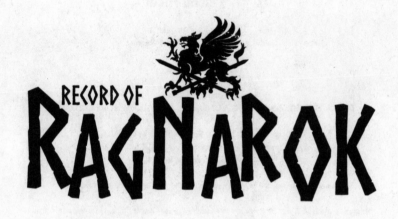

RECORD OF RAGNAROK

VOLUME 4
VIZ Signature Edition

Art by **Azychika**

Story by **Shinya Umemura**

Script by **Takumi Fukui**

Translation / Joe Yamazaki
Touch-Up Art & Lettering / Mark McMurray
Design / Julian (JR) Robinson
Editor / Mike Montesa

Shumatsu no Walkure
©2017 by AZYCHIKA AND SHINYA UMEMURA AND TAKUMI FUKUI/COAMIX
Approved No. ZCW-123W
First Published in Japan in Monthly Comic ZENON by COAMIX, Inc.
English translation rights arranged with COAMIX Inc., Tokyo
through Tuttle-Mori Agency, Inc., Tokyo

Printed in Canada

Published by VIZ Media, LLC
P.O. Box 77010
San Francisco, CA 94107

10 9 8 7 6 5 4 3 2 1
First printing, October 2022

PARENTAL ADVISORY
RECORD OF RAGNAROK is rated T+ for
Older Teen and is recommended for ages
16 and up. Contains graphic violence.

viz.com

vizsignature.com

IN THE ORIGINAL CLASSIC MANGA set in a postapocalyptic wasteland ruled by savage gangs, a hero appears to bring justice to the guilty. This warrior named Ken holds the deadly secrets of a mysterious martial art known as Hokuto Shinken—the Divine Fist of the North Star!

FIST OF THE NORTH STAR

Story by **BURONSON** Art by **TETSUO HARA**

Ex-soldier Juzo Inui has one question—
who turned him into a cyborg
and erased his memories?

No Guns Life

STORY AND ART BY
TASUKU KARASUMA

After the war, cyborg soldiers known as the
Extended were discharged. Juzo Inui is one of
them, a man whose body was transformed, his
head replaced with a giant gun! With no memory
of his previous life—or who replaced his head and
why—Inui now scratches out a living in the dark
streets of the city as a Resolver, taking on cases
involving the Extended.

VIZ

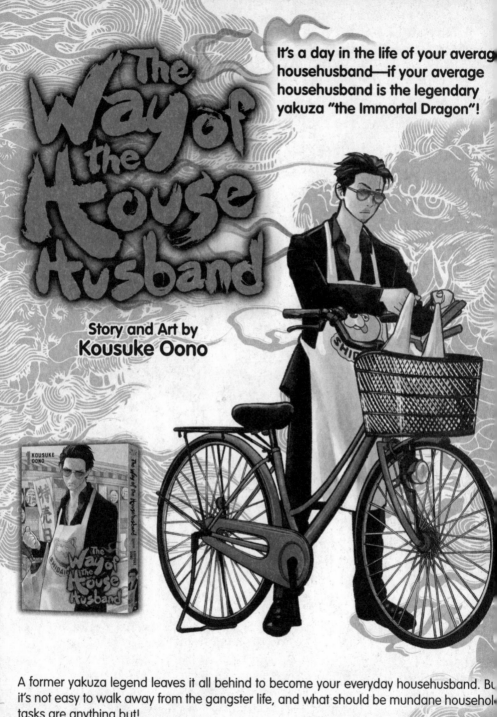

It's a day in the life of your averag
househusband—if your average
househusband is the legendary
yakuza "the Immortal Dragon"!

The Way of the House Husband

Story and Art by
Kousuke Oono

A former yakuza legend leaves it all behind to become your everyday househusband. Bu
it's not easy to walk away from the gangster life, and what should be mundane househol
tasks are anything but!

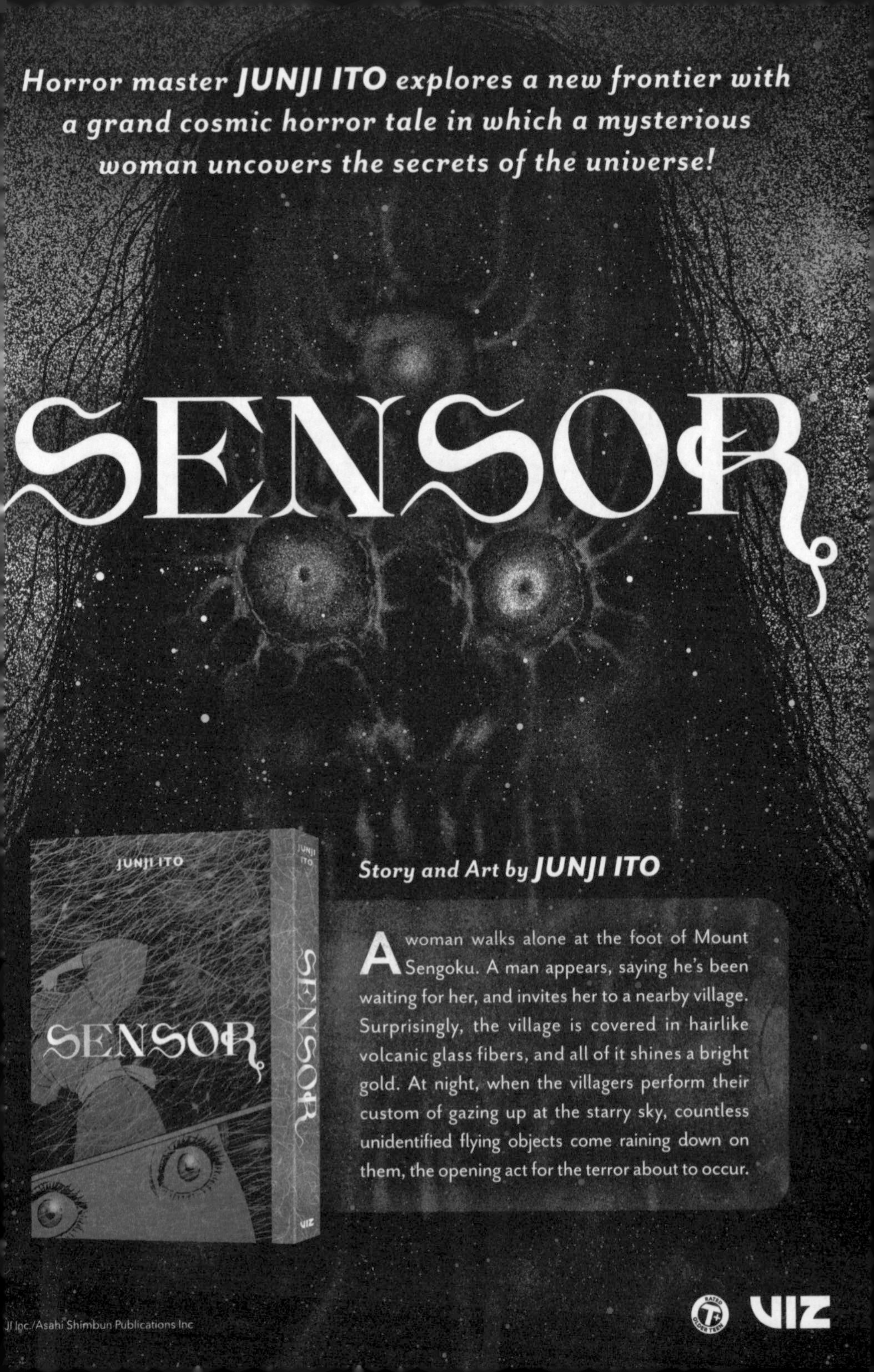
Horror master JUNJI ITO explores a new frontier with a grand cosmic horror tale in which a mysterious woman uncovers the secrets of the universe!
SENSOR
JUNJI ITO
SENSOR
JUNJI ITO
SENSOR
VIZ
Story and Art by JUNJI ITO
A woman walks alone at the foot of Mount Sengoku. A man appears, saying he's been waiting for her, and invites her to a nearby village. Surprisingly, the village is covered in hairlike volcanic glass fibers, and all of it shines a bright gold. At night, when the villagers perform their custom of gazing up at the starry sky, countless unidentified flying objects come raining down on them, the opening act for the terror about to occur.
RATED T+ OLDER TEEN
VIZ
JI Inc./Asahi Shimbun Publications Inc

TOKYO GHOUL
[ILLUSTRATIONS]
z a k k i

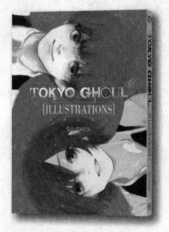

Tokyo Ghoul Illustrations: zakki features artwork and behind-the-scenes notes, commentary and ruminations from *Tokyo Ghoul* creator Sui Ishida. Discover the creative process that brought the hit manga to life, in gloriously ghoulish full color.

YOU'RE READING IT WRONG!

RECORD OF RAGNAROK

reads right to left starting in the upper-right corner. Japanese is read from right to left, meaning that action, sound effects, and word-balloon order are completely reversed from English order.

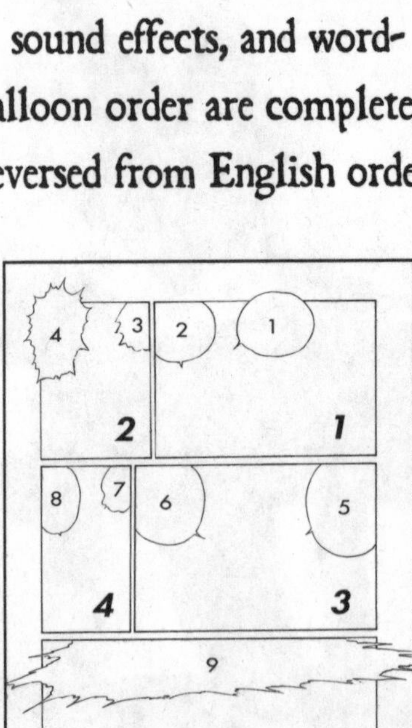

1
2
3
4
1
2
5
6
7
8
3
4
9
5
142

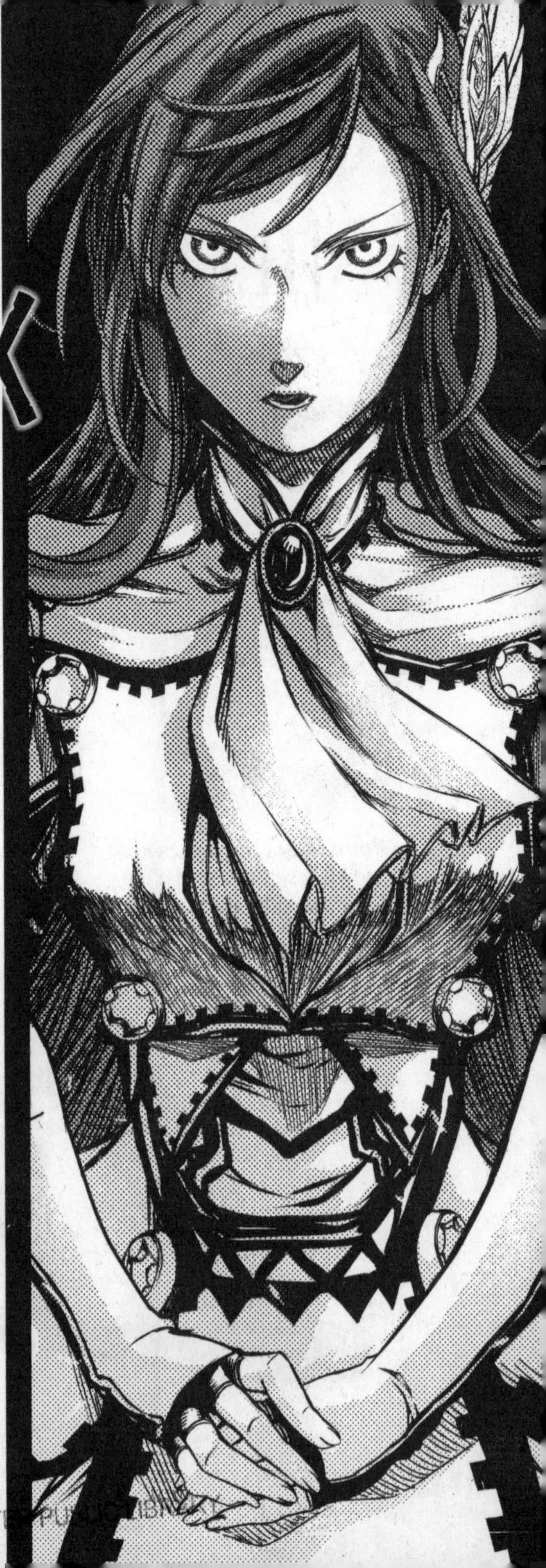

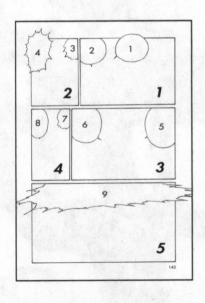